THE

MW01264649

BERLIN

REAL GUIDE CREDITS

Series Editor: Mark Ellingham
Editorial: Martin Dunford, John Fisher, Jack Holland, Jonathan Buckley
U.S. Text Editor: Melissa Kim
Production: Susanne Hillen, Greg Ward, Kate Berens, Andy Hilliard
Typesetting: Gail Jammy
Design: Andrew Oliver

Special thanks to: **Claire Terry**, for help, advice, and inspiration: without her enthusiasm and guidance this book would never have seen the light of day. To **John Gawthrop** for his contributions on the East, and to **Victor and Ina Schröder** who did much to make the East Berlin section of this book possible. Thanks also, in no particular order, to Peter Brodersen of the *Verkehrsamt Berlin*, Alexander Bidder of the Berlin Tourist Board, Paul Ayres at Berolina, Michael Prellberg, Wolfgang Zeissner, Peter Rieth, Antonio Cardillo, Louise Bourke, Gordon McLachlan, the staff at the British Military Hospital in Berlin, Peter Glencross, Natascha Scott-Stokes, Jorgos Sidiropoulos, Jonathan Buckley, Britta Zurbel, Gianni Lancellotti, Erika Brettschneider-Bass, Peter and Marlon Bork, Martin Dunford, Dave Driscoll, Petra Stüben, and Mog Greenwood.

Thanks too to all those who helped produce this book, especially Dan Richardson for editing the history, Jules Brown for proofing, Kate Berens for the checking, Gail Jammy for setting, and Susanne Hillen for never shouting at me once.

Published in the United States and Canada by
Prentice Hall Press
A division of Simon & Schuster Inc.
15 Columbus Circle
New York, NY 10023

Prentice Hall Press and colophons are registered trademarks of Simon & Schuster Inc.

Typeset in Linotron Univers and Century Old Style.
Printed in the United States by R.R. Donnelley & Sons.

Illustrations in Part One and Part Three by Ed Briant;
Contexts illustration by Simon Fell.

240p.
Includes index.

Cataloguing-in-Publication Data
is available from the Library of Congress

THE REAL GUIDE
BERLIN

Written and Researched by

JACK HOLLAND

With additional contributions by

John Gawthrop, Claire Terry, and Jill Denton

PRENTICE
HALL
PRESS

NEW YORK LONDON TORONTO SYDNEY TOKYO SINGAPORE

CONTENTS

Introduction vi

■ **CHAPTER 6 THE CITY 133**

Arriving: Friedrichsrasse and Around (137), Unter den Linden (138), The Museum Island (142), Alexanderplatz and Around (145), The Nikolaiviertel (147), Around the Center (149), Prenzlauer Berg (152), Köpenick (155), Karlshorst (159), Pankow (160), Weissensee (161), East Berlin's Museums (161).

■ **CHAPTER 7 DRINKING AND EATING 166**

Drinking: Bars (166), Cafés (169), *Eating:* Restaurants (172).

■ **CHAPTER 8 MUSIC AND NIGHTLIFE 176**

Discos and Clubs (176), Live Music (177), Theater (179), Film (181).

▨▨PART THREE▨▨ THE CONTEXTS   183

INTRODUCTION

Berlin is like no other city in Germany or indeed the world. For over a
century, its political climate has either mirrored or determined what
has happened in the rest of Europe. Heart of the Prussian kingdom,
economic and cultural center of the Weimar Republic, and, in its final
days as a united city, the headquarters of Hitler's Third Reich, it is a weather
vane of European history. After the war, the world's two most powerful military systems stood face to face here, sharing the spoils of a city for years split
by that most tangible object of the East–West divide, the Berlin Wall. As the
Wall fell in November 1989, Berlin was once again pushed to the forefront of
world events. And it's this weight of history, the sense of living in a hothouse
where all the dilemmas of contemporary Europe are nurtured, that gives
Berlin its excitement and troubling fascination.

It was, of course, **World War II** that defined the shape of today's city. A
seventh of all the buildings destroyed in Germany were in Berlin, Allied and
Soviet bombing razing 92 percent of all the shops, houses, and industry here.
At the end of the war, the city was split into French, American, British, and
Soviet sectors, according to the agreement at the Yalta Conference: the Allies
took the western part of the city, traditionally an area of bars, hotels, and
shops fanning out from the Kurfürstendamm and the Tiergarten park. The
Soviet zone contained what remained of the pompous civic buildings,
churches, and grand museums around Unter den Linden. After the building
of **the Wall** in 1961, which sealed the Soviet sector and enabled it to become
capital of the young German Democratic Republic, the divided sections of the
city developed in different ways. The authorities in the West had a policy of
demolition and rebuilding; the East restored wherever possible, preserving
some of the nineteenth-century buildings that had once made Berlin magnificent. Even now, after so much massive destruction, it's indicative of just how
great a city Berlin once was that enough remains to fill a guidebook.

Though without some knowledge of its history Berlin is impossible to
understand, it is easy to enjoy. For years its isolation in the middle of the
GDR meant that **West Berlin** has had a pressure-cooker mentality; this,
combined with the fact that a large and youthful contingent comes here to
drop out or involve itself in alternative lifestyles (Berlin residents are exempt
from the military service compulsory in the Federal Republic), has created a
vivacious **nightlife** and a sense of exhausted excitement on the streets. And
even if you try and ignore them, the constant reminders of the war years add
spice to your wanderings.

To get an idea of the city as an entity, it's essential to escape the bright
lights and consumerism of the West and make a few trips to **East Berlin**.
Following what Berliners call *Die Wende*, the change and transformation
following the hard-to-believe events in 1989–90, East Berlin is now, de facto,
part of the West, gearing itself up for that not so distant day when the two
Germanys fully unify. On first glance, it seems little different from the West,
particularly now that much of the Cold War atmosphere has vanished.

Preconceptions about drab lifestyles, food shortages, and numbing militarism quickly evaporate; it's only when you scratch below the glossy surface and fall into conversation with locals that you realize how distant these two sections of the same city really have been.

Yet, as the move to **German unification** accelerates, East and West will unavoidably meld into one—a process that has already tentatively begun, with the dismantling of the Wall hastening changes in the atmosphere of both Berlins. When the countries unify, the post-war schizophrenia that marred it will hopefully vanish—leaving Berlin the possible new capital city of the largest country in Europe, one whose exports will be of greater total worth than those of the United States. But in the final analysis, no amount of facts and figures, economics, or history can really explain the place; only by seeing it for yourself can you attempt some understanding.

Inevitably, **the pace of change** in Berlin, particularly the East, means that certain sections of this book are going to be out of date even as you read them, such is the speed of transformation in the two Germanys. For the latest information, particularly on visiting the East, contact the respective tourist authorities (see p.10).

When to Go
Lying in the heart of Europe, Berlin's climate is continental: winters are bitingly cold, summers hot. If you're hanging on for decent weather, April is the soonest you should go: any earlier and you'll need to don winter sweaters, earmuffs, and a decent pair of waterproof shoes; this said, the city (especially the East) does have a particular poignancy when it snows. Ideally, the best time to arrive is in May: June and July can be wearingly hot, though the famed Berlin air (*Berliner Luft* – there's a song about it) keeps things bracing. The weather stays good (if unpredictable) right up until October.

	DAYTIME TEMPERATURES			
	MIN		**MAX**	
	°C	°F	°C	°F
January	-12	10	9	48
February	-12	10	11	52
March	-7	19	17	63
April	-2	28	22	72
May	2	36	28	82
June	6	43	30	86
July	9	48	32	90
August	8	46	31	88
September	4	39	28	82
October	-1	30	21	70
November	-4	25	13	55
December	-9	16	10	50

PART ONE

WEST BERLIN

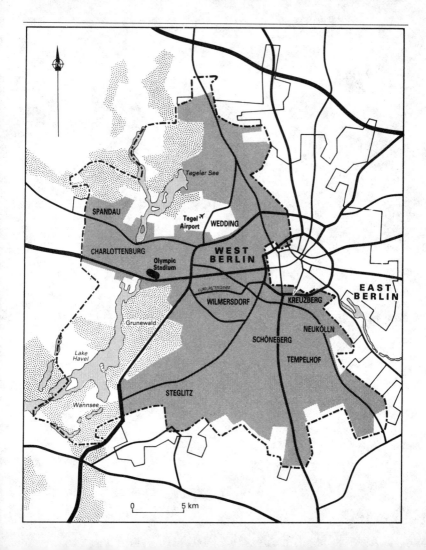

SPANDAU

Tegeler See

Tegel
Airport

WEDDING

CHARLOTTENBURG

WEST
BERLIN

Olympic
Stadium

KURFÜRSTENDAMM

WILMERSDORF

KREUZBERG

EAST
BERLIN

Grunewald

NEUKÖLLN

SCHÖNEBERG

TEMPELHOF

Lake
Havel

Wannsee

STEGLITZ

0   5 km

GETTING THERE

FLIGHTS FROM THE USA

The quickest and easiest way to get to West Berlin is to **fly**. If you're visiting the city as part of a wider European tour you have the option of flying direct to another European gateway city—such as London or Frankfurt—then on to Berlin. Many European cities have train and bus connections to Berlin, though these will invariably cost you more.

Lufthansa (☎800/645-3880) operate the most frequent services from the US to Germany. They have several daily flights from New York, Los Angeles, and Chicago, slightly fewer from other major US cities. From New York fares to Berlin range from $830 low season to $969 high season, while from Los Angeles or San Francisco prices start at $1043 in low season, rising to $1183 in the high. It's worth noting that there are no savings to be made traveling from the West Coast by separate carrier and then transferring to *Lufthansa* in New York. Of the American airlines, *TWA* (☎800/892-4141) fly to Berlin from most US cities connecting through New York and Frankfurt. Their fares from Chicago and New York are roughly comparable, rising from $700 low season to $1300 in the summer, while from Los Angeles prices rise from $800 to a steep $2200 in high season. *Pan Am* (☎800/221-1111) fares are similar from New York and Chicago, but represent a considerable saving on flights from Los Angeles, which go from as little as $800 in low season, and only $878 in the high. Most of the American carriers have the same conditions

attached to their fares, namely that they must be purchased thirty days in advance, with a seven-day minimum and 21-day maximum stay. Fares quoted are midweek rates—expect to add on anything from $50 to $100 more for weekend travel—and are mostly non-refundable, though some will give a fifty percent return on canceled tickets.

FLIGHTS FROM CANADA

From Canada, flights to West Berlin usually route through either London or Frankfurt. Again *Lufthansa* offers the most frequent service, with flights departing daily from Vancouver, Montreal, and Toronto. Of these three, fares from Vancouver are the most expensive, ranging from $990 in low season to $1210 in high season, and cheapest from Toronto, starting from as little as $750 in low season, and climbing to a high season peak of $910. *Canadian Airlines* (☎800/426-7000) also fly out of Vancouver and Toronto; fares from the latter range from $720 low season to $884 in high season, while from Vancouver they're more expensive—from $919 to $1134. Conditions attached to these fares are slightly more flexible, requiring only 14 days advance purchase, and a minimum to maximum stay range of seven days to three months.

STUDENT AND DISCOUNT FLIGHTS

If you qualify for a student or youth fare you should contact any of the specialist operators listed overleaf, who may be able to offer you substantial discounts on scheduled fares. To be eligible for these fares on most routes you'll need student ID, or proof that you're under 26, or sometimes 31; teachers can often also get discounts on most routes. If you don't fit into any of these categories you may still be able to pick up a bargain fare—flights from both coasts of the US can be found for as little as $590 in low season. The only possible drawback is that these flights may involve more stopovers than you'd want.

> Though it's invariably easier to fly to West Berlin and cross the border, it *is* possible to fly to **East Berlin**'s Schönefeld airport—see p.121 for details.

COUNCIL TRAVEL IN THE US

Head Office: 205 E. 42nd St., New York, NY 10017; ☎212/661-1450

CALIFORNIA
2486 Channing Way, Berkeley, CA 94704; ☎415/848-8604
UCSD Price Center, Q-076, La Jolla, CA 92093; ☎619/452-0630
1818 Palo Verde Ave., Suite E, Long Beach, CA 90815; ☎213/598-3338
1093 Broxton Ave., Suite 220, Los Angeles, CA 90024; ☎213/208-3551
4429 Cass St., San Diego, CA 92109; ☎619/270-6401
312 Sutter St., Suite 407, San Francisco, CA 94108; ☎415/421-3473
919 Irving St., Suite 102, San Francisco, CA 94122; ☎415/566-6222
14515 Ventura Blvd., Suite 250, Sherman Oaks, CA 91403; ☎818/905-5777

COLORADO
1138 13th St., Boulder, CO 80302; ☎818/905-5777

CONNECTICUT
Yale Co-op East, 77 Broadway, New Haven, CT 06520; ☎203/562-5335

DISTRICT OF COLUMBIA
1210 Potomac St., NW Washington, DC 20007; ☎202/337-6464

GEORGIA
12 Park Place South, Atlanta, GA 30303; ☎404/577-1678

ILLINOIS
1153 N. Dearborn St., Chicago, IL 60610; ☎312/951-0585
831 Foster St., Evanston, IL 60201; ☎708/475-5070

LOUISIANA
8141 Maple St., New Orleans, LA 70118; ☎504/866-1767

MASSACHUSETTS
79 South Pleasant St., 2nd Floor, Amherst, MA 01002; ☎413/256-1261
729 Boylston St., Suite 201, Boston, MA 02116; ☎617/266-1926
1384 Massachusetts Ave., Suite 206, Cambridge, MA 02138; ☎617/497-1497
Stratton Student Center MIT, W20-024, 84 Massachusetts Ave., Cambridge, MA 02139; ☎617/497-1497

MINNESOTA
1501 University Ave. SE, Room 300, Minneapolis, MN 55414; ☎612/379-2323

NEW YORK
35 W. 8th St., New York, NY 10011; ☎212/254-2525
Student Center, 356 West 34th St., New York, NY 10001; ☎212/643-1365

NORTH CAROLINA
703 Ninth St., Suite B-2, Durham, NC 27705; ☎919/286-4664

OREGON
715SW Morrison, Suite 600, Portland, OR 97205; ☎503/228-1900

RHODE ISLAND
171 Angell St., Suite 212, Providence, RI 02906; ☎401/331-5810

TEXAS
2000 Guadalupe St., Suite 6, Austin, TX 78705; ☎512/472-4931
Exec. Tower Office Center, 3300 W. Mockingbird, Suite 101, Dallas,TX 75235; ☎214/350-6166

WASHINGTON
1314 Northeast 43rd St., Suite 210, Seattle, WA 98105; ☎206/632-2448

WISCONSIN
2615 North Hackett Avenue, Milwaukee, WI; ☎414/332-4740

STA IN THE US

BOSTON
273 Newbury St., Boston, MA 02116; ☎617/266-6014

HONOLULU
1831 S. King St., Suite 202, Honolulu, HI 96826; ☎808/942-7755

LOS ANGELES
920 Westwood Blvd., Los Angeles, CA 90024; ☎213/824-1574
7204 Melrose Ave., Los Angeles, CA 90046; ☎213/934-8722

2500 Wilshire Blvd., Los Angeles, CA 90057; ☎213/380-2184

NEW YORK
17 E. 45th St., Suite 805, New York, NY 10017; ☎212/986-9470;☎ 800/777-0112

SAN DIEGO
6447 El Cajon Blvd., San Diego, CA 92115; ☎619/286-1322

SAN FRANCISCO
166 Geary St., Suite 702, San Francisco, CA 94108; ☎415/391-8407

TRAVEL CUTS IN CANADA

Head Office: 187 College St., Toronto, Ontario M5T 1P7; ☎416/979-2406

ALBERTA

1708 12th St. NW, Calgary T2M 3M7; ☎403/282-7687. 10424A 118th Ave., Edmonton T6G 0P7; ☎403/471-8054

BRITISH COLUMBIA

Room 326, T.C., Student Rotunda, Simon Fraser University, Burnaby, British Columbia V5A 1S6; ☎604/291-1204. 1516 Duranleau St., Granville Island, Vancouver V6H 3S4; ☎604/689-2887. Student Union Building, University of British Columbia, Vancouver V6T 1W5; ☎604/228-6890 Student Union Building, University of Victoria, Victoria V8W 2Y2; ☎604/721-8352

MANITOBA

University Centre, University of Manitoba, Winnipeg R3T 2N2; ☎204/269-9530

NOVA SCOTIA

Student Union Building, Dalhousie University, Halifax B3H 4J2; ☎902/424-2054. 6139 South St., Halifax B3H 4J2; ☎902/424-7027

ONTARIO

University Centre, University of Guelph, Guelph N1G 2W1; ☎519/763-1660. Fourth Level Unicentre, Carleton University, Ottawa, K1S5B6; ☎613/238-5493. 60 Laurier Ave. E, Ottawa K1N 6N4; ☎613/238-8222. Student Street, Room G27, Laurentian University, Sudbury P3E 2C6; ☎705/673-1401. 96 Gerrard St. E, Toronto M5B 1G7; ☎ (416) 977-0441. University Shops Plaza, 170 University Ave. W, Waterloo N2L 3E9; ☎519/886-0400.

QUÉBEC (Known as *Voyages CUTS*)

Université McGill, 3480 rue McTavish, Montréal H3A 1X9; ☎514/398-0647. 1613 rue St. Denis, Montréal H2X 3K3; ☎514/843-8511. Université Concordia, Edifice Hall, Suite 643, S.G.W. Campus, 1455 bd de Maisonneuve Ouest, Montréal H3G 1M8; ☎514/288-1130. 19 rue Ste. Ursule, Québec G1R 4E1; ☎418/692-3971

SASKATCHEWAN

Place Riel Campus Centre, University of Saskatchewan, Saskatoon S7N 0W0; ☎306/343-1601

NOUVELLES FRONTIÈRES

In the United States

NEW YORK 19 W. 44th St., Suite 1702, New York, NY 10036; ☎212/764-6494

LOS ANGELES 6363 Wilshire Blvd., Suite 200, Los Angeles, CA 90048; ☎213/658-8955

SAN FRANCISCO 209 Post St., Suite 1121, San Francisco, CA 94108; ☎415/781-4480

In Canada

MONTREAL 1130 ouest, bd de Maisonneuve, Montréal, P.Q. H3A 1M8; ☎514/842-1450

QUEBEC 176 Grande Allée Ouest, Québec, P.Q. G1R 2G9; ☎418/525-5255

SPECIALIST GDR TRAVEL AGENCIES

NEW YORK: *Anniversary Tours,* 250 West 57th St., NY 10019; ☎212/245-7501

Koch Overseas Travel, 157 East 86th St., NY 10028; ☎212/535-8600

WASHINGTON: *Travel Advisors of America,* 1413 K St. NW, Suite 800, DC 20005; ☎202/371-1440

RESTON: *Security Travel,* 1631 Washington Place, VA 22090; ☎703/471-1900

DENVER: *Travel Associates Inc.,* 7007 East Hampden Ave., CO 80224; ☎303/759-8666

SAN FRANCISCO: *Trans World Visa Service,* 790 27th Ave., CA 94122; ☎415/752-6958

GLENDALE: *Karen Travel Service,* 1131 North Brand Blvd., CA 91202; ☎818/502-9999

SOUTH MINNEAPOLIS: *Kenwood Travel,* 2002 Colfax Ave., MN 55405; ☎612/871-6399

CHICAGO: *Hapag-Lloyd Travel,* 179 W. Washington St., ILL 60602; ☎312/332-0090

OLDSMAR: *Uniglobe-Forest Lake Travel,* 1106 State Road 594 West, FLA 33557; ☎813/855-8911

SEATTLE: *Eastern Europe Tours,* 1402 Third Ave., Ste. 1127, WA 98101; ☎206/682-8911

CARSON CITY: *Bonanza World Travel,* PO Box 1734, NV 89702; ☎702/882-5856

HOUSTON: *Visa and International Passport,* 36 FM 1960 West, Ste. 150, TX 77090; ☎713/921-1661

VIA BRITAIN

If you travel to Berlin via Britain a whole range of onward travel options becomes available, again the easiest of which is to **fly**. Best way to find **bargain scheduled fares** is by scanning the travel pages of the Sunday newspapers, and, if you're in London, *Time Out* or the many giveaway magazines, such as *LAM*. Of the companies who specialize in cheap flights to West Berlin and Germany, the *German Travel Center* (8 Earlham St., London WC2; ☎071/379 5212) consistently has the most attractive prices. Like most discounted plane fares, their tickets (usually routed via Frankfurt or Hamburg) carry restrictions concerning minimum and maximum stays and the ability to change the return date, but prices are usually between £90–120 return; all flights leave from London.

Flying **directly from regional UK airports** is possible, though more expensive. Sample *British Airways* APEX/Poundstretcher fares are £149 from Manchester, £135 from Birmingham and £160 from Glasgow; standard unrestricted fares are at least twice as expensive. Any high street travel agent will have the full details.

A further cost-cutting option is to utilize the **charter flights** run by *Dan Air* (a company, incidentally, that started life helping with the Berlin airlift), which can be booked direct or through *GTF Tours* and cost around £100 return. *Dan Air* also offer a weekly flight from Manchester for the same price. Their scheduled fares, however, offer no savings over *Pan Am* or *BA*.

BY TRAIN

Unless you qualify for a discount fare, there are no savings to be made traveling to West Berlin **by train**, though you'll see more of Europe en route. **Regular return tickets** cost £137, are valid for two months and permit one stopover in West Germany en route to Berlin. The **route** from London (Liverpool Street station) crosses the Channel from Harwich to the Hook of Holland (6hr 30min), and passes through Utrecht, Hannover and Helmstedt. Once across the Channel, the ride to Berlin takes ten hours.

Rail travel is more economically feasible if you're a **student** or **under 26**, since you qualify for the discounted fares offered by *Eurotrain* (52 Grosvenor Gardens, London SW1; ☎071/730 3402), whose return fares from London are £103, and *Wasteels* (121 Wilton Road, London SW1; ☎071/834 7066).

Another cash-saving possibility for those under 26 is the **Eurail pass**, the North American equivalent of the European InterRail pass, which you must buy in the US. The under-26 Eurail Youthpass covers one month ($320) or two months ($420) of travel. If you're over 26, the regular pass covers first-class travel for 15 days ($298), one month ($470), or three months ($798).

BY BUS

Traveling to West Berlin by **bus** won't bring any major savings over the cheapest air fares, and the journey will be long and uncomfortable, interrupted every 3–4 hours by stops at motorway service stations. Services are run by *Eurolines* (52 Grosvenor Gardens, London SW1; ☎071/730 0202) from London (Victoria station), and can be reserved through most travel agents. In summer four coaches a week run to West Berlin, taking 26 hours to get there, for a fare of £90 return. Winter departures are only slightly fewer and fares are the same as during the summer. If you're **outside London**, *Eurolines* will book you a *National Express* coach to London, but with no reduction on the usual domestic fare.

There are **student** and under-26 **youth fares** on offer, but these only shave a few pounds off the adult fares.

Some **discount agents**, who you'll see advertised in newspapers and listings magazines, may also be able to reduce prices but, again, not by more than a few pounds.

POINTS OF ARRIVAL

All scheduled and charter flights arrive at **Tegel airport** (☎41011), whence frequent #9 buses run directly to the Bahnhof Zoologischer Garten (**Zoo Station**) in the city center (journey time 35min; DM2.70). Taxis cover the distance in half the time and cost DM15–25. At the airport you'll find exchange facilities but scant duty-free shopping.

If you're heading to Berlin from a central or eastern European destination and flying with *Interflug*, the airline of the GDR, you'll arrive at Schönefeld airport in East Berlin. Transit coaches connect the airport to West Berlin—for more details, see "East Berlin Basics," p.119.

You'll also arrive at the Zoo Station if coming by **train**. International **buses** mostly stop at the central bus station, west of the center near the Funkturm: regular #94 buses or the U-Bahn from Kaiserdamm station link it to the city center.

GETTING THERE FROM THE FEDERAL REPUBLIC

Officially you still need a visa to travel by road through the GDR from West Germany to West Berlin. However with the end of border controls a normal passport should suffice.

BY TRAIN

Trains connect Berlin with most West German cities, and the rest of Europe. **The usual border crossing points** are, from north to south:

Büchen (journey to Berlin approximately 3hr 15min).

Helmstedt (2hr 40min).

Bebra (5hr 40min).

Ludwigstadt (5hr).

Hof (5hr 20min).

Tickets from these towns cost between DM45 and DM75, less if you buy a youth/student ticket. If you've been traveling around the Federal Republic using one of the unlimited train passes available (the *DB Tourist Card*, or for those under 26, the *DB Junior Tourist Card*), note that you'll have to pay a supplement of around DM50 round-trip; *InterRail* passes can be used without incurring extra charges. **Transit visas** for the Democratic Republic are issued, without charge, on the train. From the border, trains are run by *Deutsche Reichsbahn*, the GDR rail company: it's important to bring your own **food** for the journey, as what's available on the train leaves a lot to be desired.

BY BUS

Connecting over 170 West German cities to Berlin, buses are slightly cheaper than trains. Certain bus operators offer a **student discount** on round-trip tickets: inquire when booking, either at any *DER* agency (found near train stations or tourist offices), many travel agents, or the central bus station in West Berlin.

BY CAR

Although there are no longer any restrictions on crossing the border, the old transit route crossing points will probably be the most convenient places to head for en route to Berlin. These are:

Gudow–Zarrentin (on the Hamburg autobahn).

Helmstedt–Marienborn (Hannover autobahn, and the fastest route, taking 2–3hr).

Herleshausen–Wartha (Frankfurt autobahn).

Rudolphstein–Hirschburg (Nürnberg autobahn).

Remember seat belts are compulsory in the GDR and there's an 80kph speed limit. Be aware also that drinking and driving is *completely* illegal.

> Once the two Germanys are fully integrated, it's envisaged that the GDR will adopt the motoring regulations and speed limits of the Federal Republic, thus cutting down on the currently slow crossing across the GDR into Berlin.

RED TAPE AND VISAS

US and Canadian citizens need only a valid passport to enter the Federal Republic of Germany and/or Berlin. For a touristic visit no visa in advance is required; you'll merely be given a ninety day date stamp in your passport on arrival (and guards at the airport tend to be lax about this).

If you know that your stay will be longer than this, apply for an extension visa from the nearest West German embassy or consulate *before* you go. In order to extend a stay once in the country, all visitors should go to the *Ausländeramt* (Foreign Police) at Friedrich-Krause-Ufer 24 (☎390550 or 39051). Since the collapse of the Wall, their capacity to administer paperwork is virtually nil: you need to be here at 7am to get an appointment. For more details on longer stays in Berlin, see "Staying On".

The Foreign Police are also the people you should see if you want to try and get a work permit (*Arbeitserlaubnis*), and should you wish to stay in Berlin full-time, you will need a residents' permit or *Aufenthaltserlaubnis*: both these documents are difficult to get hold of, and their issuance is by no means automatic (unless of course, they have been organized by your employers in the US).

If you're a national of any other country you'll need to organize a visa before you arrive: see your local West German embassy or consulate for details.

GERMAN EMBASSIES AND CONSULATES

USA
Embassy: 4645 Reservoir Rd. NW, Washington, DC 20007-1998; ☎202/298-4000
Consulates: Atlanta, Boston, Chicago, Detroit, Houston, Los Angeles, Miami, New Orleans, New York, San Francisco, and Seattle.

CANADA
Embassy: P.O.B. 379, Post Station A, Ottawa, Ont. K1N 8V4; ☎613/232-1101
Consulates: Edmonton, Montreal, Toronto, and Vancouver

HEALTH AND INSURANCE

For minor complaints, or to just get a prescription filled, you need to go to an *Apotheke*; German pharmacists are well-trained and often speak English. Outside normal hours a notice on the door of any *Apotheke* indicates the nearest one open, meaning that there's a round-the-clock service. Otherwise try *Europa-Apotheke*, Tauentzienstr. 9 (☎261 4142), which is open 9am–9pm daily.

Doctors are likely to be able to speak English, but if you want to be certain the British consulate will provide a list of English-speaking doctors (see "Listings" for the consulate's address). For an **emergency doctor**, call ☎310031; for an **emergency dentist**, ☎1141. In the event of a general **emergency**, phone ☎110 for the police, who will call an ambulance.

INSURANCE

The Federal Republic of Germany has no reciprocal health care agreements with either the USA or Canada, and with cost of care equaling or exceeding that at home, it would be wise to look into medical coverage beforehand. Before you purchase special **travel insurance**, whether for medical or property mishaps, check that you won't duplicate any **existing plans** which you may have. For example, **Canadians** are usually covered for medical expenses by their provincial health plans (but may only be reimbursed after the fact). Holders of **ISIC** cards are entitled to $2000 worth of accident coverage and sixty days ($100 per diem) of hospital in-patient benefits for the period during which the card is valid. **Students** will often find that their student health coverage extends for one term beyond the date of last enrollment. Bank and charge **accounts** (particularly *American Express*) often have certain levels of medical or other insurance included. One item which tends to be excluded by home-based insurance, however, is transportation by ambulance—this can get very expensive if you're not specifically covered. **Homeowners' or renters'** insurance often covers theft or loss of documents, money, and valuables while overseas, though exact conditions and maximum amounts vary from company to company.

Only after exhausting the possibilities above might you want to contact a specialist travel insurance company; your travel agent can usually recommend one. Travel insurance offerings are quite comprehensive, anticipating everything from charter companies going bankrupt to delayed or lost baggage, by way of illnesses and accidents. If you've purchased any sort of discounted air ticket, whether APEX, charter, or a consolidated seat, these tend to be non-refundable and often date-inflexible; thus it would be wise to consider a trip cancellation policy if nothing else; this will entitle you to compensation should you be unable to use your ticket(s) on the specified dates.

Premiums vary widely, from the very reasonable ones offered primarily through student/youth agencies (though available to anyone), to those so expensive that the price tag for anything more than two months of coverage will probably equal the cost of the worst possible combination of disasters. Note also that very few insurers will arrange on-the-spot payments in the event of a major expense or loss; you will usually be reimbursed only after going home.

A most important thing to keep in mind—and a source of major disappointment to would-be claimants—is that *none* of the policies currently available insure against **theft** of *anything* while overseas. (Americans have been easy pickings for foreign thieves—naivete on the part of the former and an all-Americans-are-rich attitude among the latter led to companies going broke paying robbery/burglary claims.) North American travel policies apply only to items **lost** from, or **damaged** in, the custody of an identifiable, responsible third party, ie hotel porter, airline, luggage consignment, etc. Even then, you will still have to contact the local police to have a complete report made out so that your insurer can process the claim. In addition, time limits for submitting claims often apply, so promptness in getting back to your insurer is essential.

COSTS, MONEY, AND BANKS

Massively subsidized by West Germany, West Berlin's opulent shops and slick restaurants were always a deliberate taunt to the relative lack of development of the Eastern Bloc. With its concentrated consumerism, and the need to "import" goods from the West, it is by no stretch of the imagination a cheap city: if you've just arrived from the Federal Republic the extra expense will come as a surprise.

Assuming you intend to eat and drink in moderate places, utilize the public transit system sparingly and not stay in the Hilton, the **minimum** you could get by on *after* you've paid for your room is $13–20 a day: a more realistic figure if you want to see as much of the city as possible and party at night would be twice that amount.

Accommodation, **transport**, and **nightlife** are most likely to run your budget up. The cheapest dormitory or basic rooms cost around $13 a night; the flat fares of about $1.50 on the bus and U-Bahn network quickly mount up, and drinking can be pricey in the more enjoyable nightspots. But eating is cheap, cheerful, and varied, and many museums are free, with others softening their charges for those with student ID.

MONEY

The currency of West Germany and West Berlin is the *Deutschmark*, which comes in **notes** of DM10, DM20, DM50, DM100, DM500, and DM1000; and **coins** of DM0.01 (one *Pfennig*), DM0.02, DM0.05, DM0.10, DM0.20, DM0.50, DM1, DM2, and DM5.

Travelers' checks are the safest way to carry your money. They can be cashed in any bank or exchange office, and used in flashier shops.

Surprisingly, **credit cards** are little used in West Berlin: only the major cards will be known and accepted, and then only in large department stores and mid- to upmarket restaurants.

Should you need **cash** on your plastic, various banks will give a cash advance against *Visa* and *Master Card*, subject to a minimum of the equivalent of US$100—stickers in the bank windows indicate which credit cards they're associated with. *American Express* card holders can use that company's facilities at Kurfürstendamm 11, 1/15, 2nd floor (Mon–Fri 9am–5pm, Sat 9am–noon; ☎882 7575).

BANKS

Banking hours are Monday to Friday 9am–noon and two afternoons a week from 2–6pm (varying from bank to bank); branches of the *Berliner Bank* have the longest hours. It may be worth shopping around several banks (including the savings banks or *Sparkasse*), as the rates of exchange offered can vary, as can the amount of commission deducted. The latter tends to be a flat rate, meaning that small-scale transactions should be avoided whenever possible. In any case the *Wechselstube* (bureaux de change) around Zoo Station offer better rates, as well as being open outside of normal banking hours. The exchange at the main entrance to the Zoo Station (Mon–Sat 8am–9pm, Sun 10am–6pm) will cash travelers' checks and give cash advances on major credit cards, though subject to a minimum of DM200.

INFORMATION AND LISTINGS MAGAZINES

Before you leave, it's worth contacting the German National Tourist Office, who have information on accommodation, what's on in town and the odd glossy brochure (see box below).

Once in West Berlin, the **tourist office**, *Verkehrsamt Berlin*, is in the Europa Center (entrance on Budapester Str.; daily 8am–11pm; ☎262 6031), with an additional office in the Zoo Station (daily 8am–11pm; ☎313 9063). It can supply a wider selection of hand-outs than the national offices, including comprehensive listings of the higher-brow cultural events, and help with accommodation (see "Finding a Place to Stay").

A better starting point for gathering more general info is the **Informationszentrum** at Hardenbergstr. 20, 1/20, 2nd floor (Mon–Fri 8am–7pm, Sat 8am–4pm; ☎310040). As well as a host of English-language leaflets on the city's history and political background (including useful material on East Berlin), they also give away the handy booklet *Berlin for Young People*. If your German's up to it the parallel version—*Berlin für Junge Leute*—is more detailed and up-to-date. The *Informationszentrum* can also help book youth hostel accommodation (see "Finding a place to stay").

GERMAN NATIONAL TOURIST ORGANIZATION OFFICES

In the US

New York 747 Third Avenue West, NY 10017; ☎212/308-3300

Los Angeles S. Flower St. Suite 220, CA 90017; ☎213/668-7332

In Canada

Montreal Place Bonaventure, Quebec H5A 1B8; ☎514/8778-9885

Next door to the *Informationszentrum* are two **cultural centers**. The *Amerika Haus*, Hardenbergstr. 22–24, 1/12 (Sept–June Mon, Wed, & Fri 11:30am–5:30pm, Tues & Thurs 11:30am–8pm; July & Aug Mon–Fri 1–5:30pm) offers US newspapers, magazines, and a well-stocked library, along with regular movies and cultural events. The *British Center*, Hardenbergstr. 20, 1/12, 1st floor (Mon, Wed, & Fri noon–6pm, Tues & Thurs noon–8pm) has a scant library and shows occasional films, but is a good source of British newspapers. While its cultural activities are not as frequent as the *Amerika Haus*, it occasionally has interesting visiting speakers.

LISTINGS MAGAZINES AND MAPS

West Berlin has two essential **listings magazines**, which come out on alternate weeks. *Zitty* (DM3) is marginally the better of the two, with

day-by-day details of gigs, concerts, events, TV and radio, theater, and film, alongside intelligent articles on politics, style and the Berlin in-crowd, and useful classified ads. *Tip* (DM3.40) doesn't quite match it for conciseness or flair. Both magazines also have extensive coverage on East Berlin. The monthly *Berlin Program* (free from the tourist office, otherwise DM2.50) has more condensed listings alongside info on opening times, and national and international train, bus and plane timetables. There's also a flimsy English-language paper, *The Berliner* (DM2.50), only worth picking up for its listings of all English-language events.

The best large-scale **map** of the city (West and East) is the ingeniously-folded *Falk Plan* (DM4), which contains an excellent gazetteer and enlarged plans of the city center. We've only been able to show major streets on our maps: the *Falk Plan* is an essential complement.

GETTING AROUND

PUBLIC TRANSPORT

Berlin is a large city, and sooner or later you'll need to use its efficient if expensive transport system. The U-Bahn, running both under and over ground, covers much of the center and stretches into the suburbs: trains run from 4am to between midnight and approximately 12:30am, an hour later on Friday and Saturday.

Sections of the system run under the border into East Berlin, and back out to the West: even if

you don't want to get off and enter East Berlin at Friedrichstrasse station, you can use these lines without fear of official hassle. For the moment , at least, it's still possible to get off at Friedrichstrasse U-Bahn and stock up on cheap East German duty-frees here. The **S-Bahn** system was severely damaged in World War II, and renovation has only recently begun. These days the service is far less frequent than the U-Bahn system, but better for covering long distances fast—say for heading out to the Wannsee lakes.

You never seem to have to wait long for a **bus**, the timetables at the stops are uncannily accurate, and the city network covers most of the gaps in the U-Bahn system. **Night buses** run at intervals of around 20 minutes, although the routes sometimes differ from daytime ones; the *BVG* (see below) will supply a map.

TICKETS

Tickets for the U- and S-Bahn system and the bus network can be bought from the orange-colored machines at the entrances to U-Bahn stations. These take all but the smallest coins, give change, and have a basic explanation of the ticketing system in English. Though it's tempting to ride without a ticket, be warned that plain-

The U & S Bahn

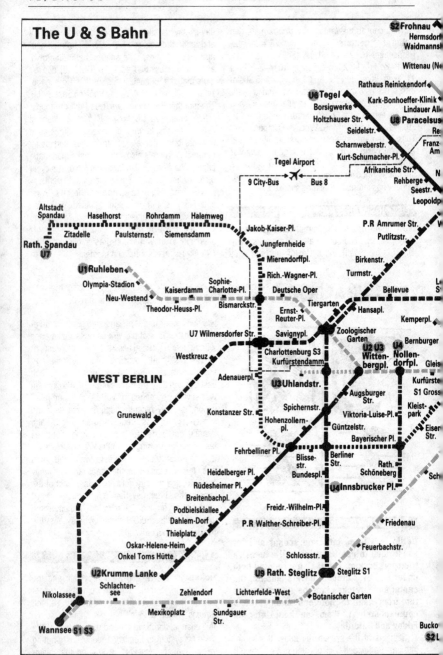

S2 Frohnau
Hermsdorf
Waidmanns

Wittenau (Ne

Rathaus Reinickendorf

U6 Tegel
Borsigwerke
Holtzhauser Str.
Seidelstr.
Scharnweberstr.
Kurt-Schumacher-Pl.
Afrikanische Str.
Rehberge
Seestr.
Leopoldp

Kark-Bonhoeffer-Klinik
Lindauer All

U8 Paracelsus
Re
Franz
Am
N

Tegel Airport
9 City-Bus   Bus 8

P.R Amrumer Str.
Putlitzstr.

Altstadt
Spandau   Haselhorst   Rohrdamm   Halemweg
Zitadelle   Paulsternstr.   Siemensdamm
Rath. Spandau
U7

Jakob-Kaiser-Pl.
Jungfernheide
Mierendorffpl.
Rich.-Wagner-Pl.

Birkenstr.
Turmstr.

U1 Ruhleben
Olympia-Stadion
Neu-Westend
Theodor-Heuss-Pl.

Kaiserdamm
Sophie-
Charlotte-Pl.
Bismarckstr.

Deutsche Oper
Ernst-
Reuter-Pl.
Tiergarten

Bellevue

L
S

Hansapl.

Kemperpl.

U7 Wilmersdorfer Str.
Savignypl.
Zoologischer
Garten

U2 U3
Witten-
bergpl.

U4
Nollen-
dorfpl.

Bernburger

Gleis

Charlottenburg S3
Kurfürstendamm

Westkreuz

WEST BERLIN

Adenauerpl.

U3 Uhlandstr.

Augsburger
Str.
Viktoria-Luise-Pl.
Güntzelstr.
Bayerischer Pl.

Kurfürste
S1 Gross
Kleist-
park
Eisen
Str.

Spichernstr.
Hohenzollern-
pl.

Konstanzer Str.

Grunewald

Fehrbelliner Pl.

Blisse-
str.
Bundespl.

Berliner
Str.

Rath.
Schöneberg

Sch

Heidelberger Pl.
Rüdesheimer Pl.
Breitenbachpl.
Podbielskiallee
Dahlem-Dorf
Thielplatz
Oskar-Helene-Heim
Onkel Toms Hütte

U4 Innsbrucker Pl.

Freidr.-Wilhelm-Pl.
P.R Walther-Schreiber-Pl.

Friedenau

Feuerbachstr.

Schlossstr.

U2 Krumme Lanke
Schlachten-
see
Nikolassee
Mexikoplatz

Zehlendorf
Sundgauer
Str.

U9 Rath. Steglitz

Lichterfelde-West
Botanischer Garten

Steglitz S1

Wannsee S1 S3

Bucko
S2 L

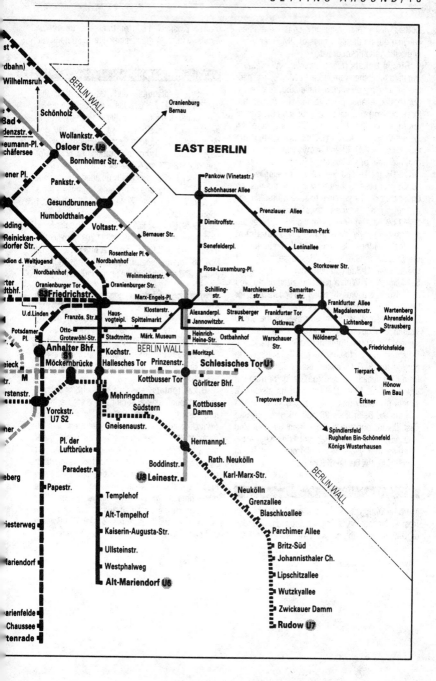

clothes inspectors frequently cruise the lines, handing out on-the-spot fines of DM60 for those without a valid ticket or pass.

Single tickets (*Einzelfahrschein Normaltarif*) common to all the systems cost DM2.70, irrespective of how far you want to travel; they're valid for two hours, enabling you to transfer across the three networks to continue your journey, and to return within that time on a different route. An *Einzelfahrschein Kurzstreckentarif*, or short-trip ticket, costs DM1.70 and allows you to travel up to three train or six bus stops (no round-trip journeys). On the U- and S-Bahn you're supposed to punch your ticket before traveling; on the bus the driver checks. It's possible to save a little money by buying a *Sammelkarte* of five tickets for DM11.50, but if you're intending to use the system frequently it's better to buy a **day ticket** (*Tageskarte*) for DM9 from any U-Bahn station or the *BVG* office on Grunewaldestrasse, 1/62, next to Kleistpark U-Bahn station (Mon–Fri 8am–6pm, Sat 7am–2pm). With a passport-sized photo, you can also buy a weekly ticket (*Wochenkarte*) for DM26, or a monthly ticket (*Monatskarte*) for DM65: these allow unlimited travel on the entire system and obviously represent a considerable saving. For more information, and a larger-scale U-Bahn map than the one on pp.12–13, it's worth getting the *BVG Liniennetz* leaflet (DM2), either from their cubicle outside Zoo Station or from the tourist office. Most U-Bahn stations also have simple giveaway maps; ask at the kiosk on the platform. U-Bahn lines #6 and #8 now run into East Berlin, and the S-Bahn from Bahnhof Zoo also now runs beyond Bahnhof Friedrichstrasse, meaning that you can travel from West Berlin directly into the center of East Berlin.

BY BOAT

More an option for a day out on the Havel lake from Wannsee or the Tegeler See from Spandau or Gatow (both to the west of the city center)

than a practical mode of transport, **boats** run regularly through the summer. For full details see p.66.

TAXIS AND CAR HIRE

Taxis are plentiful, and though expensive (DM3.40 + DM1.58 per kilometer), hardly more so than public transit, especially if you're traveling in small groups. They cruise the city day and night and congregate at useful locations, such as Savignyplatz and the Zoo Station. To phone for one, dial ☎6902, ☎240202, or ☎261026.

Though there's practically no need ever to **rent a car** in the city, one of the least expensive firms is *Mini-bus Service*, Zietenstr. 1, 1/30 (☎261 6565). Otherwise try *Allround*, Kaiser-Friedrich-Str. 86, 1/10 (☎342 5092), or *First & Second Hand Rent*, Lohmeyerstr. 7, 1/10 (☎341 7076); expect to pay around DM50 daily, plus a deposit of about DM200. International firms have offices at Tegel airport and are listed in the phone directory.

CYCLING

Cycling is a quick and convenient way of getting around the city, and—if you take your bike on the U- or S-Bahn—of exploring the countryside and lakes of the Grunewald and Wannsee areas. To take your bike on a train you'll need an extra ticket (DM1.70).

Bike rentals are available from several shops, though (unlike at cities in West Germany) not from the railroad station. Try *Fahrradbüro Berlin*, Hauptstr. 146, 1/41 (near Kleistpark U-Bahn; ☎784 5562), who charge around DM10 per day, DM50 per week; DM50 deposit and passport needed. If you're planning to stay for any length of time it works out cheaper **to buy** a second-hand machine and sell it when you leave. Try any of the bike stores like the one given above, or look under *Fahrräder* in the classified ads section of *Zweite Hand* (published Tues, Thurs, & Sat), *Die Berliner Morgenpost* (Sun), or *Der Tagesspiegel* (Sun).

FINDING A PLACE TO STAY

West Berlin has a wide range of rooms, from youth hostels to five-star hotels. Easily the best—and in the longer term, certainly the cheapest—way of finding a place to stay is through one of the accommodation agencies known as *Mitwohnzentrale* listed below. Compared to these, most other options are overpriced or inconvenient.

Hostels, at around DM23 the cheapest short-term choice, tend to be heavily booked and sometimes enforce a curfew. The **tourist office** in the Europa Center offers a hotel and pension **booking service** for DM3, though their options, especially in the high season, are limited to mid-range and upmarket places. However, you may be lucky and get something for around DM40 single, DM70 double, or be offered a cheap private room. The tourist office also provides an advance booking service: write at least two weeks before you arrive to *Verkehrsamt Berlin*, Europa Center, 1000 Berlin 30, stating the length of your stay and how much you're prepared to spend.

As a result of the tourist boom generated by the fall of the Wall, budget-range **hotel or pension rooms** aren't as easy to find as they once were. But, if you're prepared to phone around and wear out some shoe leather, it is possible to find a double room for under DM50: listings begin below.

Summer weekends are the most problematic periods, and if you're arriving on a Friday night from June to August it makes sense to have at least the first few days' accommodation booked in a hotel if you haven't been able to reserve a room from the *Mitwohnzentrale* in advance. Watch out, too, if you arrive when a popular exhibition or event (such as the Berlin Film Festival) is

taking place: see "Festivals and Events" for dates. The tourist office's leaflets *Tips für Jungendliche* and *Berlin Hotelverzeichnis* (also available from German National Tourist Offices) have useful lists of hotels and pensions.

MITWOHNZENTRALE

Mitwohnzentrale are agencies that can find just about any type of room, and for any length of time—from a week in a bedroom in a shared apartment to an entire luxury apartment for six months. In the summer, when plenty of places become available to let while people are away on vacation, your chances of their being able to find something immediately are high. But where the *Mitwohnzentrale* come into their own is for arranging **longer term stays**. Monthly charges for a self-contained apartment range from DM450 to DM700, about half to two-thirds that if you're prepared to share kitchen and bathroom facilities; agency fees are usually one percent of the annual rent per month. **Shorter stays** will work out at similar prices *pro rata*, though the shortest period of time a *Mitwohnzentrale* will book a room for is usually one week. Considering this works out at roughly DM18–25 per person per night, it clearly represents an important cost-cutting option over anything other than the cheapest dormitory hostel beds. Almost all *Mitwohnzentrale* will take advance reservations by phone, and vary only in the number of places they have on their files— and in some cases, their degree of efficiency.

Mitwohnzentrale, 3rd floor, Ku'damm Eck, Kurfürstendamm 227–8, 1/12 (☎882 6694). Mon–Fri 10am–7pm, Sat & Sun 11am–3pm. Biggest and best of the *Mitwohnzentrale*, and an easy walk from the Zoo Station. Also has rooms for women in women-only apartments, for which there's a separate phone number—☎882 6284.

Erste Mitwohnzentrale, Sybelstr. 53, 1/12 (☎324 3031). Mon–Fri 10am–8pm, Sat & Sun 10am–4pm. Second best in the city after the above. Laid back and a little disorganized.

Mitwohnzentrale, Holsteinischestr. 55, 1/31 (☎861 8222). Mon–Fri 10am–7pm, Sat 10am–2pm, Sun 11am–1pm. Friendly and fairly central, specializing in inner-city rooms. They also have women-only apartments on their lists.

Mitwohnzentrale Kreuzberg, Mehringdamm 72, 1/61 (☎786 6002). As the name suggests, their rooms tend to be in the Kreuzberg/eastern part of the city only, and therefore cheaper.

YOUTH HOSTELS

West Berlin's youth hostels are used extensively by school and sporting parties from the Federal Republic, and rooms tend to be booked well in advance: hence it's *essential* to phone first. The *Informationszentrum Berlin*, Hardenbergstr. 20, 1/12 (☎310040; see "Information and Listings Magazines" above) can book rooms in most hostels free of charge.

IYHF HOSTELS

All require an **IYHF membership card** which you can buy for about $20 from your local **American Youth Hostels Inc** branch before leaving, or from the organization's Berlin offices at Tempelhofer Ufer 32, 1/61 (☎362 3024; nearest U-Bahn Möckernbrücke). Each has a midnight curfew (frustrating in this insomniac city) and includes bedding and a spartan breakfast in the price.

Jugendgästhaus, Kluckstr. 3, 1/30(☎261 1097). Bus #29, direction Oranienplatz. Most central of the IYHF hostels, handy for the Tiergarten museums, but very solidly booked. DM20 for those under 25, DM23 otherwise, key deposit DM10. 9am–noon lockout.

Jugendherberge Wannsee, Badeweg 1, 1/38 (☎803 2034). S-Bahn #3 to Nikolassee. Very pleasantly located, with plenty of woodland walks on hand near the beaches of the Wannsee lakes, but far from the city center—and with a curfew that renders it useless if you're enjoying the nightlife. DM20 for under-25s, DM23 otherwise, key deposit DM20.

Jugendherberge Ernst Reuter, Hermsdorfer Damm 48–50 1/28 (☎404 1610). U-Bahn #6 to Tegel then bus #15 towards Frohnau. Situated so far from town that it's the least popular of the hostels and therefore least likely to fill up in summer: worth bearing in mind as an emergency option. Under-25s DM17, otherwise DM20; key deposit DM10.

OTHER HOSTELS

Bahnhofsmission, Zoo Station, 1/12 (☎313 8088). Church-run mission with limited accommodation for rail travelers (you may need to show your ticket) for one night only. No risk that you'd want to stay for any longer, since the rooms are windowless and dingy and the atmosphere starchily puritan. DM15 per person for a four-bedded cell with a meager breakfast; rise and shine by 6am. A desperate option, but worth knowing about if you're penniless or arrive in town very late.

Jugendgästhaus am Zoo, Hardenbergstr. 9a ,1/12 (☎312 9410). Zoologischer Garten U- and S-Bahn. An excellent location and extremely popular. Singles DM30, doubles DM50, triples DM70. No curfew.

Jugendgästhaus Genthiner Strasse, Genthiner Str. 48, 1/30 (☎261 1481). #29 bus direction Oranienplatz. Located near the grimmer section of the city's canal, but just ten minutes away from the nightlife of Winterfeldtplatz. Singles DM35, doubles DM66, triples DM90; breakfast included. No curfew, key deposit DM20.

Jugendhotel International, Bernburger Str. 27–28, 1/30 (☎262 3081). #29 bus direction Oranienplatz. Interesting position near the Wall. Singles DM38, doubles DM70.

Studentenhotel Berlin, Meiningerstr. 10, 1/62 (☎784 6720). #73 bus to Rathaus Schöneberg, or Eisenacherstrasse U-Bahn. Dormitory accommodation at the relaxed edge of the city's action. Doubles DM29 per person, including breakfast. No curfew, key deposit DM25.

HOTELS AND PENSIONS

SINGLES UNDER DM50

Centrum Pension Berlin, Kantstr. 31, 1/12 (☎316153). Great location, two minutes' walk from Savignyplatz and five minutes' bus ride from Zoo Station. Renovated with style, and great value at DM32 single, DM49–56 double.

Hotel De Luxe, Lietzenburgerstr. 76, 1/30 (☎882 1828). While the name may be a bit misleading, and the location—between an amusement arcade and a sex club—not the city's most salubrious, the *De Luxe* is situated just behind the Ku'damm and has a mess of good restaurants right on its doorstep. Singles DM37, doubles DM64.

Hotel Gotland, Spreewaldplatz 6, 1/36 (☎618 2094). Deep in the heart of Kreuzberg, with singles DM35–45, doubles DM60–100, breakfast included.

Hotel Savigny, Brandenburgischestr. 21, 1/15 (☎881 3001). Ten minutes south of Adenauerplatz. Singles DM42–65, doubles DM79–104.

Hotel Wendenhof, Spreewaldplatz 8, 1/36 (☎612 7046). Close to Oranienstrasse, the punks and all the anarchic delights of Kreuzberg. Singles DM40–50, doubles DM55–80.

Hotelpension am Bundesplatz, Bundesallee 56 1/31, corner of Hildegard Str. (☎853 5770). Central position five minutes by U-Bahn from Zoo Station. Singles DM40, doubles DM70–80; breakfast included.

Hotelpension am Lehninerplatz, Damaschkestr. 4, 1/31 (☎323 4282). Youth hostel-type atmosphere bang in the middle of an area that's lively at night. Dormitory accommodation in a four- or five-bedded room DM25–35 (including breakfast); singles (two rooms only) DM53 or DM63; doubles DM43–48. The single and double rooms don't include breakfast.

Hotelpension Biales, Carmerstr. 16, 1/12 (☎312 5025). A bit bleak and soulless, but on one of the prettiest streets in town, between Savignyplatz and Steinplatz. Singles DM45–75, doubles DM65–110; breakfast included.

Hotelpension Hansablick, Flotowstr. 6, 1/21 (☎391 7007). A short hop from the Tiergarten, this is one of the few "alternative" hotels in town, being run by a collective. Singles DM45, doubles DM80; breakfast included.

Hotelpension Lietzensee, Neue Kantstr. 14, 1/19 (☎321 5982). Near to an attractive lake and park, this is surprisingly good value for the quietly chic Charlottenburg area at DM45–60 for a single, DM86 double; breakfast included.

Hotelpension Pariser Eck, Pariserstr. 19, 1/15 (☎881 2145 or 883 6335). Adequate lodgings in a pleasant, leafy backstreet. Ten minutes' walk from the Ku'damm and with some classy cafés nearby. Singles DM38–75, doubles DM65–90; breakfast included.

Hotelpension Südwest, Yorckstr. 80, 1/61 (☎785 8033). Dreary part of town, but close to Kreuzberg hill and an area that's buzzing at night. Singles DM35, doubles DM60.

Pension Alexis, Carmerstr. 15, 1/12 (☎312 5144). Rather drab, but with more character than the *Biales* next door. Singles DM45, doubles DM60; breakfast included.

Pension am Savignyplatz, Grolmanstr. 52, 1/12 (☎313 8392). In the midst of Savignyplatz's nightlife; pleasantly seedy. Singles DM37, doubles DM65–75.

Pension Elfert, Knesebeckstr. 13–14, 1/12 (☎312 1236). Slightly shabby, but worth it for a location that's central by both day and night. Singles DM40, doubles DM60.

Pension Fischer, Nürnbergerstr. 24a, 1/30 (☎246808). Excellent value and near to the famed *Dschungel* disco. Singles DM35–40, doubles DM50–60.

Pension Kreuzberg, Grossbeerenstr. 64, 1/61 (☎251 1362). Close to Kreuzberg hill at the fancier end of that neighborhood. Singles DM39, doubles DM65.

Pension Niebuhr, Niebuhrstr. 74, 1/12 (☎324 9595). Clean and fresh pension in a quiet backstreet location that's within spitting distance of the Ku'damm and Kantstrasse. Singles DM35, doubles DM55–60.

Pension Peter, Kantstr. 146, 1/12 (☎312 2278). A little dismal and noisy, but as close to Savignyplatz as you can get. Singles DM45, doubles DM70.

Pension Riga, Rankstr. 23, 1/30 (☎211 1223). A few minutes from Ku'damm U-Bahn. Could do with a splash of paint, but considerably prettier than the *Austria* (see below) down the street. Singles DM35–40, doubles DM72; breakfast included.

DM50 UPWARDS

Unless otherwise stated, the following each include breakfast in the price.

Hotel Alpenland, Carmerstr. 8, 1/12 (☎312 9370 or 312 4898). Well situated and an excellent choice at this price. Singles DM60–70, doubles DM90–130.

Hotel am Zoo, Kurfürstendamm 25, 1/12 (☎884370). A gleaming gold foyer ushers you into a swish and plush hotel smack bang in the center of town. Singles DM159, doubles DM191–280.

Hotel Artemisia, Brandenburgischestr. 18, 1/15 (☎878905). The first women-only hotel in the city. Dormitory-type accommodation in a three-bedded room DM43, singles DM85–95, doubles DM120–180. Fills up quickly, so it's advisable to reserve in advance.

Hotel Bogota, Schlüterstr. 45, 1/12 (☎881 5001). Pleasant luxury at sensible prices. Singles DM50–80, doubles DM88–140.

Hotel Charlot, Giesebrechtstr. 17, 1/12 (☎323 4051). Neatly restored, efficiently run hotel near Adenauerplatz. Excellent value for money at DM50–80 single, DM85–150 double.

Hotel Comet, Kurfürstendamm 175, 1/12 (☎882 7021 or 882 7022). Airy but noisy rooms three floors above the Ku'damm. Singles DM55–95, doubles DM95–155.

Hotel Frühling am Zoo, Kurfürstendamm 17, 1/12 (☎881 8083). As central as you can get. Modern and spacious, but little more than that. Singles DM65–105, doubles DM100–165.

Hotel Heidelberg, Knesebeckstr. 15, 1/12 (☎310103). Central hotel in an area good for bars and a street noted for its bookstores. Singles DM100, doubles DM135.

Hotel Medenwaldt, Kurfürstendamm 225 1/31 (☎881 7034). Cramped but central rooms above the *Filmpalast* movie theater. Singles DM50–60, doubles DM85–120.

Hotel Meineke, Meineke Str. 10 , 1/15 (☎882 8111). Old-fashioned, typical Berlin hotel, with an amiable atmosphere and about a minute's walk from the Ku'damm. Singles DM105–129, doubles DM160.

Hotel Schweizerhof Berlin, Budapesterstr. 21–31, 1/30 (☎26960). Excellent food, service, and style. And so it should be at DM195–370 for a single, DM245–430 double. One for a splurge . . .

Hotelpension Aarona, Bleibtreustr. 32, 1/12 (☎881 6274 or 881 1818). Situated behind an unusual burnt-orange mock-Gothic facade a few minutes south of the Ku'damm. Singles DM50–65, doubles DM70–95.

Hotelpension Adria, Knesebeckstr. 74, 1/12 (☎881 6550). Convenient location, between Savignyplatz and the Ku'damm. Singles DM55–65, doubles DM85–95.

Hotelpension Alster, Eisenacherstr. 10, 1/30 (☎246952). Quiet backstreet location close to Winterfeldtplatz and its excellent nightlife. Singles DM50, doubles DM86.

Hotelpension Astrid, Bleibtreustr. 20, 1/12 (☎881 5959 or 881 8686). Rather gloomy rooms inside a pleasant old apartment building close to the Ku'damm. Singles DM60–84, doubles DM86–114.

Hotelpension Austria, Rankestr. 26, 1/30 (☎213 6018 or 213 6019). Simple, clean, and fresh. A few yards from the much cheaper *Riga* (see above); the extra marks are for the extensive modernization. Singles DM60–70, doubles DM95–120.

Hotelpension Haus Trinitatis, Imchenallee 62, 1/22 (☎365 4262). Way over to the west of the city, near the Havel lakes, and worth considering if you have your own transport. Sumptuous food, lovely rooms, and a view over the lake. Singles DM50–60, doubles DM90–100.

Hotelpension Imperator, Meinekestr. 5, 1/15 (☎881 4181 or 882 5185). Good value central, intimate hotel, situated on one of the most exclusive yet friendly streets in Berlin. Singles DM60–85, doubles DM85–100; breakfast not included.

Hotelpension Springmann, Bleibtreustr. 31, 1/12 (☎882 3091). Every possible facility squashed into the rooms, but comfortable nevertheless. Singles DM80, doubles DM120; prior reservation advisable.

Pension am Viktoria-Luise-Platz, Viktoria-Luise-Platz 12a, 1/30 (☎211 4095). A quiet haven in the older part of town, with interesting bars to explore nearby. Singles DM52, doubles DM74.

Pension Florian, Giesebrechtstr. 11, 1/12 (☎883 5062). Though the first-floor site makes the rooms a bit dingy, this is one of the most charming hotels in Berlin, with a cosy living room replete with chintzy sofas and huge oil paintings. Good value with singles for DM60 and doubles at DM80.

CAMPING

None of West Berlin's three **campgrounds** is close to the center: each requires time and effort to reach and, unlike many other European cities, there's no specifically youth-designated site. However they're all inexpensive (prices are a uniform DM5 per tent plus DM6 per person per night), well run and, with one exception, open year-round. If you are looking to cut costs, and intend to stay for a while, a *Mitwohnzentrale* apartment may work out almost as cheap.

Camping Dreilinden, Albrechts Teerofen, 1/39 (☎805 1201). From Oskar-Helene-Heim U-Bahn, take a #18 bus in the direction of Kohlhasenbrück. Open April 1–Sept 30. Close to the border in the southwest of the city, the site is one and a half miles from the nearest bus stop, and therefore inadvisable unless you have transport. Free showers and a small restaurant.

Camping Haselhorst, Pulvermühlenweg, 1/20 (☎334 5955). #10 bus in the direction of Haselhorst. The most accessible campground, but the least picturesque. A few minutes' walk from the Havel lakes, and not far from Spandau Citadel. Facilities include a restaurant, bar, showers (DM0.50), and a small shop. Four week maximum stay.

Camping Kladow, Krampnitzer Weg 111–117, 1/22 (☎365 2797). Bus #34 in the direction of Gatow or #35 direction Kladow, then change at Ritterfeld Damm for the #35E. Friendly campground with the best facilities of all the three sites, including a free nursery, bar, restaurant, shop, and showers (DM0.50). Six week maximum stay.

HOURS AND PUBLIC HOLIDAYS

Shops in West Berlin are open Monday to Friday from 9am to 6pm, 9am to 2pm on Saturday; department stores often stay open a little longer. On Thursday shops are allowed to open until 8:30pm; on the first Saturday of each month (*Langer Samstag*) and each of the four Saturdays in the run-up to Christmas, shops stay open till 6pm. A few supermarkets, located in U-Bahn stations, are open late and on Sunday (see Chapter Two, *Shops and Markets*); or you can stock up on basics in any of the Turkish shops of Kreuzberg on Saturday or Sunday afternoons. Additionally, many bakers open on Sunday from 2pm to 4pm.

Museums follow a general pattern of opening 9–5pm daily except Monday. They're open on all the public holidays listed on the next page (even Christmas), but usually close the following day.

PUBLIC HOLIDAYS
New Year's Day (Jan 1); Good Friday (changes annually); Easter Monday (changes annually); May Day (May 1); Ascension Day (changes annually); Day of German Unity (June 17); Day of Prayer and National Repentance (3rd Wed in Nov); Christmas Eve (Dec 24); Christmas Day (Dec 25); Boxing Day (Dec 26).

POST OFFICES AND TELEPHONES

West Berlin's main post office is inside the Zoo Station (Mon–Sat 8am–6pm, Sat 8am–noon; one counter open 24hr). This is the most convenient (and quickest) place to send letters home: mail to the US usually takes 4–7 days. It's also the place to send and collect letters poste restante: letters should be sent to Postlagernde Sendungen, Postamt Bahnhof Zoo, 1000 Berlin 12, and collected from the counter marked *Postla-gernde Sendungen* (take your passport).

Other, smaller post offices are dotted around town, and you can also buy **stamps** from the small yellow machines that you'll find next to some mail boxes. **Mail boxes** themselves are everywhere and unmissable, painted in bright yellow. When sending a letter, make sure you distinguish between the slots marked *Berlin (West)* and *Andere Richtungen* (other destinations). Boxes marked with a red circle indicate a faster service.

Telegrams can be sent either by dialing ☎1131, or from any post office.

INTERNATIONAL DIALLING CODES

USA 001	**Britain** 00 44	**New Zealand** 00 64
Canada 00 1	**Irish Republic** 00 353	**Australia** 00 61

USEFUL NUMBERS

Operator ☎03	**International directory assistance** ☎00118
Directory assistance ☎1188 (for West Berlin and West Germany)	**Ambulance** ☎112
Police ☎110	**Fire** ☎112

TELEPHONES

You can make **international calls** from most phone booths in West Berlin. Easiest are those that take DM1, DM2, and DM5 coins: only whole, unused coins are returned. Some boxes are marked "International," with a ringing bell symbol to indicate that you can be called back on that phone. There are international and local phones next to the post office in Zoo Station: cheapest time to call abroad is between 8pm and 8am. For **local calls** insert a minimum of DM0.30 and you can speak for as long as you like; in cafés and restaurants this minimum charge is sometimes hiked up. It's also possible to call direct to East Berlin: the code is ☎0372 (though this will probably go when the phone networks integrate) and the minimum charge is DM0.30 for six minutes.

FESTIVALS AND EVENTS

West Berlin's festivals are, in the main, cultural affairs, with music, art, and the theater particularly well catered for. Best place to find out what's on and where (and, occasionally, to reserve tickets) is the tourist office in the Europa Center (see "Information and Listings Magazines"): all mainstream events are well publicized in their leaflets and in giveaway brochures like *Berlin Program* and *Journal*. Other than this, events tend to be rather staid: one thing to look out for are the *Volksfeste*, small, local street festivals you often come across by chance.

FEBRUARY

Berlin International Film Festival. Various movie theaters around town; check *Tip* and *Zitty* for listings. After Cannes and Venice the largest film festival in the world, with around twelve days of old and new movies, art house cinema, and straightforward entertainment. Since the fall of the Wall, the festival has taken on a pan-Berlin flavor, with films from the GDR increasingly prominent. Movies are usually shown in the original versions with German subtitles.

International Tourism Exchange. Last week in February in the Funkturm Exhibition Halls. Information and goodies from over a hundred countries.

APRIL

Free Berlin Art Exhibition. Early April–early May in the Funkturm Exhibition Halls. Berlin artists show their most recent work. Painting areas for children, too.

MAY

Berlin Drama Festival. Various theaters. Large, mainly German-speaking theater event that has tended towards the experimental in recent years.

Allied Military Parade, Strasse des 17 Juni. May or June: exact date changes. Show of military strength by the three occupying powers along the city's traditional triumphal way. Starts at the Brandenburg Gate, finishes at Theodor-Heuss-Platz.

JUNE

Jazz in the Garden. Four weeks of the best international jazz artists in the gardens of the Neue Nationalgalerie.

Festival of World Cultures. Every fourth year, next in 1992. Massive program of events, exhibitions, concerts, and the like centered around one great culture or civilization.

Youth Drama Festival. End May–early June. Various sites. Experimentalism rather than professionalism is the name of the game here.

JULY

Berlin Barrel Organ Festival. In the city center for one weekend; check with tourist office for exact date and location. A gathering of the devices that people either love or hate.

The Bach Days. Second week of July. Celebration of the great Baroque composer and musician in concerts throughout the city.

A Midsummer Night's Dream. July–August. A medley of classical music, contemporary art displays, street entertainment, and rock concerts, with no real theme or purpose other than to add spice to summer evenings.

German-French Festival. End July–mid August, Kurt-Schumacher-Damm (near Tegel airport). Mini-fair with food and music and a reconstruction of a different French town each year.

SEPTEMBER

Berlin Festival Weeks. Various sites. A wide variety of events and international performers celebrate a different highlight from the history of the arts each year.

OCTOBER

Berlin Marathon. First Sunday of the month. The race begins on Strasse des 17 Juni and ends about 30 miles later, after passing through Dahlem and along the Ku'damm, back at the Kaiser-Wilhelm Memorial Church. To enter, write to SCC Berlin, Meinekestr. 13, 1000 Berlin 15: closing date for entries is one month before the marathon.

AAA Exhibition. Early October for nine days; Funkturm Exhibition Halls. Motor show organized by the German equivalent of the Automobile Association.

Lesbian Weeks. Mehringhof, Gneisenaustr. 2, 1/62. International forum for discussion, dance, music, and celebration of lesbian culture.

Jazz Festival. End October–beginning November. Jazz of every form and style. Different places each year; check program available from the tourist office.

NOVEMBER

Festival of Young Songwriters. Five days in early November; ask at tourist office for site. Forum for young songwriters to discuss and perform their work. Strongly international (and political) in tone.

DECEMBER

Christmas Street Market. Cutesy Christmas market from the first Sunday in December to December 24 in Breitscheidplatz, between the Europa Center and the Memorial Church.

People, Animals, Sensations. Circus in the Deutchslandhalle, near the Funkturm.

POLICE AND TROUBLE

The West Berlin police (*Polizei*) maintain a low profile: like the West German police, they're not renowned for their friendliness, but they usually treat foreigners with courtesy. They're unlikely to make their presence much felt unless ordered to from on high (which usually happens during demonstrations), in which case the Prussian military mentality goes into automatic pilot, resulting in robotic-type gratuitous violence.

Generally though, the police are very correct, and shouldn't subject you to any unnecessary trickery—in this country of rule and order it's more likely to be the ordinary citizen who'll spot you jay walking and reprimand you before the police even have a chance to get there.

The positive side to all this is that **petty crime** is comparatively low; probably the worst you can expect is handbag snatching in one of the main shopping malls, but keep a tight grip on your belongings and you should be okay. As far as **personal safety** is concerned, Berlin has to be one of Europe's least threatening cities; you'll be safe walking virtually anywhere alone by day or night, though avoid Kreuzberg SO36 in the dead of the night if you're female and alone. (For more on women and sexual harassment, see p.23.)

If you do have something **stolen** (or simply lost), you'll need to register the details at the local police station: this is usually straightforward, but inevitably there'll be a great deal of bureaucratic bumph to wade through.

Though **drugs** tend to be fairly commonplace in West Berlin, possession of any of the usual substances is illegal, and anyone caught with them will face either prison or deportation: consulates will not be sympathetic towards those on drugs charges.

The emergency **phone number** for the police is ☎110; occasionally you'll also see emergency posts with a direct line to the nearest police station.

WOMEN'S WEST BERLIN

There are around a hundred women's organizations and permanent locales in West Berlin, offering info and advice, performances, courses, and partying. They're testimony to a struggle for equal rights that began before the 1848 revolution and which side-stepped a complete ban from 1850 to 1908 on women's right to political assembly.

Not that women can yet afford to rest on their laurels. The election of a Red-Green senate in April 1989 opened the public purse to hitherto voluntarily-funded women's organizations but proved, perhaps inevitably, to contain more promises than pfennigs. Similarly, recent improvements in maternity provision—while long overdue and very welcome—were fueled primarily by a concern for the falling birthrate. They also help underpin a "return to family values" which, given the present unforeseen strain on resources and employment, along with the increased electoral support for right-wing parties, could mean more women carrying the burden of unpaid social welfare.

Funding to make public the more "distasteful" aspects of oppression—incest survivors' groups, rape crisis, defiant art—is already precarious, and the West Berlin Senate prefers to paint up feminism's more respectable face with prestige projects such as the *Fraueninfothek*, Leibnizstr. 57 (Tues–Sat 9am–9pm, Sun 9am–3pm; ☎324 5078), which has detailed and up-to-the-minute information on all organizations run by or pertinent to women. Its helpful staff can answer all your questions: they'll also admit to being the thick icing on a crumbling cake. The listings below cover a cross-section of women's groups: don't worry if your German is nonexistent—there's always someone around who speaks English. For **women-only bars**, see Chapter Four, *Drinking and Eating*.

Compared to many other European cities West Berlin is generally safe for women to visit. **Sexual harassment** is low, and it's safe to use the U-Bahn and walk around at night: streets are well-lit, and dawdling for hours in late-night cafés is standard practise. Obviously you should use common sense, but even the rougher neighborhoods (say of East Kreuzberg) feel more dangerous than they actually are: the run-down U-Bahn stations at Kottbusser Tor and Görlitzerbhf. (both in largely immigrant, and hence underfunded districts) look alarming when compared to the rest of the system, but wouldn't stand out in most other European cities. Kurfürstenstrasse U-Bahn is in a small red-light district, and worth avoiding if you're on your own.

HEALTH, SUPPORT, AND CRISIS CENTERS

Extra Dry, Mommsenstr. 34, 1/12 (☎324 6038). Project run by and on behalf of women in the process of kicking drug and/or alcohol abuse. Available to all women are some excellent courses—languages, tango, self-defense—and general legal advice. Drop your kids off in the cheap nursery (Sat 10am–1pm).

Feministisches Frauengesundheitszentrum, Bambergerstr. 51, 1/30 (☎213 9597). Self-help oriented women's health center.

Frauenkrisentelefon, (Mon–Thurs 10am–noon; Tues, Wed & Fri 7–9pm; Sat and Sun 5–7pm; ☎654243). Phone-in service offering sympathetic support and practical advice in a crisis.

Im 13. Mond (In the 13th Moon), Hagelbergerstr. 52, 1/61 (☎786 4047). Self-help oriented center, specializing in abortion advice, menstrual problems, self-examination courses. Fascinating courses on menses-related myth, practice, and healing.

Pro Familia, Ansbacherstr. 11, 1/30 (Mon–Thurs 6–9pm, Sun noon–2pm; ☎213 9013). Efficient and impartial abortion referral clinic, advice on pregnancy and the morning-after pill.

Rape Crisis Line. ☎251 2828. Tues–Thurs 6–9pm, Sun noon–2pm.

WOMEN'S CENTERS AND GROUPS

Frauenzentrum Berlin, Stresemannstr. 40, 1/61 (☎251 0912). Friendly and well-organized help and information center that offers advice on a wide range of subjects.

Mimi Treff, Danckelmannstr. 52a, 1/19 (Mon–Wed & Fri 2–6pm, Thurs 9am–2pm; ☎322 3087). Informal discussion groups with other women about their experiences. Run by women from the Evangelical Church.

Schokofabrik, Mariannenstr. 6, 1/36 (Sun–Fri 11am–10pm; ☎652999). One of Europe's largest women's centers, with a café/gallery, sports facilites (including a women-only Turkish bath: see p.95), and diverse events.

Selbstverteidigung für Frauen, Haupstr. 9, 3rd Gartenhaus, 3rd floor, 1/41 (Mon 4–6pm; first Wed of the month 7:30pm; Thurs 5:30–7pm). Fairly strenuous courses in self-defense.

ARCHIVES

FFBIZ (Archive of the Women's research, Education and Information Center), Danckelmannstr. 15 & 47, 1/19 (Tues 2–6pm, Fri 3–10pm; ☎322 1035). The place to make contact with the West Berlin Historians' Network, and for guided tours of Women's Berlin. On Tuesday between 10am and 1pm there's a breakfast served for women only.

See also *Spinnboden Archive* in "Lesbian West Berlin" below.

GALLERIES AND CULTURAL CENTERS

Begine, Potsdamer Str. 139, 1/30 (☎215 4325). A slightly more earnest sister to *Pelze* (see below), with lectures and films (Sept–May), and excellent performances by women musicians and dancers.

Pelze Multimedien, Potsdamer Str. 139, 1/30 (phone for opening hours; ☎216 2341). First-rate experimental art space with frequently changing exhibitions, performance, film, and art installations, occasional evening café. (Fri–Sun 10pm–late).

Das Verborgene Museum, Schlüterstr. 70, 1/12 (Thurs–Fri 3–7pm, Sat & Sun noon–4pm; ☎313 3656). A new, intriguing women's gallery.

BOOKSHOPS

Frauenbuchladen Labrys, Hohenstaufenstr. 64, 1/30 (☎215 2500). One of the first feminist bookshops in West Berlin, with a strong lesbian slant. Records and postcards available, and a small café. Some English-language books; only women admitted.

Lilith, Knesebeckstr. 86–87, 1/12 (☎312 3102). Feminist books and records, international newspapers and a good selection of fiction written by women. Also stocks a range of English-language books.

ACCOMMODATION

Frauenmitwohnzentrale. Organizations that finds rooms in all-women apartments. See

"Finding a Place to Stay" (p.15) for details and addresses.

Hotel Artemisia, Brandenburgischestr. 18, 1/15 (☎878905). The first women-only hotel in Weat Berlin, with a roof garden and exhibitions. Dormitory-type accommodation in a three-bedded rooms DM43, singles DM85–95, doubles DM120–180. All prices include breakfast, and it's advisable to reserve in advance as it fills up quickly.

GAY AND LESBIAN WEST BERLIN

Berlin has, despite the horrors of the past, a good record for tolerating an open and energetic gay and lesbian scene; as far back as the 1920s Christopher Isherwood and W.H. Auden both came here, drawn to a city where, in sharp contrast to oppressive London, there was a gay community which did not live in fear of harassment and legal persecution. And if West Berlin's gay and lesbian community is not as immediately noticeable as that of San Francisco or New York, it's still a city where there's plenty going on.

The easy-going, easy-living attitude stretches into the straight community, too, and it's not uncommon to see transvestites at their glitziest dancing atop tables at even the most conservative of bashes. The best time to arrive and plunge yourself into the hurly burly is during Gay Action Week, centered around the Christopher Street Day gay pride march on June 26 every year. For detailed **information** on the gay scene in West Berlin contact *Aha*, Friedrichstr. 12, 1/61 (☎251 2541 or 892 5601; meetings on Wed & Fri at 8pm and Sun at 3pm), or pick up a copy of *Berlin von Hinten* (DM13), the city's most useful gay guide. *Siegessäule*, a monthly gay magazine with detailed listings of events, is available from all of the groups below and most **gay bars** (listed in Chapter Four, *Drinking and Eating*), as well as at the *Prinz Eisenherz* bookshop.

CONTACTS AND INFORMATION

International Gay Association, Friedrichstr. 12, 1/61 (☎324 3277). Political pressure group with up-to-the-minute information on the latest in the international gay scene.

Neuengruppe, Friedrichstr 12, 1/61 (☎251 2541). Meets each Thursday at 8pm. Support and encouragement in groups of ten to twenty for those new on the scene in Berlin and/or just coming out.

Schwuz, Kulmerstr. 20a, 1/30 (☎215 3742/753 1321). Saturday evening meeting point for gays from all parts of the spectrum to come together and share ideas and experiences. During the week a locale for workshops and theater groups.

HEALTH AND ADVICE CENTERS

Zentrum für Sexual Wissenschaft, c/o Günther Schon, Potsdamerstr. 131, 1/30 (☎853 9401). Friendly advice and self-help groups for all aspects of sexual behavior. (Not exclusively gay.)

Deutsche AIDS-Hilfe e.V., Niebuhrstr. 71, 1/12 (☎323 6027). Mon–Fri 10am–1pm. Constructive help and information on AIDS.

Kommunikations-und-Beratungszentrum homosexueller Frauen und Männer, Hollmannstr. 19, 1/61 (☎251 0531 for men). Mon, Tues, and Thurs 5–8pm. Comprehensive advice and information center, offering single and group consultations, a small café, a telephone advisory service and lists of gay bars, activities, doctors, and therapists in the city.

Schwule Ärzte und Therapeuten Berlin e.V (☎693 4470). Mon 7–9pm. Contact number for locating sympathetic gay doctors and psychologists in West Berlin.

BOOKSHOPS AND GALLERIES

Galerie Janssen, Pariserstr. 45 1/15 (on Ludwigkirch Platz). Mon–Fri 11am–6:30pm, Sat

11am–2pm. Men's art gallery, also selling posters, postcards, and some art books.

Prinz Eisenherz, Bülowstr. 17, 1/30 (☎216 8400). Friendly and informative gay bookstore with helpful assistants. Excellent for browsing.

ARCHIVES

B/anal Graefestr. 18, 1/61 (☎691 1833). Archive on gay photography, graphics, literature, and art.

Schwules Pressearchiv im ASTA/FU, Kiebitzweg 23, 1/33. Newspaper cuttings reflecting the German-language media's attitude to homosexuality. A monthly exemplar of the latest snippets is available from the *Prinz Eisenherz* bookshop and some gay bars.

LESBIAN WEST BERLIN

Lesbians in West Berlin have a much lower profile than gay men. Perhaps because of this, there's no real distinction between bars and cafés for lesbians or straight women—see Chapter Four, *Drinking and Eating. Blattgold*, a monthly publication which lists all lesbian groups and events, *UKZ* (*Unsere Kleine Zeitung*; DM3.50) and *LesbenStich* are the main newspapers, available from most feminist meeting places and bookshops (see above). For support and information contact *Lesben Treff und Beratung*, Kulmerstr. 20a, 2nd Gartenhaus, 4th floor, 1/30 (Mon–Thurs 5–8pm; ☎215 2000). *Spinnboden* ("Archive and Treasury for Womanlove"), Burgdorferstr. 1, 1/65 (Mon–Thurs 2–5pm, Fri 5–9pm; ☎465 2021; U-Bahn Wedding; DM5 per visit) is a comprehensive archive of every aspect of lesbian experience, with a beautifully housed collection of 5000 books, videos, posters, and magazines. Foreign visitors are welcome. *Araquin*, Bülowstr. 54, 1/30 (☎215 2195), is a gallery/café that's a platform for lesbian culture and meeting point for artists' groups. Erratic hours; phone ahead.

The most important event of the year is the annual **Lesbian Weeks** at the Mehringhof, Gneisenaustr. 2, 1/61, a two-week international festival of music, dance, and political discussion held in October.

MEDIA

It's relatively easy to find American newspapers in West Berlin: *Internationale Presse* (daily 9am–10pm: corner of Hardenbergstrasse and Joachimstalerstrasse, near Zoo Station) has a good selection of international newspapers and magazines as does the *Amerika Haus* on Hardenberg-strasse (see "Information and Listings Magazines").

West Berlin produces two reputable **local newspapers**: *Die Zeit*, which comes out every Thursday and, while left-wing in stance, includes a number of independently written reports on a variety of subjects, and the Greenish/alternative *Tageszeitung*, known as the *TAZ*. It's not so hot on solid news, but has good in-depth articles on politics and ecology. Of the national dailies, the two best-sellers come from the presses of the late and unlamented Axel Springer: *Die Welt* is a right-wing heavyweight, and the tabloid *Bild* a reactionary, sleazy, and sensationalist rag that even Rupert Murdoch would be ashamed to publish. The *Frankfurter Allgemeine*, widely available in the city, is again conservative, appealing to the business community in particular.

Berlin has six main **TV channels**: ARD, ZDF, and N3 are closer to PBS in content; SAT1 is more of an entertainment channel, while the East German DDR1 and DDR2 are curious concoctions of travel documentaries, abysmal music shows, and the occasional foreign movie mixed in with heavily biased news reports. Although broadcast from the East in color, programs are in black and white on West Berlin TV unless the set is fitted with a special decoder.

There's a good chance of catching a foreign movie on any of the above-mentioned channels. If it's listed in the newspaper as *OF* it will be in the original language (usually English or French); *OmU* means that it has German subtitles. With cable TV, available in fancier hotels, you'll be able to pick up the usual European stations plus AFN, BFBS, and Tele5, which serve the US, British, and French armed forces respectively.

The only **English-speaking radio** stations are the *BBC World Service* (90.2FM), the British Forces station *BFBS* (99FM) and the American Armed Forces radio station *AFN* (88FM), which combines music charts with military news, and has to be heard to be believed.

STAYING ON

West Berlin acts as a magnet for young people from West Germany and all over Europe. Its reputation as a politicized, happening city, with a high profile in the arts and a more relaxed and tolerant attitude than its parent state, means that many people come here to live and work. That the English-speaking community—Americans, Brits, and Irish—is a large one will work to your advantage when it comes to finding out the latest situation for jobs and housing; and to your disadvantage in terms of competition.

An important **caveat** to the notes below is that things change quickly in this city, and with the influx of GDR citizens since the demise of the Wall (all of whom are guaranteed work and accommodation) it seems likely that rules, regulations, and openings will have changed at least subtly by the time you read this.

WORK

If you don't mind what you do (or what hours you do it), and are prepared to work "black" (without contract, taxes, or insurance), finding **work** in West Berlin shouldn't pose too much of a problem. If you want a **work permit**, however, then there's a large amount of of bureaucratic red tape to cut through.

Everyone is allowed to stay for three months on arrival and should register with the **Foreign Police** (*Ausländeramt*), Friedrich-Krause-Ufer 24

(Mon, Tues, & Thurs 7:30am–1pm, Fri 7:30am–noon; ☎390550 or 39051; see note in "Red Tape and Visas") on arrival if intending to stay longer than that. For all bureaucratic activities, take your passport and a couple of passport-sized photos.

American citizens and other non-European Community (EC) passport holders must go straight to the Foreign Police and apply for a **work permit** (*Arbeitserlaubnis*) *before* getting (and, legally, even applying for) a job, but permits are pretty difficult to come by and a lot of people just work black or, as a desperate final measure, marry a German national to put an end to their difficulties. If you are successful in getting a permit, you'll need to register with the Foreign Police for a **resident's permit** (*Aufenthaltserlaubnis*), for which you'll need to bring along an *Anmeldungsform* (registration certificate: see "Accommodation," below).

FINDING A JOB

Since long-term accommodation can work out quite cheaply in West Berlin, it's possible to live reasonably well on comparatively little here. Indeed, it's possible to get by on a take-home pay of DM1000–1500 a month.

Numerous *Arbeitsbüro* (job agencies) offer both temporary and permanent work—usually secretarial—but you'll obviously be expected to have a good command of German. Other than that, there are also several cleaning agencies (look in the yellow pages under *Gebäudereinigungs Firmen*) where only a minimal knowledge of the language is needed.

However, the best sources of both temporary and permanent work are certain **newspapers and magazines**: *Zweite Hand* (published on Tues, Thurs, & Sat), *Tip* or *Zitty* (bi-monthly on alternate weeks, first copies on sale on Wed). Other than personal contacts, these are also the best places to find English-language **teaching work**—either privately or in a school. For private work, the normal rate is DM20–25 per hour—don't be beaten down to anything less than that. Previous experience is not always necessary (particularly for private lessons).

Otherwise, the innumerable **cafés and restaurants** often look for workers: you'll need to tramp around town a bit first, and they'll expect a decent working knowledge of German; the good news is that you can often work black. If you do sign a contract with them it's likely that you'll need a *Gesundheitspass* (health certificate), information about which can be found at any local **Bezirksamt**. These are local official information offices (they're listed under *Senat* in the phone book, and are usually located in the local town hall), which can also advise on claiming social security and unemployment benefit.

ACCOMMODATION

Despite the lifting of the rent regulations (the *Weisser Kreis*) in 1988, an action which effectively allowed landlords to charge whatever rent they liked, **apartments** in West Berlin are still relatively cheap to rent and easy to find—assuming that you intend to stay at least a month, and don't mind the frequent moves necessitated by the preponderance of short-term leases. **Permanent accommodation** is much harder to come by, normally requiring an illegal take-over fee known as an *Abstand*. This can range from DM2000 to DM10,000, depending on fittings and the state of decoration. (It can, in turn and again illegally, normally be extracted from the person who moves in when you leave.) A *Kaution* (deposit), usually in the form of three months' refundable rent, is often also charged.

APARTMENT HUNTING

Although *Tip*, *Zitty*, *Zweite Hand*, and the Sunday newspaper *Berliner Morgenpost* advertise apartments and rooms, it's much quicker and less traumatic to sign on at one of several **Mitwohnzentrale**, accommodation agencies that specialize in long-term sublets in apartments throughout the city. (For full details see "Finding a Place to Stay.") Wherever you look, expect to pay between DM450 and DM700 for a self-contained one or two-room apartment, or between DM250 and DM400 for a room in a shared apartment. In listings or ads, the word *Warm* means that the rent is inclusive of heating and other charges; *Kalt*, non-inclusive. Incidentally, Berlin is the only city in Germany with a large number of apartments that have coal-fueled burners for heating (*Ofenheizung* in German). These are messy and inconvenient as they require constant stoking up—if you're out of the house for more than a few hours be prepared to come back to Arctic temperatures during the bitterly cold Berlin winter.

Once you've been here a while and made contact with people, **word of mouth** also works if you want a better (or cheaper) place to stay: tell everyone you're looking, and something will usually become available surprisingly quickly—there's a high turnover in apartments here.

When you finally find a place to live, you need to buy an *Anmeldungsformular* (registration form) for a few marks from any newsagent. Ask your landlord or landlady to complete this (if you don't have an apartment or room, friends will usually sign—illegally—that you're living at their home), take it to the local police station to be stamped, and you'll be able to apply to the Foreign Police for your resident's permit.

SQUATTING AND COMMUNAL LIVING

The tolerant attitude of the early 1980s is today very much a thing of the past, and although a few **radical squats** still exist (mainly in Kreuzberg—see p.45) the hassle you're likely to get from the authorities isn't really worth it for the money saved. Squatting is more of a **political gesture** than a practical alternative, and the organized groups here will want to see real evidence of commitment to their ideals before, as a foreigner, you'll be allowed to join. It remains to be seen how the Social Democratic-Green alliance that gained control of the city council in 1989 will change the situation. The Greens have responsibility for housing, and their more liberal policies offer some hope for the future.

Originating in the events of 1968, the **Wohngemeinschaften** (literally "communities") are now a firmly established part of West Berlin's "alternative" scene. Nothing like the hippy communes of yore, they are usually well-organized left-wing collectives of four to eight people (often with a few kids thrown in), who share rent, food, and, supposedly, a few ideals. A few do function well, and in any case are especially good for single mothers for the practical and emotional support offered. In the independently minded 1990s, however, the stringent requirements of being home every evening at a certain time to eat with "the family," cooking and cleaning to a strict weekly rota, the lack of privacy and heavy "talks" if you don't fulfil community expectations can seem too much for some. Having said this, the *Wohngemeinschaften* often advertise rooms to rent, and once you're in, these can be as permanent as you like.

Finally, **apartments in public housing** are few and far between, have long waiting lists and, with the influx of GDR citizens that began in 1989, are now almost beyond hope. It's worth inquiring at your local *Bezirksamt* on arrival, though, particularly if you have a "social problem" (eg pregnancy), as they're then required to find something as soon as possible.

DIRECTORY

ADDRESSES The street name is always written before the number. *Strasse* (street) is commonly abbreviated as *Str.*, and often joined on to the end of the previous word. Other terms include *Weg* (path), *Ufer* (river bank), *Platz* (square), and *Allee* (avenue). Berlin apartment buildings are often built around courtyards with several entrances and staircases: the *Gartenhaus* (garden house) and the *Hinterhof* (back house) are at the rear of the building (see "Zip Codes" below).

AIRLINE OFFICES *Pan Am*, Europa Center (☎881011); *TWA*, Kurfürsten-damm 14 (☎882 4066); *Air France*, Europa Center (☎261051); *British Airways*, Europa Center (☎691 021); *Dan Air*, Tegel Airport (☎4101 2707).

AIRPORT TAX Included in the cost of the flight.

BEACHES Believe it or not, West Berlin has a "beach" of sorts, on the Havel river at Wannsee to the west of the city center. See p.68 for more details.

CONSULATES *United States*, Clayallee 170, 1/37 (☎832 4087); *Canada*, Europa Center 12th floor, 1/30 (☎261 1161); *Britain*, Uhlandstr. 7–8, 1/12 (☎309 5292); *Ireland*, Ernst-Reuter-Platz 10, 1/12 (☎3480 0822).

CONDUCTED TOURS Unnecessary really, since there's little you can't see more fully, and more enjoyably, by yourself. Of the various tour companies, *BBS*, Rankestr. 35 (off Kurfürstendamm; ☎213 4077), and *Severin & Kühn*, Kurfürstendamm 216 (☎883 1015), have the most extensive list of trips.

CONTRACEPTION A glowing spectrum of **condoms** is available from supermarkets, anywhere selling toiletries, and vending machines in bar toilets. If you're into bizarre varieties, you'll be well catered for; if not, best bring your own. To get a prescription for **the pill** you'll need to see a doctor, so again it's worth stocking up before leaving.

DISABLED TRAVELERS The *Touristik Union International* (TUI), Postfach 610280, 3000 Hannover 61 (☎0511 5670) has a centralized information bank on many German and West Berlin hotels and pensions that cater to the needs of disabled travelers or those with specific dietary requirements—not in specially designed and separate establishments, but within the mainstream of tourist facilities. The *TUI* can put you on a package tour or organize rooms according to individual itineraries, taking into account each customer's needs, which are gauged from a questionnaire filled out before reservation arrangements commence. Their services also include such details as providing suitable wheelchairs for train travel, the transportation of travelers' own wheelchairs, and the provision of transport at airports and stations.

ELECTRIC CURRENT The supply is 220 volts, so any US equipment will need a voltage converter.

EMERGENCIES Police ☎110; Ambulance/Fire Brigade ☎112

JAYWALKING is illegal and you can be fined if caught. Even in the irreverent atmosphere of West Berlin, locals stand rigidly to attention until the green light comes on—even when there isn't a vehicle in sight. Cars are not required to stop at crosswalks—and walking on one doesn't give you any right of way.

LAUNDROMATS Dahlmannstr. 17, 1/12 (Mon–Fri 9am–1pm & 3–6pm); Uhlandstr. 53, 1/15 (6:30am–10:30pm); Hauptstr. 151, 1/62 (7:30am–10:30pm). Other addresses are listed under *Wäscherei* in the yellow pages.

LOST PROPERTY Police lost and found ☎6991; for items lost on public transit, contact the *BVG Fündbüro*, Potsdamer Str. 184, 1/30 (☎216 1413). Mon, Tues, & Thurs 9am–3pm, Weds 9am–6pm, Fri 9am–2pm. Otherwise try the police station at Platz der Luftbrücke 6, 1/42 (☎6991).

LUGGAGE CONSIGNMENT Lockers at Zoo Station. DM2 or DM3 for 24 hours. Luggage consignment at Zoo Station (Mon–Fri 6am–midnight, Sat & Sun 6am–5:40pm & 6pm–midnight); does not accept backpacks.

RIVER TRIPS From April to October *Reederei Riedel* run short trips from their jetty behind the Kongresshalle down the River Spree and the Landwehrkanal as far as the border with East Berlin. Trips cost DM7.50 and last for three hours: ☎693 4646 for more details. Other companies, also located behind the Kongresshalle, offer a variety of trips, some going as far as Spandau. See also "By Boat" in "Getting Around."

TAMPONS are available in most supermarkets and pharmacies, though much more expensively than in the US. When buying sanitary napkins, don't get the ones with the word "Deo" on the packaging—they're laced with viciously unhealthy deodorants.

TELEPHONE CODE (☎030).

TIPPING In fancier restaurants, or places where the service has been particularly good, 5–10 percent of the bill is the going rate: if there's a figure against the word *Bedienung* on the bill it means that service is included. In taxis, add a mark or two to the total.

TRAVEL AGENTS *ARTU*, Hardenbergstr. 9 (☎310 0040) and Mariannenstr. 7 (☎614 6822). Youth and student travel specialists.

VACCINATIONS None needed for Berlin, East or West.

ZIP CODES All Berlin addresses are suffixed by a code—it's important to include this when writing to distinguish between streets of the same name in different areas. In the Guide codes are given in their abbreviated form: thus Kurfürstendamm 11, 1/15 would be written in full as Kurfürstendamm 11, 1000 Berlin 15.

CHAPTER ONE

THE CITY

West Berlin is closer to Poland than the Federal Republic, and you're constantly reminded of the fact that this is occupied territory: NATO troops are everywhere, American accents twang out on the radio, and British Airways planes swoop over the Reichstag on their way to Tegel airport. Even though the Wall has crumbled and the barbed wire and watch towers that once ringed the western part of the city will soon be gone, West Berlin feels like what it is—an artificial creation, a pocket of western capitalism kept alive at great effort and expense by interested powers.

No one in their right mind comes here for light-hearted sightseeing: West Berlin is a profoundly scarred city, and even in the flashiest sections of its new center, around the **Memorial Church**, it still seems half-built, the modern buildings somehow making it look less finished and more ugly. Unlike Paris, Amsterdam, or Munich, this isn't a city where you can simply stroll and absorb the atmosphere. You need to plan your trips and target your points of interest, using the city transport system to cover what can be longish distances. Those points of interest are, almost without exception, somber: the **Reichstag**, looming symbol of the war years; the daily-decreasing remains of the garishly decorated **Wall**, facet of its aftermath; and several **museums** which openly and intelligently try and make sense of twentieth-century German history.

The brighter side is that this isn't the only face of modern Berlin. By night the city changes, awakening into a **nightlife** that's among the best in Europe—the bars here are by turn raucous, shady, stylish, and promiscuous, the discos and clubs blasting their stuff well into the early hours; restaurants are excellent, cheap, and of unequaled variety.

Culturally, the city has the advantage of massive subsidies from Bonn and a legacy of great art collections. By far the finest of these is in the suburb of **Dahlem**, where a museum complex holds everything from medieval paintings to Polynesian huts. Elsewhere, there's bound to be something to your taste. About a third of West Berlin is either **forest** or **park**, and some of these green stretches are surprisingly beautiful: in the center, **Schloss Charlottenburg** and its gardens are a great place to loll away a summer afternoon, and on the city's western outskirts, the **Havel lakes** and the **Grunewald forest** have a lush, relaxed attraction that's the perfect antidote to the city's excesses.

THE CITY CENTER

Wartime damage has left West Berlin with the appearance of a badly patched-up skeleton: beneath the surface the former street plan survives, but in a haphazard fashion and severed with cool illogicality by the erstwhile course of

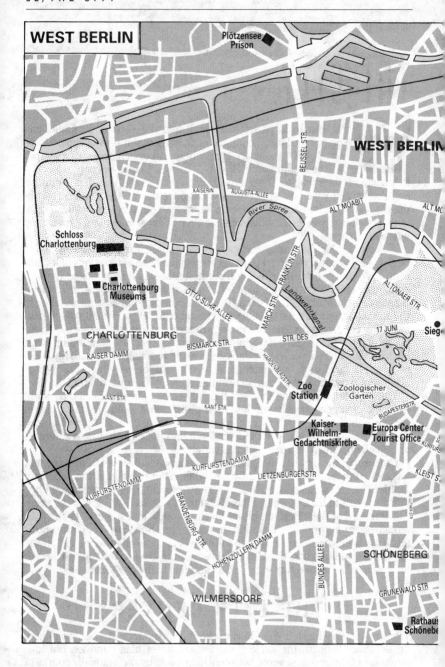

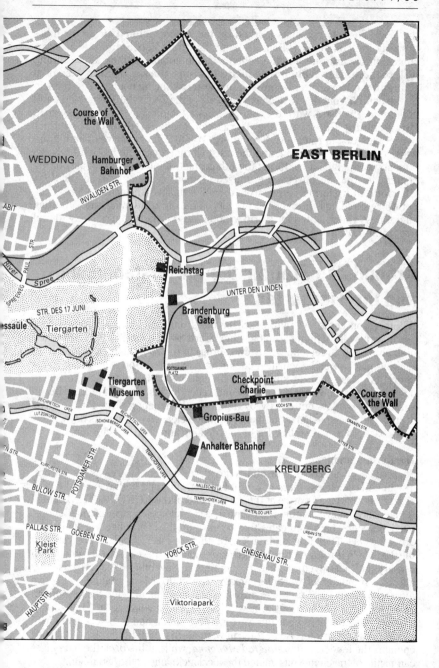

Course of
the Wall

WEDDING   Hamburger
           Bahnhof

EAST BERLIN

INVALIDEN STR.

ABIT

PAUL STR.

Spree

SPREEWEG

Reichstag

UNTER DEN LINDEN

STR. DES 17 JUNI

essaüle   Tiergarten

Brandenburg
Gate

POTSDAMER
PLATZ

Tiergarten
Museums

Checkpoint
Charlie

Course of
the Wall

REICHPIETSCH UFER

LUTZOW UFER

SCHÖNEBERGER UFER

REICHPIETSCH UFER

KOCH STR.

ORANIEN STR.

ÈN STR.

TEMPELHOFER UFER

Gropius-Bau

Anhalter Bahnhof

RITTER STR.

KURFÜRSTEN STR.

BÜLOW STR.

POTSDAMER STR.

HALLESCHES UF

TEMPELHOFER UFER

WATERLOO UFER

KREUZBERG

PALLAS STR.

GOEBEN STR.

URBAN STR.

Kleist
Park

YORCK STR.

GNEISENAU STR.

HAUPTSTR.

Viktoriapark

the Wall. The city center is marked by the **Zoologischer Garten**, or more properly the combined U-Bahn, S-Bahn, and train **Zoo Station** adjacent. A stone's throw from here is the center's single notable landmark, the rotting tusk of the **Kaiser-Wilhelm-Gedächtniskirche** (Kaiser Wilhelm Memorial Church); the **Kurfürstendamm**, an upmarket shopping boulevard, targets in on the church from the west. North and east of the Zoo is the **Tiergarten** park, ending in the east with the old **Reichstag** building and the reopened **Brandenburg Gate**. Near the **Tiergarten Museum district** the former border cuts east to run above **Kreuzberg**, West Berlin's enclave of immigrant workers, "alternative" living, and the most vibrant area at night. **Schöneberg**, a mostly residential area, forms the other point of interest in this part of the center; to the northwest the museums and gardens around **Schloss Charlottenburg** form a respite from the modernism of the center's filing cabinet office buildings. In between the city is mostly residential and suburban and, unless you've opted for a pricey hotel, this is where you're likely to find **accommodation**.

Around Zoo Station: the Kurfürstendamm and the Tiergarten

Whether you come by train, coach or bus from Tegel airport, chances are you'll arrive at Bahnhof Zoologischer Garten—**ZOO STATION**. Perched high above the street, and with views across to the Zoo, the train station is an exciting place to end a journey, conjuring memories of pre-war steam trains under its glassy roof. At street level though, it's an unkempt and conspicuously lavatorial-smelling place that until recently was run by the East Berlin authorities. By day, but chiefly by night, it's the meeting place for the city's drunks and dope pushers, but has been much cleaned up since its days, a few years back, as a marketplace for heroin dealing and child prostitution.

The Kurfürstendamm

Step out east from Zoo Station and you're in the center of the city's maelstrom, a seemingly senseless mess of bright lights, traffic, and high-rise buildings. A short walk south and you're at the eastern end of the **KURFÜRSTENDAMM** (universally known as the Ku'damm), a 3.5-kilometer strip of ritzy shops, movie theaters, bars, and cafés that zeros in on the center like the spoke of a broken wheel. The great landmark here, the one that's on all the postcards, is the **Kaiser-Wilhelm-Gedächtniskirche**, built at the end of the nineteenth century and destroyed by British bombing in November 1943. Purposefully left as a reminder of wartime damage, the church is a strangely effective memorial, the crumbling tower providing a hint of the old city. It's possible to go inside what remains of the nave (Tues–Sat 10am–6pm, Sun 11am–6pm): there's a small exhibit showing wartime destruction and a "before and after" model of the city center. Adjacent, a new, modern **Chapel** (daily 9am–7:30pm) contains the tender, sad *Stalingrad Madonna*, while at the back the blue glass campanile of the chapel has gained the local nickname of the "Soul-Silo."

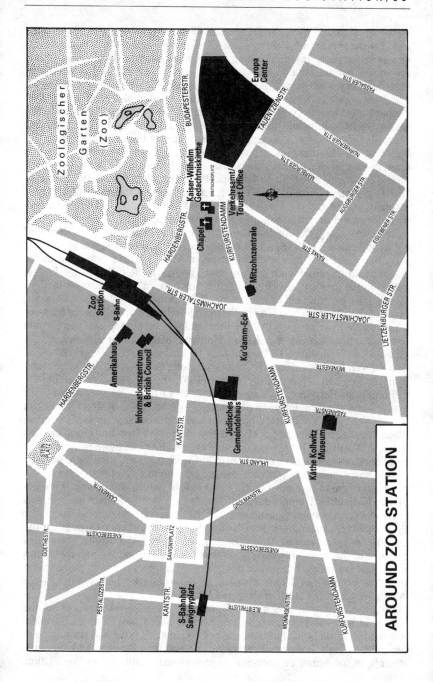

AROUND ZOO STATION

The area around the church acts as a focal point for West Berlin's punks and down-and-outs, who threaten the well-heeled Ku'damm shoppers with demands for cash. It's a menacing, unfriendly, spot and **Breitscheidplatz**, the square behind, isn't much better, a dingy concrete slab usually filled with skateboarders and street musicians. This area marks the beginning of Tauentzienstrasse, with the **Europa Center**, a huge shopping center that contains the *Verkehrsamt* (tourist office), at its head. It's worth a climb to the **observation platform** (daily 9am–11pm; DM2), under the rotating Mercedes symbol, for a preliminary reconnoiter of the center, the dazzling lights of the Ku'damm sharply contrasted with the darkened Memorial church. Farther down Tauentzienstrasse, and claiming to be the largest store on the continent, is the *Ka-De-We*, an abbreviation of *Kaufhaus Des Westens* – "the Department Store of the West." It's an impressive statement of the city's standard of living, and the seventh floor food hall is a mouthwatering inducement for one of the many exotic snacks sold there.

Turn west along the Ku'damm and you're at the beginning of its stretch of shops and cafés, which (roughly) get cheaper the farther west you go, blazing a trail at night in a dazzle of bright neon. The Ku'damm was built under Bismarck in the nineteenth century, and Thomas Wolfe called it "the largest coffee-house in Europe" when hanging out here in the 1920s; these days there's little left from either man's time. If the shops are beyond your budget, some of the street stalls selling clothes and jewelry are fun places for trinkets. There's little to do on the Ku'damm other than spend money, and there's only one cultural attraction, the **Käthe Kollwitz Museum** at Fasanenstr. 24. (Wed–Mon 11am–6pm; DM6, students DM3; buses #9, #19, or #29). The drawings and prints of Käthe Kollwitz are among the most moving to be found from the first half of this century. Born in 1867, she lived for almost all her life in Prenzlauer Berg in today's East Berlin (see Chapter Six), where her work evolved into a radical left-wing perspective. Following the death of her son in World War I, her woodcuts, lithographs and prints became explicitly pacifist, often dwelling on the theme of mother and child. When her grandson was killed in World War II her work became even sadder and more poignant. The museum's comprehensive collection of her work makes it possible to trace its development, culminating in the tense, tragic sculptures on the top floor.

Fasanenstrasse continues on the other side of the Ku'damm, and at no. 79–80 the **Jüdisches Gemeindehaus** (Jewish Community House) incorporates parts of a former synagogue attacked by the Nazis on the night of November 9, 1938, when synagogues, Jewish-owned shops, and homes throughout the country were destroyed—the *Kristallnacht* or "Crystal Night," so-named because of the mass of broken glass that resulted. Inside the hall the names of the concentration camps and wartime ghettos are inscribed; more cheerfully, the Community House also has an interesting kosher restaurant—for which see Chapter Four, *Drinking and Eating*.

By the time you reach **Adenauerplatz** the slick showrooms of the Ku'damm have died out, and the bars become affordable: although the clientele tend towards brash kids and sloshed recruits, it's not a bad starting point for an evening's boozing. Best of all for eating, drinking, and nightlife, though, is the squashed rectangle of streets south and east of Zoo Station, roughly bordered by Kantstrasse, Hardenbergstrasse, and Leibnizstrasse, and focusing on **Savignyplatz** (see Chapter Four, *Drinking and Eating*).

Hardenbergstrasse itself runs from Zoo Station, past the conveniently grouped **British Council**, **Amerika Haus**, and **Informationszentrum** ("Information and Listings", *West Berlin*), to Ernst-Reuter-Platz, a blandly modern oval named after the city's first post-war governing mayor. To the east, the **Technische Universität** (most striking of whose buildings is the huge, brilliantly painted **Umlauftank**, a hydraulics research center at the edge of the Tiergarten) marks an uncompromisingly modern start to Strasse des 17 Juni; a collection of old clothes and modern crafts makes the weekend **flea market** on the north side of the street a good place to browse.

The Tiergarten

Back in the center, the **Zoologischer Garten** forms the beginning of the **TIERGARTEN**, a restful expanse of woodland and lakes laid out under Elector Friedrich III as a hunting ground and destroyed during the Battle of Berlin in 1945—though so successful has its replanting been that these days it's hard to tell it's not original. The Zoo and its Aquarium (daily 9am–sunset; DM7.50, Aquarium DM6.50, combined ticket DM11, kids half price) are much like any the world over, and expensive to boot (see Chapter Three): better to wander through the Tiergarten tracing the course of the **Landwehrkanal**, an inland waterway off the River Spree. Near the Corneliusbrücke, a small, odd sculpture commemorates the radical leader **Rosa Luxemburg**. In 1918, along with fellow revolutionary Karl Liebknecht, she reacted against the newly formed Weimar Republic and especially the terms of the Treaty of Versailles, declaring a new Socialist Republic in Berlin along the lines of Soviet Russia (she had played an important part in the abortive 1905 revolution). The pair were kidnapped by members of the elite First Cavalry Guards: Liebknecht was gunned down while "attempting to escape," Luxemburg was knocked unconscious and shot, her body dumped in the Landwehrkanal at this point.

The broad avenue that cuts through the Tiergarten to form the continuation of Unter den Linden's triumphal way was originally named Charlottenburger Chausee. Known as the **East-West Axis**, it was a favorite strip for Nazi processions: on Hitler's birthday in 1938, 40,000 men and six hundred tanks took four hours to parade past the Führer. Now called **Strasse des 17 Juni***, its name commemorates the day in 1953 when workers in the East rose in revolt against the occupying Soviet powers, demanding free elections, the removal of all borders separating the two Germanys, and freedom for political prisoners. Soviet forces were quickly mobilized, and between two and four hundred people died; the authorities also ordered the execution of twenty-one East Berliners and eighteen Soviet soldiers—for "moral capitulation to the demonstrators." Today Strasse des 17 Juni sees only one triumphal parade—that of the occupying Allied forces in late May/early June each year, though this will probably become history once the two Germanys unite.

---

*Within hours of the opening of the border in 1989, paper strips were pasted over the street signs, renaming Strasse des 17 Juni "Strasse des 9 November," in celebration of the Wall's effective end; whether the new name will become official seems undecided.

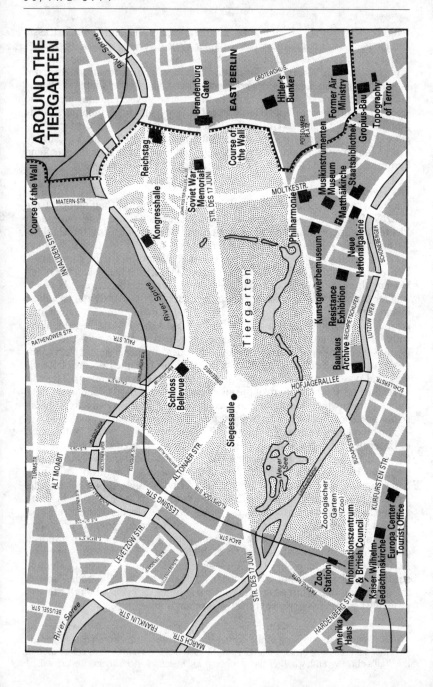

AROUND THE TIERGARTEN

Brandenburg Gate

EAST BERLIN

GROTEWÖHL-S.

Hitler's Bunker

Former Air Ministry

Gropius-Bau

Topography of Terror

Reichstag

Course of the Wall

POTSDAMER PLATZ

Musikinstrumenten Museum

Staatsbibliothek

MOLTKESTR.

Matthäikirche

Kongresshalle

Soviet War Memorial

STR. DES 17 JUNI

JOHN FOSTER DULLES ALLEE

Philharmonie

Kunstgewerbemuseum

Neue Nationalgalerie

MATERN-STR.

Course of the Wall

INVALIDEN STR.

River Spree

Tiergarten

Resistance Exhibition

REICHPIETSCHUFER

LÜTZOW UFER

RATHENOWER STR.

PAUL STR.

Bauhaus Archive

SCHILLERSTR.

Schloss Bellevue

SPREEWEG

HOFJAGERALLEE

Siegessäule

TURMSTR.

ALT MOABIT

ALTONAER STR.

KLOPSTOCK STR.

Neuer See

BUDAPESTER STR.

KURFÜRSTEN STR.

LEVETZOW STR.

LESSING STR.

BACH STR.

Zoologischer Garten (Zoo)

Europa Center

Tourist Office

River Spree

BEUSSEL STR.

FRANKLIN STR.

MARCH STR.

STR. DES 17 JUNI

FASANEN STR.

Zoo Station

Informationszentrum & British Council

Kaiser Wilhelm Gedächtniskirche

HARDENBERG STR.

Amerika Haus

At the center of the avenue is the **Siegessäule** (April–Nov Tues–Sun 9am–6pm, Mon 1–6pm, last admittance 5:45pm; DM1.20, students DM0.70; bus #16 or #24), the victory column celebrating Prussia's military victories (chiefly that over France in 1871) that was shifted to this spot from what is today's Platz der Republic on Hitler's orders in 1938. Though the boulevard approaches exaggerate its size, it's still an eye-catching city monument: 67m high, and topped with a gilded winged victory that symbolically faces France. The view from the top is one of Berlin's best—the Brandenburg Gate and the East seem tantalizingly close, the Reichstag standing like a gnarled protector at the edge of the park. Have a look, too, at the mosaics at the column's base, which show the unification of the German peoples and incidents from the Franco-Prussian War: they were removed after 1945 and taken to Paris, only to be returned when the lust for war spoils had subsided. Dotted around the Siegessäule are statues of other German notables, most imposing of which is that of Bismarck, the "Iron Chancellor," under whom the country was united in the late nineteenth century. He's surrounded by figures symbolizing his achievements; walk around the back for the most powerful.

From the Siegessäule it's a long hike down to the Brandenburg Gate and Reichstag, and most visitors take the #69 or #83 buses from the city center. If you do come this way it's worth looking out for **Schloss Bellevue**, an eighteenth-century building that was once a guest house for the Third Reich and is today the Berlin home of the Federal President—only visitable when he's not around. Farther east, on John-Foster-Dulles-Allee, sits the upturned banana of the **Kongresshalle**, an exhibition center whose concept couldn't be matched by available technology: the roof collapsed a few years back, and has only recently been rebuilt. On the southeast side of the park, the Tiergarten Museum Complex offers a variety of cultural delights (see below): few visitors venture north into Wedding, an industrial/working-class residential suburb whose charms are few, despite its former pre-war fame as a socialist heartland known as "Red Wedding." But it's worth pushing north from the park for the **Hamburger Bahnhof** at Invalidenstr. 50–51 (opening times and prices vary; S-Bahn line #3 to Lehrter Stadtbahnhof or bus #83). Like the Anhalter Bahnhof to the south (see "Kreuzberg", Chapter One), the Hamburger station was damaged in the war, though it had ceased functioning as a station as early as 1906. Fortunately it didn't suffer its twin's fate in post-war redevelopment, and is today an important forum for art exhibitions, usually of contemporary work. It's an exciting and innovative place, with a good café and bookshop.

From the Reichstag to Checkpoint Charlie

Strasse des 17 Juni comes to an end at the Brandenburg Gate, but it's better to start a little farther north—at the Reichstag.

The Reichstag—and the Remains of the Wall

Built in the late nineteenth century to house the German parliament, familiar from flickering newsreels as it burned in 1933, and the scene of Hitler's wresting of control of Germany in the same year, the **REICHSTAG** today seems lost in a sea of irony*. Inscribed with the words *Dem Deutschen Volke* ("To the German People"), what was once the symbol of national unity stands hard by the border that for years underlined its division; in front, on the broad green square, Turkish workers picnic and occupying troops play soccer. But it's not difficult to imagine the scenes the building has witnessed: in November 1918 the German Republic was declared from a balcony here, while Karl Liebknecht was busy proclaiming a Socialist Republic down the road at what is today's State Council building in East Berlin—and cementing his and Rosa Luxemburg's fate. Nowadays the Reichstag, restored following a wartime gutting, contains the fascinating exhibition *Questions on German History* (Tues–Sun 10am–5pm; free; bus #69 or #83), which chronicles the alliances and divisions, the war and rebuilding that led to West Berlin's insular existence. Inevitably the best sections are those concerning the Third Reich: photos of the 1936 Olympic Games, anti-Jewish propaganda, horrific pictures of the Plötzensee executions, and much documentary evidence of the war years that's not often seen elsewhere. Most of the commentary is in German, so it's well worth shelling out DM6 for the written English guide, or DM2 for an audio tape. With reunification seemingly inevitable, it's feasible that the Reichstag may once again become the seat of government for the united Germanys: Bonn was only made capital of the Federal Republic as an "interim measure"; Berlin, lying in the center of a greater Germany, would be the natural choice for a new seat of government.

Immediately behind the Reichstag you can still make out the course of the **Wall** that for twenty-eight years divided the city, and just to the left of the entrance, a poignant series of plaques marks the names (where known) of those killed trying to swim to the West across the nearby River Spree. Erected overnight on August 13, 1961, to cordon off the Soviet sector and corral the British, American, and French sectors of the city some 200km inside the GDR, the Wall underlined the city's schizophrenia and frenzy and marked (as Berliners are fond of telling you) the city's *raison d'être*—the "stabilization of the impossible." Late in 1989 the East German government, spurred by Gorbachev's *glasnost* and confronted by a tense domestic climate, realized it could keep the impossible stable no longer. To an initially disbelieving and then jubilant Europe, travel restrictions for East German citizens were lifted on November 9, 1989. Effectively, the Wall had ceased to matter, and pictures of Berliners East and West hacking away at the hated symbol filled newspapers and TV bulletins around the world. Eventually the Wall will be demolished entirely, to be replaced by a small border marker: while it still stands it's worth following it south from the Reichstag—and reviewing a little history.

---

* Debate as to who actually started the Reichstag fire has resumed in recent years. In a show trial, Göring, as Minister of the Interior for the State of Prussia, successfully accused a subnormal half-sighted Communist Dutch bricklayer, **Marius van der Lubbe**, of arson; he was executed the following year. It's equally likely that members of the SA, the precursors of the SS, began the fire to allow draconian measures to be brought in against the Nazi's enemies. By an emergency decree on the day after the fire, the basic civil rights guaranteed by the Weimar constitution were suspended, and the death penalty was introduced for a range of political offenses.

After the war, Berlin was split between its conquerors, as Stalin, Roosevelt, and Churchill had agreed at Yalta. Each sector was supposed to exist peacefully with its neighbor, under a unified city council, but almost from the outset antagonism between the Soviet and other sectors was high. Only three years after the war ended the Soviet forces closed down the land access corridors to the city from the Federal Republic, in what became known as the **Berlin Blockade**: it was successfully overcome by a massive Western **airlift** of food and supplies that lasted nearly a year. This, followed by the 1953 uprising, large-scale cross-border emigration, and innumerable "incidents," led to the building of what was known in the GDR as the "anti-Fascist protection wall."

When the four powers were deciding on sectors, one of the parish maps of Greater Berlin of 1920 was used to delineate them: the Wall followed the Soviet sector boundary implacably, cutting through houses, across squares and rivers with its own wild logic. One oddity about the Wall was that it was actually built a few meters inside GDR territory: the West Berlin authorities therefore had little control over the **graffiti** that covered it like a static New York subway car. Even now, as it is slowly chipped away by souvenir hunters eager to get a chunk of history before the Wall is finally demolished, it's an ever-changing mixture of colors and slogans, with the occasional burst of bitterness: *"My friends are dying behind you,"* humor: *"Last one out please turn off the lights," "Why not jump over and join the Party?"* and stupidity: *"We shoulda nuked 'em in '45 ."*

The Brandenburg Gate

Follow the course of the Wall south and you reach the **Brandenburg Gate** (*Brandenburger Tor*), another of those Berlin buildings dense with meaning and historical associations. Originally built as a city gate-cum-triumphal arch in 1791 and modeled after the Propylaea, the entrance to the Acropolis in Athens, it became, like the Reichstag later, a symbol of German unity, looking out to the Siegessäule and guarding the leafy passage of Unter den Linden, the continuation of what is now Strasse des 17 Juni, in East Berlin. In 1806 Napoleon marched under the arch and took home with him the **Quadriga**, the horse-drawn chariot that tops the Gate. It was returned a few years later, and the revolutionaries of 1848 and 1918 met under its gilded form; later the Gate was a favored rallying point for the Nazis' torch-lit marches. After the building of the Wall placed it in the Eastern sector, the observation posts nearby became the place for visiting politicians to look over from the West and secure a handy photo-opportunity—the view was apparently emotive enough to reduce Margaret Thatcher to tears on a visit here. With the opening of a border crossing here just before Christmas 1989, the East-West Axis of the city was symbolically recreated and the post-Wall mood of eagerness for unification was strengthened. When the GDR authorities rebuilt the Quadriga following wartime damage, they removed the Prussian Iron Cross from the Goddess of Victory's laurel wreath that topped her staff, on the grounds that it was "symbolic of Prussian-German militarism": when the border was reopened, it was announced that the Iron Cross would be replaced. Following the jubilation that accompanied the opening of the Gate, the area become a flea market for East German uniforms and junk; yet it's easy enough to see why some, mindful of historical precedent, still view the Gate with a frisson of unease.

From the Gate the border cuts directly south, but before following it, cross to the north side of Strasse des 17 Juni for a look at the **Soviet War Memorial** to the Red Army troops who died in the Battle of Berlin. Built from the marble of Hitler's destroyed Berlin HQ, the Reichs Chancellery, and flanked by two tanks that were among the first to reach the city, it's guarded by two Soviet troops, each under the "protection" of a British soldier. Police warn you away if you try and come too close.

Around Potsdamer Platz

Continuing south the course of the Wall passes through the edge of the Tiergarten to reach another the newly-opened **Potsdamer Platz**, the heart of pre-war Berlin and once a hub of the city's transport and nightlife. The old tramlines can still be seen, running headlong into a near-featureless no-man's land that's now filled with streams of Germans passing east and west. Nearby, to the left of the Platz, a small hummock of land marks the remains of **Hitler's bunker**, where the Führer spent his last days, issuing meaningless orders as the Battle of Berlin raged above. Here he married Eva Braun and wrote his final testament: he personally was responsible for nothing; he had been betrayed by the German people, who had proved unequal to his leadership, and deserved the future he could now envisage ahead of them. On April 30, 1945, he shot himself, his body hurriedly burned by loyal officers. In the wrangles after the war to prove his death, the Soviet Army apparently came up with Hitler's teeth, which they had managed to retrieve from the charred remains and have verified by the Führer's dentist. The latest on this apocryphal tale is that the teeth are now stored away in a museum in East Berlin.

Since *Die Wende*, the question of what to do with the remains of the bunker has reopened. Some say it should be preserved as a museum; others that it would become a shrine for rightist and neo-Nazi groups and should thus be destroyed. In June 1990, in preparation for a performance of "The Wall" by Roger Waters of Pink Floyd, engineers found another bunker farther north, filled with weapons and covered with SS murals depicting Nazi might. Whether these too will be destroyed is, as yet, undecided.

Just below Potsdamer Platz the border swings east, giving a good view of the new M–Bahn line, a showy if rather purposeless development in the city's transport network. The drab buildings on the Eastern side of the border are those of Göring's **Air Ministry**: Göring promised the people that not a single bomb would fall on Berlin during the war; if this were to happen, said Göring, he would change his name to Meyer—a common Jewish name in Berlin at the time. Ironically, the Air Ministry was one of the few buildings to remain unscathed during bombing and Red Army shelling.

Below Potsdamer Platz the woodland of the Tiergarten falls away and you enter a semi-desolate area that has never really recovered from 1945 devastation. A magnificently restored exception is the **Martin-Gropius-Bau** at Stresemannstr. 110 (Tues–Sun 10am–6pm or later; main collections DM4, though times and prices for temporary exhibitions vary; bus #24 or #29). Designed in 1877 by Martin Gropius, a pupil of Schinkel and the uncle of

Bauhaus guru Walter, the Gropius-Bau was, until its destruction in the war, home of the museum of applied art. In recent years it has been rebuilt and refurbished, and is now the city's main site for large, prestigious exhibitions. Also contained in the building are the main sections of the **Jewish Museum**, with a frightening section on the war years, and large collections of German **applied and fine art**. Its small café is a useful stopping-off point and needed pick-me-up before tackling an adjacent exhibition, **The Topography of Terror** (daily 10am–6pm; free). This is housed in a newly-built structure a little way from the Gropius-Bau, for nothing is left of the buildings that once stood here. Formerly known as Prinz-Albrecht-Strasse, Niederkirchenstrasse was the base of the Gestapo, the SS, and Reich Security offices: in buildings along here Himmler planned the Final Solution, the deportation and genocide of European Jews, and organized the Gestapo, the feared secret police. The exhibition is housed in what were once the cellars of the Gestapo headquarters, where important prisoners were interrogated and tortured. Though the photos here tell their own story, you'll need the English translation (DM2) for the main text of the exhibits.

Checkpoint Charlie

The land behind the Gropius-Bau is more wasteland; the place where West Berlin's learner's permit drivers come to practise, although the chances are the developers and construction teams will arrive soon. From here it's a ten-minute walk (or #29 bus ride) down Wilhelmstrasse and Kochstrasse to **Friedrichstrasse**, once one of the city's great streets, packed with cafés and shops, now a dusty avenue heavily pockmarked by wartime shell damage. **CHECKPOINT CHARLIE**, an allied military post and one of Berlin's more celebrated landmarks, stood at its northern end until July 1990 when it was declared redundant and removed. This building lent its name informally to the adjacent GDR border crossing (official title *"Grenzübergang Friedrichstrasse"*), which with its dramatic "YOU ARE NOW LEAVING THE AMERICAN SECTOR" signs and unsmiling border guards used to be the archetypal movie-style iron curtain crossing. In the Cold War years it was the scene of repeated border incidents, including a stand-off between American and Soviet forces in October 1961 which culminated in tanks from both sides growling at each other for a few days.

Tangible evidence of the trauma the Wall caused is still on hand at the **Haus am Checkpoint Charlie*** (daily 9am–10pm; DM4, students DM2.75; nearest U-Bahn Kochstrasse or bus #29), which tells the history of the Wall in photos of escape tunnels, and the (actual) converted cars and home-made aircraft by which people attempted, succeeded, and sometimes tragically failed to break through the border. Films document the stories of some of the seventy-five people murdered by the East German border guards, and there's a section on human rights behind the Iron Curtain, but it's a scruffy, rather

---

*An interesting—and little publicized—fact is that the Haus am Checkpoint Charlie is funded by the ruling right-wing West German CDU (Christian Democratic Union) party, who, in November 1989, also set about vote-catching by organizing free beer tents for East Germans crossing into West Germany.

dated collection, and not quite the harrowing experience that some American visitors seem to expect. For more details, pick up a copy of *It Happened at the Wall* or *Berlin—from Frontline Town to the Bridge of Europe* , both on sale here.

Walk a little down Kochstrasse and you'll see a high-rise building marked "**Axel Springer Verlag**" standing right next to the border. The late Axel Springer, extreme right-wing newspaper and publishing magnate (*Bild* magazine was his most notorious creation), deliberately had his offices built here as an act of provocation towards the GDR authorities. Today, the Springer corporation is busily buying into East German media.

The Tiergarten Museum Complex

To the west of Potsdamer Platz, the **TIERGARTEN COMPLEX** is a recently-built mixture of museums and cultural forums that could easily fill a day of your time. Far and away the finest building here is the **Neue Nationalgalerie**, Potsdamer Str. 50 (Tues–Sun 9am–5pm; main collection free; buses #29 & #83), a black-rimmed glass box that seems almost suspended above the ground, its clarity of line and detail having all the intelligent simplicity of the Parthenon. Designed by Mies van der Rohe in 1965, the upper section is used for temporary exhibits, often of contemporary art, while the underground galleries contain paintings from the late eighteenth century onwards. Many, though by no means all, of the works are German: **Menzel** begins the collection with portraits, interiors, and landscapes, followed by the more recognizable works of **Courbet**. The paintings of **Feurbach** seem thoroughly nineteenth-century and thoroughly German, and are followed by those of **Böcklin**—most typically the *Landscape with Ruined Castle*. After the bright splodges of **Lovis Corinth** and a clutch of **Monets**, the galleries move on to the portraits and Berlin cityscapes of **Grosz** and **Dix**, notably Grosz's *Gray Day* and Dix's *Maler Family*. **Kirchner** spent time in Berlin before World War I, and his *Potsdamer Platz* dates from 1914, though it might as well be in another country instead of just down the road. There's also work by Miró (*Little Blonde in an Attraction Park*), Klee, Karel Appel, Jasper Johns, and Francis Bacon: a fine, easily assimilated collection.

North of the Nationalgalerie the **Matthäikirche** (Matthias Church) stands in lonely isolation on a blitzed landscape that now forms a parking lot for the **Philharmonie**, home of the Berlin Philharmonic and, until he retired and subsequently died in 1989, their renowned conductor **Herbert von Karajan**.*

---

*Von Karajan's success in the post-war years obscured a murky past that included a close association with the Nazi party. Exactly what those associations were is unclear, though his organizing of concerts for the Führer—including an occasion when he had the audience seating arranged in the form of a swastika—is well documented, and in later years few of the world's great Jewish soloists ever performed or recorded with him. From the 1960s to the 1980s he ruled the Berlin Philharmonic with a rigid discipline that alienated many who worked under him, but proved fabulously successful in the field of popularizing classical music. Under the *Deutsche Grammophon* label, they recorded just about everything that had a chance of selling, all in the highly polished von Karajan style—a style as distinctive (and to some as likeable) as that of Mantovani.

Looking at the gold-clad ugliness of the building, designed in the 1960s by Hans Scharoun, it's easy to see how it got its nickname among Berliners of "Karajani's circus." Should you wish to reserve a ticket, the office is open Monday to Friday from 3:30pm to 6pm, Saturday and Sunday 11am to 2pm (☎261 4843): chances of getting a seat for major concerts under the orchestra's new conductor, Claudio Abbado, are slim unless you've booked months in advance, but the acoustics are so good that it's worth trying your luck for other performances under guest conductors.

Continuing the musical theme, the **Musikinstrumenten Museum** (Tues–Sun 9am–5pm; free), just below the Philharmonie, comes as something of a disappointment. Its collection of (mostly European) keyboards, wind, and string instruments from the fifteenth century to the present day is comprehensive and impressively laid out: but it's all strictly look-don't-touch stuff, with guards vigilant for the slightest tinkle. Content yourself with the pre-recorded tapes that give a taste of the weird and wonderful sounds the instruments make.

Much better is the **Kunstgewerbemuseum** (Tues–Sun 9am–5pm; free), an encyclopaedic but seldom dull collection of European arts and crafts. The top floor contains the Renaissance, Baroque, and Rococo pieces (wonderful silver and ceramics), along with Jugendstil and Art Deco objects, particularly furniture. The first floor holds the Middle Ages to Early Renaissance collections, with some sumptuous gold pieces. The highlight, though, is the basement: a small but great assembly of Bauhaus furniture, glittering contemporary jewelry, and a display of the evolution of product design.

Lastly, the **Staatsbibliothek** (Mon–Fri 9am–9pm, Sat 9am–5pm; free access) across Potsdamer Strasse from the other buildings, has over three and a half million books, occasional exhibitions, a small concert hall, a cheapish café, and a wide selection of British newspapers. The final building to be designed by Hans Scharoun, and the most popular of his works among his fans, the *Staabi's* most recent claim to fame came when it was used as an important backdrop in Wim Wenders' poetic film elegy to the city, *Wings of Desire*.

Kreuzberg

East of the Gropius-Bau the border runs from west to east, and the area directly below it forms **KREUZBERG**, famed for its large immigrant community and self-styled "alternative" inhabitants, nightlife, and goings on. Effectively there are two Kreuzbergs: the west, the area bounded by Friedrichstrasse, the Viktoriapark, and the Südstern, is a richer, fancier, more sedate neighbor to the east, which is sometimes refered to as SO 36 after its postal code. East Kreuzberg is West Berlin's "happening" quarter, a mix of punks and old hippies, and the place to hang out and hit the really raucous nightspots, names like *Trash* and *Bronx* giving you an idea of the atmosphere. It's also where the youth of the Federal Republic come to get involved in alternative politics, or avoid national service. Though there's precious little in the way of things to see, it is, in many ways, the city's liveliest neighborhood.

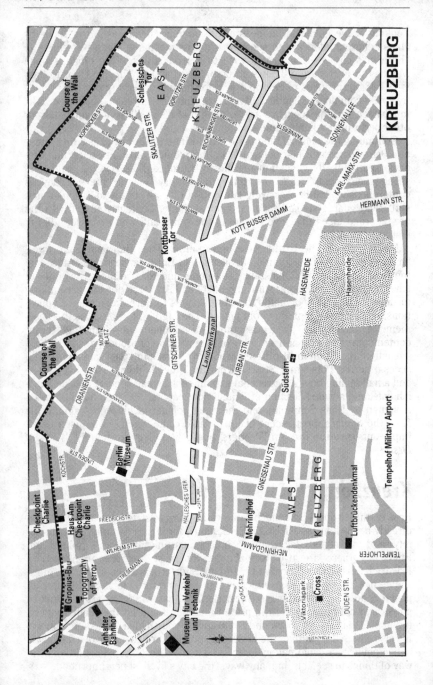

KREUZBERG

West Kreuzberg

First **the west**. It's only a short walk south, cutting down Stresemannstrasse, from the Gropius-Bau to the remains of the **Anhalter Bahnhof**, a sad reminder of misguided civic action that some would term civic vandalism. The Anhalter Bahnhof was once one of the city's (and Europe's) great rail termini, forming Berlin's gateway to the south. Completed in 1870, it received only mild damage during the war and was left roofless but substantial in 1945. Despite attempts to preserve it as a future museum building, it was blown up in 1952—essentially because someone had put in a good offer for the bricks. Now only a fragment of the facade stands, giving a hint at past glories. The patch of land that the station once covered is today a wasteland, and though there's nothing to see save a mock-up skeleton of its exit, an upturned railway engine and the paths of the old railtracks, it's an oddly atmospheric spot. The blunt and featureless building to one side, incidentally, is a fortified bunker-storehouse from the war years.

A brisk walk east from here, through streets leveled during wartime bombing, takes you to another Kreuzberg highspot, the **Berlin Museum** at Lindenstr. 14 (Tues–Sun 10am–6pm; DM3.50; buses #24, #29, and #41), which attempts to show the history and development of the city through paintings, prints and crafts. The earlier sections are reasonably successful but best are the exhibits from this century, particularly the collections of wartime posters and kids' toys, and Klaus Richter's portraits of Hitler and Göring. One unmissable attraction is the **Kaiserpanorama**, a large mid-nineteenth-century stereoscope designed to allow several viewers to see its rotating slides simultaneously. Usually it's loaded with pictures of pre-war Berlin, giving a vivid portrait of the lost city. Until a permanent site can be found, the museum also holds part of the **Jewish Museum**, a small but moving collection of Judaica chronicling the history and tragedy of Berlin's Jewish community. The remainder of the collection is in the Martin-Gropius-Bau (see above). More whimsically—and the reason most people come here—there's a mock-up of an old Berlin bar, the *Alt-Berliner Weissbierstube* (closes at 4pm at weekends, and is often crowded) which serves a traditional Berlin buffet—distinguished by being very heavy on pork.

An alternative and easier approach to the area is to catch the U-Bahn to Möckernbrücke station on line #1, an enjoyable above-ground ride through old warehouses and towering post-war redevelopment. Crossing south over the Landwehrkanal and turning right along Tempelhofer Ufer, you pass one of the decaying but still ornate **public toilets** erected in the early years of this century: Gents can pop in for a Bismarckian moment of relief. A little farther on, at Trebbiner Str. 9 is the **Museum für Verkehr und Technik** (Museum of Transport and Technology; Tues & Wed 9am–6pm, Thurs & Fri 9am–9pm, Sat & Sun 10am–6pm; DM3.50, students/children DM1.50; bus #29), one of the city's most entertaining museums and a button-pushers' and kids' delight. The technology section has plenty of experiments, antiquated machinery, and computers to play with, alongside some elegant old cars and planes. The transport museum, a collection of ancient steam trains and carriages, is even more impressive, the polished behemoths brought to rest in what was once a workshop of the old Anhalter Bahnhof.

Reaching the **Viktoriapark** (the "Kreuzberg," as it's popularly known) from here means a half-hour's walk, retracing your steps to the U-Bahn and heading south down Grossbeerenstrasse. On the slopes of a hill, the park is one of the city's most likeable, a relaxed ramble of trees and green space with a pretty brook running down the middle: on summer afternoons there's no better place to stretch out and relax. To one side is the *Golgotha Café* and disco (see Chapter Four, *Drinking and Eating*), packed on summer evenings, and atop the hill is the **Cross** (though it's more of a Neoclassical spire) from which Kreuzberg gets its name, designed by Schinkel to commemorate the Napoleonic Wars. The view is a good one too, made all the more pleasant by the wafting aromas from the Schultheiss brewery on the southern slopes. The well-restored streets that side the hill have a scattering of cafés, their tone and clientele reflecting the residents of the neighborhood, who are on the whole slightly older than those of the more youthful East Kreuzberg.

South and east of the Viktoriapark, the housing fades away to the flatlands containing **Tempelhof Military Airport**. Built by the Nazis, and once Germany's largest airport, it's still possible to see the Nazi eagles that decorate the buildings. Today it's used mainly by the US Air Force, and it was here that the Allies flew in supplies to beat the Berlin Blockade of 1948–9—an act that was to strengthen anti-Soviet feeling among West Berliners and increase the popularity of the occupying forces. At the height of the airlift a plane landed every minute, and the **Luftbrückendenkmal**, a memorial at the entrance to the airport symbolizing the three air corridors used, commemorates the seventy airmen and eight groundcrew who died in crashes while attempting to land.

East Kreuzberg: SO 36

In the 1830s, Berlin's industries started recruiting peasants from the outlying countryside to work in their factories and machine shops. It was to the small village of Kreuzberg that many came, to work in the east of the city and live in buildings that were thrown up by speculators as low-rent accommodation. Kreuzberg was thus established as a solidly working-class area and, in time, a suburb of Greater Berlin. *Siemens*, the electrical engineering giant, began life in one of Kreuzberg's rear courtyards. In the 1930s local trade unionists and workers fought street battles with the Nazis, and during the war it was one of very few areas to avoid total destruction, and among the quickest to revive in the 1950s. When the Wall was built in 1961, things changed: Kreuzberg became an eastern outpost of the city, severed from its natural hinterland in the East. Families moved out, houses were boarded up, and Kreuzberg began to die. At the same time, the city, deprived of cheap East Berlin labor to work in its factories, began to look farther afield, for the migratory workers who have come to be known as *Gastarbeiter*. Turks began to move to the city in large numbers, in time bringing their families and Islamic customs; few landlords welcomed the new workers, who gradually began to found a community in the area with the cheapest rentable property: Kreuzberg.

Throughout the 1960s and 1970s, Kreuzberg developed as West Berlin's Turkish enclave, with other *Gastarbeiter* from Yugoslavia, Spain, and Italy joining them. Along, too, came the radicals, students, and drop-outs of the

1968 generation—often attracted to the city because it was a method of avoiding national service, and to Kreuzberg because it offered vast potential for **squatting**. The ruling that pre-1950s-built apartments were subject to rent restrictions meant that speculators often allowed them to fall into disrepair, so that they could erect new buildings and charge whatever rent they pleased: squatters who maintained and developed these old apartments thus saved some of the city's old architecture.

In the 1980s Kreuzberg became the focus and point of reference for squatters throughout the Federal Republic, and the Social Democratic city government adopted a liberal approach to them, offering subsidies to well-organized squats and giving them some security of tenure. Projects like the **Mehringhof**, an adult education center and home for alternative industries and arts (actually just in west Kreuzberg at Gneisenaustr. 2), flourished.

All went well until the Christian Democrats took over the city. Using arguments over the role of city property—many of the buildings here are owned by the government—and the growing problems of crime and drug dealing, the right-wing Minister of the Interior ordered the riot police to enter Kreuzberg and forcibly close down the squats. There were riots in the streets, demonstrations all over the city, and intense political protest, which reached its peak when a fifteen-year-old boy was killed by a bus during a demonstration. Activists called a strike and the city government was forced to back down.

Which is how things have remained. The Turks and other immigrant communities are thriving, an uneasy truce exists between the radical squatters and the new civic authorities, and slowly, though perhaps inevitably, a few signs of gentrification are there, as astute Berliners (with an eye to their political profiles) move to the area. To say you live in Kreuzberg is to make a statement. At one time, if you wanted to gauge the political temperature of West Berlin, you had only to see what was happening on the streets here. The occasional spontaneous uprising still occurs, but the atmosphere is more subdued and less explosive than it was five years ago, when the tension was more explicit and frequent; the outbursts nowadays tend to be acts of unthinking violence rather than ones that spring from genuine political motivation. Nevertheless, Kreuzberg still constituted enough of a threat for the authorities to have briefly sealed off the area—even closing down the U-Bahn network locally—during a meeting of the IMF in Berlin in 1988. Despite the provocation, things—perhaps suprisingly—remained calm. With the ending of the Wall as an effective barrier it remains to be seen to what extent activists here turn their attentions away from local matters towards the unification issue.

You don't, however, need any interest in revolution or city machinations to enjoy Kreuzberg. The **nightlife** here is the city's wildest, and it's an enjoyable area to wander through by day, stopping off at one of the innumerable Turkish snack bars for a kebab, breakfasting on a 9am vodka-and-beer special at a café, or just taking in the feel of the place—which is much like an Istanbul market in an Eastern bloc housing development.

Catching U-Bahn line #1 (unkindly named the "Istanbul Express" in this stretch) to **Kottbusser Tor** or **Schlesisches Tor** stations right next to the border is a good introduction to Kreuzberg. The area around Kottbusser Tor is typical, a scruffy, earthy shambles of Turkish street vendors and cafés, the air filled with the aromas of southeast European cooking. Cutting through Dresdener Strasse, past the Turkish cinema, takes you on to Kreuzberg's main strip, **Oranienstrasse**, which from Moritzplatz east is lined with café-bars, art galleries, and clothes shops, and in a way forms an "alternative" Kurfürstendamm. Stop off at any of the bars along here for a taste of what the locals call a *Szene* place—somewhere that's in and happening.

South of Kottbusser Tor U-Bahn, it's a few minutes' walk down Kottbusser Damm to the canal. Turning left here and walking along Paul-Lincke-Ufer in an eastwards direction elicits a peculiar mix of emotions, with the beauty of the natural subverted by the derelict, deserted factories of East Berlin on the other side. Here, perhaps more than anywhere else in Berlin, the sense of despondency, of the separation that the Wall brought, feels very real: hope-fully, what Berliners call the *Wende*—"the change" brought about by the end of travel restrictions—will alter its character.

Around the Schlesisches Tor things are more residential, although for years the nearness of the Wall heightened the tension of the area. The River Spree here was in GDR territory, a strange situation for those residents of West Berlin whose apartments backed directly on to it. In the midst of the desolate buildings close by, a post-modernist construction swathed in gray and designed by the Portugese architect Alvaro Siza bears the emblem—courtesy of the local punks—"Bonjour Tristesse." At night the areas around both the Schlesisches Tor and the Kottbusser Tor seem a little sharper, dark-ness giving them an edge of danger and a sense of concealed, forbidden pleasures.

The Landwehrkanal runs south of Oranienstrasse, and below that the broad path of Hasenheide-Gneisenaustrasse marks the transition from east to west Kreuzberg. Around the Südstern (which has a convenient U-Bahn station) is another clutch of café-bars, and Gneisenaustrasse has some good restaurants; but the flavor of east Kreuzberg has gone, and things feel (and are) a lot tamer.

Schöneberg and Around

Like Kreuzberg, **SCHÖNEBERG** was once a separate suburb, one that was swallowed up by Greater Berlin as the city expanded in the late eighteenth and nineteenth centuries. Blown to pieces during the war, it's now a mostly middle-class residential area, stretching below the Tiergarten and sand-wiched between Kreuzberg to the east and Wilmersdorf to the west. Things to see are few: but what is here is both fascinating and moving.

Schöneberg officially begins south of Kurfürstenstrasse: but just north of the Landwehrkanal, on the edge of Tiergarten at Klingelhöferstr. 13–14, is the **Bauhaus Archive** (Wed–Mon 11am–5pm; DM3, students DM1; bus #29 to Lützowplatz). The Bauhaus school of design, crafts, and architecture was founded in 1919 in Weimar by Walter Gropius. It moved to Dessau in 1925 and then to Berlin, to be closed by the Nazis in 1933. The influence of Bauhaus has been tremendous, and you get some idea of this in the small collection here. Marcel Breuer's seminal **chair** is still (with minor variations) in production today, and former Bauhaus director Mies van der Rohe's designs and models for buildings show how the Modernist Bauhaus style has changed the face of today's cities. There's work too by Kandinsky, Moholy-Nagy, Schlemmer, and Klee, each of whom worked at the Bauhaus. The building, incidentally, was designed by Gropius himself.

East of the Archive, Reichspietsch Ufer follows the leafy course of the Landwehrkanal towards the Neue Nationalgalerie. **Stauffenbergstrasse**, a left turn off the Ufer, takes its name from one of the instigators of the plot to assassinate Hitler that came closest to success. **Claus Graf Schenk von Stauffenberg**, aristocratic chief of staff to the German Army Office that once stood on this street, organized the **bomb plot** of July 20, 1944. During a conference at Hitler's East Prussian headquarters in Rastenburg, von Stauffenberg placed his briefcase packed with explosives no more than four meters from the Führer, slipped out of the meeting and headed back to Berlin, where he and fellow conspirators had made extensive contacts among high ranking army officers with anti-Nazi sentiments. By some fluke Hitler escaped unscathed: von Stauffenberg and the rest of the conspirators were quickly arrested, taken to the courtyard of the Army Office, and, under the lights of assembled staff cars, shot. Throughout Berlin anyone even vaguely connected with the plot was also arrested, many meeting their fates at Plötzensee Prison (see below); recent figures estimate that almost five thousand people were killed as a result of the failed plot as the Nazis purged the German aristocracy who had supported von Stauffenberg. Today the site of the building where von Stauffenberg worked and died is occupied by the permanent exhibition **Resistance to National Socialism** (Stauffenbergstr. 14; Mon–Fri 9am–6pm, Sat & Sun 9am–1pm; free; bus #29), a well-mounted collection of photos and documents covering the suprisingly wide range of groups opposed to the Third Reich. This is one exhibition rarely highlighted to visitors, and there's little translation of material; but if you have any interest in the war years, it's deeply absorbing.

On the corner of Reichspietsch Ufer and Stauffenbergstrasse, the **Shell-Haus**—now known as the Bewag building—is one of Berlin's great buildings that substantially survived World War II, a procession of tiered levels designed by Emil Fahrenkamp in 1931 and a leading piece of Modernist architecture. Keep walking east on Reichspietsch Ufer, cross Potsdamer Strasse, and you soon come to the city's largest (and junkiest) weekend **flea market** (see Chapter Two, *Shops and Markets*). This has recently become the venue of the *"Polenmarkt"* or "Polish Market", a sorry affair where Poles sell vodka and tawdry knick-knacks at the weekend, come rain or shine. The few marks they make in a day can be stretched a long way in Poland, and the unhappy spectacle of hundreds of people selling sad, personal items, is a telling statement on the East-West economic division. If you want to take photos, ask first.

Schöneberg

Potsdamer Strasse itself leads south into Schöneberg proper, quickly becoming a broad, untidy strip of Turkish cafés, restaurants, and wholesalers, with the **Turkish Bazaar**, a market place of tacky Taiwanese junk by day (and with a wild bar that has a belly-dancing floor show at night), parked in an old U-Bahn station. A little farther south, past the prostitutes who line the street after dark and, at no. 139, the *Begine* café and *Pelze* gallery—part of a cluster of women's groups here and the only things on the street to which even money can't buy access for men—is the **Kleist Park.** This, fronted by the **Köningskolonnaden**, a colonnade of 1780 (summer 7am–8pm; winter 7am–4pm), gives the stretch a touch of dignity: on a misty morning you might be fooled into thinking you were in Paris. The **Kamergerichtesgebäude**, the building behind the park, was once the Supreme Court of Justice, where the Nazi courts under the infamous Judge Freisler held show trials of their political opponents, a prelude to the inevitable executions—which often took place in Plötzensee prison. Freisler met his unlamented end in the final few weeks of the war: on his way from the courtroom a bomb from an American aircraft fell on the building, dislodging a beam which crushed Freisler's skull. Today much restored, only thirty of the building's 486 rooms are in use, as headquarters of the Allied Air Control, which oversees safety in the air corridors leading to the city.

From Potsdamer Strasse it's a short detour west to **Nollendorfplatz**. In the Weimar Berlin of the 1920s and early 1930s, Nollendorfplatz was the center of the city's large **gay and lesbian community**. Even by contemporary standards, Berlin's gay scene in those days was prodigious: there were around forty gay bars on and near this square alone, and gay life in the city was open, fashionable, and well-organized, with its own newspapers, community associations, and art. The city's theaters were filled with plays exploring gay themes, homosexuality in the Prussian army was little short of institutionalized, and gay bars, nightclubs, and brothels proudly advertised their attractions—there were even gay working men's clubs. All this happened at a time when the rest of Europe was smothered under a welter of homophobia and repression, when to be "discovered" as a homosexual or lesbian meant total social ostracism. Under the Third Reich, homosexuality was quickly and brutally outlawed: gays and lesbians were rounded up and taken to concentration camps, branded for their "perversion" by being forced to wear (respectively) pink or black triangles*. A pink plaque in the shape of a triangle at Nollendorfplatz U-Bahn station commemorates the thousands of men and women who were murdered in the camps. Today, the area around Nollendorfplatz remains the focus of West Berlin's gay nightlife and especially its bars: for listings, see "Gay Men's Bars" in Chapter Four, *Drinking and Eating*.

As well its first-rate nightlife, Nollendorfplatz holds a couple of offbeat attractions by day. On the western side the **flea market** (Wed–Mon 11am–7pm) is one of the best in the city: housed in a group of old carriages on a disused U-Bahn station, it sells more antiques than junk, though most of the stuff here is reasonably priced. There's a bar here, too, which often has live jazz and adds to the sense of fun. Crossing back onto Nollendorfplatz, past the proto-deco **Metropol disco** (see Chapter Five, *Music and Nightlife*), Maassenstrasse leads on to Nollendorfstrasse, where at no. 17 stands the building in which **Christopher Isherwood** lived during his years in pre-war Berlin, a time that was to be elegantly recounted in perhaps the most famous collection of stories about the city ever written—*Goodbye to Berlin*:

> *From my window, the deep solemn massive street. Cellar shops where lamps burn all day, under the shadow of top-heavy balconied facades, dirty plaster frontages embossed with scroll work and heraldic devices. The whole district is this: street leading into street of houses like shabby monumental safes crammed with the tarnished valuables and second hand furniture of a bankrupt middle class.*

---

*Officially, the black triangle indicated "anti-social" offenders: in an attempt to ignore the existence of lesbianism, lesbians were arrested on pretexts such as swearing at the Führer's name. As homosexuality was, at the time, still illegal in Allied countries, no Nazis were tried for crimes against gays or lesbians at Nürnberg.

Schöneberg has since been reborn as a fancy, even chic neighborhood; the would-be Isherwoods of the moment hang out in SO 36 or Prenzlauer Berg in East Berlin. At night, this part of Schöneberg, particularly the area around **Winterfeldtplatz**, is a good one for eating and especially drinking: tidily bohemian, less sniffy than Savignyplatz, and much more middle-of-the-road than SO 36. On Wednesday and Saturday mornings the square holds an excellent **market**: see Chapter Two, *Shops and Markets*.

Schöneberg's most famous attraction actually has the least to see: the **Rathaus Schöneberg** on Martin-Luther-Strasse, the penultimate stop on U-Bahn line #4. Built just before World War I, the Rathaus became the seat of the West Berlin Parliament and Senate after the last war, and it was outside here in 1963 that **John F. Kennedy** made his celebrated statement of the Cold War political situation, just a few months after the Cuban missile crisis:

> *There are many people in the world who really don't understand, or say they don't, what is the great issue between the free world and the Communist world. Let them come to Berlin. There are some who say that Communism is the wave of the future. Let them come to Berlin. And there are some who say in Europe and elsewhere we can work with the Communists. Let them come to Berlin. And there are even a few who say it is true that Communism is an evil system, but it permits us to make economic progress.* Lässt sie nach Berlin kommen. *Let them come to Berlin . . . All free men, wherever they may live, are citizens of Berlin, and, therefore, as a free man, I take pride in the words* "Ich bin ein Berliner."

Rousing stuff. But what the President hadn't realized as he read from his phonetically-written text was that he had actually said "I am a small doughnut," since *Berliner* is the name given in West Germany to those cakes. So popular has this sub-text become that it's possible to buy little plastic doughnuts, bearing the historic words. The day after Kennedy was assassinated, the square in front of the Rathaus was given his name—a move apparently instigated by the city's students, amongst whom the President was highly popular.

If you've time and interest it's possible to climb the Rathaus tower, and see the replica **Liberty bell** donated to the city by the US in 1950, though it's more pleasant, and certainly less strenuous, to take a stroll in the small **Volkspark**, a thin ribbon of greenery that runs west from here.

Charlottenburg: the Schloss and museums

The district of **CHARLOTTENBURG** stretches north and west of the center of town, reaching as far as the forests of the Grunewald. To the west it contains a number of attractions (detailed under "Out from the Center"), but far and away the most significant target, one that needs a day at least to cover, is the **Schloss Charlottenburg and Museum Complex** on Spandauer Damm. The Schloss is open Tuesday to Sunday from 9am to 5pm: tickets, which include entrance to all other Schloss buildings, cost DM6, DM3 for students; the buses which run nearest are #54 or #74.

Schloss Charlottenburg and its museums

Schloss Charlottenburg comes as a surprise after the unrelieved modernity of the city streets. Commissioned as a country house by the future Queen Sophie Charlotte in 1695 (she also gave her name to the district) the Schloss was expanded and added to throughout the eighteenth and early nineteenth centuries, the master builder Karl Friedrich Schinkel providing the final touches. Approaching the sandy elaborateness of the Schloss at the main courtyard, you're confronted with Andreas Schlüter's **statue** of Friedrich

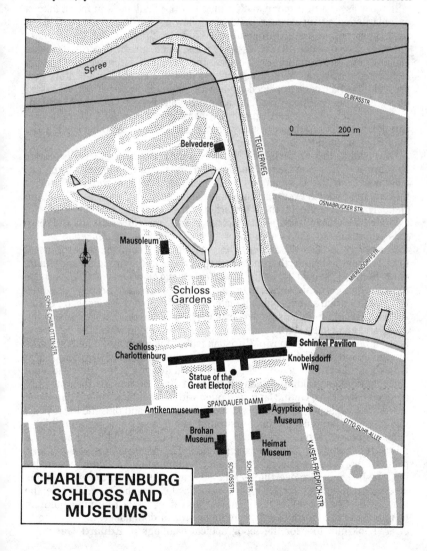

CHARLOTTENBURG SCHLOSS AND MUSEUMS

Wilhelm, the Great Elector, cast as a single piece in 1700. Immediately behind is the entrance to the Schloss. To see its central section, which includes the restored residential quarters, you're obliged to go on the conducted tour that's in German only, which makes it worth buying the detailed (English) guide-book before you start. The tour is a traipse through increasingly sumptuous chambers and bedrooms, filled with gilt and carving. Most eye-catching are the **porcelain room** packed to the ceiling with china, and the **chapel**, which includes a portrait of Sophie Charlotte as the Virgin ascending to heaven.

It's just as well to remember that much of the Schloss is in fact a fake, a reconstruction of the former buildings following wartime damage. This is most apparent in the **Knobelsdorff Wing**, to the right of the Schloss entrance as you face it; the upper rooms, such as the Rococo "Golden Gallery" are too breathlessly perfect, the result of intensive restoration. Better is the adjacent "White Hall," whose destroyed eighteenth-century ceiling painting has been replaced by a witty contemporary paraphrase. Next door, the "Concert Room" contains a superb collection of works by **Watteau,** including one of his greatest paintings, *The Embarcation for Cythera*, a deli-cate Rococo frippery tinged with sympathy and sadness. Also here is his *The Shop Sign*, painted for an art dealer in 1720.

Downstairs, the Knobelsdorff Wing currently contains the **Galerie der Romantik** (Tues–Sun 9am–5pm; free), a collection of nineteenth-century paintings from the German Romantic masters, Classical and Biedermeier movements that will eventually be transplanted to a planned extension of the Neue Nationalgalerie in the Tiergarten. Most dramatic are the works of **Caspar David Friedrich**, all of which express a powerful elemental and relig-ious approach to landscape. This is most evident in *Morning in the Riesengebirge* and *Der Watzmann*, where it seems as if some massive, primeval force is about to leap forth from the earth. Typical of the brooding and drama of his Romantic sensibility is the *Monastery among Oak Trees* of 1809, perhaps the most famous of his works. In the next room, *Moonrise at Sea* reveals some-thing of Friedrich's philosophy: initially a straightforward seascape, on closer study the painting unfolds its deeper meaning; the moon that illuminates the scene and guides the ships represents Christ; the rock on which the figures sit is a symbol of the constancy of Christian faith. This room also contains works by **Karl Friedrich Schinkel,** the architect reponsible for the war memorial in Kreuzberg, and more notably, the Neoclassical designs of the Altes Museum and many other buildings standing today in East Berlin. His paintings are meticulously-drawn Gothic fantasies, often with sea settings. *Gothic Church on a Seaside Bluff* is perhaps the most moodily dramatic, and didactic in purpose: the medieval knights in the foreground stand next to a prayer tablet—Schinkel believed that a rekindling of medieval piety would bring about the moral regeneration of the German nation. His *Medieval City on a River*, painted shortly after the end of France's domination of Schinkel's native Prussia, is even more overt in its religious and political overtones: the unfin-ished spire of the cathedral is topped by an flag bearing the imperial eagle; the king, at first barely noticeable beneath the cathedral, is returning home in triumph; and the storm clouds, symbol of French dominance, are starting to clear. Look out, too, for the topographical paintings of **Eduard Gaertner,** which show the Berlin of the early nineteenth century—and reveal just how good a restoration job the East Berlin authorities have made of Unter den Linden. Check out Gaertner's 1853 painting of that name for the evidence.

The western wing of the Schloss once sided an Orangerie (much depleted after the war) and the **gallery** there now houses major exhibitions. If what's there isn't to your taste, there are few better ways to idle away a morning in Berlin than to explore the **Schloss Gardens** (open daily, till 9pm in summer). Laid out in the French style in 1697, the gardens were transformed into an English-style landscaped park in the early nineteenth century: after severe damage in the war, they were mostly restored to their Baroque form. Though it's possible to buy a map in the Schloss, it's easy enough to wander, heading through the garden to the lake and on to the grounds behind, which do indeed have the feel of an English park. Places to head for are the **Schinkel Pavilion**, on the far eastern side (Tues–Sun 9am–5pm), designed by the architect for Friedrich Wilhelm III, and where the king preferred to live away from the excesses of the Schloss. Square and simple, it today houses Schinkel's drawings and plans. Deeper into the gardens, on the north side of the lake, is the **Belvedere** (Tues–Sun 9am–5pm), built as a teahouse in 1788 and today housing a missable collection of Berlin porcelain.

On the western side of the gardens a long, tree-lined avenue leads to the hushed and shadowy **Mausoleum** (April–Oct Tues–Sun 9am–noon & 1–5pm; DM0.50) where Friedrich Wilhelm III is buried, his sarcophagus, carved with his image, making him seem a good deal younger than his seventy years. Friedrich Wilhelm had had the mausoleum built thirty years earlier for his wife, Queen Luise, whose own delicate sarcophagus depicts her, in the euphuism of those times, not dead but sleeping. Later burials here include Kaiser Wilhelm I, looking every inch a Prussian king.

Other Museums

Though you could spend an idle morning wandering around the Schloss and its gardens, just across the way a group of excellent museums beckons. Best of these is the **Ägyptisches Museum** (Schlossstrasse 70; Mon–Thurs 9am–5pm, Sat & Sun 10am–5pm; free), the result of innumerable German excavations in Egypt from the early part of the century. The museum's pride and joy is the *Bust of Nefertiti* on the first floor, a treasure that has become a symbol for the city as a cultural capital. There's no questioning its beauty—the queen has a perfect bone structure and gracefully-sculpted lips—and the history of the piece is equally interesting. Created around 1350 BC, the bust probably never left the studio in which it was housed, acting as a model for other portraits of the queen (its use as a model explains why the left eye was never drawn in). When the studio was deserted, the bust was left there, to be discovered some 3000 years later in 1912. In the last few days of the war, the bust was "removed" from the Soviet Sector of Berlin; the authorities there would still like it back. Elsewhere in the museum, atmospheric lighting focuses attention on the exhibits, which are of a uniformly high standard. Look out for the expressionistic, almost futuristic *Berlin Green Head* of the Ptolemaic period, and the *Kalbasha Monumental Gate*, given to the museum by the Egyptian government in 1973.

Immediately south of the Ägyptisches Museum, the **Heimatmuseum Charlottenburg** (Tues–Fri 10am–5pm, Sun 11am–5pm; free) isn't anything special except for a few photos of Charlottenburg from the Weimar and wartime eras. Across Schlossstrasse, the **Antikenmuseum** (Tues–Fri 9am–5pm; free), holds Greek and Roman collections, notably the Roman silver treasure found at Hildesheim. Other highlights include Corinthian helmets and jewelry (both on the ground floor), and a collection of Greek vases, considered by those in the know to be among the finest in the world. Just south of the Antikenmuseum, the **Bröhan-Museum** (Tues–Sun 10am–6pm; DM3, students DM1.50) houses a great collection of Art Deco and Jugendstil ceramics and furniture, laid out in period rooms dedicated to a particular designer and hung with contemporary paintings—worthiest of which are the pastels of Willy Jaeckel and the uncompromisingly modern works of Jean Lambert-Rucki. Small, compact, and easily taken in, the Bröhan forms a likeable alternative to the more extensive Ägyptisches Museum or the Schloss collections.

Continuing westwards, Charlottenburg breaks out into open country and forest, with the Olympic stadium and tower the main draws (see below).

OUT FROM THE CENTER

While there's more than enough to detain you in West Berlin's center, the western **suburbs** hold a disparate group of attractions of considerable historical interest; and once you're out of the claustrophobic city, the verdant countryside and lakes come as a surprise, a reminder of Berlin's position in *Mittel-Europa*—and of the fact that one third of the city is greenery and parkland. Thanks to the efficient U- and S-Bahn system it's possible to reach the farthest limits of West Berlin in under three quarters of an hour, making the contrast between inner-city excitement and rural relaxation all the stronger.

Dahlem: The Museum Complex

The suburb of **DAHLEM** lies to the southwest of central Berlin, a neat village-like enclave that feels a world away from the technoflash city center. Mostly residential, it's home to the Free University, the better-off bourgeoisie and a group of museums that's the most important in the city—and among the best in Europe.

Housed in a large new building, the **DAHLEM MUSEUM** can be overpowering if you try and do too much too quickly: it's wiser to make a couple of trips here, taking time out to visit the Botanical Gardens nearby (detailed below). If you are pushed for time, the must-sees are the Picture Gallery and South Seas Ethnographic Collection. To reach the museums, take U-Bahn line #2 to Dahlem-Dorf and follow the signs; the main block is on Arnimallee, and open from Tuesday to Sunday 9am to 5pm. Admission to all the collections is free.

The Picture Gallery

The **Picture Gallery** is the highlight of the Dahlem Museum. Originally part of the pre-war Berlin Museum, during the war years its paintings were stored throughout the city for safekeeping, with the result that part of the collection is now contained in the Altes Museum and Nationalgalerie on East Berlin's Museum Island. But this doesn't detract from the Gallery's scope or quality: arranged in chronological order, it covers the early-medieval to late-eighteenth-century periods, the section of early **Netherlandish Painting** and later **Dutch and Flemish** works being the most authoritative.

Netherlandish Painting

The collection of **Netherlandish Painting**, works painted in the Low Countries in the fifteenth to late sixteenth centuries, begins in room 143 with the artist credited with the creation of European realism, **Jan van Eyck**: his beautifully lit *Madonna in the Church* is crammed with architectural detail, the Virgin lifted in the perspective for gentle emphasis. Nearby, his *Portrait of Giovanni Arnolfini* shows a character more famous from the wedding portrait in London's National Gallery. **Petrus Christus** may have been a pupil of van Eyck, and certainly knew his work, as *The Virgin and Child with Saint Barbara and a Carthusian Monk* reveals: in the background are tiny Flemish houses and street scenes, the artist carefully locating the event in his native Bruges. His *Last Judgement*, on the other hand, is full of medieval nightmares. **Dieric Bouts'** figures tend to be stiff and rather formalized, but his *Christ in the House of Simon the Pharisee* is filled with gesture, expression, and carefully drawn detail—especially in the food and shoes.

Much of the next room is given over to the work of **Rogier van der Weyden**, which shows the development of the Eyckian technique to a warmer, much more emotional treatment of religious subjects. The figures in his *Bladelin Altarpiece* reveal a delicacy of poise and an approachable humanity that was greatly to influence German painting in the fifteenth century. **Aelbert van Outwater** was also a major influence on his contemporaries and followers, although his *Raising of Lazarus* is the only complete work to have survived: it's a daring picture, the richly dressed merchants on the right contrasting strongly with the simplicity of the Holy Family on the left. **Geertgen tot Sint Jans** was Outwater's pupil, though his *Saint John the Baptist* is quite different from his master's painting—the saint sits almost comically impassive against a rich backdrop of intricately constructed landscape. The two other major paintings in this room (146) are both by **Hugo van der Goes**: the *Adoration of the Shepherds* (painted when the artist was in the first throes of madness) has the scene unveiled by two characters representing the prophets, while the shepherds stumble into the frame. His *Adoration of the Magi*—also known as the *Monforte Altarpiece*—has a superbly drawn realism that marks a new development in Netherlandish art, carrying precision over into a large-scale work with a deftly executed, complex perspective. The small altarpiece *Triptych with the Adoration of the Magi* by **Joos van Cleve** reveals how these themes were absorbed by Goes's successors. Room 148 moves into the sixteenth century and the works of Jan Gossaert, Quentin

Massys, and **Pieter Bruegel the Elder**, whose *Netherlandish Proverbs* is an amusing, if hard-to-grasp, illustration of over a hundred sixteenth-century proverbs and maxims. As a fascinating contrast to the fifteenth-century Netherlandish works, look out for a rare French panel painting of the same period, **Jehan Fouquet**'s *Etienne Chevalier and Saint Stephen*, which shows the Treasurer of France accompanied by his patron saint.

Medieval and Renaissance German Painting

The **German Medieval and Renaissance** rooms follow the Netherlandish sections, revealing the contrast between German and Netherlandish treatment of religious subjects: almost always, the German works are darker and more crudely drawn. Crudest of all is the large *Passion Altar* of 1437, made in the workshop of the great Ulm sculptor **Hans Multscher**; its exaggerated gestures and facial distortions mark it out as an ancient precursor of Expressionist painting. There's an interesting contrast with *Solomon before the Queen of Sheba*, painted in the same year by **Conrad Witz**, who was far more subtle in his aim of developing German painting away from its hitherto idealized forms. The exquisite *Nativity* by **Schongauer** is the most important surviving panel by the father-figure of the German Renaissance.

These apart, the best works here are by **Altdorfer**, one of the first fully-realized German landscape painters (in his *Nativity* the figures of Christ and the Holy Family seem less important than the depiction of the ruined stables), and **Dürer**—a marvelous group of portraits. There's an impressive group of works by Dürer's eccentric pupil **Baldung**, notably an exotic *Adoration of the Magi* triptych. By **Holbein the Younger** are five superbly observed portraits, most celebrated of which is *The Danzig Merchant Georg Gisze*, featuring a still-life background which is a real tour de force of artistic virtuosity. Pick of the many examples of **Cranach** is *The Fountain of Youth*, whose tongue-in-cheek humor is adroitly achieved: old women emerge from the miraculous bath as fresh young girls, whereas the men are rejuvenated merely by association.

Italian Renaissance Painting

To the right of rooms containing the German works is the collection of **French and German** painting of the sixteenth, seventeenth and eighteenth centuries. But to continue in chronological order, carry straight on to the **Italian Renaissance** section. This collection is particularly strong on works from the Florentine Renaissance: **Fra Filippo Lippi**'s *The Adoration in the Forest* is a mystical image of unusual grace and beauty, rightly among one of the most admired of all the paintings of the period. Another much-prized work is the gorgeously colorful *Adoration of the Magi* by the rarely seen **Domenico Veneziano**, which perfectly captures the full regal splendor of the subject. **Correggio**'s wonderfully suggestive *Leda with the Swan* is a good example of the classical preoccupations of the period; its subject so offended an eighteenth-century religious fanatic that he hacked it to pieces. There's work here, too, by Giotto, Verrocchio, Masaccio, Mantegna, Raphael, and Titian, and most importantly by another Florentine, **Sandro Botticelli**, whose *Virgin and Child with the Two Saint Johns*, *Portrait of a Young Woman* and *Saint Sebastian* are among the highlights of the gallery.

Dutch and Flemish Painting

On the next floor the museum reveals its second strength in the **Dutch and Flemish** collection. This begins with the large portraits of Van Dyck and the fleshy canvases of Rubens, and continues with a fine group of **Dutch interiors**, hung together and inviting comparison. The work of **Vermeer** is the most easily identifiable—though his *Woman with a Pearl Necklace* is not one of his greater works. Better is *Man and Woman Drinking Wine*, which uses his usual technique of placing furniture obliquely in the center of the canvas, the scene illuminated by window light. **De Hooch** used a similar technique in *Woman Weighing Gold*, though more complex, both compositionally and morally, is his *The Mother*, a masterly example of Dutch interior painting at its finest.

The subsequent rooms trace the development of Dutch art through the works of Maes, Terborch, Dou, Jan Steen, and Frans Hals, and, in perhaps the largest collection in the world, the paintings of **Rembrandt**. Recently, his most famous picture here, *The Man in the Golden Helmet*, was proved to be the work of his studio, though this does little to detract from the elegance and power of the portrait, its reflective sorrow relieved by the bright helmet. Other (verified) works include a 1634 *Self-Portrait*, painted at the height of the artist's wealth and fame; a *Portrait of Saskia*, Rembrandt's wife, painted in the year of her death; a beautifully warm and loving *Portrait of Hendrickje Stoffels*, the artist's later, common-law wife; and numerous other religious works.

Continuing through the painting galleries, there's work by Goya, Caravaggio (*Cupid Victorious*, heavy with symbolism and homo-eroticism), Poussin, and Claude, and a concluding clutch of Canalettos.

Other Collections and Sights

If you've just spent the morning wandering through the picture gallery, this could be the moment to adjourn to the museum's basement **café**. Alternatively, the **Sculpture Court** adjoining the Picture Gallery on the upper floor forms a good complement to the paintings: it's chiefly German and most authoritative in its sections detailing the Middle Ages—everything from simple religious artifacts to complex polychrome carvings, including work by Tilman Riemenschneider and Hans Multscher. Also included is an excellent Byzantine and early Christian section, plus works from the Italian Renaissance, notably by Donatello.

The **Ethnographic Sections** of the Dahlem Museum are worth a visit in their own right: rich and extensive collections from Asia, the Pacific, and South Sea Islands of Melanesia and Polynesia, imaginatively and strikingly laid out. In particular, look out for the group of sailing boats from the South Sea Islands, dramatically lit and eminently touchable. Other collections within the museum include Islamic, Asian, East Asian, and Indian art—dip in according to your tastes.

At Im Winkel 6, a short signposted walk from the main complex, is the **Museum für Deutsche Volkskunde** (Museum of German Ethnology; Tues–Sun 9am–5pm; free), a static and rather dull collection of furniture, tools, and costumes from the sixteenth century onwards. Of much more specialized interest, the **Geheimes Staatsarchive** (Archivstr. 12–14; reading room Mon & Thurs 1–9pm, Tues, Wed & Fri 9am–5pm) holds the once-secret Prussian State Archive, a mass of State documents, records, and files now chiefly used as a resource for academic study.

In the other direction (turn left out of the U-Bahn station and continue west along Königin-Luise-Strasse) is the **St Annenkirche**, a pretty little brick-built church that dates back to 1220. If it's open (officially Mon, Wed & Sat 2–5pm, but seemingly random), pop in for a glimpse of the Baroque pulpit and gallery, and carved wooden altar.

Finally, as an escape from cultural overload, catch a #17 bus northeast to the **Botanical Gardens** (Königin-Luise-Str. 6–8; daily 9am–sunset; DM2.50, students DM1.20; also bus #1), where you'll find palatial, sticky hothouses sprouting every plant you've ever wondered about (some 18,000 species), enticingly laid-out gardens, and an uninspiring **Botanical Museum** (Tues & Thurs–Sun 10am–5pm, Wed 10am–7pm; free).

The Plötzensee Memorial

Berlin sometimes has the feel of a city that has tried, unsuccessfully, to sweep its past under the carpet of the present. When concrete reminders of the Third Reich can be seen, their presence in the occupied, post-war city becomes all the more powerful. Nowhere is this more true than in the buildings where the Nazi powers brought dissidents and political opponents for imprisonment and execution—the **PLÖTZENSEE PRISON MEMORIAL**.

Plötzensee stands in the northwest of the city, on the border between the boroughs of Charlottenburg and Wedding. To get there, take bus #23 from Zoo Station to the beginning of Saatwinkler Damm and walk away from the canal along the wall-sided path of Hüttigpfad.

The former prison buildings are now refurbished as a juvenile detention center, and the memorial consists of the buildings where the **executions** took place. Over 2500 people were hanged or guillotined here between 1933 and 1945, usually those sentenced in the Supreme Court of Justice in the city. Following the July bomb plot (see "Schöneberg" above), eighty-nine of the two hundred people condemned were executed here in the space of a few days: Hitler ordered the hangings to be carried out with piano wire (so that the victims would slowly strangle rather than die from broken necks), and spent his evenings watching movie footage of the executions. Many of those murdered were only vaguely connected to the conspirators; several died simply because they were relatives. Today the execution chamber has been restored to its wartime condition: on occasion victims were hanged eight at a time, and the hanging beam, complete with hooks, still stands. Though decked with wreaths and flowers, the atmosphere in the chamber is chilling, and as a further reminder of Nazi atrocities an urn in the courtyard contains soil from each of the concentration camps. Perhaps more than at any other wartime site in Berlin, it is at Plötzensee that the horror of senseless, brutal murder is most palpably felt. The memorial is open from March to September 8am–8pm, October 8:30am–5:30pm, November 8:30am–4:30pm, December 8:30am–4pm, January 8:30am–4:30pm and February 8:30am–5:30pm.

Near the memorial, at Heckerdamm 230, is the church of **Maria Regina Martyrum,** a purposely somber memorial church to those who died in the Nazi years. A gaunt undecorated open-air altar stands over the church itself, which has similarly abstract S*tations of the Cross* modeled in bronze, and an apocalyptic *fresco* on the chancel wall.

Points Westward: the Funkturm, Olympic Stadium, and Beyond

Reaching the **FUNKTURM**, the skeletal transmission mast that lies to the west of Charlottenburg, is an easy matter of catching U-Bahn line #1 to Kaiserdamm, or bus #66, #92, or #94 from Zoo Station. Since being built in 1928 as a radio and TV transmitter (today it only serves police and taxi radios) it's been popular with Berliners for the toe-curling views from its 138-meter-high observation platform (daily 10am–11pm; DM4, students DM2). With the aluminum-clad monolith of the **International Congress Center** immediately below, it's possible to look out across deserted, overgrown S-Bahn tracks to the gleaming city in the distance—a sight equally mesmerizing at night.

You may have to wait in line to catch the elevator up to the observation platform; much less popular is the **Museum of Radio and Broadcasting** (Tues–Sat 10am–6pm, Sun 10am–4pm; free), housed in a former studio to one side of the tower. An assembly of old wirelesses and Rube Goldberg radio equipment, some of the shiny Bakelite contraptions are rather wonderful—the sort of thing your granny keeps on her sideboard. Tracing the development of radios, record players, and televisions from the beginning of broadcasting in Germany in 1923 until World War II, it's as much a history of design as technology, made all the more entertaining by a scattering of period rooms and a mock-up of the first-ever German radio studio.

To reach the Olympic Stadium from here, catch the #1 U-Bahn three stops westwards to the station of the same name. From there, it's a fifteen-minute signposted walk to the Stadium itself (8am–sunset; DM2). If you catch the (less convenient) bus #4 up Masurenallee towards the Stadium, you cross **Theodor-Heuss-Platz**, a huge square formerly known as Adolf-Hitler-Platz; the flame in the center will not be extinguished until Germany is unified.

The Olympic Stadium
Built for the 1936 Olympic Games, the **OLYMPIC STADIUM** is one of the few Fascist buildings left intact in the city, and remains very much in use. Whatever your feelings about it, it's still impressive, the huge Neoclassical space a deliberate rejection of the Modernist architecture then prevalent elsewhere. Hitler used the international attention the games attracted to show the "New Order" in Germany in the best possible light. Anti-Semitic propaganda and posters were suppressed, German half-Jewish competitors were allowed to compete, and when (for the first time in the history of the games) the Olympic flame was relayed from Athens, the newsreels and the world saw the road lined with thousands wearing swastikas and waving Nazi flags. To

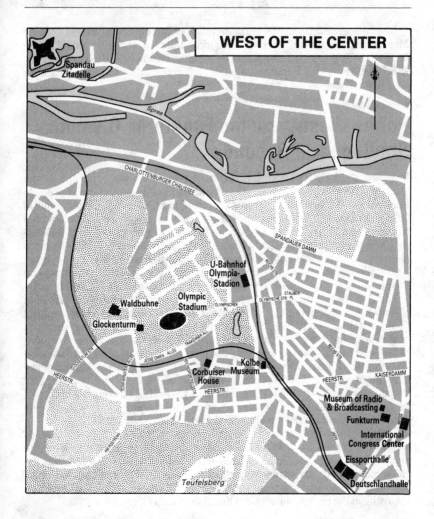

WEST OF THE CENTER

Spandau Zitadelle

Spree

CHARLOTTENBURGER CHAUSSEE

SPANDAUER DAMM

U-Bahnhof Olympia-Stadion

Waldbuhne

Olympic Stadium

Glockenturm

STAUBEN
OLYMPISCHE STR

OLYMPISCHER PL.

Kolbe Museum

Corbuiser House

HEERSTR.

HEERSTR.

HEERSTR.

KAISERDAMM

Museum of Radio & Broadcasting

Funkturm

International Congress Center

Eissporthalle

Deutschlandhalle

Teufelsberg

the outside world, it seemed that the new Germany was rich, content, and firmly behind the Führer.

Though the Games themselves were stage-managed with considerable brilliance—a fact recorded in Leni Riefenstahl's poetic and frighteningly beautiful film of the events, *Olympia*—not everything went according to official National Socialist doctrine. Black American athletes did supremely well in the games, **Jesse Owens** alone winning four gold medals, disproving the Nazi theory that blacks were "subhuman" and the Aryan race all-powerful. But eventually Germany won the most gold, silver, and bronze medals (there's a memorial at the western end of the Stadium), and the games were deemed a great success.

The area in which the Stadium stands is under the control of the British, and the fields around are used for drilling teenage recruits into shape. This means that much of the Stadium's environs are out of bounds, and probably explains its survival—the British being less eager to demolish interesting structures than the other Allies. If you cut south and west around the Stadium, down the road named after Jesse Owens, and take a right onto Passenheimer Strasse, you reach the **Glockenturm** or bell tower (April–Oct daily 10am–5:30pm; DM2.50). Rebuilt after wartime damage, it's chiefly interesting for the stupendous **view** it gives, not only over the stadium but also north to the natural amphitheater that forms the **Waldbühne**, an open-air concert site (see Chapter Five, *Music and Nightlife*), and across the beginnings of the Grunewald to the south. Central here is **Teufelsberg** (Devil's mountain), a massive mound that's topped with a faintly terrifying fairytale castle that is a US signals and radar base. The mountain itself is artificial: at the end of the war, the mass of debris that was once Berlin was carted to several sites around the city, most of the work being carried out by women known as *Trümmerfrauen*—"rubble women"*. Beneath the poplars, maples, and ski-runs lies the old Berlin, about 25 million cubic meters of it, presumably awaiting the attention of some future archaeologist. In the meantime, it's popular as a place for weekend kite flying, and skiing and tobogganing in winter. If you're a fan of French architect Corbusier, you may want to make a pilgrimage to the **Corbusier House** between Reichsportfeld, the street leading directly south of the stadium, and Heilsberger Allee; it was built as part of Berlin's International Building exhibition of 1957. More interesting, though, is the **Georg-Kolbe-Museum** at Sensburger Allee 25 (Tues–Sun 10am–5pm; DM2.50, students DM1; bus #94). Kolbe, a sculptor who died in 1947, never achieved the eminence of his contemporary Ernst Barlach—a judgement that seems reasonable when you view some of the 180 bronze figures and numerous drawings in what was once the artist's home.

Spandau

SPANDAU, situated on the confluence of the Spree and Havel rivers, about 10km as the crow flies northwest of the city center, is Berlin's oldest suburb—it was granted a town charter in 1232, and managed to escape the worst of the wartime bombing, preserving some pretty medieval streets and an ancient moated fort, the Zitadelle. But the word Spandau immediately brings to mind the name of its jail's most famous—indeed in later years only—prisoner, **Rudolf Hess**. Hess, who had marched in the Munich Beer Hall Putsch of 1923 and was subsequently imprisoned with Hitler in Landsberg jail, where he took the dictation of *Mein Kampf*, was for a time the deputy leader of the Nazi party. He flew to Scotland in 1941, ostensibly in an

---

*That the work was undertaken almost exclusively by women was a result of the virtual eradication of healthy adult men following the war and the bloody Battle of Berlin. Today Berlin has a visibly high number of elderly single and widowed women—their brothers and husbands having failed to survive World War II.

attempt to sue for peace with King George VI and ally Great Britain with Germany against the Soviet Union. Perhaps because there seems no sane reason why Hess, who was immediately arrested and held until the Nürnberg trials, should have attempted his flight, various sources have claimed that the man held in jail until his suicide in 1987 was not actually Hess—and that it would have been impossible for a 93-year-old man to have hanged himself on a short piece of lamp flex. The basis of this story came from the doctor who examined Hess's corpse; he could find no trace of the serious wounds Hess had acquired in World War I. But recently, it's been proved that Hess could indeed have killed himself using the lamp flex, and diligent research in archives in Munich has revealed that Hess's wartime wounds were in fact minor enough to have healed over the years—so putting to rest a colorful (and headline-grabbing) piece of conspiracy theory.

However there's little connection between Hess and Spandau itself. The jail, 4km away on Wilhelmstrasse, was demolished to make way for a supermarket for the British armed forces, and the chief reason to come here today is to escape the city center, wander Spandau's village-like streets, and to visit the **Zitadelle** (Tues–Fri 9am–5pm, Sat & Sun 10am–5pm; DM1.50, students DM0.50), a fort established in the twelfth century to defend the town. Surprisingly pretty from the outside, with its moat and russet walls built during the Renaissance by an Italian architect, it is explorable, if not totally engrossing. There's a small museum, a pricey *bürgerlich* restaurant and the **Juliusturm**, from which there's a good view over the ramshackle Zitadel interior and the surrounding countryside. If nothing else, it's a pleasant spot to picnic away a hot summer's day.

Other than this, **Spandau town**, a ten-minute walk from here, is of minor interest, at its best around its church (where there's a good *Konditorei*), in the playful sculptures of its modern marketplace, and in the recently restored street called **Kolk** (turn right off Am Juliusturm opposite Breite Strasse). Quickest way of getting to Spandau from the city center is to take U-Bahn line #7 to the Zitadelle station—or to Altstadt Spandau station and doubling back to the Zitadelle. It's also possible to catch **boats** from Spandau to Tegel, Wannsee, and elsewhere; see below for details.

Woodlands and Lakes: the Grunewald, Havel, and Wannsee

Few people associate Berlin with walks through dense woodland or swimming from crowded beaches, though that's just what the **GRUNEWALD** forests and beaches on the **HAVEL** lakes have to offer. The Grunewald is 32 square kilometers of mixed woodland that lies between the suburbs of Dahlem and Wilmersdorf, and the Havel lakes to the west; it's popular with Berliners for its bracing air and walks. Seventy percent of the Grunewald was cut down in the post-war years for badly-needed fuel, and subsequent replanting has replaced pine and birch with oak and ash, making it all the more popular.

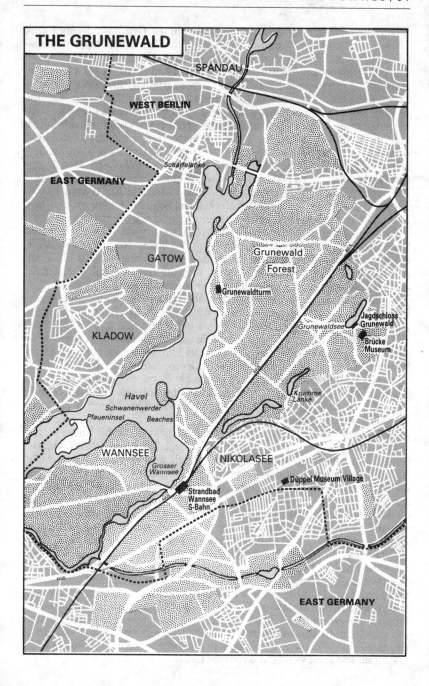

THE GRUNEWALD

SPANDAU

WEST BERLIN

Scharfelanke

EAST GERMANY

GATOW

Grunewald
Forest

■ Grunewaldturm

■ Jagdschloss
Grunewald

Grunewaldsee

■ Brücke
Museum

KLADOW

Havel

*Krumme
Lanke*

Schwanenwerder

Pfaueninsel *Beaches*

WANNSEE

NIKOLASEE

■ Düppel Museum Village

*Grosser
Wannsee*

■ Strandbad
Wannsee
S-Bahn

AVUS

EAST GERMANY

One possible starting point is the **Jagdschloss Grunewald** (April–Sept Tues–Sun 10am–6pm; March & Oct Tues–Sun 10am–5pm; Nov–Feb Tues–Sun 10am–4pm; DM2.50, students DM1.50), a royal hunting lodge built in the sixteenth century and enlarged by Friedrichs I and II. Today it's a museum, housing old furniture and Dutch and German painting, including works by Cranach the Elder and Rubens. It's refreshing to walk by the nearby lake, the Grunewaldsee, and concerts are held here on summer evenings (usually starting at 6pm; see *Zitty* or *Tip* magazines for details). To reach the Jagdschloss, take bus #60 from Blissestrasse U-Bahn to the stop at Pücklerstrasse and head west down that street into the forest. Near the Pücklerstrasse stop, incidentally, you'll find the **Brücke Museum** at Bussardsteig 9 (Wed–Mon 11am–5pm; DM3.50, students DM1.50), a collection of works by the group known as *Die Brücke* ("The Bridge") who worked in Dresden and Berlin from 1905 to 1913. The big names are Kirchner, Heckel, and Schmidt-Rottluff, who painted Expressionist cityscapes and had considerable influence over later artists.

Glance at a map of the Grunewald and you'll see a broad, ruler-straight road that runs down to the border checkpoint at Drielinden. Known as the **AVUS**, this once formed part of a pre-war motor racing circuit; today it fills a not dissimilar function, as motorists, bored with the GDR's 80kph speed limit, take out their frustration as soon as they hit straight road.

An alternative approach to the Grunewald, and with the added attraction of beginning at a strip of **beaches**, is to take the #1 or #3 S-Bahn to Nikolasee station where it's a ten-minute walk or a quick bus ride to **STRANDBAD WANNSEE**, a kilometer-long strip of pale sand that's packed as soon as the sun comes out. From here it's easy to wander into the forests, or, more adventurously, catch one of several **ferries** that leave a little way from the S-Bahn station (ask there for directions). It's possible to sail to Spandau (DM6), to Kladow, across the lake (DM2.50) or to the **Pfaueninsel** ("Peacock Island"; April & Sept daily 8am–6pm; May–Aug daily 8am–8pm; March & Oct daily 9am–5pm; Nov–Feb daily 10am–4pm; ferry DM4), whose attractions include a mini-**Schloss**, built as a folly by Friedrich Wilhelm II for his mistress, and today containing a small **museum** (April–Sept Tues–Sun 10am–5pm; Oct Tues–Sun 10am–4pm). Most enjoyable, though, are the gardens, landscaped by Peter Lenné, the original designer of the Tiergarten. No cars are allowed on the island, which has been designated a conservation zone and is home to a flock of peacocks. Between mid-April and the end of October *Stern und Kreisschiffahrt* (☎810004) run a four-hour tour that takes in the whole length of the lake systems, connecting Wannsee to Tegel; it's worth contacting them, or *Havelseenrundfahrt* (☎391 7010) for details of special and seasonal trips.

Otherwise, the whole Grunewald area is ideal for walking: targets include the **Museumdorf Düppel** (Düppel Museum Village; to the east of Strandbad Wannsee at Clauertstr. 11; May–Sept Sun 10am–1pm; DM3; bus #3 and #50), a reconstruction of a medieval country village, with demonstrations of contemporary handicrafts and farming techniques, and the surrounding, little visited **Düppel Forest**. In the middle of the western side of the forest, right next to the Havel, the **Grunewaldturm** (Grunewald Tower) was built at the end of the nineteenth century as a memorial to Emperor Wilhelm I: the tower has a restaurant and great views out across the lakes.

CHAPTER TWO

SHOPS AND MARKETS

Berlin isn't exactly a shopper's paradise, but there's an interesting selection of quirky specialist shops and earthy markets, and it's an excellent place to buy secondhand clothes. Glitz and dazzle are the prerogatives of **Wittenbergplatz** and the **Kurfürstendamm**, with its two miles of luxury galleries, antique shops, and designer clothes shops, while the areas around **U-Bahns Wilmersdorferstrasse**, **Walter-Schreiber-Platz**, and **Hermannplatz** are good for chain-store clothes and all-purpose shopping. Ethnic foods and the "alternative" businesses are mostly in **East Kreuzberg**, with a more upmarket alternative scene in **Charlottenburg**.

Normal **shop opening hours** are Monday to Friday 9am–6pm, and Saturday 9am–2pm. On the first Saturday in the month (*Langer Samstag*) and the last four Saturdays in the run-up to Christmas most major stores stay open until 6pm; on Thursdays shops are allowed to stay open until 8:30pm. Except for the larger places, **credit cards** are not widely accepted, so it's best to have cash in hand before you begin.

Art and Design

Broadly speaking, the Berlin art scene falls into two main areas: the **Kurfürstendamm** and surrounding streets for the expensive, more established galleries, and **Kreuzberg** for the "off" galleries, where younger and usually lesser-known artists have a chance to show their work. The *Berlin Arts Guide* by Irene Blumenfeld (Art Guide Publications, $10.95) gives a full, if dated, rundown of the city's private galleries, and the quarterly *Berliner Kunst Blatt* has selective listings. Check *Zitty* or *Tip* for up-to-the-minute details. Most galleries are open from about 2–7pm and close on Mondays. It's pretty easy to gatecrash openings.

Galleries

Atelier Internationale Kunst, Dahlmannstr. 11, 1/12 (☎324 4098). Dance, theater, and art under one roof. Opens at 6pm.

Galerie am Chamissoplatz, Chamissoplatz 6, 1/61 (☎692 5381). Politically oriented art, on the site of a former bakery in the heart of Kreuzberg.

Galerie Anselm Dreher, Pfalzburgerstr. 80, 1/15 (☎883 5249). Top avant-garde gallery.

Galerie Brusberg, Kurfürstendamm 213, 1/15 (☎882 7682). Excellent contemporary figurative work and sculpture.

Galerie Fahnemann, Fasanenstr. 61, 1/15 (☎883 9897). More high quality avant-garde.

Galerie Georg Nothelfer, Uhlandstr. 184, 1/12 (☎881 4405). Renowned contemporary art gallery.

Galerie Gerda Bassenge, Fasanenstr. 73 (☎881 8104). Expressionist and Impressionist art and auctions.

Galerie im Kutscherhaus, Tempelhofer Ufer 11, 1/61 (☎251 7247). Showcase for young artists, owned by Dr. Hans Stober, one of Berlin's most important collectors and patron of the arts.

Galerie in Fonte, Badstr. 38–39, 1/65 (☎494 5510). Tiny gallery for contemporary sculpture.

Galerie Nierendorf, Hardenbergstr. 19, 1/12 (☎785 6060). Mainly German Expressionism.

Galerie Pels-Leusden, in der Villa Griesebach, Fasanenstr. 25, 1/15 (☎882 6811). Renowned gallery, one of the oldest in Berlin. Specializes in classical-modern and contemporary art.

Galerie Poll, Lützowplatz 7, 1/30 (☎261 7091). Contemporary art, with an emphasis on international figurative work.

Galerie Raab, Potsdamerstr. 58, 1/30 (☎261 6098). Avant-garde and contemporary art; popular meeting place for the art "in" crowd.

Galerie Sonne Berlin, Kantstr. 138, 1/12 (☎312 2355). Young gallery with innovative avant-garde program.

Galerie Springer, Fasanenstr. 13, 1/12 (☎313 9088). Top-class contemporary stuff. One of the galleries foremost in establishing the art scene in Berlin after World War II.

Katakombe, Südwestkorso 20, 1/33. Large cellar space; presents young unknowns displaying for the first time.

Petersen Galerie, Pestalozzistr. 106, 1/12 (☎313 4508). Indefinable mix of action art and "happenings."

Posters, Prints, and Cards

Ararat, Bergmannstr. 99a, 1/37 (☎693 5080). Huge selection of cards, posters and prints.

Büchergarten, Goltzstr. 37, 1/30 (☎215 3779). Small, but highly varied selection of cards in a cosy atmosphere.

Xqutzy, Lietzenburgerstr. 74, 1/15 (☎881 2916). Unusual postcards.

Books and Magazines

Although it's not the most exciting place in the world for books, Berlin is an ideal city for leisurely, non-harassed browsing, with one bookshop, *Marga Schoeller,* even providing a few chairs for the purpose. There are quite a few places to find **English-language books**, most of them situated in or around Knesebeckstrasse, the street with Berlin's highest concentration of bookstores.

English Language/General

Autorenbuchandlung, Carmerstr. 10, 1/12 (☎310151). Some English-language books; regular readings by (non-English) authors.

Buchbandlung Assmus, Kaiser-Friedrick-Str. 1 (☎342 1137). Well-stocked bookshop with readings in spring and autumn.

Elwert & Meurer, Hauptstr. 110, 1/62 (☎784 001). Books on every subject.

The English Bookshop, Sesenheimerstr. 17, 1/15 (☎313 7622). Very good selection of secondhand paperbacks and some hardbacks at about a third of the usual price. Quiet and friendly atmosphere where you can sit down and skim-read at leisure.

Herder Buchbandlung, Kurfürstendamm 69, 1/15 (☎883 5001). Large, run-of-the-mill general bookstore.

Kiepert, Hardenbergstr. 4–5, 1/12 (☎310711). Sprawling over the corner into Knesebeckstrasse, Kiepert has an excellent selection of books under every major subject heading, with a particularly good travel department and a limited, but well-chosen, assortment of English-language books.

Marga Schoeller, Knesebeckstr. 33–34, 1/12 (☎881 1112). Rather eccentric shop assistants will point you to a good array of English fiction and non-fiction (this is the best place for esoteric topics in English) and then wrap up your purchases prettily upon request.

Ringelnatz, Zossenerstr. 15, 1/61 (☎692 4501). Good all-rounder.

Discount/Secondhand

Antiquariat, Schustehrusstr. 28, 1/10 (☎341 5833). A little of everything.

Buchbandlung Zimmermann, Schlossstr. 29, 1/41 (☎342 4044). Modern literature, specializing in feminism and psychology.

Bücherhalle, Hauptstr. 154, 1/62 (☎784 7185). Large, well-kept selection.

Knesebeck 11, Knesebeckstr. 11, 1/12 (☎312 2836). General bookstore with a section of secondhand books.

Art and Architecture

Bücherbogen am Savignyplatz, Stadtbahnbogen 593–594, 1/12 (☎312 1932). Situated under the S-Bahn railroad's arches, a nevertheless airy and spacious setting for specialist art, architecture, film, and photography books.

Galerie 2000, Knesebeckstr. 56–58, 1/12 (☎883 8467). Mainly photography; some art books and art exhibition catalogs.

Kiepert Hardenbergstr. 4–5, 1/12 (☎310711). Art books at knock-down prices usually on display on the street outside.

Kids' Books

Et cetera, Suarezstr. 31, 1/19 (☎322 8665). Large selection of children's books, wooden toys, and recycled paper.

Spiele-Shop im PZ, Berlinerstrasse, corner with Uhlandstrasse, 1/31 (☎871535). Books and toys with a strong educational slant.

Struwwellotte, Carmerstr. 11, 1/12 (☎312 5654). Alternative book and toyshop for kids; reasonably priced and some secondhand books.

Gay, Feminist, and Radical

Aurora Buchbandlung, Knobelsdorffstr. 8, 1/19 (☎322 7117). One of the best selections of anarchist literature in Germany.

Buchladenkollektiv/Politische Buchbandlung, Carmerstr. 9, 1/12 (☎313 4017). One of the last surviving left-wing bookshops in Berlin.

Frauenbuchladen Labrys, Hohenstaufenstr. 64, 1/30 (☎215 2500). Women-only feminist and lesbian bookstore, with some books in English. Also records and postcards.

Lilith Frauenbuchladen, Knesebeckstr. 86–87, 1/12 (☎312 3102). Good selection of fiction by feminist writers, some in English; records and international newspapers.

Spiritual

Adhara, Pestalozzistr. 35, 1/12 (☎312 2462). Cosy and friendly mind, body, and spirit bookshop.

Dharma, Akazienstr. 17, 1/62 (☎784 5080). Books with a slant towards occultism and oriental philosophies, with a few in English.

Kristall Buchbandlung, Weimarerstr. 16, 1/12 (☎313 8793). Large, well-stocked shop with a good variety of titles, several in English.

Theater and Film

Bücherbogen am Savignyplatz, Stadtbahnbogen 593–594, 1/12 (☎312 1932). See "Art and Architecture" above.

Kommedia Medienbuchladen, Potsdamerstr. 132, 1/30 (☎216 1369). Every aspect of media and communications thoroughly covered.

Travel

Kiepert, Hardenbergstr. 4–5, 1/12 (☎310711). See "English language/general."

Storandt, Kurfurstendamm 105, 1/15 (☎891 8233). Enormous selection of travel guides and maps.

Comics and Science Fiction

Grober Unfug, Gneisenaustr. 15, 1/61 (☎693 6413). Comics in the cellar.

Morgenwelt, Körtestr. 27, 1/61 (☎691 5550). Good variety of sci-fi books.

Roman-Boutique, Peter Skodzik, Goltzstr. 35, 1/30 (☎216 5159). Small comics and science fiction shop.

Magazines and Newspapers

The majority of places to find international newspapers and magazines are, as you might expect, clustered around the Zoo Station area, the best stocked being **Internationale Presse**, Joachimstalerstr. 1, open daily until 10pm.

They have every London-printed morning newspaper (and the International Herald Tribune) by lunchtime, and the major US newspapers the following day. Also open late and well laid out for browsing is the selection at **Ku'damm Caree**, Kurfürstendam 206–9, 1/15. Alternatively, there's a **kiosk** on the corner of Joachimstalerstrasse and the Kurfürstendamm, or try the store on the first floor of the **Europa Center**, also open daily until 10pm. The small **newsagent** just inside the main entrance to Zoo Station also has a limited selection of newspapers and US magazines.

Clothes and Accessories

Although they like to think of themselves as such, Berliners aren't exactly trend setters: the punks look like pale imitations of their London cousins, hippy fashion has never really left town, and black from head to toe seems to be the sartorial standby for everyone from fourteen to forty. Having said that, it's possible to pick up superb **bargains** at the many **secondhand** clothes stores (usually Mon–Fri 11am–6:30pm, Sat 11am–2pm): you'll find unusual (and trendy) items here at very low prices.

The main shopping areas at Wilmersdorferstrasse U-Bahn and Walter-Schreiber-Platz U-Bahn have plenty of inexpensive name-brand styles. The Kurfürstendamm has the monopoly on designer clothes shops, but unless you're very rich and very conservative, they're not worth the time. A couple of exceptions are leather jackets, which are both cheap and good quality, and, though you won't make any great savings, the excellent selection of stylish shoes.

Clothes

Secondhand

Garage, Ahornstr. 2, 1/30 (Mon–Sat noon–9pm). Largest secondhand clothes store in Europe; good for jackets, coats, and jeans. Price according to weight (the clothes', not yours).

Kauf's im Kilo, Hermannstr. 1–3, 1/61 (☎621 6325). The best of Berlin's pay-by-kilo shops; particularly good for 1950s' dresses.

Kilomanscharo, Bleibtreustr. 49, 1/15. Another pay-as-you-weigh.

Macy's, Mommsenstr. 2, 1/12 (☎881 1363). Secondhand designer clothes.

Made in Berlin, Potsdamerstr. 63, 1/30. Popular with the *Szene* crowd: excellent selection of shirts, dresses, and items in black.

Männersache, Winterfeldtstr. 45, 1/30 (☎215 1071). Scarcely-worn men's haute couture and designer for half-price.

Maria Makkaroni, Bleibtreustr. 49, 1/15 (☎312 8584). 1940s American fashions.

Nina Vorberg, Mehringplatz 36, 1/61 (☎251 8822). Clothes and exquisite marcasite jewelry.

CLOTHING AND SHOE SIZES

Dresses
American	8	10	12	14	16	18	20
Continental	40	42	44	46	48	50	52

Women's Shoes
American	5½	6	6½	7	7½	8	8½	9
Continental	36½	37	37½	38½	39	39½	40½	41

Men's Shoes
American	7	7½	8	9	10	10½	11	12
Continental	39	40	41	42	43	44	45	46

Sweaters
American	8	10	12	14	16	18	20	22
Continental	36	38	40	42	44	46	48	50

Shirts and Collars
American	14	14½	15	15½	16	16½	17	17½
Continental	36	37	38	39	40	41	42	43

Second Coming, Motzstr. 15, 1/30. Rather a raggedy selection: hunt hard enough and you might find a bargain.

Secondo, Mommsenstr. 61, 1/12 (☎881 2291). Exclusive designer clothes.

US-Waren, Gneisenaustr. 95, 1/61 (☎693 8690). American military stuff.

New and Designer Labels

Alles für Tramper, Bundesallee 88, 1/41 (☎851 8069). From ambling in the Harz to hiking in the Himalayas, you'll find everything you need here.

Blue Moon, Wilmersdorferstr. 80, 1/12 (☎323 7088). Ultra-trendy *Szene* shop.

Fantazzi, Urbanstr. 65, 1/61 (☎691 9412). Classic elegance, reasonably priced.

Hennes & Mauritz, Kurfürstendamm 20, 1/12 (☎882 6299). Inexpensive, up-to-the-minute styles.

Inge Helf, Rheinstr. 48, 1/41 (☎852 7651). International designs and young fashions, in bigger than standard sizes.

Jean Pascale, Europa Center, Tauentzienstr. 9, 1/30 (☎262 5490). Similar to *H&M*, only cheaper.

Matchball, Fasanenstr. 31, 1/12 (☎882 5297). Upmarket sports clothes.

Mike's Laden, Nürnbergerstr. 53–57, 1/30 (☎248020). Gaultier junior for men.

Molotow, Gneisenaustr. 112, 1/61 (☎693 813). The best of West and East Berlin designers; middle price range.

Noncult, Wielandstr. 31, 1/15 (☎883 3810). Classic, functional men's clothes, with an eye to unusual detail.

Seppälä, Kurfürstendamm 235, 1/15 (☎882 7195). Chic Finnish designs at low prices.

Soft, Bleibtreustr. 6, 1/15 (☎312 1403). Jean Paul Gaultier, Thierry Mugler, Montana et al.

Veni Vidi Vici, Leibnizstr. 40, 1/12 (☎323 2322). Classic styles in natural fabrics for men and women.

X-Plus, Luxemburgerstr. 2, 1/65 (☎454 3924). Oversize fashions for the extrovert.

Die Zweite Haut, Rheinstr. 62, 1/41 (☎851 9318). Made-to-measure latex designs in a multitude of colors.

7 UP'S, Bleibtreustr. 48, 1/15 (☎883 5108). Wonderful jackets.

Children

Baby-Korb, Bundesallee 17, 1/15 (☎883 3007). Accessories and European designer clothes; middle price range.

Laura, Fasanenpassage (☎882 5922). Exclusive children's shoes.

Moozy Poozy, Rheinstr. 61, 1/41 (☎852 2611). Reasonably priced jeans, underwear, and chic odds and ends.

Naturkind, Klausenerplatz 15, 1/19 (☎321 1830). Pure fibers for the rich Alternatives of Charlottenburg.

Wundertüte, Stuttgarterplatz 5, 1/12 (☎323 4054). New and secondhand clothes and accessories.

See also Chapter Three, *Kids' Stuff and Sport*.

Accessories

Bags and Belts

Sack & Pack, Kantstr. 48, 1/12 (☎312 1513). Natural and black leather bags in sporty styles.

Die Weisse Hoffnung, Schlüterstr. 50, 1/12 (☎323 6532). Men's and women's bags and large selection of way-out belts, all made on the premises.

Fabrics

Fichu, Akazienstr. 21, 1/62 (☎781 5461). A delicate assortment of materials from the 1920s onwards.

Tessuti, Pestalozzistr. 85, 1/12 (☎313 8016). Fashionable and rich display of natural fibers (no synthetic dyes) from Italy, with advice if needed.

India Import, Uhlandstr. 47, 1/15 (☎881 1563). The oriental craze hasn't caught on in Berlin as it has in the rest of Europe, so now's your chance to snap up some prints and silks before the prices rocket.

Knopf Paul, Zossenerstr. 10, 1/61 (☎692 1212). Buttons.

Leder-Adelt, Joachim-Friedrichstr. 41, 1/31 (☎891 3334). Leather.

Schwarze Mode, Grunewaldstr. 91, 1/62 (☎784 5922). Latex.

Glasses

Brillen am Winterfeldtplatz, Maassenstr. 13, 1/30 (☎216 3020). The latest in French specs with friendly and personal service.

Glasses, Nürnbergerstr. 50–56, 1/30 (☎242474). Optician's set out like a cocktail bar, if you can believe it.

Optiker Neumann, Gneisenaustr. 22, 1/61 (☎691 9334). Large variety of 1950s glasses, currently all the rage here.

Hair

Carlo Piras, Fasanenstr. 42, 1/15 (☎882 1100). Classy salon in the Italian school of hairdressing.

Hair Flair, Waitzstr. 13, 1/12 (☎324 0755). Some of their stylists are English, if you're worried about the language problem.

Jason's Hairpower, Leibnizstr. 102, 1/12 (☎341 9085). Ultra-hip and ultra-expensive barnet adjuster that has numbered David Bowie and Brigitte Nielsen among its customers.

Venus, Goltzstr. 38, 1/30 (☎216 4791). Punk and "normal" hairstyles at reasonable prices.

Perfume

Belladonna, Bergmannstr. 101, 1/37 (☎694 3731). Large choice of natural cosmetics.

Duft Fabrik, Kantstr. 106, 1/12 (☎324 3582). Mix your smells then take them away, for DM5.

Shoes

The best place to track down reasonably priced **shoes** is in the Wilmersdorferstrasse U-Bahn area, where a number of shops provide a vast selection: for something special, try **Schuhtick**, Savignyplatz 11 (☎312 4955). At the other end of the fashion spectrum, **Roots**, Kantstr. 57 (☎323 3021) specializes in comfortable "earth" styles.

Tights and Underwear

Seide Silk Soie, Oranienstr. 23, 1/36 (☎614 4712). Lingerie, tights, and kimonos in silk.

Strumpfladen, Kurfürstendamm 66, 1/12 (☎883 6254). Tights.

Department Stores

There are no surprises inside Berlin's **department stores** and, with the exception of *KaDeWe*, they're only worth popping into to stock up on essentials or to buy **concert and theater tickets** at the *Theaterkassen*. Listed below are the most central ones; check the phone book for more outlying branches.

Bilka, Joachimstalerstr. 5, 1/12 (☎881 3081). Excellent discounts on toiletries.

Hertie, Wilmersdorferstr. 118, 1/12 (☎310311) and Blücherplatz 3 (☎251 0761). Not as good a selection as at *Karstadt* (see below) and more expensive. The branch at Blücherplatz has a slightly better selection.

KaDeWe, Tauentzienstr. 21, 1/30 (☎21210). Content rather than flashy interior décor rules the day here. From designer labels to the extraordinarily good displays at the international delicatessen, where you can nibble on some piece of exotica or stock up on double price El Paso taco mix, everything the consumer's heart desires can be found at this, the largest department store on the continent.

Karstadt, Wilmersdorferstr. 109, 1/12 (☎31891), Schlossstr. 7, 1/41 (☎790010) and Hermannplatz., 1/61 (☎69081). Good basic all-rounder, classier and cheaper than *Hertie*. The branch at Hermannplatz is best stocked.

Wertheim, Kurfürstendamm 231, 1/15 (☎882061) and Schlossstr. 11, 1/41 (☎791091). A smaller and cheaper version of *KaDeWe*. Everything is beautifully laid out, with a particularly good menswear department.

F.W. Woolworth, Willmersdorferstr. 113, 1/12 (☎313 4095) and Joannisthaler Chaussee 327 (☎603 1071). Although it's a bit of a trek, the branch at Johannisthaler Chaussee has surprisingly good quality, fashionable clothes at knock-down prices.

Food and Drink

Of the city's **supermarket chains**, *Pennymarkt* is by far the cheapest for food and drink, although with a little less choice than the rest. *Ullrich*, on Hardenbergstrasse, underneath the railroad bridge by Zoo Station, has an excellent selection—though you pay over the odds for its central position, and you may find it packed with East Berliners out for the day. The city's **specialty food shops** are spread throughout the town, though the majority of Turkish shops are in Kreuzberg. The **night shops** listed below all close before midnight, and are about a third more expensive than usual: they're particularly useful when everything else has closed for the weekend.

Bread

Bäckerei, Körtestr. 32, 1/61 (☎691 8136). Berlin specialties.

Backstern, Kantstr. 95., 1/12 *Vollkorn* bread and especially delicious cakes.

Coffee and Tea

King's Teagarden, Kurfürstendamm 217, 1/15 (☎883 7059). Buy your tea downstairs or drink someone else's upstairs to a background of classical music. Open all day Saturday.

TeeHaus, Krummerstr. 35, 1/12 (☎310131). A tea lover's paradise: teas sold loose and to suit every taste. Also English jams and natural honeys.

Delicatessens and Ethnic Foods

Holland Shop, Mehringdamm 73, 1/61 (☎692 6967). Far Eastern specialties.

Ku Long, Maassenstr. 5, 1/30 (☎216 6698). Southeast Asian ingredients.

Magasin Provençal, Nollendorfstr. 15, 1/30 (☎215 3415). Traditional food from Provence.

De Milchladen, Dresdenerstr. 20, 1/36 (☎657272). Fresh milk and dairy products.

Salumeria da Pino & Enzo, Windscheidstr. 20, 1/12 (☎324 3318). Wines and yummy Italian delicacies. Mouth-watering nibbles available for lunch.

Sikasso, Dresdenerstr. 124, 1/36 (☎614 8729). African food and *objets d'art*.

Spezialitäten Kontor, Danckelmannstr. 29, 1/19 (☎322 6619). Delicatessen with fine wines and wine tasting.

Südwind, Akazienstr. 7, 1/62 (☎782 6153). Wines and products from Tuscany. Very good value.

Fish and Meats

Alternative Fleischerei, Körtestr. 20., 1/61 (☎691 6486). Cows and chickens that weren't stuffed with chemicals before they were killed.

Fische & Geflügel, Maxstr. 17, 1/65 (☎456 6807). Family-run business specializing in fish and wildfowl. A bit out of the way, but worth it.

Health Food

Mutter Erde, Behaimstr. 18, 1/10 (☎341 7955). Large stock of everything, ranging from organically grown vegetables and wines to "green" household products.

Risico, Dieffenbachstr. 32, 1/61 (☎694 2862). Health shop and café.

Sesammühle, Knesebeckstr. 89, 1/12 (☎312 5199). Health foods.

Spezialkräuterhaus, Templehofer Damm 177, 1/42 (☎751 6022). Herbal specialist.

UFA-Fabrik-Laden, Viktoriastr. 13, 1/61 (☎752 6078). Wholefoods and goods from developing and politically emergent countries.

Wines and Spirits

Der Rebgarten, Bergmannstr. 112, 1/61 (☎694 5502). Organically grown wines and juices. Open afternoons and Saturday mornings only.

La Cantina, Kreuzbergstr. 76, 1/61 (☎785 8793). Italian wines.

Wein & Glas Compagnie, Prinzregentenstr. 2, 1/31 (☎213 7879). German and French wines (and some glasses).

Weinstein, Maassenstr. 5, 1/30 (☎215 7251). Italián and French wines from the barrel, filled in the shop.

Weinwinkel, Kopischstr. 2, 1/61 (☎692 9987). Selection of fine wines, friendly service.

Night Shops

Edeka, in U-Bahn Schlossstrasse, 1/41 (Mon–Fri 3–10pm, Sat 1–10pm, Sun & holidays 10am–8pm).

Metro, in U-Bahn Fehrbelinner Platz1, 1/31 (daily 11am–10:30pm).

Metro, in U-Bahn Kurfürstendamm, 1/12 (Sun–Fri 11am–11pm, Sat 11am–midnight).

Most **Turkish shops**, the majority being in Kreuzberg and Neukölln, are open Saturday afternoon and Sunday 1–5pm.

Markets

There's a myriad of food markets within each quarter of the town, too numerous to mention here: listed below is a selection of the best **flea markets**. For **junk shops**, Suarezstrasse in Charlottenburg is the place to head for.

Flea Markets

Fehrbellinerplatz (Sun 8am–3pm). Lots of plants and old pictures.

Kreuzberger Krempelmarkt, am Reichpietsufer, corner with Linkstr. (Sat & Sun 8am–3:30pm). Dusty and sprawling market, mainly junk, but the occasional superb bargain to be had if you dig around long enough. On the street, and in the park next to it, Polish people down for the weekend try to sell anything possible, effecting a scenario that's both sad and humorous at the same time. See also p.51.

Nollendorfplatz U-Bahn (Wed–Mon 11am–7pm). Situated in the disused section of the old station, sometimes with live jazz music to accompany your browsing. High quality antiques/oddities, and not overly expensive.

Strasse des 17 Juni, north side of the road near Ernst-Reuter-Platz (Sat & Sun 8am–3:30pm). Pleasant enough for a Sunday morning stroll, but the most expensive of the flea markets, and with horribly tourist-oriented wares. Good for lace and embroidery though.

Türken-Markt, Kottbusser Damm, corner with Maybachufer. (Tues & Fri noon–6pm). Definitely worth a visit, especially on Fridays when there's a real oriental flavor. Very cheap, and a good place to hunt down fabrics and haberdashery.

Winterfeldtmarkt, am Winterfeldtplatz. (Wed & Sat mornings). Arguably the most popular market in Berlin, with brightly printed clothes, exotic smells floating in the breeze, and plenty of cafés nearby for a drink afterwards.

Zille-Hof, Fasanenstr. 17, 1/12 (Mon–Fri 8:30am–5:30pm). Not so much a flea market as an overgrown junkshop with reproduction curios, old street signs, and a miscellany of interesting junk. Not especially cheap, but good fun.

Miscellaneous and Ethnic

For a cross-section of the weird and wonderful, Berlin is hard to beat:

Allerlei zur Hexerei, Hauptstr. 4, 1/62 (☎784 2406). Wools and knitting needles.

Antike Ubren, Droysenstr. 2, 1/12 (☎323 2136). Sells and repairs antique clocks.

Apotheke am Viktoriapark, Grossbeerenstr. 52, 1/61 (☎785 0111). The only alternative pharmacy in Berlin, and therefore the best place to go for natural and homeopathic remedies.

Atzert-Radio, Kleiststr. 32, 1/30 (☎214 6044). Do-it-yourself radio and electronics paradise.

Bale-Bale, Savignyplatz 6, 1/12 (☎312 9066). Arts and crafts from India, Pakistan, and Indonesia. More a fashion store than a crafts shop.

Blumenladen, Südstern U-Bahn, 1/61 (☎691 8924). Flowers on Sunday.

Classic Bike, Oranienplatz 5, 1/36 (☎614 7046). English motorbikes.

Der Pfeifenmacher, Bismarckstr. 60, 1/12 (☎341 6303). Huge selection of tobaccos and own-brand pipes.

Die Palme, Kurfürstendamm 102, 1/15 (☎892 4640). Exotic plants and bonsai trees.

Die Schlange, Elberfelderstr. 6, 1/21 (☎391 9963). Should you feel the need to buy a snake during your stay, this is the place to come.

Dritte-Welt-Laden, inside the Gedächtniskirche, 1/12 (☎832 5497). Non-profit-making organization selling handicrafts from the Third World and books on problems facing the developing countries.

El Condor, Kantstr. 36, 1/12 (☎313 9828). Latin American crafts.

Foto Meyer, Geisbergstr. 14, 1/30 (☎247087). Reasonably priced cameras and darkroom equipment.

Hängos Tätowierstudio, Mierendorffstr. 25, 1/10 (☎344 9367). Tattooing, if that's your style.

Kelim & Kunsthandwerk, Goethestr. 34, 1/30 (☎313 9651). Polish crafts.

Narrenfreibeit, Langenscheidtstr. 6a, 1/62. Theater and clowning materials.

Ostasiatica, c/o Wolfgang Bock, Gardeschützenweg 92, 1/45 (☎833 2929). The ultimate in idiosyncracy: the only authorized dealer in Europe for Samurai swords.

Reflections, Bregenzerstr. 9, 1/15 (☎883 9869). Superb variety of Art Deco lamps, ornaments, and some smaller pieces of furniture. Reasonably priced.

Sayo, Mommsenstr. 4, 1/12 (☎882 1612). Antique shop specializing in Art Deco.

Spiel-Vogel, Uhlandstr. 137 (☎872377). Toys, games, and model-making equipment.

Take Off, Langenscheidtstr. 7, 1/62. Mickey Mouse knick-knacks and presents.

Versandstelle für Postwertzeichen, Post office at Goethestr. 2 (☎3409 2409). New and special-issue stamps.

Vom Winde Verweht, Eisenacherstr. 81, 1/62 (☎784 7769). Kites.

Zauberkönig, Hermannstr. 84 (☎621 4082). Illusions, tricks, and other magicians' equipment.

Zinnsoldaten, Skalitzerstr. 81. Enormous selection of tin figures.

Records

Although Berlin doesn't have as many large, general record stores as America, there are plenty of smaller shops dedicated to just one style:

Down-Beat, Pallasstr., opposite Winterfeldtplatz, 1/30 (☎215 7773). Reggae, soul, R&B, and jazz, with some rare items.

Gelbe Musik, Schaperstr. 11, 1/15 (☎211 3962). Avant-garde in both music and style, the place being not so much a record shop as a music gallery.

Groove Records, Pücklerstr. 36 (☎454 3417). New wave.

Jazzcock, Behaimstr. 4, 1/10 (☎341 5447). Over 5000 jazz titles; specialists in European avant-garde.

Pedro, Tegeler Weg 100, 1/10 (☎344 1875). Buys and sells secondhand records.

Rayen Records, Pestalozzistr. 96, 1/12 (☎316031). Secondhand records from the Fifties onwards.

Schallplatten, Stettinerstr. 64, 1/65 (☎322 4575). Large selection of blues, rock, jazz, and chansons.

Soundman-Shop, Urbanstr. 112, 1/61 (☎691 3718). Everything for your Walkman.

WOM, Augsburgerstr. 35–41, 1/12 (☎882 7541). Huge choice of records.

CHAPTER THREE

KIDS' STUFF AND SPORT

Berlin isn't most peoples' first choice when it comes to traveling with **kids**: but there's enough to keep them occupied during the day and, should you need them, babysitting and childminding services are good. **Sports** facilities are fine if you're participating, not so hot if you're watching.

MAINLY FOR KIDS

Attitudes to young children in Berlin strike the outsider as oddly ambivalent. While the city has a large number of single-parent families, and excellent social service provisions for them, Berliners aren't too tolerant of kids in "adult" places, such as restaurants or bars; and though the city consists of a higher proportion of lakes, park, and woodland than any other European capital, there's little in them directly geared to entertaining children. If you're bringing kids, be prepared to do Berlin versions of the obvious things—zoos, museums, and shops—rather than anything unique to the city.

Babysitting Services

Babysitter-Service, Claudiasstr. 6 (☎393 5981). Complicated and expensive payment system (it works out to between DM12 and DM20 an hour), but offering an all-night service.

Hernzelmännchen der Freien Universität Berlin, Unter den Eichen 96, 1/46 (☎831 6071). Reservations for sitters taken Mon, Tues & Thurs 7am–6pm, Wed & Fri 7am–5pm.

Mary Poppins, Uhlandstr. 113 (☎861 2947). Centrally located.

TUSMA der Technischen Universität Berlin, Hardenbergstr. 35, 1/12 (☎313 4054). Reservations for sitters taken Mon–Fri 7am–7pm, Sat 8am–1pm. Rates approximately DM13 per hour.

Parks, Playgrounds, and Trips

With over a third of Berlin being forest or parkland, often with playgrounds dotted around, there's no shortage of spaces for children to go and let off steam. The most central and obvious choice is the **Tiergarten** northeast of Zoo Station, though this is rather tame compared to the rambling expanses of the **Grunewald** (S-Bahn Grunewald): in both parks paddle and rowing boats are for rent, bikes too at Grunewald S-Bahn station. The Grunewald borders the **Wannsee** lake, and it's fun to take the ferry over to the **Pfaueninsel** (Peacock Island) where there's a castle and plenty of strutting peacocks; see p.68 for details. **Freizeitspark Tegel** (U-Bahn Tegel, walk to the lake, then turn right) has playgrounds, trampolines, table tennis, and paddle boats. There's also a good **adventure playground** at Sodenerstr. 29–41 (U-Bahn Rüdesheimerplatz or buses #60 or #86), open from Monday to Saturday noon to 6pm, Thursday from 3pm to 6pm. The **Teufelsberg** ("Devil's Mountain," bus #94 to Teufelsee Chaussee and then a good fifteen minutes' walk down the same road), a large hill to the west of the city, is the place to go kite flying on weekends.

Educationally oriented **Kinderbauernhöfen**, or children's farms, can be fun without knowing the language: they're to be found at Wienerstr. 59 (U-Bahn Görlitzer Bahnhof or bus #29 then follow footpath; summer Mon, Tues, Thurs & Fri 10am–7pm, Sat & Sun noon–7pm; closes at 5pm during winter months) and in the UFA-Fabrik, Viktoriastr. 13–18 (U-Bahn Ullsteinstrasse or bus #25; open daily from 10am).

Of the city's sports facilities, of most interest to kids is probably **Blub**, a slick indoor and outdoor pool complex at Buschkrugalle 64 (U-Bahn Blaschko Allee; Mon–Fri 10am–11pm, Sat & Sun 9am–midnight; adults DM16, children 6–17 DM9). It's a bit of a trek out, and expensive to boot, but worth it for the waterfalls, whirlpools, 12-meter shoot and wave machine, to name but a few facilities.

For views of Berlin from on high (in ascending order of terror) try the **Siegessäule** (not for little legs; see p.39), the top floor of the **Europa Center** (p.36), and the **Funkturm** (p.63).

Older children might appreciate a visit to the **Zeiss Planetarium**, Munsterdamm 90 (S-Bahn Priesterweg, buses #25, #68, #76 and #83; guided tours at 8pm Tues–Sun; adults DM4, children DM3).

Circuses, Amusement Parks, and the Zoo

The UFA-Zirkus at the UFA-Fabrik, Viktoriastr. 13, 1/61 (☎752 8085), is a residential **circus** offering an inventive alternative to the usual lions-and-clowns stuff. Circus troupes visit the city regularly during the summer months. To find out where and when, contact the *Zirkusdirektorenverband*, Xantenerstr. 9 (☎8881 4660).

Small **amusement parks** can be found almost year-round in Berlin on the small patches of park that dot the city. Check with the tourist office in the Europa Center for locations.

The **Zoo**, Hardenbergplatz 8, 1/30 (☎261 1101; daily 9am–dusk, DM7.50, children 3–15 DM3.50), near to the railroad station of the same name, has an array of exotic animals in surroundings that attempt to mimic their natural habitat. Of most interest to kids will be the monkeys, orangutans and gorillas, the nocturnal rooms (a darkened area where varieties of gerbilly-type creatures do their thing), pony and horse and trap rides around the zoo, and a playground. The **Aquarium** nearby, Budapesterstr. 32, 1/30 (☎261 1101;

daily 9am–6pm, last Sat in month & public holidays until 10pm; DM6.50, children 3–15 DM3.25; combined tickets with Zoo DM11/5.50), is also well worth the money, though probably best seen on a separate trip from the Zoo.

Museums

Dahlem Junior Museum, Arnimallee, near U-Bahn Dahlem-Dorf, 1/33 (Tues–Sun 9am–5pm; free). Plenty for the kids to finger and touch, especially in the ethnographic sections of the main museum, where boats and huts from the South Seas are just waiting to be climbed on and crawled into.

Düppel Museum Village, Clauertstr. 11, 1/37 (May–Sept, Sun only 10am–1pm; DM3; bus #3 and #50). Reconstruction of a medieval country village, with demonstrations of the handicrafts and farming methods of those times. Better for older children.

Panoptikum, 4th floor, Ku'damm Eck, Kurfürstendamm 227–228, 1/12 (daily 10am–11pm; DM5, kids under 11 DM3). Tawdry waxworks.

Museum of Transport and Technology, Trebbinerstr. 9, 1/61 (Tues–Fri 9am–6pm, Sat & Sun 10am–6pm; DM3.50, children DM1.50). Lots of gadgets to experiment with, plus a great collection of old steam trains and carriages. Highly diverting; the perfect thing for a wet afternoon. See "West Kreuzberg", Chapter One.

Wilmersdorf Community Gallery—Children's Gallery, Hohenzollerndamm 176, 1/30 (Mon–Fri 10am–6pm, Sun 11am–5pm). Plenty of free material with which children can paint, draw, and build, plus films of their choice. The local history museum next door has exhibitions on how the young and old of Wilmersdorf used to live (Mon, Wed & Fri 10am–2pm, Tues & Thurs 2–6pm; free).

Theaters and Cinemas

Berliner Figurentheater, Yorckstr. 59, 1/61 (☎786 9815). Constantly innovative puppet theater with superbly crafted dolls. Like the other puppet theaters listed below, kids don't need a knowledge of German to enjoy what's going on.

Fliegenotes Theater, Gneisenaustr. 2, in the Mehringhof, 1/61 (☎693 3791). Puppet theater.

Grips, Altonaerstr. 22 (☎391 4004). Top class children's/young people's theater; usually all improvised. German-speaking only.

Kino Museum, Grossbeerenstr. 57, 1/61. Tiny place with old cinema furniture. Shows old slapstick movies on Wednesday, Friday, and Sunday at 6pm.

Klecks, Schinkestr. 8–9 (☎693 7731). Puppet theater aimed specifically at the 3- to 8-year-old age group.

Multivisions-Theater, 1st floor, Europa Center, 1/30 (daily at 9am, 10am, noon, 1:30pm, 3pm & 4:30pm; DM8, children 6–9 DM5). The history of Berlin in glorious Technicolor; headsets available with an English translation. Suitable for older children.

Shops

Baby-Korb, Bundesallee 17, 1/15 (☎883 3007). Accessories and European designer clothes; middle price range.

Die Schlange, Elberfelderstr. 6, 1/21 (☎391 9963). Snakes!

Et Cetera, Suarezstr. 31, 1/19 (322 8665). Large selection of kids' books and wooden toys.

Grober Unfüg, Gneisenaustr. 15, 1/61 (☎693 6413). Comics in the cellar.

Narrenfreiheit, Langenscheidtstr. 6a, 1/62. Theater and clowning materials. Open Mon–Fri 1–6pm.

Spiele-Shop im PZ, Berlinerstrasse, corner of Uhlandstrasse, 1/31 (☎871535). Books and toys with a strongly educational slant.

Spiel-Vogel, Uhlandstr. 137, 1/15 (☎872 377). Toys, games, and model-making equipment.

Struwwellotte, Carmerstr. 11, 1/12 (☎312 5654). Alternative book and toy shop for children; reasonably priced, with a selection of secondhand books.

Take Off, Langenscheidtstr. 7. Mickey Mouse knick-knacks and presents.

Versandstelle für Postwertzeichen, Post Office at Goethestr. 2, 1/12 (☎3409 2409). New and special issue stamps and franking. Several shops nearby sell stamps and coins.

Vom Winde Verweht, Eisenacherstr. 81, 1/62 (☎784 7769; Mon–Fri 2–6:30pm, Sat 10am–1pm). Kites—the place to come before heading off for the Teufelsberg hill.

Wundertüte, Stuttgarterplatz 5, 1/12 (☎323 4054). New and secondhand kids' clothes and accessories.

Zauberkönig, Hermannstr. 84, 1/61 (☎621 4082). Illusions and tricks for magicians and their apprentices.

Zinnsoldaten, Skalitzerstr. 81, 1/36 (Mon–Fri 4–6pm, Sat 1am–1pm). Enormous selection of tin soldiers and figures.

SPORT

While West Berliners go in for healthy eating in a big way, they're not famous for being fitness fanatics—they need all their energy for the frenetic night life. But there is a surprising variety of **participatory sports** available in the city if you feel like flexing all your muscles and not just those in your right arm.

Spectator sports aren't so well catered for. There's no city soccer team (East Berlin has two), and what sporting events are held here are rarely on an international level.

For a complete rundown of all annual sporting events visit the **Landesportbund Berlin e.V**, Jesse-Owens-Allee 1–2 (☎300020), where you can pick up a copy of the yearly *Freizeitsports Kalender* which has full details of both spectator and participatory sports.

Boat Rental and Ice Skating

Paddle and rowing boats are a pleasant, if rather strenuous, way of enjoying Berlin's lakes during the summer. Try Strandbad Wannsee, the Neuer See in Tiergarten, or the quieter Schlachtensee. For other waterborne trips, see "Getting Around", in *West Berlin Basics*.

Some of the city lakes are also good for **ice skating**, but if they haven't frozen over and you're forced indoors, there are rinks at **Eissporthalle Berlin**, Jafféstrasse, 1/33, an indoor rink with a disco on Wednesday evenings during the winter from 7:30 to 9:45pm (☎3038; DM5) or **Eisstadion Berlin-Wilmersdorf**, Fritz-Wilding-Strasse 9, 1/33 (☎823 4060; DM3), an outdoor rink with a limited skating time of up to two hours.

Fishing

There's plenty of choice for fishing and angling spots in Berlin: for detailed information and the necessary visitor's fishing license (*Fischereischein*), contact the **Fischereiamt beim Senator für Stadtentwicklung und Umweltschutz**, Havelchaussee 149–151 (☎305 2047), who can also advise on the best places to rent the necessary equipment.

Jogging

The most convenient but crowded spot is around the Tiergarten, just behind Zoo station. It's worth trekking up to the area just south of the Tempodrom where some very pretty and quiet wooded glades surround a small stream.

If you're into long-distance running, a trip round Grunewald lake should be more of a challenge, or there's always the **Berlin Marathon** on the first Sunday in October. This starts on Strasse des 17 Juni and ends nearly 50km later, after passing through Dahlem and along the Kurfürstendamm, back at the Kaiser-Wilhelm Memorial Church. To enter, write to **SCC Berlin**, Meinekestr. 13, D-1000 Berlin 15 (☎882 6405): closing date for entries is one month before the marathon. The *SCC* can also supply details on numerous other meetings, including the 10-km race along the **Kurfürstendamm** in July.

Mini-Golf

Hasenheide 81, 1/61 (☎693 1362). April–Oct daily 11am–10pm.

Munsterdamm, Prellerweg, 1/41 (☎796 1558). April–Oct daily 11am–10pm.

Sechserbrücke, Berlin Tegel, 1/27 (☎433 7690). April–Oct daily 10am–sunset.

Roller-Skating

Apart from zooming round Breitscheidplatz or the outskirts of the Nationalgalerie, try:

Rollerskating-center, Hasenheide 108, 1/61 (☎621 1028), Hermannplatz U-Bahn. Tues–Fri 3–6:30pm & 8pm–midnight, Wed & Thurs 3–6:30pm & 8–11pm, Sat 2–7pm & 8pm–2am, Sun 2–11pm. DM4–6 entrance (limited time); skate rental DM3–4.

Z.B. Stadion Wilmersdorf, Fritz-Wildung-Str., 1/33 (☎824 1012). Outdoor rink May–Sept Tues–Fri 9am–4pm.

Skiing

Believe it or not, there are five ski slopes in Berlin and in the case of heavy snowfalls, skiing lessons on the *Teufelsberg* take place both day and night (DM10 for a double lesson). Contact the **Skiverband Berlin e-V im Landessportbund Berlin**, Bismarckaltee 2, 1/33 (☎891 9798), for more information. You can rent skis from *Ski-sport-stadl*, Lützowstr. 104, 1/30 (☎261505).

Swimming Pools

Bad am Spreewaldplatz, Wienerstr. 59H (☎258 85813). Popular indoor pool with sauna and wave machine. Tues–Fri 8am–9pm, Sat & Sun 1–9pm; Tues and Thurs women only, Wed men only, Fri, Sat & Sun mixed; closed Mon.

Blub, Buschkrugallee 64 (☎606 6060). Magnificent indoor and outdoor pool with wave machine, 120-meter chute, whirlpools, waterfalls, sauna, and fitness center. Daily 10am–11pm, Sat & Sun 9am–midnight. DM16 for 4 hours including sauna.

Stadtbad Wilmersdorf, Mecklenburgische Str. 80 (☎868 9523). Indoor pool with solarium, easily accessible from the city center. Mon & Sat 7am–7pm, Tues–Fri 7am–9:40pm, closed Sun.

Strandbad Wannsee, Wannseebadweg (☎803 5450). Outdoor pool with beach nearby, lots of activities going on in the summer and usually packed. May–Sept daily 7am–8pm; DM3.

Other outdoor pools include:

Freibad Halensee, Königsallee 5a (☎891 1703). Lake-side pool.

Olympia-Schwimmstadion, Olympischer Platz (Osttor), 1/19 (☎304 0676). Part of the Olympic Stadium complex (see"Points Westward", Chapter One).

Sommerbad Lichterfelde, Hindenburgdamm 9–10, 1/45. Summer pool open till 8pm May 15 to July 31.

Sommerbad Neukölln, Columbiadamm 160–190. Open from May to mid-Sept.

Tennis

Apart from private clubs, some parks have tennis courts, notably the **Freizeitpark Tegel**, 1/27 (next to Tegeler See). Mid-April–mid-Oct Mon–Fri 8am–4pm; DM18 per hour from 4–9pm, bookable up to six days in advance (☎434 6666).

Tobogganing

A favorite winter pastime in Berlin—and not just for children. The **Teufelsberg**, and to the north of the city, the **Freizeitpark Lübars**, have the most hair-raising slopes, or for more nervous souls there's the **Rodelbahn Goethepark**, Transvaalstr., 1/65, and the **Rodelbahn Humboldthain**, Gustav-Meyer-Allee, 1/65. The **Senator für Stadtentwicklung und Umweltschutz**, Lindenstr. 20–25, 1/61 (☎2586/2497), has details of the best tobogganning spots.

CHAPTER FOUR

DRINKING AND EATING

owhere is more than a stone's throw from a **bar** in Berlin. Just about every street corner has a small *Kneipe*, ranging from lugubrious beer-swilling holes to slick, upscale hangouts for the city's night people. You'll find that most places stay open later than anywhere in West Germany; it's quite feasible to drink around the clock here, the result of a law that requires bars only to close for an hour a day for cleaning.

The city's compressed, cosmopolitan nature means that the range of **restaurants** is wider than in any other German city: indeed the national cuisine takes a back seat to Greek, Turkish, Balkan, Indian, and Italian food, and plenty of places exist where a meal costs under DM15. Almost all the better bars serve food, too, and this can be a bargain—though beware the most chic places, where that interesting-looking item on the menu turns out to be a plate of asparagus tips for DM25. For cheap, on-your-feet **snacks**, hit an *Imbiss* kiosk—a few marks for a *Wurst* or burger.

DRINKING

The basic, no frills drinking hole is known as a **Kneipe** (bar), found on street corners throughout the city and identifiable by its general gloom and all-male clientele. *Kneipen* are the cheapest places to drink (a small beer costs around DM3) and can be fun if the regulars decide to befriend you. Unaccompanied women should bear in mind that such befriending may have unwanted over-tones: as a rule, local women do not frequent these places, choosing instead to head for more mixed and more **upmarket bars and cafés**. It is these places that make up the bulk of the listings below: Berlin has a great variety of upscale bars—often referred to as *Szene* ("Scene") hangouts—where pose (or self-conscious lack of it) is all; and numerous other theme-type places that are, quite simply, fun places to drink in. While the trendier-looking bars are more expensive, few are outrageously so; and, given their tendency to clus-ter, it's easy to bar-hop until you find a favorite. Most bars **open** at lunchtime and close at 1–2am, with many staying open till 3–4am. **Gay men's** and **Women's** bars are listed at the end of the section.

Berlin **beer specialties** include *Berliner Weisse*, a watery top-fermented wheat beer that's traditionally pepped up by adding a shot of fruity syrup or *Schuss*. Ask for it *mit grün* and you get a dash of woodruff, creating a greeny brew that tastes like liquid silage; *mit rot* is a raspberry-flavored kiddy drink that works wonders at breakfast time.

Bars and Cafés

Though it's fun enough to dive into any bar that takes your fancy, West Berlin has three focal points for drinking, each with more than enough bars to tackle through the course of an evening, and each with a subtly differing character. Those **around Savignyplatz** are the haunt of the city's conspicuous good-timers; the area **around Nollendorfplatz and Winterfeldtplatz** is the territory of burnt-out all-nighters and the pushing-on-forty crew. **Kreuzberg** drinkers include political activists, punks, and the Turkish community, in a mix that forms this area's appeal. Unless you're into brawling soldiers or sloshed businessmen, avoid the Ku'damm and the rip-off joints around the Europa Center.

Savignyplatz and Around

Café au Lait, Kantstr. 110, 1/12. Small and individualistic bar-restaurant with a relaxed atmosphere and Latin American music.

Café Bleibtreu, Bleibtreustr. 45, 1/12. One of Savignyplatz's more disreputable cafés. Pleasantly down-at-the-heel, and cheap.

Café Savigny, Grolmanstr. 53, 1/12. Bright, sharp café on the edge of Savignyplatz catering to an arty/media crowd. Mildly gay.

Café Tiago, Knesebeckstr. 9, 1/12. Brash decor—rather like a yuppie living room—but lively.

CUT, Knesebeckstr. 16, 1/12. Over three hundred cocktails to be imbibed in a cocoon of black.

Departure Lounge, Schlüterstr. 72, 1/12. What in America would be called a "theme bar," this is decked out with old aircraft seats, plastic planes, and international tack. A bit like O'Hare on Acid, and great fun.

Dicke Wirtin, Carmerstr. 9, 1/12. Noisy, boozy, and popular place, more for the 1970s rock crew than anyone else. Excellent bowls of filling stew for DM3.50 are the main draw.

DRINKS GLOSSARY

Wasser	water	*Orangensaft*	orange juice
Sprüdel	sparkling mineral water	*Tomatensaft*	tomato juice
Milch	milk	*Zitronenlimonade*	lemonade
Milchshake	milk shake	*Bier*	beer
Kaffee	coffee	*Weisswein*	white wine
Kaffee normale	coffee with milk	*Rotwein*	red wine
Milchkaffee	coffee	*Roséwein*	rosé wine
Tee	tea	*Sekt*	sparkling wine
Zitronentee	lemon tea	*Glühwein*	hot mulled wine
Kräutertee, Pflanzentee	herbal tea	*Apfelwein*	apple wine
Kakao	cocoa	*Weinbrand*	brandy
Schockolade	hot chocolate	*Korn*	rye spirit
Apfelsaft	apple juice	*Likör*	liqueur
Traubensaft	grape juice	*Grog*	hot rum

Dralles, Schlüterstr. 59, 1/12. Notably more expensive than other bars in the area, *Dralles* is *the* place to see and be seen: the 1950s decor is chic and understated, the clientele aspire likewise. Go beautiful and loaded, or not at all . . .

Filmbühne, corner of Hardenbergstrasse and Steinplatz, 1/12. One of the least pretentious and more original cafés in Berlin, with friendly service to boot.

Galerie Bremer, Fasanenstr. 37, 1/12. Meeting point for actors and artists of every age and bent.

Grolman's, Grolmanstr. 21, 1/12. Swish bar-restaurant with slick sitting area and a thirty-ish business crowd with a scattering of moneyed punks. Food DM15–30.

Hegel, Savignyplatz 2, 1/12. Tiny café on the southeastern side of Savignyplatz that attracts an older crowd. Gregarious fun when someone starts up on the piano.

Herta, Schlüterstr. 75, 1/12. Nothing special—except for the clientele who are so normal as to be unclassifiable in this city of categories.

Kant Billard-Café, Kantstr. 38, 1/12. Style and political persuasions are momentarily forgotten as grannies and punks alike lunge across the billiard tables.

Lentz, Stuttgarter Platz 20, 1/12. Earnest intellectuals and artists on the pick-up.

Mimikry, Kantstr. 29, 1/12. Ultra hip hangout—though, apart from the fact that it starts serving breakfast at 3am, it's hard to figure out why.

Paris Bar, Kantstr. 152, 1/12. More famous for its restaurant (see p.106) this was once the local of the city's actors and film crowd, though today it seems to live on a long-dead reputation. Middle-aged, sedate, and very expensive.

Rosalinde, Knesebeckstr. 15, 1/12. Upmarket café with an unusual variety of breakfasts: their *Fitness Frühstück* (granola, fresh fruit, and nuts) does the trick after a rough night out, and there's hot food until 2am.

Schwarzes Café, Kantstr. 148, 1/12. Kantstrasse's best hangout for the young and chic, with a relaxed atmosphere, good music, and food (including breakfast day and night, with a special of black coffee, a Sobranie Black Russian cigarette, and black bread). Although perhaps dated, still a classic Berlin bar (open 24 hours, closed Tues 8am–8pm).

Shell, Knesebeckstr. 52, 1/12. The archetypal Berlin posing parlor, the air thick with the sipping of Perrier and the rustle of personal organizers. Slick, starchy, and self-consciously superior. Vegetarian food.

Wirtshaus Wuppke, Schlüterstr. 21, 1/12. Old-fashioned *Kneipe* without the sleaze.

Zillemarkt, Bleibtreustr. 48, 1/12. Wonderful if shabby bar that attempts a fin-de-siècle feel. Unpretentious and fun, and a good place to start Savignyplatz explorations—it's by the S-bahn. Serves breakfast till 6pm.

Zwiebelfisch, Savignyplatz 7, 1/12. Corner bar for would-be arty/intellectual types. Lots of jazz and earnest debate. Good cheap grub.

Around Nollendorfplatz and Winterfeldtplatz

Bei Spatz, Kurfürstenstr. 56, 1/30. Spruced-up corner *Kneipe* with a rustic feel to match the low prices.

Café am Arsenal, Fuggerstr. 35, 1/30. New Italian-style coffee-house furnishings, usefully near the *Arsenal* cinema (which often shows films in English).

Café Belmundo, Winterfeldtstr. 36, 1/30. Relative peace and calm—despite the shrieking color scheme—in one of the busiest areas at night.

Café Berio, Maassenstr. 7, 1/30. Quiet and civilized bar for those who prefer conversation to music.

Café Einstein, Kurfürstenstr. 58, 1/30. Housed in a seemingly ancient mansion, this is about as close as you'll get to the ambience of the pre-war Berlin *Kaffeehaus*, with international newpapers and breakfast served till 2pm. Literary readings and other activities, plus a good garden. Expensive and a little snooty.

Café Lure, Kyffhäuserstrasse/corner with Barbarossastr., 1/30. Classic Alternative crowd; not terribly exciting.

Café Lux, Goltzstr. 35, 1/30. A definitely desirable alternative to the shrill atmosphere of the *Café M* a few doors away. Open (and packed) till late.

Café M, Goltzstr. 34, 1/30. Though littered with dingy plastic chairs and precious little else, *M* is Berlin's most favored rendezvous for self-styled creative types and the conventionally unconventional. The cool thing to drink is Flensburger Pils, from the bottle. Usually packed, even for its famous breakfasts.

Café Mainstreet, Mansteinstr. 17, 1/30. Mixed crowd heads here for exotic cocktails at the weekends and live heavy rock on Friday evenings.

Café Niemandsland, Goltzstr. 17, 1/30. Appropriately named bar ("No Man's land") with few furnishings and few customers.

Café Savarin, Kulmerstr. 17, 1/30. Chiefly popular for its all-day breakfasts, homemade quiches and pastries.

Café Sidney, corner of Maassenstrasse and Winterfeldtstrasse, 1/30. Big and brash modern meeting place, especially for breakfast on Saturday mornings. Good snacks.

Café Swing, Corner of Kleiststrasse and Motzstrasse, 1/30. Plastic-y modern café a little way from *Metropol*. Convivial new-wave atmosphere, with live music, especially on Monday and Thursday.

Café Winterfeldt, Winterfeldtstr. 37, 1/30. Sparsely decorated with a narrow drinking area, but a relaxing alternative to other places around this area—when it's not full.

Forum-Café, Akazienstr. 19, 1/62. Perfectly normal café with rather comical aspirations to being a literary mecca for budding writers and poets to declaim their works. Easy amusement if you can stifle the sniggers.

Havana, Winterfeldtstr. 50, 1/30. Golden oldies and Salsa mixed in with the cocktails.

Mediencafé Strada, Potsdamer Str. 131, 1/30. Self-styled café for media types, with a few foreign newspapers thrown in for effect. Imaginative food.

Metropol, Nollendorfplatz 5, 1/30. Warehouse-sized Art Deco dance hall (for which see Chapter Five, *Music and Nightlife*), with a downstairs bar fine for vegging out in front of the enormous TV screen. Popular with all-nighters and transvestites.

Sexton, Winterfeldtstr. 35, 1/30. Dimly-lit hell-hole of hard rock and denims. Low on the trendiness scale, but always full.

Slumberland, Goltzstr. 24. The gimmicks here are sand on the floor and a tropical theme. Laid back, likeable, and one of the better bars of this area.

Kreuzberg

The lifespan of bars and cafés in Kreuzberg is notoriously unreliable, with places opening and closing almost weekly. Use these listings as a base for your explorations, but don't be suprised if characters have changed, or addresses disappeared.

Café Anfall, Gneisenaustr. 64, 1/61. Sharp, punk-filled bar that looks as if it were thrown together from junkshops. Music at maximum distortion level.

Café am Ufer, Paul-Lincke-Ufer 43, 1/36. Good views of the Landwehrkanal if you sit outside and of the frequent fights if you stay inside. Nevertheless a fun place, and with all-you-can-eat breakfasts for DM10 at weekends.

Café Jedermann, Dieffenbachstr. 18, 1/61. Recently opened up-dated traditional style bar.

Café Jonas, Naumannstr. 1, 1/62. An unrepentant freak's delight.

Café Marilyn, Muskauerstr. 23, 1/36. Charming and cosy, replete with marble and the usual posters.

Café Mora, Grossbeerenstr. 57a, 1/61. Noisy café-gallery.

Café Stresemann, Stresemannstr. 90, 1/61. Large, traditional *Berliner Kneipe* style café at the Anhalter Bahnhof.

Café Ubersee, Paul-Lincke-Ufer 44, 1/36. Great location by the canal and a slightly upmarket atmosphere for the area.

Cazzo, Orianienstr. 187, 1/36. Trendy *Szene*/gay bar, and a good place to sample the austere cosiness of contemporary Kreuzberg.

Debut, Cuvrystrasse/corner with Görlitzer Str., 1/36. Very black, very loud, very Kreuzberg. Billiards.

Die Rote Harfe, Oranienstr. 13, 1/36. Extreme left-wing ideologists knocking back some of the cheapest beer around.

Elefant, Oranienstr. 12, 1/36. More intense discussions on how to change the world.

Ex, Mehringhof, Gneisenaustr. 2, 1/61. Low prices and occasional live music in the bar of the famous alternative Mehringhof collective.

Golgatha, Viktoriapark, 1/61. Enormous open-air café perched near the top of Kreuzberg's hill. Enormously popular with everybody.

Graeffitti, Graefestr. 92, 1/61. Contrary to the name, there's no scribbling on the walls but rather elegantly hung paintings in the white-washed interior.

Heidelberger Krug, Arndtstr. 15, 1/61. Another favorite meeting place for Kreuzberg's self-styled intelligentsia.

Homo-Bar (aka *Oranienbar*), Oranienstr. 168, 1/36. Famed Kreuzberg watering hole, which despite a recent name change is by no means solely a gay bar. The interior is half-plastered (as are most of the clientele), giving it a sort of post-nuclear chic. At the time of writing, its future looked uncertain.

Intertank, Manteuffelstr. 47, 1/36. Fill up on a large supply of cocktails. More room at the bar than at the tables.

Locus, Marheinekeplatz 4, 1/61. Somewhat sober and proper decor for the location. Small garden open in the summer, Mexican food.

Madonna, Wiener Str. 22, 1/36. Grimy paint job and a sparse interior, but nevertheless one of West Berlin's "in" places. Loud music.

Max und Moritz, Oranienstr. 162, 1/36. Old fashioned bar-restaurant that, while it's a world away from the *Szene* places down the street design-wise, still packs in a youthful crowd.

Minitropa, Wrangelstr. 24, 1/36. The whole place is decked out, floor to ceiling, in Caribbean-Brazilian style. The novelty wears off pretty quickly.

Pinox, Oranienstr. 45, 1/36. Typical Kreuzberg drinking spot, popular with locals and open late.

Riehmers, Yorckstr. 83, 1/36. Large, packed, slightly seedy but fun, with a very mixed public and dance floor.

Senso Unico, Dresdener Str. 121–122, 1/36. The *Szene* goes upmarket with red velvet sofas and incongruous dancing to the taped "swing."

Tango, Baerwaldstr. 52, 1/61. Likeable bar-restaurant in a scruffy street. Homely and welcoming with good, straightforward food at around DM10.

Weinkeller Ratte, Spreewaldplatz 2, 1/36. A wine bar where it shouldn't be.

Wirtschaftswunder, Yorckstr. 81, 1/61. Young international crowd comfortably seated on early 1960s living-room furniture.

Yorckschlösschen, Yorckstr. 15, 1/61. Firmly entrenched hippy and alternative crowd; live music on Sunday.

Zaubergarten, Paul-Lincke-Ufer 11, 1/36. Prettily located garden pub.

Zum Alten, Dresdener Str. 17, 1/36. Once a haunt of Kreuzberg's smack heads, now much cleaned up but still fairly stoned. The spirit of 1976 lives on . . .

Elsewhere

Adams, Pariserstr. 18, 1/15. Breakfast café, mini-restaurant, and pub rolled into one.

Blisse 14, Blissestr. 14. Café-bar designed especially, but not exclusively, for disabled people. A good meeting place.

Café Adler, Friedrichstr. 206, 1/61. Small café whose popularity came from the fact that it is next to the site of the Checkpoint Charlie border crossing.

Café Hardenberg, Hardenbergstr. 10, 1/12. Large, old fashioned café with excellent and cheap food that draws in local students. Recommended.

Café Knobelsdorff, Knobelsdorffstr. 38, 1/19. Charming café with Viennese specialties and popular breakfasts.

Café New York, Olivaer Platz 15, 1/15. Clean-cut, pop-loving teenagers' hangout.

Café Solo, Pariserstr. 19, 1/15. Fine example of the classy bars dotted all along this street.

Café Voltaire, Stuttgarter Platz 14, 1/12. Dire bar-restaurant whose only claim to fame is the fact that it never closes. Reasonably-priced food, good value breakfasts.

DA DA DA, Kurfürstendamm 73, 1/31. Bright 'n' brash 'n' loud with constant videos blaring over the pool tables and a clientele that's a mix of Berlin sharks, local pool hustlers, and recruits. Open 11pm–8am.

Feinbäckerei, Vorbergstr. 2, 1/62. Good wine in a former bakery.

Frische Brise, Holsteinischestr. 40, 1/31. Young and old from every conceivable profession mingle in all that a good pub should be.

Galerie Helion, Zähringerstr. 33, 1/31. Reasonably priced bar-cum-gallery.

Graffiti, Naumannstr. 3, 1/62. Like its namesake over in Kreuzberg, the scrawlings here have gone but the name's remained the same. Cheap.

Holst am Zoo, Joachimstaler Str. 1, 1/12 (in the arcade southwest of Zoo Station). The bar for soccer fans: walls plastered with pix of favorite teams and assorted ephemera, lively conversation for would-be John Maddens.

Jimmy's Diner, Parisertr., corner of Sachsische Str., 1/15. A real American diner with a replica 1950s interior. Serves American food, open late.

Kastanie, Schlossstr. 22, 1/19. Amiable bar near Schloss Charlottenburg that's best on summer evenings for its small beer garden.

Kempinski-Eck, Kurfürstendamm 27, 1/12. A classy slice of strict conservatism for when you tire of being trendy.

Khan, Pariserstr. 20, 1/15. The decor—with one or two minor adjustments—has remained faithful to the bar's origins in the students' movement of twenty years ago.

Kleisther, Hauptstr. 5, 1/62. Large and always crowded with the more style-conscious Alternatives of Schöneberg. Open till 3am-ish

Kronenbar Zur Weissen Maus, Ludwigkirchplatz 12, 1/15. Chic 1920s-style bar with reproductions of Otto Dix and Max Beckmann reflected in the mass of mirrors. Popular with older artists, opens around 10pm.

Kronenbourg Café, Pfalzburgerstr. 11, 1/15. Friendly, classy café in Schöneberg serving German nouvelle cuisine at the usual inflated prices.

Kumpelnest 3000, Lützowstr 23, 1/30. Carpeted walls and a mock-Baroque effect attract a rough-and-ready crew of under-30s to this erstwhile brothel. Usually gets going around 2am.

Leuchtturm, Crellestr. 41, 1/62. Another homage to '68. For nostalgites.

Loretta im Garten, Lietzenburger Str. 89, 1/15. Though it's angled mainly at tourists, this large beer garden can be fun if you're in the mood.

Luise, Königin-Luise-Str. 40, 1/33. A smaller and more convivial beer garden, just a stone's throw from the Dahlem museums. Usually packed with students from the nearby Free University.

Malustra, Martin-Luther-Str. 42. Smoky student bar.

Monte Video, Motzstr. 54, 1/30. Mirror-lined locale for intimate soirées.

Pinguin Club, Wartburgstr. 54, 1/62. Tiny and cheerful bar with 1950–60s America supplying its theme and background music.

Resonanz, Ebersstr. 66, 1/62. Green and *Alternative Liste* meeting point.

Rümpelstilzchen, Quitzowstr. 108, 1/21. The epitome of Alternative, from the clientele and decor to the oven heating.

Sabine II, Pichelswerder Süd, 1/20. Converted houseboat in the middle of one of the more picturesque strips in Berlin.

Saftladen 2, Wegenerstr. 1, 1/31. When the booze gets too much for you this could be the place: it specializes in alcohol-free drinks, some of which are quite inventive.

Strassenbahn, Laubacher Str. 29, 1/33. Formerly a train station, this is now a popular *Szene* hangout.

Tomasa, Motzstr. 60, 1/30. Rather tacky interior design, but one of the best breakfasts in town.

UFA-Café, Viktoriastr. 13, 1/42. Amazingly cheap bar/café in the middle of the huge UFA complex.

Wintergarten, Fasanenstr. 23, 1/12. Part of the *Literaturhaus*, an institution given over to poetry readings and other bookish events, this has a beautifully renovated interior and a small garden that's a welcome break from nearby Ku'damm. Moderate prices.

Zur Linde, Sophie-Charlotten-Str. 19, 1/19. Run by a collective and very good value for money.

Gay Men's Bars

The most concentrated area of gay men's **bars** is between **Wittenbergplatz and Nollendorfplatz**, south of Kleiststrasse. For more detailed listings, pick up a copy of *Berlin von Hinten* or *Siegessäule*, available from most bars, and see also "Gay and Lesbian West Berlin" in *West Berlin Basics*.

Anderes Ufer, Hauptstr. 157, 1/62. Quiet Schöneberg café-bar favored by students and "alternative" types. Lesbians welcomed. Serves breakfasts.

Andreas' Kneipe, Ansbacher Str. 29, 1/30. A good place to begin wanderings in the Wittenbergplatz area.

BiBaBo, Platzburger Str. 5, 1/15. A small and friendly bar, with a welcoming atmosphere.

Blue Boy Bar, Eisenacher Str. 3, 1/62. Tiny, convivial, and relaxed bar, far less raucous than many that surround it.

Come Back, Lietzenburgerstr. 77, 1/15. Small bar with an older clientele humming along to the corny German songs on the jukebox. A short walk from the Ku'damm.

Fledermaus, Joachimstaler Str. 14–19, 1/15. Bar and coffee shop popular with tourists as well as locals; one of the city's most relaxing gay bars.

Fingerhut, Damaschkestr. 12, 1/19. Popular with media types, and a little upmarket.

Flip-Flop, Kulmerstr. 20, 1/30. Imaginatively decorated bar-cocktail lounge that attracts a diverse clientele.

Homo-Bar/Orianienbar, Orianienstr. 168, 1/36. Nightly from 10pm. Pre-clubbers congregate to cruise the cool clique: mixed, gay—and fun.

Kleine Philharmonie, Schaperstr. 14, 1/15. Shoe-box sized place packed with antiques. Unavoidably intimate.

Pool, Motzstrasse 25, 1/30; adjacent to *Tom's Bar*. Disco with Acid House-style music. Lesbians also welcome.

Rosa Salon, Frei Universität. In the Rostlaube, 1st floor, K-Gang, 30. Strasse, 1/30. (Mon–Thurs 10am–6pm, Fri 10am–4pm during term-time only). Rather ramshackle, but welcoming, gay café that's good for a quiet chat.

Tom's Bar, Motzstr. 19, 1/30. Dark, sweaty, and wicked cruising bar with a large back room.

Zufall, Pfalzburger Str. 10a, 1/15. Mixed gay and lesbian bar: ring the bell to gain admission. Open till late.

Women's Cafés and Bars

Many of Berlin's women-only bars have a strong lesbian following, though straight women are welcome everywhere.

Begine, Potsdamerstr. 139, 1/30 (women only). Stylishly decorated bar-bistro/gallery with limited menu. See also "Women's West Berlin" in *West Berlin Basics*.

Bid's Café-Bar, Kaiserin-Augusta-Allee 48. Lively bar popular with women, mixed.

Café V, Lausitzerplatz, 1/36. Relaxed place for a drink and good vegetarian food. Mixed.

La Chiantina, Paul-Lincke-Ufer 44, 1/36. Pleasant women-run restaurant with exhibitions.

Dinelo, Vorbergstr. 10, 1/62 (closed Mon; women only). Traditional, comfortable pub with pool table. Serves salads and hefty German dishes, DM8–17.

Extra Dry, Mommsenstr. 34 , 1/12 (closed Mon; women only). Light and airy café that serves exclusively non-alcoholic drinks, best of which are the delicious fruit cocktails. There's also good—and very inexpensive—food. See also "Health, Support, and Crisis Centers" in *West Berlin Basics*.

Frauencafé Glogauerstrasse, Glogauerstr. 22, 1/36. Amiable café that's a meeting point for women to share and discuss ideas. Info and advice available (Mon & Thurs 3–5pm, children welcome).

Hofgarten, Regensburgerstr. 5, 1/36. Classy and friendly bar for men and women, with a strong feminist following.

Lärm und Lust, Orianienstr. 189, 1/36, to the right of the rear courtyard, 3rd floor. Women's musicians' collective and occasional cabaret with a diverse program. Open sessions Friday nights.

Lipstick, Richard-Wagner-Platz 5, 1/10 (women-only Mon, Fri & Sat; open to all on first Friday of every month). Lesbian cocktail bar that welcomes straight women; stylish and lively disco. Difficult to find: look out for the white entrance door.

Pour Elle, Kalckreuthstr. 10, 1/30 (closed Mon; women only except Tues). Intimate disco-bar popular frequented by the straighter sort of (generally older) lesbian. Pricey.

Schoko-Café, Mariannenstr 6, 1/36, on Heinrichplatz (closed Sat; women only). Very alternative converted warehouse housing a health-conscious café and info on the many activities organized by the Schokoladenfabrik collective. Cliquey atmosphere that's a little intimidating if you're new to the place. The women-only Turkish baths next door are open from September to the end of May (see "Women's West Berlin" in *West Berlin Basics*).

Steps, Grossbeerenstrasse, 1/61. Basement bar with women-only evenings Tuesday (for motorbikers' meeting) and Friday. Monthly disco.

Swingtime, Fürbringerstr. 29, 1/61 (closed Sat: women only). Friendly, laid-back lesbian bar-café run by a volunteer collective. If you're lucky, there might just be something on the stove at 11pm. At time of writing, its future seemed uncertain.

Die Zwei, corner Martin-Lutherstrasse and Motzstrasse, 1/30. Berlin's tacki-est best, a determinedly (non-exclusive) lesbian bar with music from Marlene via Iron Butterfly to Madonna and a similarly wide range of clientele. Unmissable.

EATING

You can spend as much or as little as you like on **food** in Berlin; it's one item, at least, that won't break the bank. What follows is an overview of eating in the city, along with a glossary of food terms that's also applicable to East Berlin; listings of places to eat begin on p.103.

Breakfast

The majority of West Berlin's hostels, hotels, and pensions include **breakfast** (*Frühstück*) in the price of the room. Although some places go in for the spartan French affair of rolls, jam, and coffee, the normal breakfast lies midway

A LIST OF FOODS AND DISHES

Basics

Frühstück	breakfast	Brötchen	bread roll	Zucker	sugar
Mittagessen	lunch	Butter	butter	Pfeffer	pepper
Abendessen	supper, dinner	Butterbrot	sandwich	Salz	salt
Messer	knife	Belegtes	open	Öl	oil
Gabel	fork	Brötchen	sandwich	Essig	vinegar
Löffel	spoon	Marmelade	jam	Senf	mustard
Speisekarte	menu	Honig	honey	Sosse	sauce
Teller	plate	Käse	cheese	Reis	rice
Tasse	cup	Fleisch	meat	Spätzle	a kind of
Glas	glass	Fisch	fish		shredded
Vorspeise	appetizer	Eier	eggs		pasta
Hauptgericht	main course	Gemüse	vegetables	Maultaschen	form of ravioli
Nachspeise	dessert	Obst	fruit	Rechnung	bill
Brot	bread	Joghurt	yogurt	Trinkgeld	tip

Soups and Appetizers

Suppe	soup	Ochsenschwanzsuppe	oxtail soup
Erbsensuppe	pea soup	Flädlesuppe,	clear soup with pancake
Linsensuppe	lentil soup	Pfannkuchensuppe	strips
Bohnensuppe	bean soup	Leber Pastete	liver paté
Zwiebelsuppe	onion soup	Lachsbrot	smoked salmon on bread
Hühnersuppe	chicken soup	Melone mit Schinken	melon and ham
Gulaschsuppe	thick soup in imitation	Grüner Salat	mixed green salad
	of goulash	Gurkensalat	cucumber salad
Leberknödelsuppe	clear soup with liver	Fleischsalat	cut sausage salad with
	dumplings		onions
Fleischsuppe	clear soup with meat	Schnittlauchbrot	chives on bread
	dumplings	Sülze	jellied meatloaf

Meat and Poultry

Aufschnitt	mixed slices of cold sausage	Gyros	kebob
		Hackbraten	mincemeat roast
Bockwurst	chunky boiled sausage	Hackfleisch	mincemeat
Bratwurst	grilled sausage	Hammelfleisch	mutton
Currywurst	sausage served with piquant sauce	Hase	hare
		Herz	heart
Eisbein	pig's trotters	Hirn	brains
Ente	duck	Hirsch, Reh	venison
Fasan	pheasant	Huhn, Hähnchen	chicken
Fleischpflanzerl	Bavarian-style meatball	Innereien	innards
Frikadelle	meatball	Jägerschnitzel	cutlet in wine and mush-
Froschschenkel	frogs' legs		room sauce
Gans	goose	Kanninchen	rabbit
Geschnetzeltes	shredded meat, usually served with rice	Kassler Rippen	smoked and pickled pork chops

Meat and Poultry (continued)

Kotelett	cutlet (cheapest cut)	Schnitzel Natur	uncoated cutlet (usually pork)
Krautwickerl	cabbage leaves filled with mincemeat	Schweinebraten	roast pork
Lamm	lamb	Schweinefleisch	pork
Leber	liver	Schweinehaxen	pig's knuckle
Leberkäse	baked meatloaf served hot or cold	Speck	bacon
		Truthahn	turkey
Lunge	lungs	Weisswurst	white herb sausage made with veal and pork
Nieren	kidneys		
Ochsenschwanz	oxtail	Wiener Schnitzel	thin cutlet in breadcumbs
Rahmschnitzel	cutlet in cream sauce	Wienerwurst	standard boiled pork sausage
Rindfleisch	beef		
Schaschlik	diced meat with piquant sauce	Wild	wild game
		Wurst	sausage
Schinken	ham	Wildschwein	wild boar
Schlachtplatte	mix of cured meats, including blood sausage, liver sausage and boiled meat	Zigeunerschnitzel	cutlet in paprika sauce
		Saure Lunge	pickled lungs
		Sauerbraten	braised pickled beef
Schnecke	snail	Zunge	tongue

Fish

Aal	eel	Muscheln	mussels
Forelle	trout	Sardinen	sardines
Hering, Matjes	herring	Schellfisch	haddock
Hummer	lobster	Scholle	plaice
Kabeljau	cod	Schwertfish	swordfish
Karpfen	carp	Seezunge	sole
Kaviar	caviar	Skampi	scampi
Krabben	crab	Tintenfisch	squid
Lachs	salmon	Thunfisch	tuna
Makrele	mackerel	Zander	pike-perch

Vegetables

Bohnen	beans	Pellkartoffeln	baked potatoes
Bratkartoffeln	fried potatoes	Pilze, Champignons	mushrooms
Brokkoli	broccoli	Pommes frites	french fries
Erbsen	peas	Salzkartoffeln	boiled potatoes
Grüne Bohnen	green beans	Reibekuchen	potato cake
Gurke	cucumber	Rosenkohl	brussel sprouts
Karotten, Möhren	carrots	Rote Rübe	beetroot
Kartoffelbrei	mashed potatoes	Rotkohl	red cabbage
Kartoffelpuree	creamed potatoes	Rübe	turnip
Kartoffelsalat	potato salad	Salat	salad
Knoblauch	garlic	Sauerkraut	pickled cabbage
Knödel, Kloss	dumpling	Spargel	asparagus
Lauch	leeks	Tomaten	tomatoes
Maiskolben	corn on the cob	Weisskohl	white cabbage
Paprika	green or red peppers	Zwiebeln	onions

Fruits

Obstsalat	fruit salad	Mandarine	tangerine
Ananas	pineapple	Melone	melon
Apfel	apple	Orange	orange
Banane	banana	Pampelmuse	grapefruit
Birne	pear	Pfirsich	peach
Datteln	dates	Pflaumen	plums
Erdbeeren	strawberries	Rosinen	raisins
Feigen	figs	Schwarze	blackcurrants
Himbeeren	raspberries	Johannisbeeren	
Johannisbeeren	redcurrants	Trauben	grapes
Kirschen	cherries	Zitrone	lemon
Kompott	stewed fruit or mousse		

Cheeses and Desserts

Emmentaler	Swiss Emmental	Kaiserschmarrn	shredded pancake served
Käseplatte	mixed selection of cheeses		with powdered sugar,
Schafskäse	sheep's cheese		jam, and raisins
Weichkäse	cream cheese	Kasekuchen	cheesecake
Ziegenkäse	goat's cheese	Keks	cookie
		Krapfen	doughnut
Apfelstrudel mit	apple strudel with fresh	Nüsse	nuts
Sahne	cream	Nusskuchen	nut cake
Berliner	jam doughnut	Obstkuchen	fruitcake
Dampfnudeln	large yeast dumplings	Pfannkuchen	jam doughnut (or) pancake
	served hot with vanilla	Schokolade	chocolate
	sauce	Schwarzwälder	Black Forest cake
Eis	ice cream	Kirschtorte	
Gebäck	pastries	Torte	cake, tart

Common Terms

Art	style of	Geräuchert	smoked
Eingelegte	pickled	Gutbürgerliche	traditional German
Frisch	fresh	Küche	cooking
Gebacken	baked	Hausgemacht	home-made
Gebraten	fried, roasted	Heiss	hot
Gebraten ...'blau'	cooked rare	Kalt	cold
Gedämpft	steamed	Spiess	skewered
Gefüllt	stuffed	Topf (Eintopf)	stew, casserole
Gegrillt	grilled	Vom heissen Stein	raw meats you cook your-
Gekocht	cooked		self on a red hot stone

between this and the elaborate Scandinavian cold table. Typically, you'll be offered a small platter of **cold meats** (usually sausage-based) and **cheeses**, along with a selection of marmalades, jams, and honey. Granola or another cereal is sometimes included as well, or as an alternative to the meats and cheeses. You're generally given a variety of **breads**, one of the most distinctive features of German cuisine. Both brown and white rolls are popular; these are often given a bit of zap by the addition of a condiment, such as caraway, coriander, poppy, or sesame seeds. The rich-tasting black rye bread, known as *Pumpernickel*, is a particular favorite, as is the salted *Bretzel*, which tastes nothing like any foreign imitation.

Coffee (which is usually freshly brewed) is the normal accompaniment, and **tea**—whether plain or herbal—is also popular, while hot chocolate is another common alternative. A glass of fruit juice—almost invariably orange—is sometimes included as well.

If breakfast isn't included in your accommodation, it can be bought at certain **cafés**, many of which continue to serve breakfast through the afternoon and into the evening. Prices start at around DM5 for a basic bread, eggs, and jam affair rising to DM20+ for more exotic, champagne-swigging delights. Several cafés also have eat-as-much-as-you-like buffets for a reasonable set price. For a quick reference of cafés that serve breakfast, see overleaf.

If finances are tight, best bet for a stand-up morning snack is in one of the bakeries (*Bäckereis*), where coffee and cake will set you back a couple of marks.

Snacks and Cheap Eats

Easiest option for a quick **snack** is to head for one of the ubiquitous *Imbiss* stands found on street corners, where for a few marks you can fill up on *Currywurst*—curry flavored sausages that originated in Berlin—and fries. Chinese and Greek *Imbiss* stands have recently become popular, with Greek doner kebabs known as *gyros*, served in a puffy pitta-ish bread, generally with *tsatziki* as a sauce and great value at DM4–5. For something more substantial but not that much more expensive, try any one of the six sit-down *Imbiss* **restaurants**, which charge between DM5 and DM12 a meal, or, at lunch time, either of the city's **Mensas**, officially for university students only but usually open to anyone who broadly fits that description and always to those with *ISIC* cards. In either case, make sure you head for the *Bargeld* (cash) line.

Otherwise, **fast-food places** and **burger bars** are everywhere, especially around Zoo Station in the center. Takeout **pizzas** are a major boon if you're on a tight budget, with prices as low as DM1.50 for a square of cheese, tomato and salami pizza. The city's large Turkish community, particularly in and around Kreuzberg, means that **kebab** places are also common.

Around lunch time in the main shopping areas, such as those around Wilmersdorferstrasse and Walter-Schreiber-Platz U-Bahns, it's worth trying some of the **fish shops**, which sell rolls with a good variety of fishy fillings. A few bakeries in these places also sell filled rolls for around DM3.

In the afternoon, it's traditionally time for *Kaffe und Kuchen* (coffee and cakes) in one of the self-conciously elegant (and, therefore, ultra-expensive) cafés in the city center. Although indelibly associated with Austria, they're just as popular an institution in Germany. Serving various types of coffee to the accompaniment of cream cakes, pastries, or handmade chocolates, they're the ideal place to head for should your your mid-afternoon blood sugar level need pepping up.

Restaurants . . . and German Food

The city's compressed, cosmopolitan nature means that the range of **restaurants** is wider than in any other German city: indeed the national cuisine takes a back seat to Greek, Turkish, Balkan, Indian, and Italian food, and plenty of places exist where a meal can be bought for less than DM15. Almost all the better **bars** serve food too, and this can be a bargain—though the chic places serving *Neue Deutsche Küche* (the German equivalent of *nouvelle cuisine*) can seem very expensive for what you get.

If you're on a budget, Greek, Italian, or Yugoslav eateries often provide the best bargains (Greek places in particular are remarkably inexpensive). As a bonus, each can usually rustle up something for vegetarians, though a small number of vegetarian restaurants provide a welcome relief from salads. With money to splurge, there are excellent French and Japanese places well worth trying out. By law, all restaurants have to display their menu and prices by the door, as well as indicating which is their *Ruhetag/e* (closing day/s).

German Restaurants

German restaurants are, as a rule, expensive for what's on the menu, and the only places really worth going to are those out from the city center, where wild game is served up (at equally wild prices). It does help if you share the national penchant for solid, fatty food accompanied by compensatingly healthy fresh vegetables and salad. The **pig** is the staple of the German menu—it's prepared in umpteen different ways, and just about every part of it is eaten. Pork also forms the main ingredient for **sausages**, which are not only the most popular snack but are also regarded as serious culinary fare. *Kassler Rippen* (smoked and pickled pork chops) and *Eisbein* (pig's feet) are Berlin favorites—although the fatty *Eisbein* tend to be more of a winter specialty, as is *Boulette*, a sort of German hamburger. *Königsberger Klopse* (meat dumplings in a caper and lemon flavored sauce), though not originally from Berlin, is also to be found on many menus here. Unusual things are done with potatoes, too: try *Kartoffelpulver* (flour and spuds rolled into a ball) or *Pellkartoffeln mit Quark und Leinöl*, a stomach-churning combination of baked potatoes, curd cheese, and linseed oil that's best digested with quantities of beer or schnapps.

Desserts in Berlin's German restaurants are something of an anti-climax, where they exist at all. *Rote Grütze* (jello eaten hot or cold with cold vanilla sauce) is one of the few distinctive dishes. Otherwise it's the usual selection of fresh and stewed fruits, cheeses, and ice creams: if you have a sweet tooth, best head for a café that serves one of the delicious cakes of which Germans are so fond.

Breakfast Cafés—A Checklist

The following all serve breakfast at the hours shown: for more details see "Bars and Cafés" under *Drinking*.

Savignyplatz and around

Café au Lait, Kantstr. 110, 1/12. From 10am.

Café Bleibtreu, Bleibtreustr. 45, 1/12. 9:30am–2pm.

Café Savigny, Grolmannstr. 53, 1/12. 10am–4pm.

Café Tiago, Knesebeckstr. 9, 1/12. Mon–Fri 8am–3pm, Sat 8am–6pm, Sun 10am–6pm.

Filmbühne, corner of Hardenbergstrasse and Steinplatz, 1/12. 10am onwards.

Mimikry, Kantstr. 29, 1/12. 3–9am.

Rosalinde, Knesebeckstr 15, 1/12. 9:30am–noon.

Schwarzes Café, Kantstr. 148, 1/12. 24hr. Closed Tues 8am–8pm.

Around Nollendorfplatz and Winterfeldtplatz

Café am Arsenal, Fuggerstr. 35, 1/30. 9am–5pm.

Café Berio, Maassenstr. 7, 1/30. 9am–midnight.

Café Einstein, Kurfürstenstr. 58, 1/30. 10am–2pm

Café M, Goltzstr. 34, 1/30. 9am–3pm.

Café Savarin, Kulmerstr. 17, 1/30. Noon–midnight.

Café Sidney, corner of Maasenstrasse and Winterfeldtstrasse, 1/30. 9am–5pm.

Café Swing, Corner of Kleiststrasse and Motzstrasse, 1/30. 10:30am–5am.

Kreuzberg

Café am Ufer, Paul-Lincke-Ufer 43, 1/36. From 10am.

Café Mora, Grossbeerenstr. 57a, 1/61. 11am–11pm.

Café Stresemann, Stresemannstr. 90, 1/61. 10am–4pm.

Golgotha, Viktoriapark, 1/61. 11am–3pm.

Elsewhere

Café Hardenberg, Hardenbergstr. 10, 1/12. 9am–midnight.

Café Knobelsdorff, Knobelsdorffstr. 38. 8am–4pm.

Café New York, Olivaer Platz 15, 1/15. 2am–6pm.

Café Voltaire, Stuttgarter Platz 14, 1/12. 24hr.

Tomasa, Motzstr. 60, 1/30. 10am–4pm.

Wintergarten, inside the *Literaturhaus*, Fasanenstr. 23, 1/12. From 10am.

Imbiss Restaurants and Mensas

Ashoka-Imbiss, Grolmanstr. 51, 1/12 (off Savignyplatz). Daily 11am–midnight. About the best of the lot, dishing up good portions of tremendous-bargain Indian food. Vegetarian options.

Fuji-Imbiss, Goethestr. 6, 1/30 (near Knesbeckstrasse). Mon–Sat noon–11pm. Japanese snacks and light meals.

Guru, Kurfürstendamm 156, 1/15. Tues–Sun noon–3am. Indian fast-food place with snacks and meals.

Japan Imbiss, Winterfeltstr. 7. and Kantstr. 118, 1/12. Wide selection of dishes at knock-down prices.

Mensa of the Free University, Habelschwerdter Allee, at the junction with Thiel Allee, 1/33 (nearest U-Bahn #2 to Dahlem-Dorf). Mon–Fri noon–2pm. Only worth considering if you're spending the day at the Dahlem museums. Around DM3, *ISIC* advisable.

Rani Indischer Imbiss, Goltzstr. 34, 1/30. Noon–midnight. Another budget-priced Indian, ideal for cheap eats when exploring the bars of Winterfeldtplatz.

TU Mensa, Hardenbergstr. 34, 1/12. Mon–Fri 11:15am–2:30pm. Meals around DM4, buy your meal ticket before getting your food.

Restaurants

The following listings detail budget options and sit-down restaurants, and the prices quoted are for main courses, exclusive of appetizers, drinks, or tips. Don't forget that many of the bars listed earlier can be excellent (and inexpensive) choices for food, especially breakfast.

Chinese, Japanese, and Indonesian

Bambus, Knesebeckstr. 49, 1/12. Vietnamese food in a pleasant area. DM15–20.

Dschingis Khan, Martin-Luther-Str. 41, 1/30. Asian cuisine, predominantly Chinese, but with a decor more in keeping with the origins of the name than the food. DM9–20.

Ho Lin Wah, Kurfürstendamm 218, 1/15. The former Chinese embassy transformed into a Chinese restaurant. An oddity.

Kyoto, Wilmersdorferstr. 94, 1/12. Excellent Japanese locale and *sushi* to your heart's content. DM15–25.

Mahachai, Schlüterstr. 60, 1/12. Traditional Thai food and service. DM12 and up.

Petit Chinois, Spandauerdamm 82, 1/19. Excellent Chinese food made from fresh ingredients. Decor is unnervingly like that of a corner *Kneipe*.

Sapporo-Kan, Schlüterstr. 52, 1/12. Admire the wax culinary creations in the window, then eat the real thing inside. Japanese restaurant that's a popular lunch-time spot for people working nearby. DM10–20.

Sawaddi, Bülowstr. 9, 1/30. Thai through and through, but rather pricey. DM20.

Tuk-Tuk, Grossgörschenstr. 2, 1/30. Amiable Indonesian near Kleistpark U-Bahn. Enquire about the heat of your dish before ordering. DM10–20.

Vietnam, Suarezstr. 61, 1/19. One of the city's most favored Vietnamese restaurants, quietly situated in a street of junk shops. Meals are broadly similar to Chinese, but spicier. DM10–30.

French

Aristide, Knesebeckstr. 92, 1/12. Stylish French interior decor and food. DM13–20.

Café Einstein, Kurfürstenstr. 58, 1/30. Elegant literary café (see "Drinking") with pricey French-style food served in a lovely tree-filled garden.

Chamisso, Willibald-Alexis-Str. 25, 1/61. Long-established *Szene* eating spot, with French and Italian food on the menu. DM15–25.

Chapeau Klack, Pfalzburgerstr. 55, 1/15. Discreet and elegant French restaurant. Upmarket menu with prices to match. DM20 plus.

Cour Carrée, Savignyplatz 5, 1/12. Deservedly popular French restaurant with fin-de-siècle decor and garden seating. DM15–25.

Epikur, Prinzregentenstr. 53, 1/31. French bistro with a solid variety of country cuisine on offer. DM10 and up.

German and Eastern European

Alfons, Wilmerdorferstr. 79, 1/12. The five cooks not only serve up their food personally, but sing and play the piano too. DM15 and up.

Ax-Bax, Leibnizstr. 34, 1/12. Limited menu of Viennese dishes, with yummy cakes and desserts. Favourite stomping ground for arts and film people. DM10–25.

Cava, Pariserstr. 56, 1/15. Vegetarian and South German dishes. Open all night. DM12–20.

Exil, Paul-Lincke-Ufer 44, 1/36. Popular with the Kreuzberg arts crowd for its attractive site next to the canal and its moderate to expensive Viennese food. Something of a bohemian meeting place.

Florian, Grolmanstr. 52, 1/12. Leading light of the new German cuisine movement in Berlin, this is as much a place to be seen in as to eat. The food, similar to French *nouvelle cuisine*, is light, flavorful—and expensive. DM20 and up.

Gusto, Mehringdamm 80, 1/61 (south of Kreuzbergstrasse). Large corner restaurant with pleasant outdoor seating. Mixed menu of German cuisine along with pizzas, steaks, and breakfasts. DM9–25.

Haus Trinitas, Inchenallee 62, 1/22. Glorious views over the Havel river in this restaurant that serves up fresh fish in a villa far removed from the hustle of the city center. DM20 and up.

Henne, Leuschnerdamm 25, 1/36 (☎614 7730). Pub-style restaurant with the best chicken (expensive) in Berlin. Advisable to reserve in advance. DM9–15.

Historische Gaststätte auf der Zitadelle, Am Juliusturm, Spandau Zitadelle, Spandau, 1/20. Witches' lair-effect in a cellar serving sumptuous portions of good *Bürgerliche* food. Can be a bit overpowering both gastronomically and socially, but the scenic surroundings of Spandau Citadel go some way to make up for it. DM10–30.

Jagdhütte, Eisenzahnstr. 66, 1/15. Wild game and traditional German fare near Adenauerplatz. DM20 and up.

Paris Bar, Kantstr. 152, 1/12. This was once the city's most famous meeting place for artists, writers, and intellectuals. Now high prices (DM30 plus) mean that it's wholly the preserve of the moneyed middle classes. The food is Viennese in style and the service immaculate. Credit cards not accepted.

Samowar, Luisenplatz 3, 1/10. Expensive but exquisite Russian cooking. DM18 and up.

Schipkapass, Hohenzollerndamm 185, 1/31. Bohemian and Czechoslovakian cuisine in a rather ramshackle atmosphere. DM15–25.

Suppenkasper, Motzstr. 63. Hearty soups and stews to fill you up before a serious evening's drinking. DM6–12.

Tegernseer Tönnchen, Mommsenstr. 34, 1/12. Bavarian cuisine—which means enormous dishes of *wursts* and *schnitzels* washed down with pitchers of beer. Given the quantity placed in front of you, excellent value at DM10–17.

Weissbierstube, in the Berlin Museum, Lindenstr. 14, 1/61. Recreation of a traditional German buffet-restaurant, serving local specialties and very heavy on pork. Often packed; closed Mondays. Complete meals for under DM15.

Zlata Praha, Meinekestr. 1, 1/15. Classy Czech restaurant with nouveau-riche clientele. DM15–30.

Greek

Akropolis, Wielandstr. 28, 1/15. Taped Greek communist songs accompany the moussaka in a tranquil locale. More expensive than the average Greek restaurant. DM12–20.

Athener Grill, Kurfürstendamm 156, 1/15. Fairly ordinary Greek fast-food place and rather heavy on the grease. DM5–12.

Dimokritos, Arndstr. 12, 1/61. Cosy and kitschy Greek eatery. DM9–20.

Dionysos, Schöneberger Ufer 47, 1/30. Slightly more expensive than most Greek restaurants, but miles better price-wise than any of the cafés in the surrounding Tiergarten museums. DM8–20.

Lissos, Pfalzburgerstr. 83, 1/15. One of the first Greek restaurants in Berlin, the original Greek *Gastarbeiter* diners now having been replaced by hordes of Alternatives and students. DM10–20.

To Steki, Kantstr. 22, 1/12. Mountains of inexpensive (DM7–15) Greek food, boisterous live music and dancing till four in the morning at weekends. A great place, and conveniently close to the bars of Savignyplatz.

Indian

Ashoka Taj, Leibnizstr. 62, 1/12. Graded degrees of fire-in-the-belly, reasonably priced Indian food. DM8–15.

Golden Temple, Rankestr. 23, 1/30. Friendly restaurant serving up not-so-hot Indian food and lots of vegetarian dishes. DM10–25.

India-Palace, Leibnizstr. 35, 1/12. Incredible variety and low prices. DM10–14.

Kalkutta, Bleibtreustr. 17, 1/12. Arguably the finest Indian restaurant in Berlin. DM20 and up.

Maharadscha, Fuggerstr. 21, 1/30. Though the ambience is one of a German farmhouse, the food is pure Indian in style. DM10–15.

Italian

Aroma, Hochkirchstr. 8, 1/61. Inexpensive Italian with photo gallery and Italian films on Thursday evenings. DM8–14.

Bar Centrale, Yorckstr. 82, 1/61. Chic Italian locale, popular with Alternatives transforming themselves into yuppies, and exiled Italians. DM10–20.

Cafe Tucci, Grolmannstr. 52, 1/12. New Italian bar with emphasis on simple but fresh Italian delights. Always full.

Capri, Lietzenburgerstr 76, 1/15. Friendly and noisy all-night Italian restaurant; favored by night-clubbers. DM8–15.

Casa Leone, Hasenheide 69, 1/61. Top class and varied Italian cooking, with a pretty outside terrace in the summer. DM10–20.

La Cascina, Delbnickstr. 28, 1/33. Quality Italian restaurant beloved of the Berlin film crowd. Pricey.

Hostaria del Monte Croce, Mittenwalderstr. 6 (Hinterhof). Small, expensive Italian locale, but worth it for the feast of assorted first courses and desserts. Advisable to reserve in advance: ☎694 3968.

Osteria No.1, Kreuzbergstr. 71, 1/61. Classy Italian restaurant run by a collective. DM10–20.

Pizzeria al Castello, Spandauer Damm 23, 1/19. Cheap pizza and pasta, handy for lunch if you're tackling Schloss Charlottenburg and the museums nearby.

Primo, Südstern 3, 1/61. Smoothly attractive upscale Italian. Good value. DM9–20.

Mexican and Latin American

La Batea, Krummer Str. 42, 1/12. Latin American food in a convivial atmosphere with frequent live music. DM7–15.

Carib, Motzstr. 31, 1/30. Classical Caribbean cuisine, friendly service. DM10–22.

La Estancia, Bundesallee 45, 1/31. Very good value for money Latin American restaurant, patronized mainly by environmentally and politically conscious Berliners. DM8–15.

Los Indios, Xantenerstr. 63, 1/15. Centrally located with reasonably priced Mexican food as its specialty. DM8–20.

El Perron, Carmerstr. 13, 1/12. Solid Latin American food, and good fun when patrons leave their tables to tango. DM15–30.

Estoni, Vorbergstr. 11, 1/62. Small tucked-away bar with tapas or full scale meals. Trendy.

Som Tropical, Kaiser-Friedrich-Str. 40, 1/12. Small South American restaurant with live music at weekends. DM7–20.

Middle Eastern and Egyptian

Der Ägypter, Kantstr. 26, 1/12. Egyptian falafel-type meals. Spicy, filling and an adventurous alternative to the safe bets around Savignyplatz. Good vegetarian selections. DM10–15.

Altin Köse, Dresdenerstr. 126, 1/36. Solid Turkish cooking, favored both by Turks and native Kreuzbergers. DM10–20.

Istanbul, Knesebeckstr. 77, 1/12. Arabian-nights-type interior and equally fairytale prices. DM15 and up.

Kurdistan, Kaiser-Friedrich-Str. 41, 1/15. Exotic Kurdish delicacies in a fitting atmosphere. Worth a visit despite the cost. DM18 and up.

Restaurant am Nil, Kaiserdamm 114, 1/19 (near Sophie-Charlotte-Platz). Moderately priced Egyptian, easy-going service. DM10–30.

Spanish and Portuguese

Algarve, Waitzstr. 11, 1/12. Pleasant Portuguese restaurant with a huge variety of fish on the menu and very reasonably priced. DM12–25.

Goya, Bismarckstr. 28, 1/12. Tiny Spanish restaurant, favored by locals. DM12–20.

Litfass, Sybelstr. 49, 1/12. Don't be put off by the bunker-like exterior of this restaurant: great portions of Portuguese food, with particularly tasty seafood dishes. DM10–20.

El Pulpo Flamenco, Kantstr. 137, 1/12. Done out in such extraordinary bad taste that it has a class all of its own. Always packed, mainly because of the bravura of the owner, who's apt to burst into spontaneous operatic renderings of "Una Paloma Blanca" and the like. DM15 and up.

Vegetarian

Baharat Falafel, Winterfeldtstr. 35, 1/30. The best falafels this side of Baghdad—to the swaying and rippling of a (German) belly dancer. DM5 and up.

Einhorn, Mommsenstr. 2, 1/12. Vegetarian wholefood at its best, in a friendly and relaxed atmosphere. DM6–9.

Escargot, Brüsselerstr. 39, 1/65. Large portions of cheap, imaginative veggie food make this café-restaurant well worth the trek to little-visited Wedding.

Hakuin Martin-Luther-Str. 3, 1/30. Japanese vegetarian-macrobiotic à la Zen. DM30–50.

La Maskera Koburger Str. 5, 1/62 (just south and east of Rathaus Schöneberg). Among the best vegetarian places in town, with an Italian slant adding color to the food and atmosphere. Wholemeal pizzas and pasta, along with egg and tofu dishes. DM8–20.

Meta-Café, Barbarossastr. 32, 1/62. Lacto-vegetarian, non-smoking restaurant which strives so hard with its health-conscious menu and chic Greek decor that it almost invites a debauched-ridden evening afterwards to relieve the stress. DM10–20.

Restaurant V, Lausitzer Platz 12, 1/36. Upmarket for Kreuzberg-wholefood locale run by a collective. DM9–15.

Thurnagel, Gneisenaustr. 57, 1/61. Small, nice, friendly vegetarian in west Kreuzberg. DM10–20.

Other

Café Voltaire, Stuttgarterplatz 14, 1/12. Primarily an all-night bar, but serving hot, inexpensive meals (pasta, quiche) until 5am. DM10 and up.

Jewish Community Center Restaurant, Fasanenstr. 79, 1/12. Wonderful kosher delights in a good atmosphere.

Kopenhagen, Kurfürstendamm 203, 1/15. Danish and pricey for what you get. DM15 and up. Full of German busines men and old ladies.

Pik-As, a boat: from Kottbusser Tor U-Bahn, head along Plan-Ufer, 1/36. Eat as you rock on a floating restaurant, with Kreuzberg's alternative crowd above deck, and their ideological opposites, the corner-*Kneipe*-crowd, below. Varied menu, dancing on Friday and Sunday.

Simsalat, Ansbacherstr. 11, 1/30. Salads of every conceivable variety. You pay by weight: DM1.80 per 100 grammes. Open till midnight, closed Sun.

CHAPTER FIVE

MUSIC AND NIGHTLIFE

Since the time of the Weimar Republic, and even through the lean post-war years, Berlin has had a reputation for having the some of the best—and steamiest—nightlife in Europe, an image fueled by the cartoons of George Grosz and films like *Cabaret*. Today, it's still a city that wakes up when others are going to sleep. **Musically** there's much of appeal here: places cover a breadth of tastes, and are rarely expensive. **Clubs and discos** range from slick hangouts for the trendy to dingy, uninviting punk dives: as ever, it's the tension the city seems to generate that gives the nightlife its color.

Berlin's reputation as a leader of the avant-garde is reflected in the number of small, often experimental **theater groups** working here. The scene is an active one, though it's worth remembering that many theater companies take a break in July and August. **Classical music** has long been dominated by the world-class Berlin Philharmonic, though other orchestras play in the city, and museums and historic buildings often host chamber concerts and recitals.

Two of the city's sites are unclassifiable: the *Waldbühne* is a large outdoor amphitheater on the Hollywood Bowl model, just west of the Olympic Stadium. It presents everything from opera to movies to hard rock—unbeatable in summer. The *Tempodrom*, two tents in the Tiergarten, hosts concerts and circuses in the larger tent, cabaret and more intimate performances in the smaller.

Ticket Agencies and Offices

Ticket offices or *Theaterkassen* are usually the easiest (and occasionally the only) way of buying tickets for all major music, theater, and dance events. They're central, open during working hours (or longer) and charge only a small commission on the ticket price.

KaDeWe, Tauentzienstr 21, 1/30 (☎882 7360).

Theaterkasse Centrum, Meinekestr. 25, 1/12 (☎882 7611).

Theaterkasse Sasse, Kurfürstendamm 24, 1/12 (☎882 7360).

Wertheim, Kurfürstendamm 231, 1/15 (☎882 2500).

Wildbad–Kiosk, Rankestr. 1, 1/12 (☎881 4507).

Discos and Clubs

Berlin's discos are smaller, cheaper, and less exclusive than their counterparts in New York or most other European cities—and fewer in number. You don't need much upstairs to work out that the places along the Ku'damm are tourist rip-offs: the real all-night sweats take place in Kreuzberg and Schöneberg, where glitz is out and post-punk cool in. Admission is often free—when you do pay, it shouldn't be much more than DM10. Like most cities, Berlin's turnover in nightspots is rapid: expect the following listings to have changed at least slightly by the time you arrive.

Abraxas, Kantstr. 134, 1/12 (☎312 9493). Tues–Sun 10pm–5am; free during the week, DM6 Fri & Sat. Hot and sweaty dance floor, specializing in salsa and Latin American sounds.

Basement, Mehringdamm 107, 1/61. Daily 10pm–6pm; free. Competitively trendy atmosphere, occasional performance happenings.

Big Eden, Kurfürstendamm 202, 1/15 (☎882 6120). Sun–Fri 7pm–4am, Sat 7pm–7am. Enormous disco popular with teenagers: check out the dance floor first on the video monitors on the street outside. Admission for women is, rather tackily, free: it's also free for everyone Sun–Thurs, but drinks are expensive.

Blue Note, Courbièrestr. 13, 1/30 (☎247248). Tues–Sun 10pm–5am. DM6 entrance on Fri & Sat. Eclectic mix of rock, Latin, and (chiefly) jazz sounds. Small dance floor.

Bronx, Wiener Str. 34, 1/36 (☎611 8445). Daily, 10pm onwards; free. Chic and popular Hip-Hop disco, done out in bomb-damage decor.

Cha-Cha, Nürnberger Str. 50, 1/30 (☎214 2976). Tues–Sun 11pm–6am. Tues, Wed, Thurs, Sun entrance DM5; Fri & Sat DM10. Currently the number one *Szene* spot in the city, ousting even *Dschungel*, next door.

Chic Afrik, Martin-Luther-Str. 19, 1/30 (☎213 3881). Tues–Sun 10pm–6am. African music and a small dance floor on which to pulsate to the rhythm.

Dschungel, Nürnberger Str. 53, 1/30. Wed–Mon 11pm–3am (☎246 698). DM10, free on Mon. The Berlin nightclub scene how you always imagined it. Mixed crowd of nightpeople, all heavily into style, posing and dancing to the excellent music. Not cheap, but essential.

Far Out, Kurfürstendamm 156, 1/31 (near Lehniner Platz; ☎320 0723). Tues–Thurs 10pm–3am, Fri & Sat 10pm–6am. Formerly a Bhagwan disco, now a friendly nightspot for offbeat conservatives and tourists.

Golgatha, in the Viktoriapark, Kreuzberg, 1/61 (☎785 2453). Kreuzberg's popular hillside café hosts a daily alfresco disco from 10am–6pm in summer months: good fun on warm evenings.

Havana Club, Winterfeldtstr. 50, 1/30. Daily, 11pm onwards. Rock 'n' roll bar for youthful and ageing rockers alike. Pure sweaty pleasure.

Linientreu, Budapesterstr. 40, 1/30. Daily from 9pm. A very mixed crowd bop on one of the best dance floors in Berlin.

Lipstick, Richard-Wagner-Platz 5, 1/10 (☎342 8126). Biggest and best of the gay nightclubs. Women-only Mon, Fri and Sat; mixed on Sun, Tues, and Thurs; closed Wed. Good music; DM3 admission.

Madow, Pariser Str. 23, 1/15. Wed–Sun 10pm onwards. Big unpretentious disco, ideal for a no-nonsense boogie in a friendly atmosphere.

Metropol, Nollendorfplatz 5, 1/30 (☎216 4122). Fri–Sat 10pm–4am; DM10. The city's largest—though rather ordinary—disco, in a marvelous Art Deco building. Occasional live bands.

Pool, Motzstr. 25, 1/30 (☎247529). Gay men's disco. Acid House-style music.

Scope, Gneisenaustr. 18, 1/61 (☎692 8132). Daily, from 11pm; free. A 1970s funk and soul freak's delight, in a cool atmosphere.

Surprise, Rheinstr. 45, 1/41. Weds–Sun 9pm–3am; DM5 entrance Fri & Sat. Heavy metal music in a converted music hall.

Sox, Oranienstr. 39, 1/36 (☎614 3573). Wed–Mon 11pm onwards. Small but lively split-level bar/disco in the center of the Kreuzberg action; music has something for everyone, especially devotees of funk and rap .

Trash, Oranienstr. 40, 1/36. Tues–Sun 11pm onwards. Current home of Berlin youth's weirder elements. Black walls, black clothes, and UV lights, Hip-Hop/New Wave sounds.

Turbine Rosenheim, Eisenacher Str. 40, 1/62 (☎248 7888). Tues–Sun 11pm–6am. Spartan rough-and-ready disco-bar for night zombies that kicks into action as the bars of Schöneberg close.

Wu-Wu, Kleiststr. 4, 1/30 (☎213 6392). Daily 10pm–7am. Gay mens' disco, popular at weekends.

Zeleste. Marburgerstr. 2, 1/30. Fri & Sat from 10pm. American-style jazz and blues club with a rather rarefied atmosphere.

Live Music

The way to find out exactly what's on and where is in the listings magazines *Tip* and *Zitty*, *Berlin Program*, or on the innumerable fly posters about town.

Major Spots

The following are the sort of places you can expect to find international super-groups playing. Book well in advance for anything even vaguely popular. Invariably you can't buy tickets from the places themselves, but need to go to one of the ticket agencies listed above.

Alte TU-Mensa, Hardenbergstr. 34, 1/12 (☎311 2233). Part of the Technological University.

Deutschlandhalle, Messedamm 26, 1/19 (☎30381). Like the Eissporthalle below, part of the Congress Center west of the city.

Eissporthalle, Jafféstr. 1, 1/19 (☎3038 4387). Another large site. The *Sommergarten im Messegelände* nearby (around the Funkturm) has, as the name suggests, outdoor concerts in summer.

ICC Berlin, Messedamm, 1/19 (☎30381). Vast, soulless hall for trade fairs that often hosts gigs.

Waldbühne, corner of Glockenturmstr. and Passenheimer Str., 1/19 (☎304 0676). Open air spot in a natural amphitheater near the Olympic stadium that features movies, bands, classical concerts, and other diverse entertainments. Great fun on summer evenings, but arrive early as it often gets crowded.

Contemporary

Remember that many bars and cafés often have live music: skim through *Zitty* and *Tip* magazines for up-to-the-minute listings.

Blockshock, Körtestr. 15/Hasenheide 54, 1/61 (☎694 2265). Place for live bands in the heart of the Kreuzberg underground movement, though thanks to action by its complaining neighbors, no longer as lively as it was.

Café Swing, corner of Motzstrasse and Kleiststrasse, off Nollendorfplatz, 1/30. A tiny club, but one offering free concerts on Monday and Thursday at around midnight or 1am. Anything is possible, from avant-garde performance art to straight rock and roll.

Ecstasy, Hauptstr. 30, 1/62 (☎788 1401). Hardcore underground bands from Germany and around the world. Wild, manic, and fun.

K.O.B., Potsdamer Str. 157, 1/30. A pub in a (now legally) squatted house which on weekdays hosts interesting groups at low prices (DM5). R&B, jazz, and psychedelic sounds play here, but the favorites are local anarcho- and fun-punk bands.

Kongresshalle, John-Foster-Dulles-Allee 10 (☎394031). Under the name of *Haus der Kulturen der Welt*, often hosts world music and allied events.

The Loft, part of the *Metropol*, Nollendorfplatz 5, 1/30 (☎216 1020). Features a whole range of independent artists, with a view to innovation and introducing new music. Also organizes larger concerts in the *Metropol* itself.

Metropol, Nollendorfplatz 5, 1/30 (☎216 4122). Well-known, if not mega, names play frequently in this large dance space.

Miami Nice, Potsdamerstr. 82, 1/30 (☎261 6656). Salsa and other sounds.

Quartier Latin, Potsdamer Str. 96, 1/30 (☎261 3707). Seated club that often hosts middle-league touring bands. Consistently good and varying selections of contemporary groups.

Tempodrom, near the Kongresshalle on John-Foster-Dulles-Allee (☎394 4045). Two tents, the larger hosting contemporary bands of middling fame.

Jazz, Folk, and Blues

Badenscher Hof, Badensche Str. 29, 1/31 (☎861 0080). Lively café-restaurant that draws in the Schöneberg crowd for its frequent jazz concerts, the best of which are at weekends.

Blues Café, Körnerstr. 11, 1/30 (☎261 3698). Hiding away in a small street off Potsdamer Strasse, this low-profile café is the place to head for if you like your blues pure and original.

Flöz, Nassauische Str. 37, 1/31 (☎861 1000). Basement club that's the meeting point for Berlin's jazz musicians, and a testing ground for the city's new bands. Also offers occasional salsa and cabaret. Can be wild.

Go-In, Bleibtreustr. 17, 1/15 (☎881 7218). The place for folk music on an international level, with musicians from the Philippines to the Pyrenees, from India to Scotland. But despite the cosmopolitan acts, the *Go-In* still doesn't seem to have discovered the full potential of world music.

The Irish Inn, Damaschkestr. 28, 1/31. Sing-along Irish folk music, plenty of booze.

Jazz for Fun, Kurfürstenstr. 10, 1/30 (☎262 4556). A place to bring your own instrument and join in the jam session. Informal and free.

Quasimodo, Kantstr. 12a, 1/12 (☎312 8086). Berlin's best jazz spot, with daily programs starting at 10pm. A high quality mix of international stars and up-and-coming names.

Classical

For years classical music in Berlin meant one man and one orchestra: Herbert von Karajan and the Berlin Philharmonic. Since his death in 1989 the orchestra has retained its popularity under new conductor Claudio Abbado, and tickets for their home with near-perfect acoustics, the **Philharmonie**, are still extremely difficult to get. Try calling at the box office at the Philharmonie at Kemperplatz, Matthäikirchstr. 1, 1/30 (Mon–Fri 3:30–6pm, Sat & Sun 11am–2pm; ☎261 4883) as far in advance as possible.

Thankfully, the Philharmonic is by no means the only option. The **Berlin Radio Symphony Orchestra** also plays at the Philharmonie, and, as well as opera and ballet, the *Deutsche Oper*, Bismarckstr. 34, 1/12 (☎341 0249), has good classical concerts with tickets selling for as little as DM10 for a seat in the gods.

The *Urania*, An der Urania 17, 1/30 (249091), has a wide-ranging program and reasonably priced seats, and many smaller orchestras play at sites in and around the city. As ever, see *Zitty* and *Tip* for listings. For opera listings, see the following section.

Theater

Sad to say, the mainstream **civic and private theaters** in Berlin are on the whole dull, unadventurous, and expensive—and though it's often possible to cut costs by buying student standby tickets, you'll find little in English save for the work of a couple of small, roving theater groups.

But Berlin's reputation as Germany's *Theaterstadt* still holds firm for the thousands of eager young West Germans who flock to the city every year, rent a space, and stage their work. In recent years, however, many professional people have left the birthplace of experimental theater and returned to Munich, and the lure of the film business. Nevertheless, Berlin is still a major ground for **experimental work**, and if your German is up to it a number of groups are worth the DM3–30 ticket price; check under "Off-Theater" in *Tip* or *Zitty* for up-to-the-minute listings. Groups that have the word *Freie* in their name indicate that they're not dependent on city or state subsidies, which often impose creative constraints on a group's output.

You can get **tickets** for almost all theater performances other than "Free" theater at the ticket offices listed under "Ticket Agencies and Offices" at the beginning of this chapter; you'll pay between DM5 and DM40.

Civic and Private Theaters

Deutsche Oper Berlin, Bismarckstr. 34, 1/12 (☎341 4449). Major mainstream opera and ballet (see listing under "Dance and cabaret," overleaf).

Hansa-Theater, Alt-Moabit 47, 1/12 (☎391 4460). Traditional and folk theater.

Komödie, Kurfürstendamm 206, 1/15 (☎882 7893). Period and contemporaray comedies.

Schaubühne am Lehniner Platz, Kurfürstendamm 153, 1/15 (☎890023). State-of-the-art equipped theater, that hosts performances of the classics, and some experimental pieces.

Schiller-Theater, Bismarckstr. 110, 1/12 (☎319 5236). The best state-run theater in West Berlin. Three stages and as experimental as can be.

Theater am Kurfürstendamm, Kurfürstendamm 209, 1/15 (☎882 3789). Run-of-the-mill plays and comedies that are of little interest to non-German speakers.

Theater des Westens, Kantstr. 12, 1/12 (☎312 1022). Musicals and light opera.

Experimental and Free Theater Groups

BELT, Stierstr. 5, 1/41 (offices ☎801 3467). The Berlin English-Language Theater group. No permanent home but occasionally play in cafés and smaller clubs. Check *Zitty*, *Tip* or phone for further information.

Berlin Play Actors (offices ☎784 7362). Another English-speaking group playing in various places about town.

Berliner Figurentheater, Yorckstr. 59, 1/61 (☎786 9815). Experimental puppet theater group dealing with topical issues; constantly innovative. Superbly crafted dolls.

Freie Theateranstalt Berlin, Klausenerplatz 19, 1/19 (☎321 5889). Experimental and political theater.

Freie Volksbühne, Schaperstr. 24, 1/15 (☎881 3742). Not as radical as it once was, but with a reputation for excellent stage designs.

Grips, Altonaerstr. 22, 1/21 (☎391 4004). First rate children's/young people's theater; usually all improvised.

Neuköllner Oper, Karl-Marx-Str. 131, 1/44 (☎687 6062). Opera and musicals, often obscure or unknown.

Schiller-Theater-Werkstatt, Bismarckstr. 110, 1/12 (☎319 5236). The experimental group of the Schiller Theater.

UFA-Fabrik, Viktoriastr. 13, 1/61 (☎752 8085). The most famous, and most efficiently run, cultural factory, with just about every aspect of the performing arts on offer. The UFA-Fabrik acts as an umbrella group for all kinds of performances—theater, dance, music, and film—and it's always worth checking out what's on.

Dance and Cabaret

Though there are few **dance groups** in Berlin, those that exist are of a high quality: expect to see plenty of original, oddball, and unusual performances.

In the 1920s and 1930s, Berlin had a rich and intense **cabaret scene**. Hundreds of small clubs presented acts that were often deeply satirical and political: when the Nazis came to power these quickly disappeared, to be replaced with anodyne entertainments in line with party views. Sadly the cabaret scene has never recovered: most of what's on show today is either semi-clad titillation for tourists, or that most German of predilections, the drag show. However a few places are worth trying for political cabaret: your German will need to be pretty good to appreciate the gags.

Dance

Deutsche Oper Berlin, Bismarckstr. 34, 1/12 (☎341 4449). Performances of classical ballet and, to a lesser extent, contemporary work, both rather lacking in flair and inspiration.

Die Etage, Hasenheide 54, 1/61 (☎691 2095). Contemporary dance and mime.

Phantoms-Mimentheater, Pfalzburgerstr. 72, 1/15 (☎881 8103). Mime group which brings myths and fables into a contemporary setting.

Tanz Tangente, Kuhligkshofstr. 4, 1/41 (☎792 9124). Highly praised modern dance company that works closely with jazz musicians. Often has visiting international groups.

Tanzfabrik Berlin, Möckernstr. 68, 1/61 (☎786 5861). Experimental and contemporary works, usually fresh and exciting.

Cabaret

Bügelbrett, Hardenbergstr. 12, 1/12 (☎312 9012).

CaDeWe, Gneisenaustr. 2A, 1/61 (☎691 5099).

Die Drei Tornados, Möckernstr. 79, 1/61.

Klimperskasten, Otto-Suhr-Allee 100, 1/10 (☎313 7007).

Stachelschweine, Europa Center, 1/30 (☎261 4795).

Wühlmause, Nürnberger Str. 33, 1/30 (☎213 7047).

Film

When the all-night drinking in Kreuzberg starts to get too much, it's always possible to veg out in front of the silver screen. The movie theaters along the Ku'damm and around the Gedächtniskirche show major international releases, with ticket prices from DM10–15; one day a week, usually Wednesday, is designated *Kinotag*, when prices are reduced to around DM6. Language can be a problem: if a film is listed as **OF** (*Originalfassung*) it's in its original language; **OmU** (*Originalfassung mit Untertiteln*) indicates German subtitles. Otherwise, the film will have been dubbed into German.

A host of **smaller movie theaters** show art house and independently-made movies, and some of the more interesting places are listed below. *Tip* and *Zitty* have alphabetical listings of all the films showing each week.

Should you be here in February, the **Berlin Film Festival** dominates the city's cultural life. Second only to Cannes in European terms, it has increasingly showcased East German and East European films alongside important releases from around the world. For details of screenings, see the listings magazines or inquire at the Verkehrsamt in the Europa Center.

Amerika Haus, Hardenbergstr. 22–24, 1/12 (☎819 7661). Classic US movies along with films of more specialized interest.

Arsenal, Welserstr. 25, 1/30 (☎246848). Specializes in retrospectives and series, with a second screen showing experimental work.

British Council Film Club, Hardenbergstr. 20, 1/12 (☎310716). Occasional British movies.

Cinema, Bundesallee 111 (☎852 3004). Screen works by and for women.

Odeon, Hauptstr. 116, 1/62 (☎781 5657). Recent English-language films

Thalia 2, Kaiser-Wilhelm-Str. 71, 1/46 (☎774 3440). Films in English.

PART TWO

EAST BERLIN

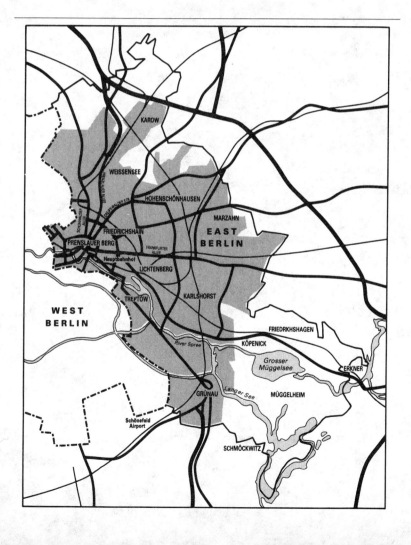

GETTING THERE

From the United States the best and cheapest way to get to East Berlin is via West Berlin (see *West Berlin Basics*).

East Berlin does have an **international airport** called **Schönefeld**, but there are no direct flights to or from American cities—although it is possible to fly to and from Leipzig with *Interflug*, the GDR state airline, and take a connecting flight if you're visiting the country as part of a pre-arranged package.

It's worth knowing that you can fly relatively cheaply to Schönefeld airport from most Eastern European cities or from Athens and Istanbul, where **bucket shop** bargains are often available. Should you arrive at Schönefeld en route to West Berlin, a transit bus will take you to the Funkturm bus station (see p.7); to get to the center of East Berlin, take the S-Bahn to Friedrichstrasse station. The S-Bahn line also continues into West Berlin.

GETTING IN

In theory, US and Canadian citizens still require visas to visit East Berlin. However, since July 2, 1990, border controls have effectively ceased to exist and visa regulations are no longer actually enforced. This means that you will have no problems entering the country with valid documentation for West Berlin (See *West Berlin Basics*).

Since the opening up of the border you can cross into East Berlin wherever you want. The most direct way into the heart of East Berlin is to take S-Bahn line #3 from Bahnhof Zoo in West Berlin (make sure you take an east-bound train—don't get on a Wannsee train). This line will take you to Friedrichstrasse, Alexanderplatz, and beyond. U-Bahn lines #U6 and #U8 will also take you into central East Berlin. The S-Bahn train winds its way over nondescript West Berlin streets, past the Reichstag and into East Berlin by way of the erstwhile *Todesstreife* (Death Strip), a vacant no-man's land now awaiting the attention of the developers.

> Much of the information in this section will be out of date even as you read it, such is the pace of the change in the GDR. Contact the *German National Tourist Office* (see *West Berlin Basics*) for the latest details on entering and staying in the country.

VISAS AND LONGER STAYS

As stated above, visas are no longer actually issued, and border controls are increasingly non-existent. For longer stays, the East German tourist authorities in the US are recommending that people make arrangements six to eight weeks in advance through a travel agency specializing in GDR tours (see box in *West Berlin Basics*) which will arrange a visa and confirm accommodation. However, this is no longer necessary—there's nothing to stop you turning up and booking into a hotel on the spot. Once in Berlin, Americans can arrange longer trips to East Germany with overnight stays.

> Should you wish to prolong your stay in East Berlin or travel further into the GDR, contact one of the specialist GDR travel agents listed under "Getting There" in *West Berlin Basics*

HEALTH AND INSURANCE

For medical and other needs it is worthwhile taking out an appropriate insurance policy before your departure—see *West Berlin Basics*.

There's a **casualty department** at the hospital at Marienburger Strasse 41–46 in Prenzlauer Berg (tram #20 from Hackescher Markt). Bear in mind that the GDR health service is badly run-down at the moment; if you need treatment head back to West Berlin unless it's an **emergency**, in which case phone ☎115 for an ambulance, but remember that there's unlikely to be an English-speaker at the end of the line. To call out a doctor, ring ☎1259. You should have more luck finding an English-speaker at one of the larger *Apotheken*, but don't bank on being able to find a particular medication. It goes without saying that you should bring with you any prescription drugs you may be taking.

CHEMISTS (*APOTHEKEN*)

Apotheke am Alexanderplatz, Hans-Beimler-Str. 70–72, 1020 (☎212 5766).
Dorotheenstädtische Apotheke, Friedrichstr. 154, 1080.
Kronen Apotheke, Friedrichstr. 165, 1080.
Robert-Koch-Apotheke, Karl-Marx-Allee 101, 1020.

MONEY AND BANKS

On July 2, 1990, currency and economic union of the two Germanys was effected. The Deutschmark replaced the Ostmark, banishing the tedious process of lining up to change money and putting hard currency hustlers out of a job. The downside of this has been a degree of fiscal chaos, spiraling prices, and an end to East Berlin as an absurdly cheap destination. You can now expect to spend as much money on a day out in East Berlin as you would in the western sector. West Berlin banking hours and regulations now apply to banks in East Berlin.

TRAVELERS' CHECKS AND CREDIT CARDS

Visa, **American Express**, **Diners Club** and **Eurocards** and **travelers' checks** are accepted by *Interhotel* hotels like the *Grand*, *Palast*, and *Metropol* (see "Hotels" under "Finding a Place to Stay"), some restaurants and nightclubs (usually the expensive ones), big department stores, and some specialist shops. As a rule, don't bank on being able to use plastic outside of the *Interhotels*, though this situation should improve.

INFORMATION AND MAPS

For general information about East Berlin head for the tourist office in the *Reisebüro der DDR*, Alexanderplatz 5, Berlin 1026. On the second floor there's an office (Mon–Fri 8am–8pm, Sat & Sun 9am–6pm; ☎215 4402) dealing specifically with foreign visitors.

Here you'll find some English-speaking staff who'll be able to provide you with guidebooks, maps, and English-language information. They'll also be able to offer you some help with hotel accommodation, theater tickets, trips on the *Weisse Flottte* cruise ships, domestic train tickets and international train reservations. Also available here is the useful monthly listings brochure *Wohin in Berlin*.

There's a smaller **tourist office** at Charlottenstr. 45 (Mon, Tues, Thurs, & Fri 9:30am–5pm, Wed 10am–5pm) which also sells international train tickets, and an **Informationszentrum** under the Alexanderplatz TV tower (Mon 1–6pm, Tues–Fri 8am–6pm, Sat & Sun 10am–6pm; ☎212 4675) which also sells maps and has information about what's on in East Berlin.

Information and street plans for central East Berlin are also available in West Berlin from the *Informationszentrum*, 2nd Floor, Hardenbergstr. 20 (Mon–Fri 8am–7pm, Sat 8am–4pm). The best large-scale **map** of East Berlin is the *Falk Plan* (DM4), which has a gazetteer and enlarged plans of the city center. Remember, too, that both *Tip* and *Zitty* magazines have condensed **listings** for events in East Berlin.

GETTING AROUND

The city center has a good bus, tram, and U-Bahn network which extends out to most of the suburbs. For longer journeys use the S-Bahn which runs out to the city limits and

beyond. Note too that fares quoted here will almost certainly rise in the near future, bringing them in line with the western sector of the city.

Apart from longer hauls on the S-Bahn, the standard **fare** across the network is DM0.20. Twenty-four-hour passes (*Touristenfahrkarten*) costing DM2 are available from U- and S-Bahn stations, and are valid for East Berlin's entire public transit network. Services on the network run from 4am until about midnight, when less frequent night services on bus and tram routes take over. The **Service Städtischer Nahverkehr** (☎246 2255) at S-Bahnhof Alexanderplatz will fill you in on transport details.

Although it's tempting not to pay when using East Berlin's public transit this can prove to be a false economy as, since the recent increase in the number of westerners visiting the city, inspectors (a hitherto almost unknown phenomenon) have

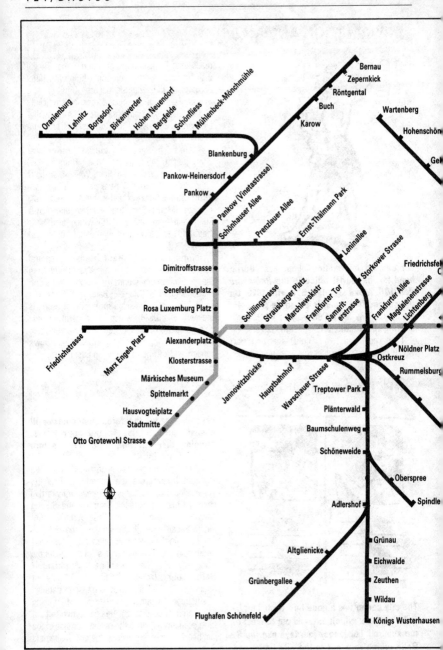

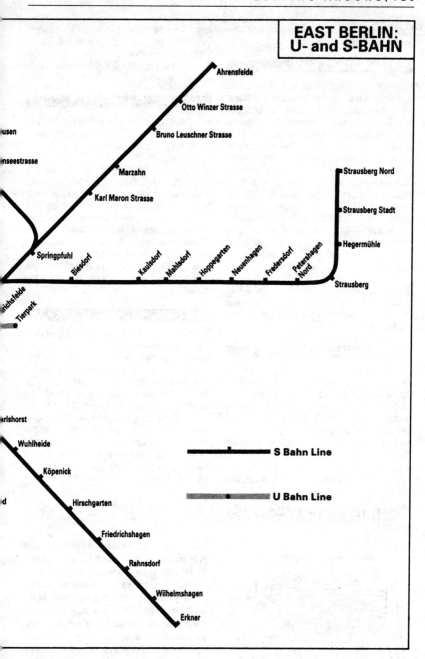

**EAST BERLIN:
U- and S-BAHN**

Ahrensfelde

Otto Winzer Strasse

Bruno Leuschner Strasse

Marzahn

Karl Maron Strasse

Strausberg Nord

Strausberg Stadt

Hegermühle

Springpfuhl

Biesdorf

Kaulsdorf

Mahlsdorf

Hoppegarten

Neuenhagen

Fredersdorf

Petershagen Nord

Strausberg

Tierpark

Karlshorst

Wuhlheide

Köpenick

Hirschgarten

Friedrichshagen

Rahnsdorf

Wilhelmshagen

Erkner

S Bahn Line

U Bahn Line

been roving rail and bus routes dishing out DM60 on-the-spot fines to fare-dodgers.

THE U-BAHN AND S-BAHN

While not as slick as the West Berlin system, East Berlin's **U-Bahn** network is fast and efficient. Ticket dispensers and hole-punches are located at the head of platforms, and most U-Bahn stations also have automatic ticket machines and ticket offices where you can buy a *Touristenfahrkarte*. Since the *Wende*, a number of U-Bahn stations which had been closed since the Wall went up have been reopened. The comprehensive **S-Bahn** network is ideal for longer suburban trips, with fares ranging from DM0.20 for the city center area (designated as *Preisstufe 1*) to DM1.30 depending on the length of journey. You'll find yourself using the S-Bahn more frequently than its counterpart in the Western sector of the city. Tickets, available from booking hall machines or from ticket offices, must be validated before boarding. Twenty-four-hour *Touristenfahrkarten* for S-Bahn services only are available for DM1, though they're only worth getting if you intend to travel out to the suburbs.

TRAMS AND BUSES

Fares for **trams and buses** are paid into a sort of honesty box: you're expected to put money in rather than, as is possible, simply pulling a lever and tearing off a ticket from the dispenser without paying. Tickets must be validated by one of the onboard hole-punches.

Tram termini in the center of town are at **Am Kupfergraben** near Friedrichstrasse and **Hackescher Markt** near Marx-Engels-Platz, and many bus routes converge in the Alexanderplatz

area. A number of bus routes now run between East and West Berlin; check with the Service Städtischer Nahverkehr at S-Bahnhof Alexanderplatz or with the BVG information booth outside Zoo station.

TAXIS

In the old days, taxis in East Berlin were relatively cheap, by western standards. However, as market forces start to take hold you can expect to be paying pretty much the same as you would in West Berlin before long. Away from the city center taxis aren't always easy to find but quite a few car owners earn a bit on the side as unofficial taxi-drivers, so it's always worth sticking your thumb out and see. There are **taxi stands** at the northern entrance to Friedrichstrasse station, the *Centrum* department store, and *Einrichtungshaus* entrances to the Alexanderplatz S-Bahnhof, at the *Hotel Stadt Berlin* nearby, and at the *Palasthotel* on Unter den Linden. To phone for a taxi, call ☎3644.

BOAT TRIPS

The *Weisse Flotte* line operates a number of **river and lake cruises**, which form a good way of exploring the lakes to the southeast of the city. From April to October, at 11am & 3pm, cruises run from **Treptow Hafen** (to get there take the S-Bahn to Treptower Park) out to the Grosser Müggelsee and back. Tickets cost DM5–6 but are in great demand and unlikely to stay this cheap for long. The *Weisse Flotte* also operate various other routes; for details and reservations check with the *Reisebüro* in Alexanderplatz. There's talk of extending *Weisse Flotte* operations to West Berlin's lakes and it's worth checking for details.

FINDING A PLACE TO STAY

The cheapest option for stays in East Berlin is in private rooms. Though this scheme is in its infancy, it does seem reasonably well-organized: addresses are listed in *Herzlich Willkommen—27, 500 Privatquartiere in der DDR* (Mair DM19.50; from any bookshop). Rooms, while nothing fancy, are a bargain compared to even the cheapest hotel. Another source of private accommodation is the bed & breakfast agency run by Frau

Neugebauer, 206 Wilhelm-Pieck-Strasse (☎281 5841), who can put you in touch with private householders who rent out rooms from about DM25 per person. Also worth checking out is the state bed & breakfast accommodation register at the foot of the TV Tower near Alexanderplatz.

For normal hotel accommodation you can expect to pay upwards of DM170 for a single room (DM240 double) at one of the big tourist hotels. Other options include youth hostels and camping.

It's possible to arrange youth hostel and hotel accommodation in advance via Berolina Travel who can confirm reservations within two or three days. In East Berlin the new **Travel Service InterHotel DDR**, Unter den Linden/ Friedrichstrasse, 1080, will be able to provide information about hotel possibilities.

HOSTELS AND CAMPING

East Berlin's **youth hostels** can be reserved on the spot or via the *Reisebüro der FDJ*, "*Jugendtourist*," 1026 Berlin, Alexanderplatz 5 (Mon–Fri 8am–4pm; ☎215 3633). Recommended hostels are the *Egon-Schultz-Jugendtourist-Hotel*, Franz-Mett-Str. 7, 1136 (U-Bahnhof Tierpark), and, on the very edge of town in the suburb of Grünau, the **Jugendherberge Berlin-Grünau**,

Dahmestr. 6 (reached by taking bus #86 as far as the school) .

There are **Camping facilities** at the *Intercamping* site by the Krossin See, just outside the village of Schmöckwitz on the southeastern edge of East Berlin. To reach the site from the center of town take the S-Bahn to Grünau or Köpenick and then tram #86 to the end of the line. From here it's a walk of about 2km if you can't get one of the occasional buses.

HOTELS

East Berlin's **top hotels** are costly enough to be out of reach of anyone traveling on a budget.The *Grand Hotel*, Friedrichstr. 158–164, 1080, is one of the most expensive at about DM300 for a single and DM450 for a double. *Hotel Metropol*, Friedrichstr. 150–153, 1080, and the *Palasthotel*, Karl-Liebknecht-Str. 5, are the most favored— and highly booked. The *Hotel Stadt Berlin*, Alexanderplatz, 1026, and the *Hotel Unter den Linden*, Unter den Linden 14, 1080, aren't a great deal less expensive.

Cheaper hotels include the *Christliches Hospiz*, Auguststrasse 82, 1040, and the *Hospiz am Bahnhof Friedrichstrasse*, Albrecht Str. 8, where you'll pay about DM100 per person a night. Also worth trying is the slightly more expensive *Hotel Adria*, Friedrichstr. 134, 1040.

OPENING TIMES, FESTIVALS, AND PUBLIC HOLIDAYS

Opening times can be a frustration. On the whole shops open from 9am–6pm during the week and 9am–noon on Saturday; certain shops stay open till 8pm on Thursday.

Restaurants, bars, and cafés are a different matter. Most have a set *Ruhetag* each week when they are closed all day (often, but by no means always, Sunday or Monday) and where possible these details are included in our listings. One scourge of East Berlin gastronomic life is the sudden closure of places, announced by a white card in the window saying that the business in question is closed until further notice because of "illness" or "technical reasons." A lot of these appeared after the exodus of 1989, and with some businesses now going under in the new harsh economic climate it's still a problem. Most **museums, monuments, and theaters** are

closed on Monday, making this the one day to avoid coming if you've limited time for trips from the West.

FESTIVALS

East Berlin boasts a few **festivals** and regular cultural events, but most of these have tradition-ally been over-worthy and dull, organized by the Party or the state. One exception is the *Fest des politischen Liedes* ("Festival of Political Song"), held in mid-February in the Palast der Republik, the Werner Sellenbinder Hall, and the Babylon cinema. In the past this has attracted popular punk, new wave, and experimental acts, who managed to inject a bit of life into an otherwise very politically correct program. There's a good chance that this could be one to watch in the future. The *Musik Biennale Berlin* which also takes place in February aims to showcase new music but doesn't really amount to much.

More important is the *Berlin Film Festival* in February, originally a West Berlin event but increasingly one picked up on in East Berlin's movie theaters: see *West Berlin Basics* for more details.

During the summer most of the districts of the city have their own *Volksfeste* (fairs) which are usually an excuse for open-air music and general partying.

The *Feste an der Panke* in **Pankow** in September is fun and the *Köpenicker Sommer* held in **Köpenick** in the second half of June is usually worth visiting.

PUBLIC HOLIDAYS

New Year's Day (Jan 1); Good Friday (changes annually); May 1; Whit Monday (changes annually); Republic Day (Oct 7); Christmas (Dec 25 & 26).

POLICE AND TROUBLE

The green-uniformed *Volkspolizei* or *Vopos* constitute the city's everyday police force: if you don't bother them, they won't bother you.

The most frequent crime committed by tourists is jaywalking, for which there are on-the-spot fines—even if there's not a car in sight. Try and avoid getting drunk and disorderly, and never drink and drive, as driving after consuming even a small amount of alcohol is totally banned.

In the event of an **emergency** the police can be reached by dialling ☎110. Should you need to report a **loss or theft**, inquire at the *Reisebüro* as to the location of the appropriate police station. Concerning which, you ought to be aware that East Berlin is by no means crime-free. Away from the center of town it's wise to exercise the same kind of caution at night as you would at home;

muggings and casual violence are not unknown in this city, and some of the high-rise satellite towns like **Marzahn** have the same problems you'd find on similar developments in the west. Watch out, too, for the skinheads as they are just as violent and fascistic as their western role models ever were, and are quite likely to harass you if you look non-European or in any way out of the ordinary. It's a frightening fact that this kind of trouble is on the increase at the moment.

Crime in general seems likely to increase, at least temporarily, as the social dislocation associated with the process of gradual unification takes hold. Many East Berliners are already suffering the effects of redundancy and unemployment, and some are taking out their resentment on well-heeled visitors.

POST OFFICES AND TELEPHONES

East Berlin's main post office is in the Palast Der Republik at Marx-Engels-Platz (daily 10am–10pm). Other offices are dotted around town and have varying opening hours: most open on Saturday mornings.

For **inquiries**, try the Central Postal Information service (☎212 5151), but don't expect an instant answer or an English-speaker. The GDR postal service, never renowned for speedy delivery of international mail, now seems to be coming into line with its West German counterpart.

TELEPHONES

Central East Berlin is fairly well provided with **public telephones**, which is fortunate as

USEFUL NUMBERS

Operator ☎180.
International operator ☎181.
Directory inquiries ☎180.
Ambulance ☎115.
Police ☎110.
Fire ☎112.

private ones aren't too common. Look out for either yellow phone booths or phones attached to walls. Phones are in the process of being adapted to take Deutschmarks. **Local calls** are cheap and not usually problematic but **international calls**, even those to West Berlin, can require patience. You may have to keep trying for some time before you get through, and once you've actually got a connection you'll need a good supply of marks to keep it. Call the International Operator for details on whether it's possible to dial direct, and for info on codes. As the city's phone service is overhauled and new lines opened, the situation should improve but all in all, it's still easier to make calls from West Berlin. The code for West Berlin **from East Berlin** is ☎849, though this should soon be dropped as the two networks integrate.

EAST BERLIN POST OFFICES

Berliner Str. 12, 1100 (Mon–Fri 7am–6pm, Sat 8–11:30am).

Eberswalder Str. 6–9, 1058 (Mon–Fri 7am–6pm, Sat 8am–1pm).

Frankfurter Allee 204–206, 1035 (Mon–Fri 7am–8pm, Sat 8am–noon).

Französische Str. 9–12, 1080 (Mon–Fri 7am–8pm, Sat 8am–1pm).

Friedrichstrasse Station, 1080 (Mon–Fri 7am–8pm, Sat 8–11:30am).

Palast der Republik, Marx-Engels-Platz, 1020 (daily 10am–10pm).

Schillerpromenade 1, 1160 (Mon–Fri 7am–8pm, Sat 8am–1pm).

Strasse der Pariser Kommune 8–12, 1017 (at the Hauptbahnhof; 24-hour).

Rathausstr. 5, 1020 (Mon–Fri 7am–8pm, Sat 8am–1pm).

MEDIA

Since the *Wende* the GDR's media has undergone a massive process of liberalization. Although the newspapers are fairly uninspiring to western eyes, and treatment of current affairs seems tame, the very fact that issues are now discussed and debated publicly is an achievement in itself.

The future of the GDR media looks decidedly shaky in the face of sophisticated western competition but it's probable that at least some vestiges will survive in the new Germany.

NEWSPAPERS

Although **English-language newspapers** are not yet widely available in East Berlin, the situation is likely to improve gradually as part of the general opening up of the city.

Home-grown newspapers are still in a state of flux but a cursory glance reveals that they have lost some of their old turgidity. The newest and best is the *TAZ*, an East Berlin cousin of the West Berlin alternative daily of the same name. The city's first independent newspaper in fifty years, it's produced with help from the publishers of the West Berlin *TAZ*. The other local paper is the *Berliner Zeitung*, which has undergone cautious liberalization, a process that should continue in the face of competition from *TAZ*. In addition to local news it also covers international stories. Also available is the tabloid *BZ am Abend*, which is good for local listings. For a more interesting read check out *Junge Welt*, a "left-wing socialist youth newspaper" published by the *Freier Deutsche Jugend*, the official party youth organization. Also worth checking out for a lively view of events within the GDR is *Der Morgen*, the newspaper of the liberal-democrat *LDPD*.

Nationally, the biggest paper is *Neues Deutschland*, the PDS organ which still follows the party line but not quite as inflexibly as in the past. These days it does actually contain news, domestic and foreign, rather than endless columns about the achievements of the GDR. West German newspapers are easy to pick up in the east and many are sold at discounted prices by western media giants anxious to secure a slice of the burgeoning market. For much the same reasons, western newspaper barons are falling over themselves to buy into existing East German publications.

TV AND RADIO

The GDR has two **TV stations**, traditionally unwatchable but today featuring some interesting investigative programs and heated debate. *DDR1* is the mainstream station, featuring sports,news, and lighter entertainment and broadcasting from early morning to late evening. *DDR2*, which usually comes on the air in the afternoon, offers educational programs until early evening when it switches over to plays and movies.

There are five GDR **radio** stations in the Berlin area: *DDR1* (95.8FM) for easy listening light music; *DDR2* (99.7FM) for classical music and educational programs; *Berliner Rundfunk* (91.4FM) for current affairs and drama; *Stimme der DDR* (97.7FM) for MOR music and occasional jazz; *DT64* (93.1FM) for pop music and youth-oriented broadcasts.

Most East Berliners, however, still prefer to tune into West German TV and radio stations.

GAY EAST BERLIN

The GDR was the most liberal of the former Eastern Bloc countries when it comes to gay rights, and the population as a whole is no more tolerant or intolerant than in West Germany.

The age of consent for men is 18 and there are a number of gay groups (mostly set up under the auspices of the Protestant church). On the whole East Berlin gays are eager to meet up with gays from the west, and there a couple of gay or semi-gay bars and nightspots, which are included in Chapters Seven and Eight (best of these is the *Schoppenstube* on Schönhauser Allee). One other place worth checking out is the *Mehrzweckgebäude*, Buschallee 87, Weissensee, 1120 (tram #70 from the Kupfergraben in the city center), where there are discos (Wed 7pm–midnight, Fri & Sat 8:30pm–3am, Sun 7pm–1am) in a big canteen building. It's hugely popular and packed with a youngish gay crowd of both sexes.

DIRECTORY

CONTRACEPTIVES Condoms are available from pharmacies and dispensing machines, but are seemingly manufactured from used tractor tires—best bring your own.

EMBASSIES AND CONSULATES *Britain*, Unter den Linden 32–34, 1080 (☎220 2431); *Bulgaria*, Unter den Linden 40, 1100 (☎229 2072); *Czechoslovakia*, Otto-Grotewohl-Str. 21, 1080 (☎439 4113); *Hungary*, Otto-Grotewohl-Str. 6, 1080 (☎212 3559); *Poland*, Unter den Linden 72, 1080 (☎589 4530); *United States*, Neustädtische Kirchstr. 4–5, 1080 (☎220 2741) *USSR*, Unter den Linden 65, 1080; *West Germany*, Hannoversche Str. 30, 1040.

EMERGENCIES Police ☎110; Ambulance ☎115; Fire ☎112.

FILM Bring your own and process it back home or in West Berlin. Don't try and use GDR-produced *ORWO* film as you won't be able to get it processed when you return home: getting it developed locally takes several weeks.

INTERTANK GAS STATIONS Chauseestr. 98, 1040; Prenzlauer Allee 1–4, 1055; Holzmarktstr. 36–42, Friedrichshain, 1017 (24hr).

LAUNDROMATS Very few, unfortunately. There's a **dry cleaning** service in the Berolinahaus at Alexanderplatz which offers a 30-minute service.

LOST PROPERTY Wilhelm-Pieck-Str. 164, 1040 (☎282 6135 or ☎282 3472); Tues & Thurs 10am–1pm & 2–6pm, Fri 10am–1pm. For items lost on trains try *Fundbüro der Deutschen Reichsbahn*, S-Bahnhof Marx-Engels-Platz, 1020 (☎492 1671); Mon–Fri 8am–5pm.

LUGGAGE CONSIGNMENT Luggage lockers (0.50M) at Friedrichstrasse station, with an office for the deposit of larger items.

TELEPHONE CODE ☎0372.

TIPPING 5–10 percent is expected in most restaurants, and it's normal to leave a tip in cafés and bars.

ZIP CODES A four-figure code is written after the street name.

CHAPTER SIX

THE CITY

A fter the Berlin Wall went up on August 13, 1961, **East Berlin** was reduced to a kind of psychological gray area for most people. It was easy to forget that behind the tourist attraction that the Wall became there was a city of a million people, also calling itself Berlin. Since the events of November 9, 1989 however, East Berlin has undergone something of a renaissance. West Berliners, who for years had regarded the "other Berlin" as a wasteland without culture or consumer durables, have re-discovered the city, encouraged as much by the simple fact of the opening of the border as by the apparent burgeoning of democracy.

Even at the height of its isolation East Berlin was never a wasteland. Neither was it—or is it—a cut-price shadow of a city, a second-best imitation of West Berlin. In many ways East Berlin *is* Berlin, home of its historic heart—unlike West Berlin which really amounts to little more than a collection of suburbs without a real center. Berlin grew up around an area that today forms the center of East Berlin, and even in the days of the Kaisers the political and cultural core of the city lay on what is now the eastern side of the border. The division of the city into zones of occupation in 1945, although seemingly arbitrary, actually followed local government boundaries, and the Soviet sector, later to become East Berlin and the capital of the GDR, encompassed the city center *Bezirk* (or district) of Mitte. Division left East Berlin home to the lion's share of the city's treasures, including Karl Friedrich Schinkel's Neoclassical architectural legacy and most of the old museums.

However, there's more to East Berlin than past glories. Although a modern city, it is one which has developed along very different lines to West Berlin. After the war, as American aid flooded in to West Berlin, the East Berliners watched the Russians dismantle and ship east practically everything that was still in working order—even whole factories*. Despite this they managed to rebuild their almost totally destroyed city with little outside help, preserving much more of its historic identity than did their counterparts in West Berlin.

But increasingly, as Berlin becomes a unified city, the distinctions between East and West will blur—it seems only a matter of time before the opinions, based on the forty-five-year-old divide of the city, that inform these pages, will no longer hold true: part of the excitement of being in Berlin, particularly the East, is the speed of change, of the rush (some would say the dangerous haste) of the German people to become "Ein Volk" once again.

---

*It is one of many ironies of the post-war history of the Soviet Union that once the factories and plant of the GDR had been carefully dismantled and shipped out to the USSR, they lay useless—no-one had made any notes on how to reassemble them.

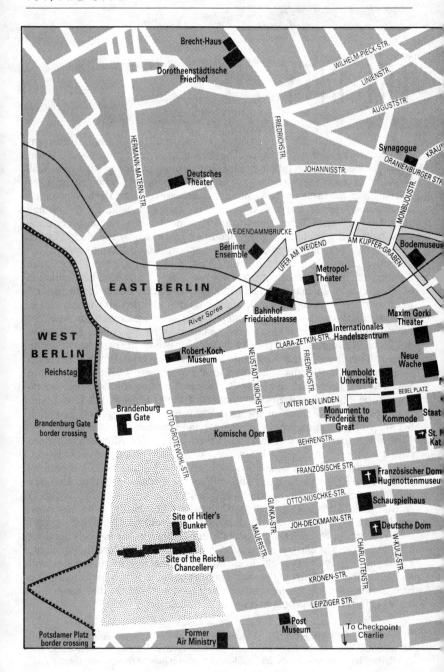

Brecht-Haus

Dorotheenstädtische
Friedhof

WILHELM-PIECK-STR.

LINIENSTR.

AUGUSTSTR.

HERMANN-MATERN-STR.

FRIEDRICHSTR.

Synagogue

KRAU

JOHANNISSTR.

ORANIENBURGER STR.

Deutsches
Theater

MONBIJOUSTR.

WEIDENDAMMBRUCKE

Berliner
Ensemble

UFER AM WEIDEND

AM KUPFER-GRABEN

Bodemuseu

Metropol-
Theater

EAST BERLIN

River Spree

Bahnhof
Friedrichstrasse

Internationales
Handelszentrum

Maxim Gorki
Theater

WEST
BERLIN

Reichstag

Robert-Koch-
Museum

NEUSTADT. KIRCHSTR.

CLARA-ZETKIN-STR.

FRIEDRICHSTR.

Humboldt
Universität

Neue
Wache

BEBEL PLATZ

UNTER DEN LINDEN

Brandenburg
Gate

OTTO-GROTEWOHL-STR.

Monument to
Frederick the
Great

Kommode

Staat

Brandenburg Gate
border crossing

Komische Oper

BEHRENSTR.

St.
Kat

FRANZÖSISCHE STR.

Französischer Dom
Hugenottenmuseu

OTTO-NUSCHKE-STR.

Schauspielhaus

GLINKA-STR.

JOH-DIECKMANN-STR.

Deutsche Dom

Site of Hitler's
Bunker

MAUERSTR.

Site of the Reichs
Chancellery

CHARLOTTENSTR.

W.KULZ-STR.

KRONEN-STR.

LEIPZIGER STR.

Post
Museum

To Checkpoint
Charlie

Potsdamer Platz
border crossing

Former
Air Ministry

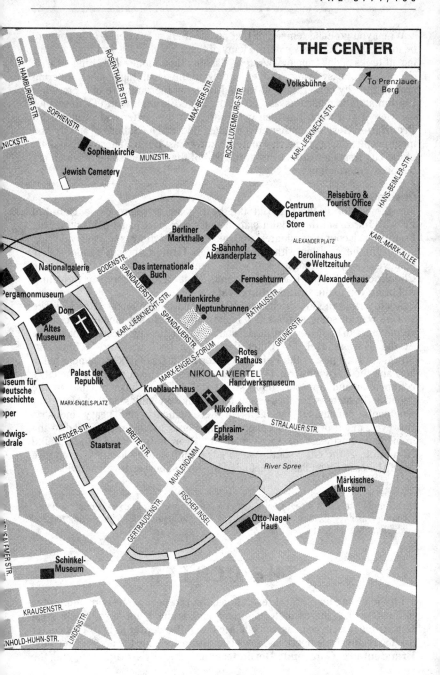

THE CENTER

To Prenzlauer Berg

GR. HAMBURGER STR.

ROSENTHALER STR.

MAX-BEER-STR.

ROSA-LUXEMBURG-STR.

KARL-LIEBKNECHT-STR.

HANS-BEIMLER-STR.

Volksbühne

SOPHIENSTR.

NICKSTR.

Sophienkirche

MUNZSTR.

Jewish Cemetery

Reisebüro &
Tourist Office

Centrum
Department
Store

KARL-MARX-ALLEE

Berliner
Markthalle

ALEXANDER PLATZ

Nationalgalerie

BODENSTR.

SPANDAUERSTR.

Das internationale
Buch

S-Bahnhof
Alexanderplatz

Berolinahaus
Weltzeituhr

Pergamonmuseum

Fernsehturm

Alexanderhaus

Dom

KARL-LIEBKNECHT-STR.

SPANDAUERSTR.

Marienkirche
Neptunbrunnen

RATHAUSSTR.

GRUNERSTR.

Altes
Museum

useum für
Deutsche
Geschichte

oper

dwigs-
edrale

Palast der
Republik

MARX-ENGELS-FORUM

Rotes
Rathaus

NIKOLAI VIERTEL
Handwerksmuseum

MARX-ENGELS-PLATZ

Knoblauchhaus

WERDER-STR.

BREITE STR.

Nikolaikirche

STRALAUER STR.

Staatsrat

Ephraim-
Palais

MÜHLENDAMM

River Spree

Märkisches
Museum

GERTRAUDENSTR.

FISCHER INSEL

Otto-Nagel-
Haus

Schinkel-
Museum

RICKAI EMER STR.

KRAUSENSTR.

LINDENSTR.

NHOLD-HUHN-STR.

When you go East, remember that people there aren't necessarily going to be in thrall to all things western. Plenty of them justifiably resent the patronizing attitudes of day-tripping "*Wessis*," flashing their money and airing an arrogance born of easy living. Also, try and avoid the usual trap of just wandering around the city center; take in the old Imperial thoroughfare of **Unter den Linden** and the museums, and go up the huge **Fernsehturm** (TV tower) for the view if you want, but then get away from the center and head out for **Prenzlauer Berg** or another area detailed under "The Suburbs," and try and meet people; the only real way to get to know East Berlin. There's a round-up of the city's smaller **museums** at the end of the chapter, some of which are bizzarely entertaining.

Orientation

For the visitor to East Berlin the best point of reference is **Bahnhof Friedrichstrasse**, the S-Bahn station that's the most usual point of arrival. From here, a couple of minutes' walk along **Friedrichstrasse** itself will bring you to the intersection with the **Unter den Linden**, the city's most stately boulevard. If you head straight you'll eventually come to what used to be **Checkpoint Charlie**, leading back into West Berlin, whereas a right turn will bring you to the **Brandenburg Gate**.

A left turn at the Friedrichstrasse/Unter den Linden intersection will take you by way of some of the city's finest eighteenth- and nineteenth-century architecture to the **Museuminsel**, island home to the city's leading museums. At the Museuminsel, the Unter den Linden becomes **Karl-Liebknecht-Strasse**, which passes the **Palast der Republik** (the GDR parliament building) and the **Fernsehturm** TV tower and leads to **Alexanderplatz**, the city's commercial and transport hub, where rail and bus links run out to the suburbs. To an outsider these suburbs look like an endless sprawl of pre-war tenements punctuated by high-rise developments and heavy industry. However, much of the atmosphere of old Berlin has been preserved to the immediate northeast of the center in **Prenzlauer Berg**, and around **Köpenick**, at the city's southeastern edge, high density living starts to give way to lakes and woodland, punctuated by small suburban towns and villages.

It's highly likely that **streets** named after lesser stars of the Marxist panoply will be changed as liberalization sweeps the city. While confusing, it'll be interesting to see which names fall first...

THE CENTER

With the easing up of travel restrictions, the prospect of spending more time in East Berlin is increasingly appealing, and, arguably more so than in West Berlin, this is a city with as much to see out of **the center** as in it. That center itself is relatively compact, and few visitors stray outside the area between the **Brandenburg Gate and Alexanderplatz**—the city's main strip, and the place where you'll find most of the conventional tourist pulls. If you don't have the time or the inclination to roam farther afield then there's certainly plenty to keep you occupied here, amidst the museums and monuments. So successful has the restoration of **Unter den Linden** been, for example, that looking at the magnificent eighteenth- and nineteenth-century buildings that line its course, it's difficult to believe that as late as the early 1960s large patches of the center were little more than rubble. Like an archaeologist trying to picture a whole vase from a single fragment, the city builders took a facade, or just as frequently a small fraction of it, and set about recreating the whole. And even though much of what can be seen today is a fraud, it's often easy to suspend your disbelief and imagine an unbroken architectural continuity.

The city center rejuvenation scheme is still going on. Since the mid-1980s massive and expensive building and reconstruction projects have had a transforming effect. This is most notable on the **Platz der Akademie**, where less than ten years ago the twin Neoclassical churches which now grace the square were little more than bombed-out shells. A little farther east, planners have attempted to recreate the almost totally destroyed core of medieval Berlin in the **Nikolai Viertel** development. Today, building continues along **Friedrichstrasse** and elsewhere in the center, breathing life back into what was once the heart of Berlin.

Despite the effort of the GDR authorities to restore the shell-damaged buildings of earlier centuries, much of central East Berlin is ill-informed high-rise modernist blight: **Alexanderplatz**, once the nerve center of Weimar Berlin, is now a concrete and glass wilderness with few redeeming features, and a perverse abundance of the soulless architecture central government considered indicative of "progress"—a suitable jewel for its showcase capital city.

But more noticeable on a visit to the city center is the feeling of change in the air. Although for many people the future seems at best uncertain, there is a feeling that East Berliners at last have a chance to shape their own futures after so many years of stultifying state control. Go into any bar in the center and, if you speak a little German, it's likely you'll fall into conversation about the new Germany and its role in the Europe of the 1990s: it's a fascinating time to be here and you may find yourself staying longer than you'd planned.

Arriving: Friedrichstrasse and Around

The first thing that hits you as you step out of Bahnhof Friedrichstrasse is the distinctive East Berlin street smell; a cloying mixture of two-stroke fuel for the ubiquitous Trabant cars, unfiltered heavy industry emissions, and the coke which powers the city's central heating systems. Savour it while you can; as Polos replace Trabants and West German-style pollution regulations come into force, it looks set to become a thing of the past. You're now on **Friedrichstrasse**, one of East Berlin's main thoroughfares, and the streetscape is one in flux. Once East Berlin seemed sluggish when compared to frenetic, crowded West Berlin, but now this half of the city is starting to catch up with a vengeance.

Directly opposite you at Friedrichstr. 101 is the **Admiralspalast**, a *Jugendstil* building which houses the *Metropol Theater*, purveyor of indifferent musical light entertainment, and *Die Distel* theater, the sorry heir to Berlin's legendary inter-war cabaret tradition (see "Theater" in Chapter Eight, *Music and Nightlife*). Turn right under the Friedrichstrasse railroad bridge, where a plaque commemorates two young Wehrmacht soldiers executed for "desertion" by the SS during the last hopeless days of the Battle of Berlin; it's one of many reminders of the cataclysm which shaped this city and which has left indelible scars on its fabric. On the northern side of Friedrichstrasse is a symbol of Honecker-era East Berlin in the shape of the Japanese-built **Internationales Handelszentrum**, a giant piece of self-consciously modernist architecture whose main purpose was to show that West Berlin didn't have a monopoly on thrusting, commercial dynamism.

Unter den Linden

A few hundred meters farther along you come to **Unter den Linden**, once the main east–west axis of Imperial Berlin and still the site for many of the city's foreign embassies. Connected to Berlin's pre-war west end by the Charlottenburger Chaussee (later known as Strasse des 17 Juni and now provisionally renamed Strasse des 9 November), until recently the Unter den Linden was a broad boulevard going nowhere. It led only to the **Brandenburg Gate** (see p.39), the great triumphal arch that was until recently backed by the Wall, which used to mark the end of the road for East Berliners. However, since November 1989 and the gradual erosion of the central stretches of the Wall, new life has been breathed into Unter den Linden and it's now crowded with tourists heading both east and west. As the two Berlins draw together it's inevitable that the Unter den Linden will be in the forefront of development. Already some of its buildings have been taken over by West German concerns, and it can only be a matter of time before it becomes one of the focal points of the revitalized city.

From here, turn around and head back up Unter den Linden. On the right is the massive **Soviet Embassy** and a little farther up is the Friedrichstrasse intersection. Before the war this was one of the busiest crossroads in the city, a focal point for cafés and hotels that included the famous *Café Kranzler*. Like most of the rest of Weimar Berlin the café vanished in the debris of the war, although it was later re-established on the Kurfürstendamm in West Berlin. These days the **Lindencorso**, a restaurant, café, and bar complex attempts to keep the flag flying, but the area is a mere shadow of its former self. Directly across Unter den Linden from the *Lindencorso* is the **Deutsche Staatsbibliothek**, the GDR state library which is housed in the one-time Prussian State Library, a typically grandiose edifice dating from the turn of the century. It's mainly the haunt of Humboldt University students now, but you can sit in the pretty courtyard by the fountain if you feel like a break.

A couple of hundred meters beyond here is an equestrian **monument to Frederick the Great**, the enlightened despot who laid the foundations of Prussian power. After the war "Der alte Fritz," as the statue was popularly known, was removed from Unter den Linden, and only restored to its city center site in 1980 after a long exile in Potsdam. His re-instatement reflected an odd revaluation by Honecker's GDR of the pre-socialist past. No longer were figures like Frederick the Great, Blücher, Scharnhorst, *et al* to be reviled as imperialistic militarists; they were, rather, accorded the status of historic figures worthy of commemoration. Even Bismarck, the arch imperialist of Wilhelmine Germany, was recognized as having "in his *Junker* way played a progressive historical role."

This monument is the vanguard of a whole host of historic buildings, survivors of nineteenth-century Berlin, restored over the last forty years from the post-war rubble. On the left-hand side of the street is the **Humboldt Universität**, a restrained and dignified Neoclassical building from 1748, originally intended as a royal palace. Philologist, writer, and diplomat, Wilhelm Humboldt founded a school here in 1809 which was later to become the University of Berlin, and be renamed in his honor in 1946. Flanking the entrance gate are statues of Wilhelm and his brother Alexander, famous for his exploration of South America. Alumni of the university include Karl Marx, Friedrich Engels, and Karl Liebknecht, the socialist leader and proclaimer of the first German republic who was murdered by right-wing *Freikorps* members in 1919. The philologists Jacob and Wilhelm Grimm (better known as the Brothers Grimm) and Albert Einstein are some of the better known former staff members. During the Nazi period the university was a center of opposition, and many students and staff members were imprisoned and executed.

Directly opposite the university is **Bebelplatz**, formerly Opernplatz, the scene on May 11, 1933 of the infamous *Buchverbrennung*, the burning of books which conflicted with Nazi ideology. Thousands of books went up in smoke, including the works of "un-German" authors like Erich Maria Remarque, Thomas Mann, Heinrich Mann, Stefan Zweig, and Erich Kästner along with volumes by countless foreign writers, H.G. Wells among them. The most fitting comment on this episode was made with accidental foresight by Heinrich Heine during the previous century: "Where they start by burning books, they'll end by burning people."

On the western side of Bebelplatz is the **Alte Bibliothek**, an old library building known colloquially as the **Kommode** (chest of drawers), thanks to its curved Baroque facade. Lenin spent some time here poring over dusty tomes while waiting for the Russian Revolution, and despite the fact that the building suffered serious damage during the war it's been immaculately restored. On the north side of the square is the **Deutsche Staatsoper**, another flawless eighteenth-century Neoclassical building by the architect Georg von Knobbelsdorff which, like everything else around here, has been almost totally reconstructed since 1945 (see "Live Music" in Chapter Eight, *Music and Nightlife*). Just behind is **St Hedwigs-Kathedrale** which was built for the city's Catholic minority in 1747 and is still in use. It's thought to have been designed by Knobelsdorff, with "advice" from Frederick the Great himself—which was bad news for the Catholics who had to pay for it, because the resulting pantheon-like structure isn't really suited to the demands of the liturgy. Next door to the Deutsche Staatsoper, the **Palais**

Unter den Linden was built in 1663 and given a Baroque facelift in 1732. One wing of this palace now houses the **Operncafé**, one of East Berlin's tackier bar/restaurant/disco complexes. Just behind the Palais Unter den Linden, housed in the **Friedrichwerdersche Kirche**, in the shadow of the huge Foreign Ministry, is the **Schinkel-Museum**, on Am Werderschen Markt, a museum about the life and work of Karl Friedrich Schinkel, the architect who gave nineteenth-century Berlin its distinctive Neoclassical stamp (see "East Berlin's Museums"). Directly opposite the Operncafé is one of Schinkel's most famous buildings, the **Neue Wache**, built between 1816 and 1818 as a sort of Neoclassical police station to house the royal watch.

Today the building, which looks like a stylized Roman temple, houses the "Memorial to the Victims of Fascism and Militarism." It's here that one of East Berlin's better-known ironies is played out when the guard of honor is changed: as one detachment goose-steps out, another goose-steps in. The main changing of the guard with full pomp and ceremony takes place every Wednesday at 2:30pm (also on public holidays) but a more restrained version takes place at the same time on the other days of the week. If you're really desperate to see some goose-stepping, but can't make it to any of these displays, then the guard is changed routinely, but without the full military works, every hour. This is yet another symbol of the pre-*Wende* GDR which may well soon become a thing of the past.

Next door, housed in one of East Berlin's finest Baroque buildings, the old Prussian Arsenal, is the **Museum für Deutsche Geschichte** (see "East Berlin's Museums"). There was much excitement here on June 14, 1848, when, during the revolutionary upheavals, the people of Berlin stormed the building which was then still in use as an arsenal. A number of people were killed, and no weapons were found, but it gave the authorities the excuse to bring troops into the city and ban various democratic newspapers and organizations. In the **Schlüterhof**, the museum's inner courtyard, look out for the twenty-two contorted faces of dying warriors, by the eighteenth-century sculptor Andreas Schlüter, which adorn the walls. Just behind the Museum für Deutsche Geschichte is the **Maxim-Gorki-Theater** (see "Theater" in Chapter Eight, *Music and Nightlife*).

South of Unter den Linden

To the south of Unter den Linden is the **Platz der Akademie**, the former Gendarmenmarkt, an historic cluster of restored buildings which was once considered one of the most beautiful squares in Europe. Here you'll find the **Französischer Dom**, built for Berlin's influential Hugenot community at the very beginning of the eighteenth century. It's a classically-influenced building which has now been completely restored, after having been all but totally destroyed during the war. In the tower of the church there's a smart restaurant (see Chapter Seven, *Drinking and Eating*)—and a great view from the balcony. On the ground floor is the Hugenottenmuseum (see "East Berlin's Museums"). Nearby, the **Deutscher Dom** was built around the same time for the city's Lutheran community, and is the stylistic twin of the Französischer Dom. Between the two is Schinkel's Neoclassical **Schauspielhaus**, a former theater, now home to the Berlin Symphony

Orchestra (see "Live Music" in Chapter Eight, *Music and Nightlife*) which fits in well with the two churches, making this one of the most striking and architecturally balanced corners of the city. During the last days of the war Platz der Akademie was the scene of heavy fighting as the Russians attempted to drive out SS troops who had dug themselves in here. This, coupled with the effects of Allied bombing, left the area in ruins, and it's only within the last few years that things have once again been put right.

A little farther to the south is Leipziger Strasse, once a main Berlin shopping street and now a lifeless showpiece of housing and commercial development dating from the 1970s "big is beautiful" phase of East Berlin town planning. You might notice that the buildings on the south side of the street are higher than those on the north side—at this height they conveniently block off the offices of right-wing publisher Axel Springer just over the border.

On June 16 and 17, 1953, this street was the focal point of a nationwide **uprising**. General dissatisfaction with economic and political conditions in the eastern half of the city came to a head when building workers (the traditional proletarian heroes of GDR mythology) working on the prestigious Stalinallee construction project went on strike, protesting at having to work longer hours for the same pay. On June 16 they marched on the **Haus der Ministerien** (Göring's former Air Ministry) at the end of Leipziger Strasse, which was at that time the seat of the GDR government. Here they demanded to speak to GDR Minister President Otto Grotewohl and SED General Secretary Walter Ulbricht. These two declined to make an appearance, so speakers from the crowd got up to demand the dissolution of the government and free elections.

News spread across the country and in the morning of the following day, there was a wave of strikes and demonstrations throughout the GDR. Tools were downed, and in many parts of East Berlin trafffic came to a standstill: clashes with the police followed as demonstrators attacked SED party offices and state food stores. The GDR authorities proved unequal to the situation, and at 1pm the Soviet military commandant of the city declared a state of emergency. It's estimated that several hundred people died as Soviet tanks moved in to restore order. Afterwards Bertolt Brecht sardonically suggested that the GDR government should "dissolve the people, and elect another." Today bland and functional high-rise buildings are set on either side of a six-lane boulevard and the whole street has a desolate feel, almost as if it was built to prove some bombastic architectural point rather than to provide homes and shops for real people.

At the end of Leipziger Strasse is **Potsdamer Platz**, re-opened to traffic in the aftermath of November 9, 1989, and the site of what in pre-war days was said to be the busiest square in Europe. Now once again traffic streams through, mostly East German vehicles heading West, and another once-desolate corner of Berlin has been reborn.

If you turn right out of Leipziger Strasse into Otto-Grotewohl-Strasse at the Haus der Ministerien and walk the hundred meters or so to Voss Strasse you come to a site which played an infamous role in Berlin's history. There's not actually anything to see but just to the left, closed off to the general public, is the former site of Hitler's **Reichskanzelei** (Reichs Chancellory) and **Hitler's bunker**. Although both structures survived the war more or less intact (less rather than more in the case of the Reichskanzelei) they were later destroyed. A small grassy mound visible from one of the observation platforms on the western side of the border marks the spot—see "From the Reichstag to Checkpoint Charlie" in Chapter One for more details.

The Museum Island

At the eastern end of Unter den Linden is the **Karl-Liebknecht-Brücke** (formerly the Marx-Engels-Brücke, and before that the Schlossbrücke), designed by Schinkel. The classical statues which line each side of the bridge were removed once the bombing started during the war: after the division of the city they ended up in West Berlin and were only returned to the east in 1981. Look out, too, for the Schinkel-designed dolphin and sea horse motifs in the cast-iron balustrades of the bridge.

The bridge leads onto **Karl-Liebknecht-Platz** (until recently Marx-Engels-Platz), former site of the old Imperial Palace, the remains of which were demolished after the war. Only the balcony from which Karl Liebknecht proclaimed the German revolution in 1918 was preserved and has since been incorporated into the **Staatsrat** (State Council) building on the south side of the square. Karl-Liebknecht-Platz now forms the mid-point of a large city center island in the River Spree.

The northwestern part of the island, extending peninsula-like from Karl-Liebknecht-Platz, is known as the **Museumsinsel** (Museum Island) and it's here that you'll find the best of East Berlin's **museums**. Your main problem will be finding enough time to see everything: it almost goes without saying that your best bet is to pick out one collection in particular rather than trying to cram them all into a single day. Remember that all except the Pergamon are **closed on Monday**, and be prepared for disappointment: often whole sections of the museums are closed for vaguely defined "technical reasons." **Admission charge** for nearly all museums is DM1.05, DM0.50 for students with an ISIC card, though these unrealistic pre-*Wende* prices will probably rise soon.

The Altes Museum

Directly to the north of Marx-Engels-Platz, the **Altes Museum** (Wed, Thurs, Sat & Sun 9am–6pm, Fri 10am–6pm), is another heavily Neoclassical Schinkel building which now houses an art museum. The post-war and GDR section is basically a large collection of state-sponsored and state-promoted artists brought together in an attempt to foster home-grown GDR art. Only Albert Eberd's quasi-religious scenes seem to break away from the pedestrian conformity or, at best, conventional experimentalism of the other artists represented. With luck you may also be able to see the **Kupferstichkabinett** (Print Collection), a large collection of engravings and prints founded in 1831 thanks to the generosity of Wilhelm Humboldt. It contains 57 exquisite drawings by Botticelli for Dante's "Divine Comedy" and also includes works by Rembrandt, Dürer, and Lucas Cranach. The nineteenth- and twentieth-century German graphic art collection has works by Käthe Kollwitz and Max Slevogt; a further section contains prints by Daumier, Manet, Degas, Rodin, Renoir, Munch, and Toulouse-Lautrec.

The Neues Museum and Nationalgalerie

Just behind the Altes Museum is the **Neues Museum**, one of East Berlin's few remaining war ruins, which is now being gradually restored to house the overflow from other museums. Next door is the **Nationalgalerie** (Wed, Thurs, Sat & Sun 9am–6pm, Fri 10am–6pm), a slightly exaggerated example of post-Schinkel Neoclassicism, which now contains East Berlin's largest art collections. The first floor **nineteenth-century section** is full of dull portraiture and landscapes, a legacy of the conservatism of Kaiser Wilhelm II, who vetoed a decision by the gallery to buy Impressionist works. Apart from a couple of Cézannes and, thanks to the Kaiser, a very small Impressionist section, it's pretty uninspiring. The **twentieth-century section** is good on the Expressionist, Bauhaus, and *Neue Sachlichkeit* (New Objectivity) movements, with work by the Dresden and Munich Expressionist collectives *Die Brücke* and *Der Blaue Reiter*. Also worth checking out are works by Otto Dix, John Heartfield's highly political 1920s and 1930s photomontages, and the expressive realism of Ernst Barlach's sculptures.

The Pergamonmuseum

To the north of the Neues Museum is the **Pergamonmuseum** (Sat–Thurs 9am–6pm, Fri 10am–6pm), accessible from Kupfergraben on the south bank of the Spree. It's a massive structure, built in the early part of this century in the style of a Babylonian temple to house the treasure trove of the German archaeologists who were busy plundering the ancient world, packaging it up and sending it back to Berlin. The museum is divided into four sections, the most important of which, the **Department of Antiquities**, contains the **Pergamon Altar**; a huge structure, dedicated to Zeus and Athena, dating from 180 to 160 BC, which was unearthed in Turkey and brought to Berlin in 1903. The **frieze** shows a battle between the gods and giants, and it's a tremendously forceful piece of work, the powerfully depicted figures writhing in a mass of sinew and muscle. The section also contains other pieces of Hellenistic architecture (albeit on a smaller scale), including a **market gate** from the Turkish town of Miletus and various examples of Greek sculpture.

The **Western Asian Section** has items going back four thousand years to Babylonian times, including the enormous **Ishtar Gate**, the **Processional Way**, and the facade of the **Throne Room** from Babylon, all of which date from the reign of Nebuchadnezzar II in the sixth century BC. While it's impossible not to be awed by the size and remarkable state of preservation of the deep blue enameled bricks of the Babylon finds, it's as well to remember that much of what you see is a mock-up, built around the original finds. Look out for the weird mythical creatures that adorn the Ishtar Gate, and check the small model of the whole structure to get some idea of its enormous scale.

The museum's **Islamic Section** contains the facade of a Jordanian **Prince's Palace** at Mshatta from AD 743, presented to Kaiser Wilhelm II by the Sultan of Turkey, as well as a host of smaller but no less impressive exhibits from Arabia and Persia. Finally, the **East Asian Collection** has a large collection of ceramics, lacquer-work, and jade spanning four thousand years.

The Bodemuseum

At the northeastern tip of the Museumsinsel is the **Bodemuseum** (Wed–Sun 10–6pm), housed in an impressive, not to say intimidating, turn-of-the-century neo-Baroque building. The collection itself is very traditional and divided into museums within a museum. The **Egyptian Museum/Papyrus Collection** contains art and papyri from 5000 BC to the third century AD, plus mummies, grave artifacts, friezes, weapons, and jewelry. The **Early Christian and Byzantine Section** has an extensive range of objects, mainly religious in nature, from the pre-medieval eastern Mediterranean. Worth checking out are the sixth century mosaic from the church of San Michele in Ravenna, the Eastern Orthodox icons, and the Coptic art exhibits. In the **Picture Gallery** there's an extensive, albeit unremarkable collection of German, Italian, Dutch, and Flemish Old Masters. More worthwhile is the **Museum for Ancient and Early History** which has archaeological material from all over Europe right up to the eleventh and twelfth centuries, including the **Heinrich Schliemann Collection**, consisting of items unearthed by the great German archaeologist on the site of ancient Troy during the nineteenth century. Tragically, the best of the Schliemann Collection was destroyed during the war, crushed in the rubble of the supposedly impregnable Tiergarten flak tower, where many of the city's finest treasures had been stored for safekeeping. The **Sculpture Gallery** has eighteenth-century pieces with a few interesting late Gothic German and early Renaissance Italian examples.

Elsewhere on Museum Island

From the Bodemuseum it's a short walk back to Karl-Liebknecht-Platz. Adjacent to the Altes Museum is the **Berliner Dom**, built at the behest of Kaiser Wilhelm II between 1894 and 1905 on the site of an eighteenth-century cathedral. With its distinctive dome and towers it was intended to serve the House of Hohenzollern as a family church, and its vault contains the remains of various members of the family. The building was badly damaged during the war, but has undergone a long period of reconstruction: although it's not completely open to the public yet, it is possible to step inside and admire the interior from a distance. Opposite the Dom stands the **Palast der Republik** which houses the *Volkskammer*, the GDR's parliament, and an entertainment complex including restaurants, cafés, a theater, and a bowling alley (none of which are recommended), and a useful post office. Irreverently dubbed "Erichs Lampenladen"—Erich's lamp shop—this huge angular building with its bronzed, reflecting windows was completed in less than a thousand days and was a source of great pride to the Honecker regime. At the southern tip of the mid-Spree island is an area known as the **Fischerinsel** (Fisherman's Island), home to yet another 1970s high-rise development which, considering its showpiece status, is spectacularly shoddy when seen from close quarters.

Alexanderplatz and Around

Alexanderplatz is the commercial hub of East Berlin. If Unter den Linden represents the glories of Berlin past, then Alexanderplatz and the area around it represent the glories of East Berlin present, although only time will tell whether the concrete giganticism of the new capital will wear as well as the efforts of Schinkel and company. To get to "Alex" from the Palast der Republik head up **Karl-Liebknecht-Strasse**, a big shopping street, where, on your left stands the **Palasthotel**, one of East Berlin's most modern and expensive hotel complexes. It has seven restaurants but they're only worth going to if you've got money to burn. A little farther along and to the left, at Spandauer Str. 4, is the **Das internationale Buch**, a large international bookstore which occasionally has good art books and bargain-priced English versions of Marx and Lenin—though probably not for much longer. Farther up Karl-Liebknecht-Strasse are the Hungarian and Polish cultural centers (full of folksy tack) and the **Berliner Markthalle**, a large covered market, worth a quick skim round.

On the other side of the street is the **Marienkirche**, a thirteenth-century Gothic parish church (the oldest in Berlin): pop in to escape the bustle of Alexanderplatz and listen to a free organ recital (daily, 3.30–4pm). The Marienkirche is overshadowed by the gigantic **Fernsehturm** or TV tower (May–Sept daily 8am–11pm; Oct–April daily 9am–11pm, 2nd and 4th Tues in month 1–11pm; 3M, student 1.50M) that dominates the East Berlin skyline like a displaced satellite sitting on top of a factory chimney. The tower does have a couple of positive features: it makes a good orientation point if you get lost, and there's a tremendous view (40km on a rare clear day, although the top is often shrouded in cloud) from the observation platform.

Above the observation platform is the *Tele-Café*, a café whose main attraction is that it turns on its own axis once every hour (you have to buy a DM5 ticket for the privilege of being able to sit here). When the sun shines on the globe of the tower, the reflected light forms a cross visible even in West Berlin, much to the reported chagrin of the old authorities and amusement of the Berliners, who call it the "Pope's revenge." If you want to go up, bear in mind that that there are usually long lines. At the foot of the tower there's a jumble of cafés, restaurants, and glass-fronted exhibition halls, all welded together by a series of walkways. Occasionally interesting exhibitions are staged, and the *Espresso Café* is where the city's youth head after a hard day's skateboarding on the concrete surfaces around and about.

In front of the TV tower is the **Neptunbrunnen**, a fountain incorporating statues of Neptune and friends, built in 1891. This stands directly in front of the **Rotes Rathaus** (tours Sat 11:15am, 11:30am, noon & 12:30pm from the main entrance), the "Red Town Hall," so called because of its bricks rather than its politics. It's a grandiose, almost Venetian-looking building, which has lost some of its impact now that it's been hemmed in by new buildings to the southwest. The Rathaus was badly knocked around in 1945, but has made a good comeback: at its front is a statue of a **Trummerfrau**—a "Rubble Woman," commemorating the women who set to work in 1945 clearing up the 100 million tons of rubble created by wartime bombing and shelling.

Alexanderplatz

From the Rathaus, follow the pedestrianized section of Rathaus Strasse, past what passes for a luxury shopping complex, as far as **S-Bahnhof Alexanderplatz**. After going under the railroad bridge walk through the gap between the **Alexanderhaus** and the **Berolinahaus**, two buildings designed at the beginning of the 1930s by the architect and designer Peter Behrens, whose ideas influenced the founders of the Bauhaus. In fact Behrens employed Walter Gropius and Mies van der Rohe, who were to become leading lights of the Bauhaus, as juniors in his architectural practice. These two buildings, which now house a bookshop and the Central Berlin District Council, are the only two Alexanderplatz structures to have survived the war. Alexanderplatz itself, named after the Russian Czar Alexander I who visited Berlin in 1805, and made famous by Alfred Döblin's novel of life in the Weimar era, *Berlin Alexanderplatz* (subsequently filmed by Fassbinder), is a huge, windswept pedestrianized plaza surrounded by high-rises.

Alexanderplatz has always figured prominently in the city's history. In 1848 it was barricaded by revolutionaries (whose ranks included the writer Theodor Fontane) and in 1872 it was the site of a demonstration by an army of homeless women and children. During the revolution of 1918, sailors occupied the Alexanderplatz police headquarters and freed all the prisoners held there. More recently Alexanderplatz was the focal point of the million-strong city-wide **demonstration** of November 4, 1989, which formed a prelude to the events of November 9. Hundreds of thousands of people crammed into the square to hear opposition leaders speak. Veteran writer Stefan Heym summed up the mood in his speech to the crowd: "Power belongs not to one, not to a few, not to the party and not to the state apparatus. The whole people must have a share."

Today Behrens' buildings, once the tallest in the area, have been put in the shade by the ugly **Hotel Stadt Berlin**, from whose thirty-seventh floor *Panorama-Restaurant* there's a fairly stupendous view (make a reservation via the *Reisebüro* or grease someone's palm—it's popular and the food is all right), and the huge and even uglier **Reisebüro der DDR**. In the center of Alexanderplatz is the sorry-looking **Brunnen der Völkerfreundschaft** (Friendship of the Peoples Fountain) which used to be a hang-out for prostitutes who promoted friendship between the peoples in their own ways. A more famous monument is the **Weltzeituhr** (World Clock) in front of the Alexanderhaus. East Berlin's most famous rendezvous point, this tells the time in different cities throughout the world, and looks like a product of the same architectural school responsible for the Fernsehturm.

Before the war, Alexanderplatz was one of the city's main shopping meccas and boasted two top people's department stores; *Tietz* and the Jewish-owned *Werthheim*. The latter, the biggest department store in Germany, stood on the opposite side of the S-Bahn to the Alexanderhaus, on a site now occupied by fast-food booths, and was "Aryanized" by the Nazis in 1933. These days commercial life on Alexanderplatz centers around the **Centrum** department store. By GDR standards it was always very well stocked, but it remains to be seen whether it will survive the competition of *KaDeWe*, *Karstadt* et al.

Nikolaiviertel

Slightly to the southwest of the Rotes Rathaus lies the **Nikolaiviertel**, a recent development which attempts to recreate the old pre-war heart of Berlin. This compact network of streets was a radical architectural departure for the old-style GDR. No longer, it seems, did the city planners feel compelled to build enormous monuments to the concrete pourer's art; most of the Nikolaiviertel buildings are no more than four or five storys high, and a concerted effort was made to inject a bit of vernacular individuality into the designs. The Nikolaiviertel consists partly of exact replicas of historic Berlin buildings which didn't make it through to the post-war era, such as the *Zum Nussbaum* pub (see Chapter Seven, *Drinking and Eating*), and partly of stylized buildings not based on anything in particular but with a distinct "old Berlin" feel to them, or at least an approximation thereof. Sometimes it doesn't quite come off, and the use of obviously prefabricated pillars and gables isn't always too convincing, but all in all the Nikolaiviertel represents a commendable effort to get away from the monumentalism of a lot of earlier post-war construction projects. It also represents an attempt to attract big-spending tourists, with a series of expensive restaurants, cafés, and *Gaststätten* (again see Chapter Seven for details). The development does however include apartments which house about 1500 people and some pricey stores, including clothes shops worthy of the dreaded sobriquet "boutique."

At the center of it all is the Gothic **Nikolaikirche**, which has been restored to its twin-towered pre-war glory and now houses a museum about the development of medieval Berlin. Nearby, on Poststrasse, is the **Knoblauchhaus**, built in 1759 and a rare survivor of the war. Inside is a museum devoted to the eighteenth-century German Enlightenment and some of the figures associated with it, while on Mühlendamm the rebuilt Rococo **Ephraim-Palais** is home to another museum, this time recording the city's development from "Electoral residence to bourgeois great city of the nineteenth century": for full accounts of all three, see "East Berlin's Museums." The original Ephraim-Palais was built by Frederick the Great's jeweler and mint master Veitel Heine Ephraim and, with characteristic Nazi sensitivity and forethought, was demolished to make way for a road in the mid-1930s. Parts of the facade were preserved and later turned up in West Berlin from whence they were returned. Nearby at Mühlendamm 5 is the **Handwerksmuseum** (again, see "East Berlin's Museums").

Nearby, on the southern side of **Molkenmarkt** is the Ministry of Culture complex which includes the former **Palais Schwerin** and the **Berliner Münze** (Berlin Mint). This area was once Berlin's medieval ghetto, and one of the adjacent streets still bears the name Jüdenstrasse. From Molkenmarkt go up Stralauer Strasse and then turn up into Kloster Strasse, which will bring you to the **Parochialkirche**, a partially restored sixteenth- and seventeenth-century Baroque church. Nearby, **Parochialstr. 1** was the site of the first meeting of Berlin's post-Nazi town council, headed by future SED chief Walter Ulbricht, even as fighting still raged a little to the west. Ulbricht and his comrades had been specially flown in from Soviet exile to lay the founda-

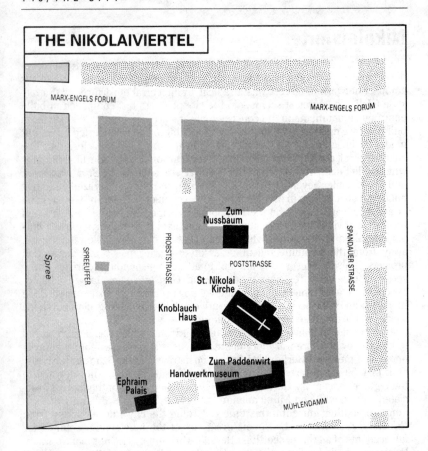

THE NIKOLAIVIERTEL

MARX-ENGELS FORUM

MARX-ENGELS FORUM

Spree

SPREEUFER

PROBSTSTRASSE

SPANDAUER STRASSE

Zum Nussbaum

POSTSTRASSE

St. Nikolai Kirche

Knoblauch Haus

Zum Paddenwirt

Handwerkmuseum

Ephraim Palais

MUHLENDAMM

tions for a future communist civil administration and moved in here, having been unable to set up shop in the still-burning Rotes Rathaus.

On the same street is the **Haus der Jungen Talente**, a big youth arts center (Mon–Sat 3–10pm) which has a good restaurant inside and is an ideal place to meet people. At the top of Klosterstrasse is the gutted thirteenth-century **Franziskaner-Kirche** which was destroyed by bombs in 1945 and has been left a ruin as a warning against war and fascism. Also in the neighborhood, between Waisenstrasse and Littenstrasse, is a crumbling fragment of Berlin's medieval **Stadtmauer** or city wall. If you're feeling hungry and thirsty then try Berlin's oldest pub, *Zur letzten Instanz* (see Chapter Seven, *Drinking and Eating*) on Waisenstrasse.

From this neck of the woods you can take the U-Bahn from Klosterstrasse to Märkisches Museum station on the southern side of the Spree (you can also walk via the Fischerinsel). The **Märkisches Museum** itself is at Am Köllnischen Park, and not far away, at Märkisches Ufer 16–18, is the **Otto-Nagel-Haus**, a museum of "proletarian and revolutionary art" (see p.161).

Around the Center

If, instead of turning right out of Bahnhof Friedrichstrasse, you had turned left and made your way north along Friedrichstrasse, you would have been heading away from the city center. To your immediate left is a triangle of land between Friedrichstrasse itself and the Spree. Before the Nazis came to power, a long-running architectural competition was held in search of a suitable design for a building to fill what was then an unsightly vacant lot. Some incredibly imaginative and improbable proposals were submitted, many of which were way ahead of their time. One entrant was Mies van der Rohe, who proposed filling the gap with an immense, tri-cornered glass and steel tower. History overtook the various projects and today the site is occupied by the Friedrichstrasse border crossing entrance for west-bound travelers, now redundant but scene of many a poignant farewell in the bad old days.

From this sorry spot, cross the wrought-iron **Weidendammbrücke** over the Spree. Immediately to the left on Bertolt-Brecht-Platz is the **Berliner Ensemble** theater (see "Theater" in Chapter Eight, *Music and Nightlife*), the official Brecht theater, although now only the invocation of Brecht's name bears witness to the greatness of the man who was once the main driving force behind modern German drama. The theater has an opulent neo-Baroque interior, with the red cross painted through the coat of arms on the royal box by Brecht on his return to Berlin in 1949 still visible.

A few streets away at Schumannstr. 13a is the **Deutsches Theater** (see Chapter Eight). In 1905 Max Reinhardt, who was to dominate Berlin theater for nearly three decades, took over as director, and in 1922 a young and unknown Marlene Dietrich made her stage debut here. It's estimated that millions were spent on restoring the interior to its turn-of-the- century splendor.

Diagonally opposite the junction of Friedrichstrasse and Reinhardtstrasse is the **Friedrichstadt Palast** theater (again, see Chapter Eight). From here head north on Friedrichstrasse towards Oranienburger Tor into Chausseestrasse. On the left is the **Dorotheenstädtische Friedhof**, East Berlin's VIP cemetery, which contains the graves of Bertolt Brecht and his wife Helene Weigel, the author Heinrich Mann, John Heartfield (the Dada luminary and inter-war photomontage exponent), the philosopher Georg Hegel, whose ideas influenced Marx, and Berlin's great nineteenth-century Neoclassical architect Karl Friedrich Schinkel. Just beyond the cemetery at Chausseestr. 125 is the **Brecht-Haus**, Brecht's last home and workplace. It now houses a Bertolt Brecht archive and there are half-hourly guided tours of the rooms where the playwright worked and lived (see "East Berlin's Museums").

If you take the next left turn after the Brecht-Haus into Invalidenstrasse you'll come to the **Naturkunde Museum**, the city's natural history museum. To be frank, you'd do better to make your way back to Oranienburger Tor and turn down into Oranienburger Strasse, where, a few hundred meters along on the left-hand side, is the old **Synagoge**, built in Moorish-Byzantine style.

Inaugurated in the presence of the Kaiser and Bismarck in 1866 it was Berlin's central synagogue, until it was burned out by the Nazis on *Kristallnacht*, the night of November 9–10, 1938, when the Nazis launched an all-out assault on Germany's Jewish community. *Kristallnacht*, so-called after the sound of breaking glass as Jewish businesses and institutions were wrecked, marked an intensification of Nazi attacks on the Jews, preparing the ground for the horror of the Final Solution. Apart from additional wartime damage, the Oranienburger Strasse synagogue has not been touched since that violent night in 1938, and remains a desolate reminder of the savagery of Nazi rule.

A little farther to the east on Grosse Hamburger Strasse is the site of Berlin's oldest **Jewish cemetery** (established in 1672) and the first Jewish old people's home to be founded in the city. In 1943 the Nazis dug a slit trench through the cemetery, using gravestones to shore it up, and turned the old people's home into a detention center into which Berlin's Jews were rounded up before being shipped off to concentration camps. A few old gravestones with Hebrew inscriptions can be seen in the wall of a neighboring house. The only stone to be found in the graveyard itself commemorates the philosopher Moses Mendelssohn, a leading figure of the German Enlightenment, and was erected after the war.

Just off Grosse Hamburger Strasse is the **Sophienkirche**, dating back to 1734: one of the city's finest Baroque churches, and the only central Berlin church to survive the war intact. The ground on which it was built was actually a gift from the Jewish community to the Protestant community, who at the time were slightly financially embarrassed. A little farther along a sharp turn to the right takes you into **Sophienstrasse**, a restored nineteenth-century street which now houses a number of arts and crafts workshops. In places the restoration is only skin-deep and the pastel facades of the old apartment houses conceal squalid, crumbling courtyards. House no. 11 dates back to 1780 and the **Handewerkervereinshaus** at Sophienstr. 18 used to be the headquarters of the old Craftsmens' Guild, which, until the founding of German Social Democrat Party (SPD), was the main focus of the Berlin workers' movement. While in the area, it's worth visiting the Sophieneck Café at Grosser Hamburgerstr. 37, where in warm weather you can sit out in the little tree-filled courtyard.

Farther East: towards Friedrichshain

From Sophienstrasse, Neue Schönhauser Strasse leads to Münzstrasse. Beyond here, between Alte Schönhauser Strasse and Karl-Liebknecht-Strasse, is the old **Scheunenviertel** quarter, an old working-class enclave and one-time center of the city's scrap-iron and rag-and-bone trades. Before World War I the area was fairly lawless in a revolutionary sort of way, and the authorities were constantly trying to find ways to justify pulling it down. At one point they refused to put down cobblestones for fear that the inhabitants would rip them up and use them to build barricades. In 1913 money raised by public subscription was used to build the **Volksbühne** theater (see "Theater" in Chapter Eight, *Music and Nightlife*) on Rosa-Luxemburg-Platz. It became Berlin's people's theater and, daringly for that time, put on plays by Hauptmann, Strindberg, and Ibsen.

Heading down Rosa-Luxemburg-Strasse and then turning right down Memhardstrasse leads to Alexanderplatz. From here a short walk leads (not necessarily in chronological order) through several distinct phases of GDR architectural development. From the eastern end of Alexanderplatz head down **Karl-Marx-Allee** (formerly Stalinallee). The section between Alexanderplatz and Strausberger Platz went up during the early to mid-1960s and is correspondingly stark and angular. From Strausberger Platz onwards things get more interesting. It was here that one of the first big post-war **reconstruction projects** was started in September 1951, when the foundation stone of what was to become an ornately monumental high-rise apartment building was laid at Weberwiese, just south of Marchlewskistrasse U-Bahn station. Over the next few years similar buildings were built from Strausberger Platz to Frankfurter Tor, which marks the eastern limit of the old Stalinallee. Look out in particular for the twin-tiered towers at Strausberger Platz, which flank the route into central East Berlin, and for the buildings at Frankfurter Tor topped by ecclesiastical-looking towers which are based on the towers of the Französische Dom and Deutsche Dom. Although generally derided in the west as examples of *Zuckerbäckerstil* (wedding-cake architecture) the buildings of Stalinallee were a well-thought out and relatively soundly constructed attempt to build housing which would live up to the great architectural tradition of Berlin. Ironically it was striking workers from the Stalinallee construction project, angry at government attempts to increase production, who sparked off the uprising of June 1953.

Another name from the socialist hall of fame crops up a little north of Strausberger Platz at **Leninplatz,** which is the center of a none-too-beautiful late-1960s and early-1970s housing complex. At the center of it all stands a 19-meter-high statue of the man himself, which can't be too different from the tens of thousands of others between here and Vladivostock. Just north, a little way along Friedenstrasse, is the **Volkspark Friedrichshain**, the city's oldest and largest park and really rather pleasant. Just for the record, the part of the park immediately adjacent to Friedenstrasse is one of East Berlin's better known outdoor gay cruising/pick-up points.

At the western entrance to the park, where Friedenstrasse and Am Friedrichshain meet, is the **Märchenbrunnen** (Fairy Tale Fountain), a neo-Baroque fountain with statues of Brothers Grimm characters. A few hundred meters to the southeast of here is a monument to the men and women of the International Brigades who fought against the fascists in Spain. Among their number were five thousand Germans (including many leading communists) of whom three thousand did not return. The rest of the park is full of the kind of worthy sporting amenities and giant chess sets which keep Germans of both East and West amused during their leisure hours. Also here are the not-so-worthy *Harzer Köhlerhütten*, a fake village with beer and food counters where even less worthy Germans like to drink beer, eat *Bockwurst*, and shout a lot. The two hills in the park are actually *Bunkerberge*, built over the remains of two wartime bunkers and post-bombing rubble. At the eastern end of the park is the **Sport und Erholongszentrum**, a big modern sports center with several swimming pools, a wave machine, an ice- and roller-skating rink, a sauna, a bowling alley, and various cafés.

THE SUBURBS

Behind the scenes in East Berlin is another city, a real one where people live and work, and which has nothing to do with the tourist attractions of the center. Most of this is located in **the suburbs**, which are each as different in character as in any western city. **Prenzlauer Berg**, a part working-class, part Bohemian district, is the most important and interesting of East Berlin's various outlying areas. If you have time you should also try to get out to the lakes and woods around **Köpenick**, which are surprisingly pleasant and unspoiled. All of the places listed below are easily reached by S- and U-Bahn, tram, or bus, and if you don't make an effort to get out to them you'll only see a minute part of what East Berlin is all about.

Prenzlauer Berg

One place you should definitely head for when you're in the city is **Prenzlauer Berg**. This run-down working-class district fans out from the northeastern edge of the city center and is East Berlin's hidden heart. During the war it was fought over (bullet holes and shrapnel scars on the building facades testify to this) but not flattened, and most of the tenement buildings put up in the late nineteenth century and early twentieth century to house the city's rapidly expanding factory worker population are still standing. Many of the blackened buildings, with their overgrown *Hinterhöfe* (courtyards), look as if they haven't been renovated since the war, and in many cases this is probably the case; behind crumbling facades paint peels in gloomy stairwells, and every year a few lives are claimed as overhanging balconies crash onto the streets below.

The quickest way to get to Prenzlauer Berg is to take the U-Bahn from Alexanderplatz and head for either Dmitroffstrasse or Schönhauser Allee U-Bahn stations. For a more atmospheric approach take tram #46 from Am Kupfergraben, or tram #49 from Hackescher Markt. Either of these will take you through some of East Berlin's lesser-known back streets and provide a good impression of the *real* city. They'll also take you past the **Zionskirche**, which was a live music club until neo-fascist skinheads broke up a gig here in October 1987. Also near here at Griebenow Str. 16 is the **Umwelt Bibliothek**, an environmental library run from church-owned premises, which attempts to keep tabs on use and abuse of the environment within the GDR and provides an information service about worldwide environmental issues. The genesis of the various opposition groups which emerged shortly before the *Wende* can in part be traced back to the Umwelt Bibliothek, which acted as an organized focus for reformists of all political complexions from the mid-1980s onwards. The library is open from Tuesday to Thursday from 6pm to 10pm and there's also a gallery and café open Tuesday, Wednesday, and Saturday from 7pm to 10:30pm, although these times may be subject to change—and it's rumored that the whole project may move to Schliemannstr. 22 soon. If you're feeling energetic you can also walk to Prenzlauer Berg from Rosa-Luxemburg-Platz. The district starts at the beginning of Schönhauser Allee and if you follow this street for about ten or fifteen minutes you'll find yourself at Dmitroffstrasse.

Schönhauser Allee itself is Prenzlauer Berg's main artery, an old-fashioned shopping street with an almost pre-war feel, and scene of some unrestrained police brutality during the October 7 demonstrations. The U-Bahn, which goes overground and becomes an elevated railroad (known popularly as the *"Magistratschirm"* or "council umbrella") just beyond Senefelderplatz gives it a distinctive, almost gloomy atmosphere. Nearby, at the Bornholmer Strasse border crossing at 9:15pm on November 9, 1989, a couple crossed the border into West Berlin without visas, becoming the first East Berliners to take advantage of the opening of the Wall (see "1989–Die Wende" in *Contexts*). However, it's in the maze of run-down streets bounded by Schönhauser Allee in the west, Prenzlauer Allee in the east, Dmitroff

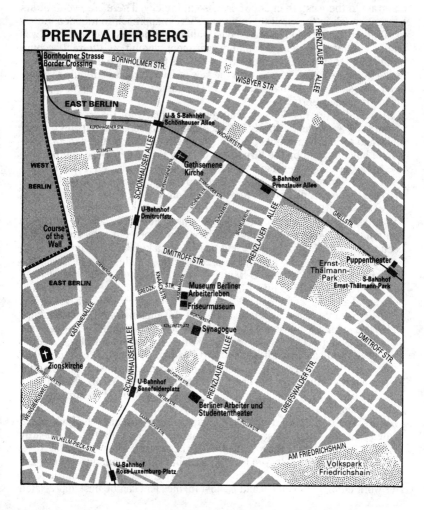

PRENZLAUER BERG

Strasse in the south, and Wisbyer Strasse in the north that the real attraction of Prenzlauer Berg lies. Here you'll find some of the best cafés and bars in the whole city (see Chapter Seven, *Drinking and Eating*). Also here, at the intersection of Stargarder Strasse and Greifenhagener Strasse, is the **Gethsemene Kirche**, which was an important focal point for reformist activities.

Prenzlauer Berg, just like Kreuzberg in West Berlin, has had a big influx of alternative lifestyle adherents and artists who chose this district to live on the edge of established GDR society—which, given the hitherto all-embracing nature of the state here, was not as easy as in "alternative" West Berlin. It was no coincidence that during the Honecker years more cars here flew white ribbons from their radio aerials, signalling that the owners have applied to emigrate to the west, than anywhere else in the city. There are even **squats** here, although in the GDR there was a different approach to the idea; rather than merely occupying a place illegally (although this also happened), it was often a case of moving into an empty apartment, finding out the rent account number and then paying the rent. However this too was illegal and there were frequent clashes with the police. In the face of East Berlin's continuing accomodation crisis it's likely that squatting will continue to be a prominent aspect of life in Prenzlauer Berg.

Historically, the district is a relatively new one. Until the mid-nineteenth century the area was positively bucolic in atmosphere, lying outside the city limits and even producing its own wine. Industrialization resulted in an explosion of building, and by the turn of the century Prenzlauer Berg had become one of Berlin's most densely populated tenement suburbs. Over the last few years the city authorities have wised up to the potential appeal of the Prenzlauer Berg, and although they don't exactly encourage tourists to go into the seedier parts, they have started to include the more accessible and presentable streets on the tourist itinerary. Foremost among these is **Husemannstrasse**, an old nineteenth-century tenement street which has been restored to its former glory and turned into a kind of living museum in a unique and encouraging attempt to preserve the grandeur of old Berlin. To reach it from Dmitroffstrasse U-Bahn station, walk along Dmitroffstrasse itself and then take the third turn on the left. This way, you get an interesting before-and-after effect as the top part of the street, above Sredzkistrasse, has yet to be restored. The spruced up section of Husemannstrasse features shops and cafés with appropriate nineteenth-century decor—but the prices and goods are modern. There's also an expensive antique shop and a livery stables from which you can rent a horse and cart if you really want to get into the *fin-de-siècle* swing of things. The street also has a couple of East Berlin's better museums; the **Museum Berliner Arbeiterleben um 1900** (Museum of Working Class Life) and, a couple of doors down, the **Friseurmuseum** (Hairdressing Museum; see "East Berlin's Museums").

At its southern end, Husemannstrasse opens out onto **Kollwitzplatz**, named after the artist Käthe Kollwitz, who lived in nearby Weissenburgerstrasse (now called Kollwitzstrasse) from 1891 to 1943. Kollwitz's home was destroyed in an air raid, but today a sculpture entitled *Die Mutter*, based on one of her drawings, stands in the little park on Kollwitzplatz. Her work embraced political and pacifist themes and can be best appreciated in the Käthe Kollwitz Museum in West Berlin (see "Around Zoo Station" in Chapter One).

Between Kollwitzstrasse and Schönhauser Allee is another Jewish cemetery, and not far away in Rykestrasse is East Berlin's only functioning **synagogue**. If you turn out of Kollwitzstrasse on to Belforter Strasse you'll notice an 1870s water tower, now a protected historic building, which has been converted into a grandiose apartment building. In 1933 the bodies of 28 workers murdered by the Nazis were found in the underground pipe network. A memorial stone commemorates them: "On this spot in 1933 decent German resistance fighters became the victims of fascist murderers. Honor the dead by striving for a peaceful world." At Belforter Strasse 15 is the **Berliner Arbeiter und Studententheater**, also known as BAT, a workers' and students' theater which is actually part of the School of Dramatic Art (see "Theater" in Chapter Eight, *Music and Nightlife*).

At the end of Belforter Strasse cross Prenzlauer Allee into Heinrich-Rolle-Strasse which leads down to Greifswalder Strasse. On the right is an old and overgrown cemetery dating back to the early nineteenth century (access from Greifswalder Strasse) with some elaborate old tombstones. Greifswalder Strasse itself looks very spick-and-span with its freshly-painted facades. In pre-*Wende* days traffic came to a standstill along the side streets a couple of times a day as a convoy of black Citroens and Volvos sped by whisking high ranking government members (notably Erich Honecker himself) from the Palast der Republik to their homes in the now infamous lakeside town of Wandlitz to the north of Berlin. But behind the immaculate facades the *Hinterhöfe* of Greifswalder Strasse are just as run down as those in the backstreets.

From the Heinrich-Roller-Strasse/Greifswalder Strasse intersection either turn right and head back to Alexanderplatz (a walk of about fifteen minutes) or make a left for the delights of the **Ernst-Thälmann-Park** (if you're feeling lazy, take tram #24 or 28, or bus #30). This is a model housing development, set in a small park and fronted by a gigantic sculpture of the head and clenched fist of Ernst Thälmann, the pre-1933 Communist leader who was imprisoned and later murdered by the Nazis. About four thousand people, mostly from the more privileged sections of society, live here, in big high-rise buildings with restaurants, shops, nurseries, and a swimming pool all immediately at hand. The development is on the site of an old gasworks, which by the look of a few surviving buildings had more architectural merit than its replacement.

Finally, on the opposite side of Greifswalder Strasse, on the other side of the Ernst-Thälmann-Park S-Bahn bridge, you'll find East Berlin's **Puppentheater**, a puppet theater which puts on shows for both children and adults (see "Theater" in Chapter Eight, *Music and Nightlife*).

Köpenick

Köpenick is one of East Berlin's more pleasant suburbs, located on the banks of the Spree towards the southeast edge of the city, and easily reached by S-Bahn from Alexanderplatz (change at Ostkreuz). It's a sleepy kind of place, but good to visit as an escape from the city center. A town in its own right during medieval times, it has since been swallowed up by Greater Berlin, but still retains a distinct identity. The presence of a number of major factories in the area meant that Köpenick always had a reputation as a "red" town. In March 1920, during the Kapp *putsch* attempt, workers from Köpenick took on and temporarily drove back army units who were marching on Berlin in support of the coup. The army later returned, but its success was short-lived as the *putsch* foundered—thanks mainly to a highly effective general strike. This militancy was to continue into the Nazi era: on January 30, 1933, the day Hitler came to power, the red flag could be seen flying from the chimney of the brewery in nearby Friedrichshagen. This defiance was punished during the *Köpenicker Blutwoche* ("Kopenick Week of Blood"), during which the SA attacked the homes of social democrats and communists. Five hundred people were imprisoned and ninety-one murdered.

If you feel the urge to know more about the history of Köpenick then visit the **Heimatgeschichtliche Kabinett Köpenick** at Elcknerplatz 8 next to the S-Bahnhof. From a sightseeing point of view Köpenick's **Altstadt** makes the best starting point: from the S-Bahnhof it's best reached by tram #84, #86, or bus #27. Situated on a peninsula between the Spree and Dahme rivers, the Altstadt's streets run more or less true to the medieval town plan. At the moment they look slightly neglected, but a big renovation project already in progress is intended to jazz them up over the next few years. On another peninsula, jutting out into the Dahme from the Altstadt, is Köpenick's Baroque **Schloss**, which is really more of a fortified manor house and now houses the **Kunstgewerbemuseum** (Museum of Applied Art; see "East Berlin's Museums"). Concerts are held in the Schloss concert hall and in the seventeenth-century chapel on weekends. From the Dammbrücke near the Rathaus you can rent boats, and on the other side of the Spree bridge there's a small park containing the **Mecklenburger Dorf**, an open-air collection of bars and *Imbiss* stands in a setting which is supposed to conjure up the ambience of a north German village. In reality it's pretty hideous, but there always seems to be a lot of people getting drunk and amusing themselves in dubious ways.

A few minutes' ride from the Spree bridge by tram #25, #26, or #82 is the **Pionierpark "Ernst Thälmann,"** a large amusement park for kids which takes up a sizable chunk of the Wühlheide woods. It's all a bit worthy, with lots of workshops and sports facilities, but the main attraction seems to be the seven-kilometer-long **Pioniereisenbahn**, a narrow gauge railroad, formerly manned by members of the *FDJ* Prty youth organisation, which is open from 2pm to 6pm all year round, weather permitting.

Oberschöneweide, a little to the east of the Pionierpark, boasts buildings designed by the architect Peter Behrens (see p.145). Opposite the Pionierpark itself, at An der Wühlheide 192–194, is a boathouse which used to be owned by AEG and there are also a couple of his factory buildings at Wilhelminenhofstrasse 83–85 (on the route of trams #25, #26 or #82). Nearby, Zeppelinstrasse 11–71, Roedernstrasse 8–14b, and Fontanestrasse 8a–12c are all examples of Behrens-designed residential housing.

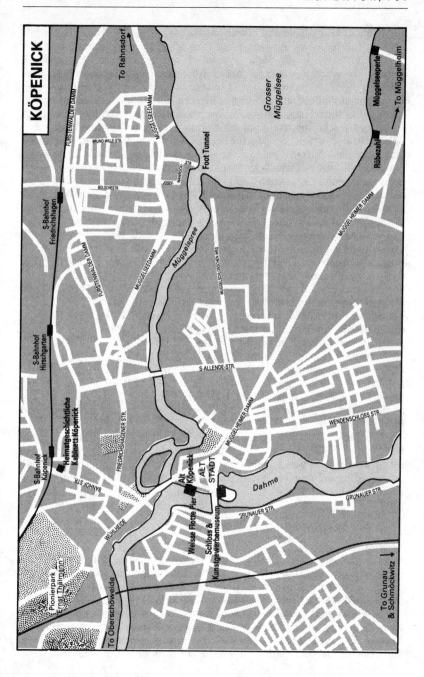

KÖPENICK

To Rahnsdorf

FÜRSTENWALDER DAMM

MÜGGELSEEDAMM

BRUNO-WILLE-STR.

NAHMITZER STR.

JOSEF STR.

BOLSCHESTR.

Foot Tunnel

Grosser Müggelsee

Müggelseeperle

To Müggelheim

Rübezahl

MÜGGELHEIMER DAMM

S-Bahnhof Friedrichshagen

Müggelspree

MÜGGELSEEDAMM

FÜRSTENWALDER DAMM

MÜGGELSCHLÖSSCHEN WEG

S-Bahnhof Hirschgarten

S-ALLENDE-STR.

WENDENSCHLOSS STR.

MÜGGELHEIMER DAMM

FRIEDRICHSHAGENER STR.

S-Bahnhof Köpenick

Heimatgeschichtliche Kabinett Köpenick

BAHNHOF STR.

Alt Köpenick

ALT STADT

Dahme

GRUNAUER STR.

Weisse Flotte Pier

Schloss & Kunstgewerbemuseum

GRUNAUER STR.

WÜHLHEIDE

Pionierpark Ernst Thälmann

To Grunau & Schmöckwitz

To Oberschöweide

The Grosser Müggelsee and Friedrichshagen

Back in the Köpenick Altstadt, from Luisenhain opposite the Rathaus, it's possible to take a *Weisse Flotte* boat to the nearby **Grosser Müggelsee**, a largish lake a few kilometers east of Köpenick itself. Another method of reaching the Grosser Müggelsee is to take the S-Bahn to **Friedrichshagen**, a small town founded in 1753 as a settlement for cotton spinners who, as a condition of their being allowed to live here, were required by law to plant mulberry trees for the rearing of silk worms. From the S-Bahnhof walk down Bölschestrasse which, despite the fact that Friedrichshagen is little more than a glorified village, is said to have some of the best shops in East Berlin. A number of the older, smaller houses along this street date from the original eighteenth-century settlement, and if you look carefully there are still a few mulberry trees dotted about. To get to the lake go down Josef-Nawrocki-Strasse, at the end of which you'll find a small park. Here, there's a *Weisse Flotte* pier and a foot tunnel which takes you under the Spree, which flows into the Grosser Müggelsee at this point.

If you take the foot tunnel to the other side and look back across to Friedrichshagen you'll see the brewery from whose chimney the red flag flew on January 30, 1933. From this point it's possible to follow the path through the woods around to the lakeshore *Gaststätten* at **Rübezahl** and **Müggelseeperle** (both of these can be reached on the *Weisse Flotte* boats). The Rübezahl *Gaststätte* is a real architectural eyesore, looking like it's been transplanted from Alexanderplatz, but you can eat well here (see Chapter Seven, *Drinking and Eating*). Just to the south, and a fairly untaxing walk away through the woods, is the **Müggelberge**, a gentle hill on top of which stands the **Müggelturm** observation tower with its café, bar, restaurant, and great view of the lake and woods around and about (this can also be reached directly from Köpenick on bus #27). Beware though: it gets very crowded at all times of the year—in summer people swarm here for sun and sailing, and in winter to ice skate.

At the east end of the Grosser Müggelsee the little town of **Rahnsdorf** can be reached by S-Bahn, or by tram #25 from Friedrichshagen. During the nineteenth century this was a fishing village, and the old core of the place is well-preserved in and around Dorfstrasse. Just off Fürstenwalder Damm, on the northern shore of the Grosser Müggelsee between Rahnsdorf and Friedrichshagen, there's a *FKK* (*Freikörperkultur*) nudist beach for hardy souls.

Grünau

A farther possible local destination is **Grünau** on the Dahme, just to the south of Köpenick. Tram #86 runs directly from Köpenick,and there are various S-Bahn connections. Grünau has a slightly sleepy atmosphere which is quite at odds with traditional images of East Berlin.

There isn't a great deal in terms of sights, but you could do worse than go for a walk along the quiet banks of the **Langer See**, as the Dahme is called beyond Grünau. The Langer See itself is a watersports center, and a beach of sorts lies just outside town. Tram #86 passes through the tranquil villa settlement of Karolinenhof to **Schmöckwitz**, which has been settled since prehistoric times. From there, you can take a bus to one of East Berlin's main campgrounds.

Karlshorst

If you take a walk through the streets of **Karlshorst** (S-Bahn from Alexanderplatz, change at Ostkreuz) in the Lichtenburg *Bezirk*, you're more likely to hear Russian spoken than German, as the area has in effect become East Berlin's Russian quarter. The Russians have been here since the end of the war when the unconditional surrender of the German armed forces was accepted on May 8, 1945.

A former Wehrmacht barracks now serves as the HQ of the Soviet garrison in East Berlin, and the streets of Karlshorst are full of Russian soldiers and their families who have taken over the local apartment blocks. There are shops where you can buy Russian food, books, newspapers and papirosi cigarettes (which have cardboard filters and will turn your lungs inside out). What place the Red Army will have in the united Germany of the 1990s remains to be seen; the old GDR government subsidized their presence here, but the prospect of the new Germany stumping up hard currency to support an occupying army seems improbable.

At the end of Fritz-Schmenkel-Strasse, the building where the German surrender was signed contains the **Berlin-Karlshorst Museum** (see "East Berlin's Museums"); it's run by the Soviet army and details the war from their point of view. Another esoteric local attraction is the **Trabrennbahn Karlshorst**, where from 3pm onwards on Wednesday, Saturday, and Sunday you can have a day at the races East Berlin-style for DM2. The racetrack is best reached via Hermann-Duncker-Strasse.

Treptow

The Soviet theme continues in **Treptow**, location of the huge and sobering **Sowjetisches Ehrenmal**, the Soviet war memorial in the **Treptower Park**. It commemorates the Soviet soldiers killed during the Battle of Berlin in April and May 1945 and is the burial place of five thousand men. Approaching via the Am Treptower park entrance, you pass first through a triumphal arch, then see a sculpture of a grieving mother; a quick right turn and you're suddenly face to face with a vast symbolic statue fashioned out of marble from Hitler's Chancellory. Over eleven meters high, it shows a stylized Russian soldier clutching a saved child and resting his sword on a shattered swastika. This isn't exactly a cheerful place, with busloads of Soviet tourists coming here to pay their respects to their war dead, but it's worth visiting just to appreciate the reasons behind why history unfolded the way it did in postwar Berlin. In January 1990 the monument was defaced, allegedly by neo-Nazis: but many East Berliners reckon that this was a put-up job, engineered by the still-communist government, or its supporters, hoping to use the traditional far-right bogeyman to rebuild support for the Party.

Most guided tours of the city include a visit to the memorial: otherwise take the S-Bahn from Treptower Park, or catch buses #47, #64, #65, #66 & #67.

Beyond the war memorial is an observatory and farther still are a couple of *Gaststätten*, *Zenner*, and *Plänterwald*. Behind these is the **Insel der Jugend**, an island in the Spree where there's a good view across to the Stralau peninsula. Here, at Alt Stralau 18, is one of the many former residences of Karl Marx during his student days. Beyond the Insel der Jugend are the *Plänterwald* woods where, in the optimistically-named **Kulturpark**, there's an amusement park with all the usual attractions of ferris wheel and carousels.

At the southeastern edge of Treptow is the **Gartenstadt Falkenberg** (best reached from Grünau S-Bahnhof), a model housing settlement designed by the architect Bruno Taut. These family houses can be found around the Akazienhof and on Bruno Taut Strasse: they were built for the workers of Berlin in 1913 and 1914, in response to the slum conditions of the city center tenements. A plaque at Akazienhof used to state, without irony: "Many of the founder members [of the settlement] were active opponents of war and fascism. Their ideals have become reality in the German Democratic Republic."

Pankow

Pankow, the northernmost of East Berlin's suburbs before the city gives way to open countryside, has a slightly different atmosphere to other East Berlin suburbs. This stems mainly from its erstwhile special status as home to so many *Parteibonzen* (Party bigwigs) of the old regime, and the location of the GDR's most prestigious government guest house, the seventeenth-century **Schloss Niederschönhausen**, where the more important state visitors are entertained. Up until the 1960s Pankow and Schloss Niederschonhausen were perceived in the West as being the real centers of power in the GDR, the Schloss being the official residence to the GDR's first president, Wilhelm Pieck, and then to SED General Secretary Walter Ulbricht, the man who took the decision to build the Wall.

These days the business of governing the GDR is carried out from the Palast der Republik in the city center, but Schloss Niederschönhausen and its extensive grounds are still out of bounds to the public. However, you can visit the **Bürgerpark**, a one-time private park with an impressive entrance portal symbolic of nineteenth-century Pankow's status as a villa quarter for Berlin's more well-to-do citizens. To the north of the Bürgerpark is the **Volkspark Schönholzer Heide**, in whose northwestern corner there's a Soviet cemetery which contains the remains of 13,200 soldiers in dozens of communal graves.

To reach Pankow, tram #49 from Hackescher Markt clatters up through the streets of Prenzlauer Berg, or for something slightly more atmospheric, catch the S-Bahn from Schönhauser Allee. On this latter option the train passes through what used to be the so-called "*Todesstraeife*" or "Death Strip", which separated East Berliners from the Wall proper. Until November 9, 1989, this was, for many East Germans, the closest they were ever likely to come to the West.

Weissensee

Weissensee lies directly to the northeast of Prenzlauer Berg, but could hardly be more different in character—a predominantly middle-class area with an almost village-like atmosphere. Take tram #23 or #28 from Hackescher Markt. The main attraction is the park which contains the **Weisser See** itself, the lake which gives the district its name. You can rent boats on the lake (which features some un-spectacular fountains) and there's an open-air stage and a *Gaststätte* nearby. There's also an open-air swimming pool which is fed by an underground spring. If you come here looking for excitement you'll be disappointed, but in terms of atmosphere Weissensee shows another side of East Berlin, and hints at the open countryside only a few kilometers away. To the north of the park is the **Radrennbahn Weissensee**, an open-air cycle track where rock concerts are occasionally held.

Ten minutes south of Klement-Gottwald-Allee, by foot, at the end of Herbert-Baum-Strasse, is the **Jüdischer Friedhof Weissensee**, a large Jewish cemetery which was opened in 1880. Just beyond the right-hand entrance portal is a memorial to the six million Jews who died in the Holocaust. Tablets set in a circle bear the names of all the large concentration camps, and gravestones commemorate non-Jewish Berliners murdered by the Nazis for opposition activity. Like many memorials to the war years in the city, it's a poignant monument to the horrors that occurred, and succeeds in being less inflated and militaristic than many others.

EAST BERLIN'S MUSEUMS

East Berlin is not short of **museums**—it has around forty, of all descriptions, and of varying levels of interest. After the division of Berlin the East inherited the best of what was left of the pre-war collections and the **Museuminsel** in the city center holds the most prestigious ones (see "The Museum Island," p.142). But most of the remaining museums are equally interesting in different ways. The fixed **admission charge** for nearly all museums is DM1, DM0.50 for students with an ISIC card—though you can expect this to rise sharply in the near future. Most museums in the East are **closed on Monday**: bear in mind also that many tend to close off whole sections indefinitely for vaguely defined "technical reasons"—usually slow-moving restoration.

Museum Berliner Arbeiter Leben um 1900
Husemannstr. 12 , 1058 (Prenzlauer Berg). Tues, Thurs & Sat 11am–6pm, Wed 10am–8pm, closed Monday. U-Bahn Dmitroffstrasse; buses #4 & #13.

Housed in a restored tenement building in a street which has been turned into a kind of "living museum," this concentrates on the living conditions of Berlin's working class population around the turn of the century which, you might be tempted to conclude after a stroll through the streets of Prenzlauer Berg, haven't changed much since. There's an interesting (really) section on the allotments (publicly rented gardens) which Berliners lived off, and occasionally in, during the lean 1920s, and info about Nazi attacks on the workers' movement during the 1920s and 1930s.

Berlin-Karlshorst Museum

Fritz-Schmenkel-Strasse, 1157 (Karlshorst). Tues–Fri 9am–1pm & 3–6pm, Sat 9am–2pm, Sun 9am–4pm; closed last Sat in month.

Also known as the **Kapitulationsmuseum** and run by the Soviet army (which has a large barracks nearby), this museum commemorating the day the Nazis capitulated is appropriately housed in the heart of East Berlin's Russian quarter. Contained in the building where the *Wehrmacht* surrendered unconditionally to the Soviet army on May 8, 1945, the museum features fourteen rooms of vivid battlefield recreations and dioramas, telling the story of World War II from the Soviet point of view.

Brecht Haus

Chausseestr. 125, 1040. Tue, Wed & Fri 10am–noon, Thur 10am–noon & 5–7pm, Sat 9:30–11:30am & 12:30–2pm. S-Bahn Fridrichstrasse; buses #57 & #59.

In 1949 Brecht moved back from the United States to his native Germany: this house was his last home and workplace, and today contains the Bertolt Brecht archive, with guided tours through the great man's work and living rooms every half-hour. Brecht's wife and collaborator, Helene Weigel, lived here until her death in 1971, and a small collection of artifacts commemorate her life.

Museum für Deutsche Geschichte

Unter den Linden 2, 1086. Mon–Thur 9am–6pm, Sat & Sun 10am–5pm. S-Bahn Friedrichstrasse or Marx-Engels-Platz; bus #57.

Although for non-German speakers it can be a bit impenetrable, most of this is adequately interesting, particularly the later sections which deal with aspects of German history like the inter-war worker's movement and communist-inspired resistance to the Nazis. The GDR section was closed after the *Wende*, and it remains to be seen how recent history will be re-interpreted.

Ephraim-Palais

Am Mühlendamm, 1020 (junction of Mühlendamm with Poststrasse). Mon 10am–4pm, Tues & Sun 10am–5pm, Wed & Sat 10am–6pm. U- and S-Bahn Alexanderplatz; buses #9, #32, #57, #78 & #79.

This rebuilt Rococo palace houses exhibits detailing the growth of Berlin from "Electoral residence to bourgeois great city of the nineteenth century," and numerous maps and pictures supply a good impression of how the place looked in pre-war, pre-Wall days. There's a selection of glass and silverware, and you have to wear giant overshoes to protect the floor as you admire it all.

Friseur Museum

Husemannstr. 8, 1058 (Prenzlauer Berg). U-Bahn Dmitroffstrasse; trams #4 & #13.

The famous hairdressing museum, and eminently interesting it is too. The proprietor (it's a private museum) is of the same opinion, and will give you a guided tour of his domain—which includes exhibits on everything to do with hairdressing from prehistory to date. So overwhelming is his enthusiasm that you may find it difficult to escape. The opening hours are a little erratic: knock on the door, and if there's anyone around you'll be able to take a look.

Handwerkmuseum

Am Mühlendamm 5, 1020 (junction of Mühlendamm with Poststrasse). Mon 10am–5pm, Tues & Wed 9am–5pm, Sat & Sun 10am–6pm. U- and S-Bahn Alexanderplatz & U-Bahn Spittelmarkt; buses #9, #32, #57, #78 & #79.

A more entertaining than average look at the various trades of old Berlin.

Hugenottenmuseum

Französische Dom, Platz der Akademie, 1080. Mon–Fri 10am–5pm. U-Bahn Hausvogteiplatz.

On the first floor of the Dom, this museum details the flight of the Huguenots from France after the Edict of Nantes and the subsequent settling of 20,000 Huguenots in Berlin. There's also a section on the history of the Dom itself.

Knoblauchhaus

Poststr. 4, 1020. Wed & Sat 10am–6pm, Thurs & Sun 10am–5pm, Fri 10am–4pm. U- and S-Bahn Alexanderplatz & U-Bahn Spittelmarkt; buses #9, #32, #57, #78 & #79.

A collection of items relating to the eighteenth-century German Enlightenment. Particular attention is paid to the lives and works of Gotthold Ephraim Lessing (1729–1781), the poet and dramatist (author of the play *Minna von Barnhelm*, often called the first German comedy), Moses Mendelssohn (1729–1786), the Jewish philosopher, and Christoph Friedrich Nicolai (1773–1811). Lessing and Mendelssohn were great friends and played a leading role in the shaping of eighteenth-century German drama and thought. After 1933, Lessing, already dead for more than 150 years, achieved the distinction of having his work banned by the Nazis.

Kunstgewerbemuseum

Köpenicker Schloss, 1170 (Köpenick). Wed–Sat 9am–5pm, Sun 10am–6pm. Tram #84, #86 or bus #27 from S-Bahnhof Köpenick.

An applied art museum with an extensive selection of porcelain, glass, textiles, leather, jewelry, tin, iron, gold, and silver work from the Middle Ages through to the present day. The treasury has an opulent hoard of gold and silver, highpoint of which is the eleventh-century *Giselaschmuck*. Also shinily impressive is the *Berliner Silberbuffet*, a set of silver tableware made for the Brandenburg prince who was to become King Friedrich I of Prussia. There's a disappointingly small *Jugendstil* section, and a collection of contemporary GDR art.

Märkisches Museum

Am Köllnischen Park, 1020. Wed & Sun 9am–6pm, Thurs & Sat 9am–5pm, Fri 9pm–4pm. U-Bahn Märkisches Museum or S-Bahn Jannowitzbrücke.

Covering the history of Berlin and the Mark Brandenburg, the oldest exhibit here is the seventh century BC Berlin Biersdorf deer mask, which is the earliest relic of human settlement in the area. There's a lot of material on the development of Berlin and its twin Cölln from 1307, through to nineteenth-century industrialization and the revolution of 1848. The growth of arts and handicrafts is also covered, with a special section on the theater. Particularly interesting is the display on Heinrich Zille (1858–1929), a Berlin artist who produced critical/satirical drawings of Berlin life.

Naturkunde Museum

Invalidenstr. 43, 1040. Tues–Sun 9:30am–5pm. Bus #57.

Unless you're a natural history enthusiast this collection of rocks, bones, and stuffed animals is probably not worth going out of the way for—there's nothing here you won't find in any other natural history museum.

Nikolaikirche

Nikolaikirchplatz, 1020. Sun & Mon 10am–5pm, Thurs & Sat 10am–6pm, Fri 10am–4pm. U- and S-Bahn Alexanderplatz & U-Bahn Spittelmarkt; buses #9, #32, #57, #78 & #79.

Located in the old Nikolaikirche in the Nikolaiviertel, this is a permanent exhibition about the development of Berlin and Cölln, which, with maps and models, gives a good overview of how the basis of modern Berlin emerged from what were little more than riverside villages.

Otto-Nagel-Haus

Märkisches Ufer 16–18, 1020. Sun, Mon, Tues & Thurs 10am–6pm, Wed 10am–8pm. U-Bahn Märkisches Museum or S-Bahn Jannowitzbrücke.

According to the official guide, this is a collection of proletarian revolutionary and anti-fascist art based around the work of Otto Nagel (1894–1967). Nagel, a prominent figure in the art world of inter-war Berlin, was jailed by the Nazis in 1936, and this collection of (relatively) modern art doesn't disgrace him. His own pictures are gloomy indictments of the hardship of life for the masses in Weimar Berlin, and share the gallery with work by the like of Ernst Barlach, Käthe Kollwitz, Otto Dix, Kurt Querner, and Konrad Felixmüller. Most of the pictures are examples of sound, upright revolutionary art but no less enjoyable for all that; on the other hand, many of them are awful.

Postmuseum der DDR

Junction of Leipzigerstrasse and Mauerstrasse, 1056. Tues–Fri 10am–5pm. U-Bahn Klosterstrasse; buses #32, #57 & #79.

If you're a philatelist then this is a must; if not you'll probably only want to drop in if you get caught in a rainstorm. Opened in 1872 and, by the looks of things, pretty much unchanged since.

Robert Koch Haus

Clara-Zetkin-Str. 96, 1080 (part of the Humboldt University). Wed 9am–6pm or by prior arrangement. S-Bahn Friedrichstrasse.

All about the life and work of Robert Koch, the founder of experimental bacteriology. You have been warned.

Schinkel Museum
Am Werderschen Markt, 1020. Times vary.

Architect Karl Friedrich Schinkel gave nineteenth-century Berlin its distinctive Neoclassical stamp, and this record of his life and works is housed in the Friedrichswerdersche Kirche, one of his own buildings. A permanent exhibition in the church's upper gallery gives a full rundown of Schinkel's achievements, in the context of the times.

CHAPTER SEVEN

DRINKING AND EATING

G eographically, there are two main clusters of places to **drink and eat** in East Berlin: the city center and Prenzlauer Berg. Most of the bars, cafés, and restaurants listed below are in these two areas. Bars are often a better bet than restaurants for food, both economically and gastronomically, and the best of everything tends to be in Prenzlauer Berg. Before monetary union took place on July 2, 1990, East Berlin's restaurants and bars were always considerably cheaper than those of the West: however, since it seems certain that prices will be in a state of flux for some time, we've avoided quoting prices here. But as a rule of thumb, expect to spend between DM10 and DM20 for a meal in a city centre restaurant, DM8–15 elsewhere: a beer will cost you roughly the same as in the West. Tipping (about 10 percent) is expected, and if you're a vegetarian then you'd better bring your own food—East Berlin is a carnivorous city. A number of new bars and restaurants have opened recently but the present precarious economic climate means that some of them may have gone under by the time you arrive (this goes for some of the more established places too).

DRINKING

While East Berlin doesn't yet have the variety of drinking spots of its western neighbor, it's more than possible to have an enjoyable night out here—whether in one of the innumerable bars, or the more restrained cafés. The following listings detail both, in the center and the suburbs.

> **For a glossary of German food and drink terms, see p.89 and pp.98–100**

Bars

There are basically two kinds of **bar** in East Berlin: the traditional German *Kneipe*, where the main business is beer drinking, and the *Speisegaststätte* where you can usually have a full sit-down meal. Both are generally open from late morning to around midnight and offer a cheap and unpretentious environment in which to eat and/or drink. Since the currency reform, however, prices have fluctuated and in some city center establishments they have been jacked up considerably. Most places are fairly civilized, although some get a bit wild—avoid the ones where there are people lying in the street outside. Be warned also that perhaps even more than in the west, bars out of the center can be all-male meeting places and intimidating—though seldom dangerous—for unaccompanied women.

The Center

Zur alten Münze, Memhardstr. 3, 1020. A would-be old Berlin interior which doesn't quite come off, attached to one of the modern shopping center developments near Alexanderplatz. Try the *Harzer Käse* if you can handle it—a real German culinary experience involving over-ripe cheese and drippings of fat.

Die Bärenschänke, Friedrichstr. 124, 1040. This cheap *Speisegaststätte* makes a good starting (or ending) point for a night of bar-hopping. It's usually full of workers letting off steam at the end of the day and tourists heading for nearby Bahnhof Friedrichstrasse. Closed every second Monday in the month.

Zum Fernfahrer, Wallstr. 68, 1020. Not a bad little place, slightly off the beaten track, near the Märkisches Ufer.

Gambrinus, Linienstr. 134, 1040. Very typical and very cheap, this one has succumbed to the craze for pseudo-old Berlin interiors, but remains popular with its working-class clientele.

Gontard Stube, Platz der Akademie, 1080. A small bar and *Imbiss* in the shadow of the Französischer Dom.

Zur Letzten Instanz, Waisenstr. 14–16, 1020. Near the old city wall this is one of the oldest and best city bars, the kind of place where you end up getting into heated political discussions with complete strangers. It's popular with people from the nearby youth arts and drama center. Wine upstairs, beer downstairs, and in summer there's a beer garden.

Matthias Keller, Karl-Marx-Allee 91, 1020. In the same building as the *Haus Budapest* restaurant, this purports to be a Hungarian wine cellar. The vault-like decor reflects this, but everything gets a bit kitsch in the evening when the gypsy band strikes up. The staff aren't renowned for their politeness but you can drown your sorrows with *palinka*, a fiery Hungarian spirit.

Zum Nussbaum, Propstrasse/Am Nussbaum, 1020. In the heart of the Nikolaiviertel, overshadowed by the redbrick Nikolaikirche, this is an exact replica of a pre-war pub that was destroyed in a war-time air raid. It verges on the expensive and flirts dangerously with kitsch, but the garden in the front is a good place to drink yourself under the table in summer.

Zum Paddenwirt, Nikolaikirchplatz 6, 1020. Another pseudo-old Berlin *Speisegaststätte* but not too bad. On Sunday morning you can enjoy the old German tradition of *Frühschoppen*—Sunday morning drinking, while indulging in a game of cards or dice.

Probierstube, Sophienstrasse 11, 1020. On a recently restored street, which has some fine nineteenth-century facades, this is East Berlin's only tasting house. It's privately owned and you can try out the wines and spirits with the option of buying more of the same to take home. There's a good range of East European wines, spirits, and champagnes.

Zur Rippe, Poststrasse/Mühlendamm, 1020. Another Nikolaiviertel *Speisegaststätte* in old Berlin style.

Tante Olga, Linienstr. 71, 1054. An old Berlin pub that's for real. A backstreet spit 'n' sawdust establishment not much bigger than someone's living room with just a few sit-down tables and a *Stehtisch*, a circular counter around which you can stand. The cheapest beer in town.

Wernersgrünerbierstuben, Karl-Liebknecht-Strasse 11, 1020. A city center cellar *Speisegaststätte* opposite the TV tower. A lot of locals come here but it's equally popular with tourists who like the rustic decor and cheap food and beer. For minimal outlay you should be able to shock a rumbling stomach into submission. No smoking from 11am–3pm.

The Suburbs

Alt Berliner Bierstube, Saarbrückerstr. 18, 1055. A gay pub, although not exclusively so, as by day it's often invaded by busloads of Polish and Hungarian tourists. At night there's a cruising atmosphere in the front bar. Usually open until 2am but closed every fourth Monday of the month.

Zum Anker, Greifenhagenerstrasse/Sredzkistrasse, 1058. A run-of-the-mill Prenzlauer Berg place with middle of the range prices. There's a disco here at weekends (see "Discos and Clubs" in Chapter Eight, *Music and Nightlife*).

Budike Nr 15, Stargarderstrasse/Sredzkistrasse, 1058. Ersatz old Berlin bar, but recommended nevertheless. Turn-of-the-century decor with up-to-date prices.

Gambrinus, Johannes-R.-Becher-Str. 16, 1100 (Pankow). Unpretentious and cheap with a summer terrace. No smoking from 11am–2pm. Closed on week-ends, serves food.

Helmholtzklause, Schliemannstrasse/Lettestrasse, 1058. A lively, not to say rowdy, clientele make this otherwise slightly spartan bar in the heart of Prenzlauer Berg worth checking out. *Skat* tournaments are an occasional attraction.

Zur Hutte, Berlinerstr. 116, 1100 (Pankow). An inexpensive *Speisegaststätte* with a stomach-churning *Schlachteplatte* (selection of cured meat and sausage) on the menu.

Kastanien Eck, Kastanienallee/Oderbergerstrasse, 1058. Popularly known as the *Trummerkutte*, this is the kind of place where there are people stand-ing outside waiting to get in at 7am.

Am Markt, Johannes-R.-Becher-Strasse 14, 1100 (Pankow). A fine collection of cacti in the window make this *Eintopfstube* stand out; inside, those German staples, stew and potato soup, are served up.

Metzer Eck, Metzer Str. 33, 1055. Founded in 1913, *Metzer Eck* is popular with the Prenzlauer Berg *Szene* crowd. It's also a favorite with actors (includ-ing some from West Germany) whose signed photos adorn the walls.

Müggelseeklause, Müggelsee Damm/Bruno-Wille-Strasse, 1162 (Friedrichshagen). A stone's throw from the Grosser Müggelsee lake, and with a bit of old Berlin panache. Art exhibitions are put on here too. Closed Monday.

Offenbachstuben, Senefelderstrasse/Stubbenkammerstrasse, 1058. Highly recommended for both food and drink, a young, eclectic crowd makes this one of the best places to head for in Prenzlauer Berg. The decor has a theatri-cal theme and the intimate seating niches are great for drunken late-night conversation. Also popular with the gay crowd. Closed Sunday and Monday.

Panke Eck, Wolfshagenerstrasse/Eintrachtsstrsasse, 1100 (Pankow). An atmospheric little drinking place down a turn-of-the-century side street. It's frequented by the local arty/intellectual crowd and the interior was designed by a Pankow artist. This is a good place to strike up a conversation with people who like to talk, and, more importantly, who actually have something to say.

Zur Pappel, Pappelallee/Raumerstrasse, 1058. A pretty basic Prenzlauer Berg bar with a slightly *Jugendstil* feel to it. Popular with lunchtime drinking workers during the day and a younger crowd at night.

Restauration 1900, Husemannstrasse/Wörtherstrasse, 1058. A well-known artists' hangout (although some would suggest that it's for people who prefer talking about it to actually doing it), this rather pricey *Speisegaststätte* is part of the Husemannstrasse restoration scheme. Food served.

Zur Sonne, Greifenhagenerstrasse/Stargarderstrasse, 1058. A real working-class bar, diagonally opposite *Zum Anker* and popular with East Berlin's *Knastis*—ex-cons instantly recognizable by their self-inflicted tattoos. Very male, rough, and ready but cheap and atmospheric in a sleazy sort of way.

Zur Traube, Senefelderstrasse/Raumerstrasse, 1058. A smoky old dive which has escaped renovation and prettification.

Cafés

In East Berlin people tend to go to bars to drink beer, eat, and then drink more beer; they meet in **cafés** to talk and exchange ideas. At the moment the cafés seem to be the real focal point of Berlin social and cultural life—and for that reason you should make a point of visiting at least one. They are good places to get to know people, a process which is made easier by the fact that most of them get very crowded and you're likely to find yourself sharing a table, which makes conversation almost inevitable.

UNOFFICIAL CAFÉS

Since the opening up of East Berlin a number of unofficial cafés, usually based around squats or occupied buildings, have made a dramatic appearance on the scene. Although not officially sanctioned they are tolerated and could be about to form the basis for an unprecedented nightlife explosion. At the time of writing details are hazy and there's no guarantee of longevity, but the following should provide you with something to go on. **Café Zapata** in Oranienburgerstrasse is an anarchic café/gallery housed in a derelict warehouse. **Café Westphal** on Kollwitzplatz in Prenzlauer Berg may have a little more staying power than some of the others, with its recently refurbished interior. Nearby is **Endstation**, which stays open all night and retains a raw edge, more in keeping with the spirit of the area. Other names to look out for include **Klub Chaos**, **ZK**, **Eimer**, and **KVU**. Ask around the cafés for details of others.

The Center

Alt Berliner Conditorei, Neue Schönhauser Strasse/Weinmeisterstrasse, 1020. Old in name only, this modern glass-fronted café-patisserie has a mouth-watering range of cakes which are served with mountains of whipped cream.

Bar Espresso Vis-a-vis, Friedrichstr. 130, 1040. Don't be put off by the dreadful mid-1970s decor, this is actually one of the city's better cafés, permanently packed with students from the nearby Humboldt University. Close to Bahnhof Friedrichstrasse.

Café Arkade, Französische Strasse (opposite the Platz der Akademie), 1080. An affluent and arty bunch comes here, drawn by the sinfully good ice cream and coffee specialties. Snack-type dishes are available too.

Café Flair, Am Marstall, 1020. This expensive café on the edge of the Nikolaiviertel is usually full of tourists and rich East Berliners and has the usual range of coffee specialties, ice creams, and mixed drinks.

Café Friedericke, Friedrichstrasse/Claire-Waldorff-Strasse, 1040. A slightly pricey new café not far from Bahnhof Friedrichstrasse.

Café Jugendmode, Karl-Marx-Allee 77–85, 1020. Newly opened and very stylish—the designer disease hits East Berlin. It's part of the *Berliner Jugendmode* store and looks set to become a major rendezvous for East Berlin's hip young things.

Café im Palais, Poststrasse 16, 1020. Part of the Ephraim-Palais Museum this café has a very pre-war feel (pre-World War I that is) and is full of extremely well-spoken and correct ladies who come here for gossip and nostalgia over *Kaffee und Kuchen*, to the strains of an ancient violin and piano duo.

Café 130 Radke, Chauseestr. 130, 1040. Another favorite student hangout, with an incredible selection of ice cream (made on the premises) and milk shakes—try their strawberry milk shake with egg liqueur. Closed every first Monday in the month.

Café Spreeblick, Spreeufer, 1020. A typical Nikolaiviertel café where you can sit outside in summer and gaze across the murky waters of the Spree.

Chez Felix, Schiffbauerdamm, 1040. an expensive little place in the shadow of Bahnhof Friedrichstrasse, which seems to be patronized mainly by tourists and well-heeled East Berliners.

Kaffeestube, Poststrasse, 1020. A pricey little Nikolaiviertel café which tries a little too hard to evoke the atmosphere of a pre-war coffee house.

Kisch Kaffee, Unter den Linden 60, 1080. Enjoying something of a boom at the moment thanks to the proximity of the Brandenburg Gate border crossing, which makes it the West German tourists' favorite.

MME Bar, Karl-Marx-Allee 35, 1020. An ice-cream parlor with a slightly retro atmosphere. Good ice cream and milk shakes.

Sophieneck, Grosse Hamburgerstrasse/Sophienstrasse, 1040. At the end of the recently renovated Sophienstrasse this one attracts both the local arty/trendy contingent and the elderly *Kaffee und Kuchen* crowd. There's a beer garden at the back in summer.

Tutti Frutti, Spandauerstr. 4, 1020. The city's most infamous *Schickey Mickey* (money, nice clothes, and minds untroubled by thought) joint, full of disco kids showing off their gear amid the tacky decor (blurred photos of people on U-Bahn escalators).

The Suburbs

Café Binz, Binzstrasse/Berlinerstrasse, 1100 (Pankow). A small, expensive café with a dance floor (see "Discos and Clubs" in Chapter Eight).

Café Ecke Schönhauser, Schönhauser Allee/Kastanienallee, 1058. A gayish café just off Prenzlauer Berg's main thoroughfare. Worth checking out.

Café Flair, Stargarderstr. 72, 1058. Also known as *Café Lila*, this is one of the best in the city, owned by an eccentric, music-loving couple who have made a valiant attempt to recreate a nineteenth-century Parisian café in the heart of Prenzlauer Berg. This is the original *Café Flair*—beware of expensive imitations in the Nikolaiviertel.

Café Lolott, Schönhauser Allee, 1058. An older and less arty crowd than most Prenzlauer Berg places, despite the management's attempts to spice things up with pseudo-*Jugendstil* posters of naked lovelies cavorting with panthers (see also "Discos and Clubs" in Chapter Eight).

Café Lotos, Schönhauser Allee 45, 1058. The decor would have been very up-to- date in 1975 but it somehow suits the *Schickey Mickey* crowd. Expensive by East Berlin standards.

Café Milchbar zur Post, Berlinerstr. 13, 1100 (Pankow). A typical East Berlin café (spartan and crowded) with a good selection of cholesterol-rich cakes, which are very tasty indeed.

Café Mozaik, Stubenkammerstrasse/Prenzlauer Allee, 1058. An East Berlin *Szene* café and erstwhile *Ausreisler* (people who applied to emigrate to the West pre-*Wende*) hangout. Food served. Closed every third Monday.

Café Papillon, Greifenhagernerstr. 16, 1058. Another East Berlin "must," with a great atmosphere and a young crowd. There's a garden at the back which is part of a tenement *Hinterhof* (courtyard). Closed Friday.

Eistüte, Wörtherstrasse/Husemannstrasse, 1058. A cheap-and-cheerful ice-cream parlor which is part of the Husemannstrasse development.

Inseraten, Schönhauser Allee 58, 1058. Decor here is early Halloween in the extreme but otherwise not a bad little café. Also serves as a kind of East Berlin "swap 'n shop"—on the bar there's a book containing small ads covering everything from old clothes to personals.

Kaffeestube, Husemannstrasse, 1058. Replica old Berlin café, complete with marble-topped tables and *Jugendstil* wall hangings for *fin-de-siècle* atmosphere. Reasonably priced and, for local color, the customers sometimes include liveried employees from the nearby horse and carriage stables.

Kleines Café, Johannes-R.-Becher-Str. 23, 1100 (Pankow). Expensive, and the main hangout for Pankow's disco kids with a teeny disco called "Top Secret" in the evenings.

Leyer's Laden, Bölschestr. 101, 1162 (Friedrichshagen). A second-hand shop and café combined. If you can't pick up anything interesting in the shop at the front you can always have *Kaffee und Kuchen* at the back.

Mokkastube, Berlinerstrasse/Elsa-Brandström-Strasse, 1100 (Pankow). Not too expensive, but it gets crowded because it's at the intersection of Pankow's main public transit routes.

Wiener Café, Schönhauser Allee 68, 1058. Formerly the *Café Schröder* this one attempts to recreate the atmosphere of old Vienna for its arty clientele.

EATING

In East Berlin you can eat cheaply and you can eat well—and occasionally you can do both. But on the whole the city's cuisine tends to revolve around a basic steak and fries theme, particularly in the bland and expensive city center hotel restaurants. At the very bottom of the price scale are the ubiquitous *Imbiss* and *Grilletta* stands where you can buy a *Bockwurst* and roll with mustard or a *Grilletta*, East Berlin's answer to the hamburger. Some stands also sell a kind of hot dog affair called *Ketwurst*, or pancakes with sweet fillings called *Pallatschinken*. Most stands sell sodas and beer.

Also worth investigating are the *Goldbroiler* chain of restaurants which sell anything remotely connected with chicken. The chicken is sold by weight and you can get alcoholic drinks and sodas too. There are also plenty of cafeteria-style places where you can eat solid if basic meals for a minimum outlay. It's likely that western fast food chains will be setting up shop soon, probably supplanting home-grown concerns.

Restaurants

If you're after something substantial in more salubrious surroundings, then it's worth remembering that East Berlin **restaurants** can get very crowded—it's advisable to try and make a reservation beforehand, particularly in the smaller places outside the city center. Where booking is advisable, the listing includes the phone number.

The choice of food is pretty much standard—overdone meats and underdone fish—and, at the moment, a meal out can be a pretty drab affair when compared to eating in the west. However there are exceptions, and in the places listed below you have a good chance of avoiding the city's endemic lack of culinary verve. Check the food glossaries in Chapter Four if you're unsure of your way around the menu.

The Center

Am Marstall, Marx-Engels-Forum, 1020. An expensive tourist restaurant, and only worth it if you have money to burn.

Ephraim Palais, Poststr. 16, 1020 (☎2171 3164). A plush and pricey restaurant overlooking the Spree. Not cheap, but better than the big tourist hotels.

Ermeler Haus, Am Märkischen Ufer 10, 1020 (☎275 5113/275 5125). Inside this Spree-side building check out the *Raabediele*, an unpretentious basement restaurant where you can get well-priced traditional German dishes in slightly folksy surroundings, and where there are usually a few tables free.

Fondue, Poststr. 16, 1020 (☎2171 3296). Smart fondue restaurant in the same building as the Ephraim Palais restaurant. Fondue for four people by prior arrangement.

Gastmahl des Meeres, Spandauerstr. 4, 1020. A city center fish restaurant which tends to get crowded with tourists. It makes a change from the usual steak and fries formula with eels in aspic and carp promised on the menu, although these tend to be subject to availability and you're more likely to end up with *Kabeljau*—cod.

Gerichtslaube, Poststr. 28, 1020. Three possibilities in this reconstruction of Berlin's medieval courthouse; the *Bierschänke* and *Weinschänke* are basically spruced up tourist restaurants with inflated prices. The food in both is all right, although not exactly imaginative. The *Weinschänke* has an extensive wine list with everything from low-grade Algerian engine oil to vintage French (the latter at a price of course). Best value for money is the pizzeria above these two which does a passable, if slightly esoteric, interpretation of pizza.

Haus Budapest Berlin, Karl-Marx-Allee 91, 1020. In this supposedly Hungarian restaurant most of the dishes are German, but with paprika. It's quite classy in an old-fashioned sort of way and not too pricey.

Hospiz Friedrichstrasse, Albrechtstrasse/Marienstrasse, 1040. Good staple German fare, reasonably priced.

Keller Restaurant Brecht Haus, Chauseestrasse 125 (☎282 3848), 1040. This atmospheric cellar restaurant, decorated with Brecht memorabilia, is in the basement of Brecht's old house. It's one of the few good ones in the area, and gets crowded—book if at all possible.

Moscau, Karl-Marx-Allee (☎279 4052). Don't be put off by this disgustingly designed building, as the food, ambience, and the nimble fingers of the pianist more than make up for it. Listen to the day's recommendations; the chicken Kiev is good.

Nationalitätengaststätte Prag, Leipzigerstr. 49, 1080. A Czech specialty restaurant which pays lip service to the idea of ethnic cuisine.

Nationalitätengaststätte Sofia, Leipzigerstr. 46, 1080. An ugly, nominally Bulgarian, restaurant where you may well be "entertained" by a dire Bulgar band. Also a fast-food bar which isn't too terrible.

Neubrandenburger Hof, Wilhelm-Pieck-Strasse/Borsigstrasse, 1040. Good food, good value for money and easily reached from the Bahnhof Friedrichstrasse area. One of the few restaurants in central Berlin deserving an unqualified recommendation. Specialty of the house is Mecklenburg cuisine; try *Gefüllte Schweinerippen mit Apfelrotkohl und Kartoffelklösse*— stuffed pork chops with red cabbage and potato dumplings.

Peking Restaurant, Friedrichstr. 58, 1080 (☎200415). East Berlin's only Chinese restaurant complete with tacky decor and a smallish, pricey menu aimed mainly at western tourists. Reservations necessary in the evening.

Ratskeller, in the Berliner Rathaus, 1020. The food isn't bad and the prices aren't too high, although it does get crowded.

Restaurant Ganymed, Schiffbauerdamm 5, 1040. An opulent interior in which crisply uniformed waiters attend subserviently to the needs of Allied officers who occasionally have regimental dinners here, in an example of the bizarre interchange between East and West that goes on under the four power agreement.

Restaurant Wolga, Haus der sowjetischen Wissenschaft und Kultur, Friedrichstrasse/Otto-Nuschke-Strasse, 1080. A Russian specialty restaurant but a samovar by way of decoration seems to be about as Russian as it gets, despite a much-vaunted Soviet master-chef. There's also a bistro which sells snack bar variations on the same pseudo-Russian theme.

Turmstuben, Französischer Dom, Platz der Akademie, 1080 (☎229 3463). In the tower of the Französischer Dom this classy restaurant is the flagship of the new-look East Berlin the authorities are trying to create. Book if possible; it can get crowded in the evenings. Go while you can since it will doubtless become impossibly expensive in the not too distant future.

The Suburbs

Chez Danny, Langhansstr. 55, 1120 (Weissensee; ☎365 0959). Pseudo-French place but not bad for all that (apart from the dreadful piped music). Kangaroo tail soup makes an appearence on the menu.

Die Spindel, Bölschestr. 59, 1162 (Friedrichshagen; ☎645 2937). In an old two-floor building, dating back to the foundation of Friedrichshagen, this restaurant has a good and imaginative menu including Chinese dishes at prices which verge on the expensive.

Gaststätte Rübezahl, Grosser Müggelsee, 1170. A big lakeside restaurant with good, typically German food.

Krusta Stube, Stargarderstr. 3, 1058. Prenzlauer Berg's only full-scale pizza house, although the pizzas might raise a few eyebrows in Italy. No smoking.

Park Idyll, Schulstr. 27, 1100 (Pankow). Claims to be a Swiss and farmhouse specialty restaurant, and for once this doesn't mean the usual range of German dishes with fancy names.

Pfeffermühle, Gaudystr. 6, 1058. Everything comes heavily sprinkled with pepper here (the name means "Pepper Mill").One of the most popular in Prenzlauer Berg, so try and book a table.

Ratskeller Köpenick, Alt Köpenick (Köpenick). Always a handy standby for decent cheap food.

Zum Maulbeerbaum, Bölschestr. 120, 1162 (Friedrichshagen; ☎645 8130). An atmospheric restaurant with a good range of traditional German cuisine.

Ratskeller Pankow, Johannes-R.-Becher-Strasse, 1100. Reasonably priced, and with food a cut above the average Ratskeller.

Restaurant Aphrodite, Schönhauser Allee 61, 1058. A good restaurant with a vaguely Mediterranean accent. Not over expensive, closed Sunday.

Restaurant Rosengarten, Ernst-Thälmann-Park, 1055. More interesting from a sociological than a culinary point of view, this restaurant is patronized by the well-to-do inhabitants of the showpiece Ernst-Thälmann-Park development—the city's yuppies if you like. Closed first Thursday of the month.

Stilbruch, Bahnhofstr. 1, 1123 (Karow; ☎249 0066). It's worth making the long and convoluted S-Bahn journey out to the suburbs to visit this privately-owned place. There's a good, if slightly pricey, restaurant, and a café-patisserie. It stays open all night and there's a disco in the evening.

Speiserestaurant Theater Klause, Rosa-Luxemburg-Str. 39, 1020. Opposite the Volksbühne theater, this great big barn of a place is popular with the theatrical crowd despite its station waiting room decor.

Venezia, Schönhauser Allee/Gleimstrasse, 1058. A cheap fast-food joint. Haute-cuisine it ain't, but you can eat your fill here for next to nothing.

Zum Wildschutz, Greifswalder Str. 208, 1055. Reasonably priced game dishes. Closed Monday.

CHAPTER EIGHT

MUSIC AND NIGHTLIFE

M usically, there's a lot happening in East Berlin, from doomy electronic experimentation and rap to classical concerts. As ever, the *Reisebüro* on Alexanderplatz has details of mainstream concerts, and can book tickets for the theater, too. East Berlin's **nightlife** takes some finding, and unless you know where to go you're likely to come away with the impression that this city shuts down at 11pm. Avoid the city center tourist hotel discos, which serve mainly as pick-up joints bringing prostitutes into contact with rich foreigners, and be prepared to voyage into the suburbs for more offbeat attractions.

Discos and Clubs

Of the city's **discos**, a few in Prenzlauer Berg and Pankow are just about bearable, with taped western chart music and lots of polite boys and girls trying to pick each other up. Most of these have dress restrictions, so try and avoid ripped jeans and battered leather jackets. However, if you do encounter any problems in this department, letting slip that you're a tourist often has a magical door-opening effect (either that, or they'll knock your teeth out). Admission will be between DM4M and DM6.50, and drinks will be a little more expensive than normal.

As for vaguely "alternative" nightlife the best bet is, surprisingly enough, the discos run in some of the clubhouses of the *FDJ* (the party youth organization), or in some of the *Kreiskulturhäuser* (arts centers) which are to be found in different East Berlin districts. In many of the FDJ clubs the youths are taking over themselves and dramatic developments seem imminent.

Bear in mind though, that much of the really good music and the arts in East Berlin tends to happen behind the scenes in private apartments and tenement building courtyards, news circulated only by word of mouth. The only way to find out about these private initiatives is to get into the bars and cafés listed in Chapter Seven and meet the East Berliners.

Alibi, Saarbrückerstr. 14, 1055 (Prenzlauer Berg). One of the area's fancier discos, attracting a *Schickey Mickey* crowd. Open until 2am most nights, closed Tuesday.

Café Binz, Binzstrasse/Berlinerstrasse, 1100 (Pankow). In the daytime it's a café, but after hours you can dance the night away until 5am on a postage stamp-sized dance floor. Relaxed atmosphere, expensive drinks.

Café Lolott, Schönhauser Allee, 1058 (Prenzlauer Berg; table reservations ☎448 4415). The afore-quoted telephone number gives you some idea that the joint isn't exactly jumping. A fancy pick-up place where you sit around the dance floor, rising to shake your thang occasionally. Open from Monday to Saturday until 6am but closed every fourth Wednesday.

Café Nord, Schönhauser Allee, 1058 (Prenzlauer Berg). Retro in an unstylish sort of way, with a small town disco feel, this isn't too bad by East Berlin standards.

Friedrichshof, Bölschestrasse, 1162 (Friedrichshagen). A restaurant, disco, and bar for the *Schickey Mickey* crowd. Closed Monday.

Nachtbar Adria, *Hotel Adria*, Friedrichstr. 134, 1040. A dire band belts out almost unrecognizable chart hits of yesteryear, as a crowd of dubious provenance dances around a fountain. Good if you want to wallow in tack.

Nachtbar Pinguin, Rosa-Luxemburg-Str. 39, 1020. An uninspiring corridor-like club in the city center which is, nevertheless, usually packed. Popular with the city's gays.

Nachtbar Xenon, Thürnagelstr. 8, 1070 (Köpenick). A run-of-the-mill disco and bar opposite Köpenick S-Bahnhof.

Party Thek, Arkonastrasse/Borkumstrasse, 1100 (Pankow). A friendly and, by East Berlin standards, quite trendy nightclub which attracts a slightly older crowd. Bizarre point of reference; it's opposite the former detention jail for political prisoners. Open Wednesday to Saturday until 6am.

Riff, Müggelsee Damm/Josef-Nawrocki-Strasse, 1162 (Friedrichshagen). Open from 10am until very late every day except Monday, with a garden out the back; attracts a chic, early 20s clientele. You pay slightly less if you just want to go in for a drink.

Schoppenstube, Schönhauser Allee, 1058 (Prenzlauer Berg). More of a gay wine-bar really, but the atmosphere approaches that of a western club. It's a small, crowded, and intimate place, but although it's overtly gay you shouldn't feel intimidated if you're straight. Cruisers, head for the cellar bar.

Yucca Bar, Wisbeyer Strasse/Neumannstrasse, 1078. (Prenzlauer Berg). An expensive *Schickey Mickey* bar and disco. Hard to miss thanks to a mock-up British red telephone booth outside. You can eat here, too.

Live Music

There's a good **music scene** in East Berlin, and people here are quick to pick up on what's going on in the West. This means that there are dreadful bands churning out bastardized western pop pap, but also plenty of bands who pick up on elements that interest them, and fuse them with their own ideas to create a specifically East Berlin musical identity. The *FDJ* clubs and *Kreiskulturhäuser* are often the best spots for gigs by smaller local bands. There are also occasional concerts by big name western bands which are usually held in big stadiums like the *Radrennbahn* in Weissensee. Fairly recent attractions have included James Brown, ZZ Top, and Genesis.

For information about gigs and other less mainstream cultural events (film, theater, art exhibitions, etc) check the poster-covered pillars called

Litfasssaule, which can be found on most East Berlin main streets. Another source of information is a tourist office handout called *Wohin in Berlin* ("Where to Go in Berlin") available from the Alexanderplatz tourist office.

Good local bands come and go fairly rapidly, breaking up and resurfacing a few weeks later with a new name. Personnel also seem to be fairly inter-changeable and it often happens that Friday night's avant-garde electronic experimenter will turn up in Saturday night's guitar-based Hip-Hop outfit. The following clubs and *Kreiskulturhäuser* can usually be relied on to come up with good gigs and events, so check their notice boards for forthcoming attractions.

Places

Club Insel des Jugends, Insel des Jugends, 1193 (Treptow). A reliable spot, situated on an island in the Spree in the Treptow Park.

Club 29, Rosa-Luxemburg-Str. 29, 1020 The whole range of musical styles, from indie rock to jazz with the occasional disco thrown in.

Erich-Franz-Club, Schönhauser Allee 36–39, 1054 (Prenzlauer Berg). A wide-ranging program taking in everything from amateur theater to gigs.

FDJ Jugendclub, Sophienstrasse, 1020 (Mitte). Plays host to the best up-and-coming local bands.

Haus der jungen Talente, Klosterstr. 68–70, 1020 (Mitte; ☎210 9201). The city center's premier arts locale which puts on just about everything; concerts, film shows, theatrical productions, dance, cabaret, and exhibitions by young artists. Definitely worth checking out.

Kreiskulturhaus "Erich Weinert", Johannes-R.-Becher-Str. 43, 1100 (Pankow; ☎482 7378). A similar program to the Erich-Franz-Club. The club-house and bar are sites for gigs and discos.

Kreiskulturhaus "Prater", Kastanienallee 7–9, 1058 (Prenzlauer Berg; ☎448 5020). One of the biggest and best known places. Part arts center, part workingmens club, there's a beer garden outside for gigs and parties.

Kreiskulturhaus Treptow, Puschkin Allee 8, 1193 (Treptow) (272 7952). A good site for jazz concerts with a reputation for putting on experimental/avant-garde music, dance, theater, film, and art events.

Jazz and Folk

Few specific clubs exist, so use the available information sources to check out who is playing the various *Kresikulturhäuser*. There are regular jazz evenings in the *Haus der jungen Talente*, at the *Deutsche Theater*, in the *Erich-Franz-Club*, and in the *Haus der Freundschaft*, Puschkin Allee, Treptow.

Classical and Opera

Although Berlin's musical tradition goes back a long way, the glories in East Berlin tend to be more historical than actual. There are a number of very capable orchestras, choirs, and operatic ensembles, but on the whole you're unlikely to come across anything really worth writing home about. The best source of tickets is the Alexanderplatz *Reisebüro*, where they'll also be able to give you information about current worthwhile events. The following listings detail the best East Berlin orchestras and ensembles.

Berlin Sinfonie Orchester, Oberwall Str. 6–7, 1080. Founded in 1952, and based in Schinkel's recently restored Schauspielhaus, this is East Berlin's main symphony orchestra. In the summer it puts on concerts every Thursday at 7:30pm in the Schlüterhof at the Museum für Deutsche Geschichte, Unter den Linden,which always attract a good crowd. Box office open Tuesday and Thursday 10am–noon & 2–6pm.

Komische Oper, Behrenstr. 55–57, 1080 (box office ☎229 2555). The house orchestra performs classical and contemporary concerts, and some very good opera productions are staged here.

Metropol Theater, Friedrichstr. 101–102, 1080 Generally fairly low-brow operetta and musical productions, but tickets sell out very quickly.

Staatskapelle, Unter den Linden 7, 1080. Founded in 1570, the State Choir numbers Herbert von Karajan, Wilhelm Fürtwangler, and Otto Klemperer among its past directors. The repertoire includes both classical and modern works. Box office open Mon–Sat & noon–6pm.

Staatsoper, Unter den Linden 5–7, 1080 (box office ☎207 1362). Excellent operatic productions, particularly of the *Niblungen Lied* and the Ring Cycle. Classical concerts are staged in the Apollo Hall.

Theater

East Berlin has a rich theatrical tradition to draw on: until 1933 the city's theaters were the focus of some of the most innovative theatrical experimentation in Europe, under the direction of world-renowned exponents of dramatic art like Max Reinhardt and Erwin Piscator. Today East Berlin can still boast a large number of theaters of varying degrees of distinction, but the restraints of the past forty years have taken their toll, and it remains to be seen whether new found freedom of artistic expression will be able to repair the damage.

Unfortunately there are no regular **English language productions** in East Berlin, so what follows will probably only be of interest to German-speakers and/or real theater enthusiasts. It's difficult to categorize the various theaters as most put on productions which range from the frankly turgid to the occasionally daringly experimental. As a tourist you'll have to rely on luck or word of mouth, and if something good comes up then you'd be well advised to catch it while you can, as really outstanding productions tend to be infrequent or even one-night affairs. You'd be well-advised to get your tickets in advance from the *Reisebüro*.

BAT (Berliner Arbeiter und Studenten Theater), Belforter Str. 15, 1055 (Prenzlauer Berg; ☎448 2857). A "workers' and students' theater," founded in 1975, which can usually be relied on to come up with challenging experimental offerings, including theater student graduation projects. A meeting point, both physical and spiritual, for everyone interested in theater.

Berliner Ensemble, Bertolt-Brecht-Platz 1, 1040 (box office ☎282 3160 or ☎288 8155). The official Brecht theater offering a recommended, if slightly lackluster, diet of staple Brecht fare like "The Caucasian Chalk Circle," "Galileo Galilei," etc. They also dish up Dario Fo, Shakespeare and a droll version of Zuckmayer's "*Der Hauptmann von Köpenick* ." Occasional experimental productions on the *Probebühne* (rehearsal stage). Box office Mon 11am–5pm, Tues–Fri 11am–1:30pm & 2–6pm, Sat 5–6pm.

Deutsches Theater, Schumannstr. 13a–14, 1040 (box office ☎287 1225 or ☎287 1226). East Berlin's best theater until a few years ago, thanks to the inspired direction of Alexander Lang. However Lang is now in the West, and the quality of the productions has fallen off slightly.

Die Distel, Friedrichstr. 101 (in the Admiralspalast), 1080 (☎207 1291) and at Degnerstr. 9 (at the *Venus* cinema in Höhenschönhausen, 1092 ☎376 5179). The slightly sorry heir to Berlin's legendary inter-war cabaret tradition, a cabaret ensemble putting on satirical shows which are often quite daring politically and give people a chance to let off steam.

Friedrichstadt Palast Revue Theater, Friedrichstr. 107, 1040 (box office ☎283 0479). Apart from the satirical ensemble "*Das Ei*," who puts on skits, pseudo-cabaret, and some serious dramatic productions, the repertoire here is fairly unimaginative. Ticket sales are guaranteed though, because of block reservations from the big state organizations and companies. In the same complex, reached via Ziegelstrasse, is the *Kleine Revue* which puts on the occasional good satirical show and, for anyone on an Isherwood trip, a transvestite cabaret.

Maxim Gorki Theater, Unter den Linden, Am Festungsgraben 2, 1080 (box office ☎207 1790). Consistently good productions including a lot of Soviet works. Not surprisingly, Gorki figures highly. Box office Mon–Fri noon–2pm & 2:30–6pm.

Puppentheater, Greifswalderstr. 81–84, 1055 (☎365 0696). Puppet shows for both children and adults, including reworkings of traditional Eastern European folk tales and more modern productions. Tickets are available from Grellstr. 36 Mon–Fri 10:30am–3pm.

Theater der Freundschaft, Hans-Rodenburg-Platz, 1156 (Lichtenburg; box office ☎557 0306). A theater for children and young people which puts on some surprisingly sophisticated productions; mainly fairly tales, and classical and modern plays from the Soviet Union and other Eastern European countries.

Theater im Palast, Palast der Republik, Marx-Engels-Platz, 1020 (box office ☎238 2559). The only interesting feature about this theater is the fact that there's no stage, just a performing area in the midst of the audience. Unfortunately the program is so unadventurous that even this unusual feature doesn't make it worth a visit.

Volksbühne, Rosa-Luxemburg-Platz, 1026. Reliable across-the-board productions. One of their more celebrated efforts in recent years has been a reworking of Bulgakov's satire of 1930s Moscow,"The Master and Margarita," which in pre-*Wende* days included close-to-the-bone references.

Film

Most East Berlin movie theaters used to show East German, Soviet, and Eastern European films plus some western films—which normally arrived a year or two after their first release date. In the old days conservative censorship meant that some films didn't make it on to the screen, including from time to time the occasional *glasnost*-influenced Soviet film. With the *Wende,* many previously withheld films are now being shown publicly for the first time in decades, and mainstream western films are beginning to supplant more traditional cinematic fare. Performances of art-house movies are often one-night affairs, and it's rare for a really sought-after film to run for a week in one cinema. Usually a film will be shown on different and not necessarily successive nights in various movie theaters across the city. Western films are usually dubbed into English and there are no regular showings of English-language films in East Berlin.

Babylon, Rosa-Luxemburg-Str. 40, 1020. East Berlin's best repertory cinema, and also home to a cinematic art museum. At the time of writing its fate hangs in the balance. It has been closed down, apparently because the heating system is unsafe, but a massive public campaign is going on, which may save it yet.

Colosseum, Schönhauser Allee 123, 1058 (Prenzlauer Berg). A local cinema with an occasionally interesting program.

Kosmos, Karl-Marx-Allee 131a, 1034. One of the city's biggest movie theaters, with a Dolby stereo sound system. In November it's the site of the Soviet film festival.

International, Karl-Marx-Allee/Schillingstrasse, 1020. A big, comfortable, modern cinema which often shows relatively new western films and also plays host to theater and music events, and discussion evenings.

Vorwärts, Herman-Duncker-Str. 115, 1157 (Lichtenberg). A small rep cinema which often unearths pre-war classics.

CONTEXTS

THE HISTORICAL FRAMEWORK

Few cities have a history as tangible as that of Berlin. It's impossible not to be aware of the forces which have shaped the city as you walk through its streets—they have left physical reminders in the shape of shrapnel scars on buildings and, most telling of all, a huge dead swathe right through the middle of the city.

This is the key to the city's atmosphere. Here the past and present co-exist. Talk of history and you're talking of events which have a direct bearing on what you see before you. If any city embodies the twentieth century it is Berlin. Even after the darkest days of the Cold War, when agreements between the great powers put an end to the city's role as the prime focus for international tension, Berlin still somehow symbolized the post-war order. And this whole process continues. Today world history's next installment is starting to unfold and once again Berlin is the setting.

BEGINNINGS

Archaeologists reckon that people have lived around the area of modern-day Berlin for about 60,000 years. Traces of hunter-gatherer activity dating from about 8000 BC and more substantial remains of Stone Age farming settlements from 4000 BC onwards have been discovered. The Romans regarded this as barbarian territory and left no mark on the region. Although **Germanic tribes** first appeared on the scene during the fifth and sixth centuries AD, many of them left during the great migrations of later centuries, and the vacated territories were occupied by **Slavs**. Germanic ascendancy only began in the twelfth and thirteenth centuries, when Saxon feudal barons of the Mark of Brandenburg expelled the Slavs. The **Saxons** also granted municipal charters to two humble riverside towns—where the Berlin story really begins.

THE TWIN TOWNS

Sited on marshlands around an island (today the Museuminsel and Fischerinsel) at the narrowest point on the River Spree, **Berlin** and **Cölln** were on a major trade route to the east, and began to prosper as municipalities. Despite many links (including a joint town hall built in 1307), they retained their separate identities throughout the fourteenth century, when both received the right to mint their own coinage and pronounce death sentences in local courts. Their admission to the powerful **Hanseatic League** of city-states (1369) confirmed their economic and political importance. By 1391, Berlin and Cölln were virtually autonomous from the Mark of Brandenberg, which grew ever more chaotic in the early years of the fifteenth century.

Order was eventually restored by **Friedrich Hohenzollern**, burgrave of Nuremburg, whose subjugation of the province was initially welcomed by the burghers of Berlin and Cölln. However, when his son Johann attempted to treat them likewise, they forced him to withdraw to Spandau. It was only divisions within their ranks that enabled **Friedrich II**, Johann's brother, to take over the two cities. Some of the guilds offered him the keys of the gates if he'd take their part against the Berlin-Cölln magistrates: Friedrich obliged, then built a palace and instituted his own harsh rule, forbidding any further union between Berlin and Cölln.

After swiftly crushing a **rebellion** in 1448, Friedrich imposed new restrictions. To symbolize the **consolidation of Hohenzollern power**, a chain was placed around the neck of Berlin's heraldic symbol, the bear, which remained on the city's coat of arms until 1875. After the Hohenzollerns moved their residence and court here, Berlin-Cölln assumed the character of a *Residenzstadt* (royal residence) and rapidly expanded, replacing its old wattle and daub dwellings with more substantial stone buildings—culminating in a Renaissance *Schloss* finished in 1540. Yet life remained hard, for despite being involved in the Reformation Berlin-Cölln lagged behind the great cities of western and south Germany, and in 1576 it was ravaged by plague. The **Thirty Years' War** (1618–1648) marked a low point. After repeated plundering by Swedish troops, the twin city had lost half its population and one third of its buildings by the end of the war.

THE GREAT ELECTOR

The monumental task of post-war **reconstruction** fell to the Mark's new ruler, Elector **Friedrich Wilhelm of Brandenburg** (1620–1688), who was barely out of his teens. Massive fortifications were constructed, besides the residences and public buildings necessary to make Berlin-Cölln a worthy capital for an Elector. (Seven Electors—three archbishops, a margrave, duke, count, and king—were entitled to elect the Holy Roman Emperor.) In recognition of his achievements, Friedrich Wilhelm came to be known as **the Great Elector**. After defeating the Swedes at the Battle of Fehrbellin in 1675, the Mark of Brandenberg was acknowledged as a force to be reckoned with, and its capital grew accordingly. Recognizing the value of a cosmopolitan population, the Elector permitted Jews and South German Catholics to move here and enjoy protection as citizens.

A later wave of immigrants affected Berlin-Cölln even more profoundly. Persecuted in France, thousands of **Protestant Hugenots** sought new homes in England and Germany. The arrival of 5000 immigrants—mostly skilled craftsworkers or traders—revitalized Berlin-Cölln, whose own population was only 20,000. French became an almost obligatory second language, indispensible for anyone looking for social and career success. Another fillip to the city's development was the completion of the **Friedrich Wilhelm Canal**, linking the Spree and the Oder, which boosted its status as an east–west trade center.

Carrying on where his father had left off, Friedrich III succeeded in becoming King of Prussia to boot (and thus gained the title of Friedrich I), whilst Berlin continued to expand. The **Friedrichstadt and Charlottenberg quarters** and the **Zeughaus** (now the *Museum für Deutsche Geschichte* in East Berlin) were created during this period, and Andreas Schlüter revamped the Elector's palace. In 1709, Berlin-Cölln finally became a single city named **Berlin**. None of this came cheap, however. Both Berlin and the Mark Brandenberg were heavily in debt by the end of Friedrich's reign; he even resorted to alchemists in the hope of refilling his treasury.

BERLIN UNDER THE SOLDIER KING

The next chapter in the city's history belongs to Friedrich I's son, **Friedrich Wilhelm I** (1688–1740). Known as the "**Soldier King**" and generally reckoned to be the father of the Prussian state, he dealt with the financial chaos by enforcing spartan conditions on his subjects and firing most of the servants at court. State revenues were henceforth directed to building up his army, and culture took a back seat to parades (eventually he even banned the theater). While the army marched and drilled, the populace had a draconian work ethic drubbed into them—Friedrich took to walking about Berlin and personally beating anyone he caught loafing.

Friedrich tried to introduce conscription but had to make an exception of Berlin when the city's able-bodied young men fled en masse to escape the army. Despite this, Berlin became a **garrison town** geared to maintaining the army; the Lustgarten park of the royal palace was transformed into a parade ground, and every house was expected to have space available for billeting troops. Much of modern Berlin's shape and character can be traced back to Friedrich—squares like **Pariser Platz** (the area in front of the Brandenburg Gate) began as parade grounds, and **Friedrichstrasse** was built to link the center with Tempelhof parade ground. When Friedrich died after watching rehearsals for his own funeral (and thrashing a groom who made a mistake), few Berliners mourned.

FREDERICK THE GREAT AND THE RISE OF PRUSSIA

His son, Friedrich II—known to historians as **Frederick the Great** (1712–1786), and to his subjects as "*Der alte Fritz*"—enjoyed a brief honeymoon as a liberalizer, before reverting to his father's ways. Soon Prussia was drawn into a series of wars which sent Berlin taxes through the roof, while the king withdrew to Sansouci Palace in Potsdam, where only French was spoken, leaving the Berliners to pay for his military adventurism. Friedrich's saving grace was that he liked to think of himself as a philosopher king, and Berlin's **cultural life** consequently flourished during his reign. This was thanks in part to the work of leading figures of the German Enlightenment, like the playwright Gotthold Ephraim Lessing and the philosopher Moses Mendelssohn, both of whom enjoyed royal patronage.

It was the **rise of Prussia** which alarmed Austria, Saxony, France, and Russia into starting the **Seven Years' War** in 1756. Four years later they occupied Berlin and demanded a tribute of 4,000,000 thalers, causing City President Kirchstein to faint on the spot. This was later reduced to 1,500,000 when it was discovered that the city coffers were empty. Berlin was eventually relieved by Friedrich, who went on to win the war (if only by default) after Russia and France fell out. Victory confirmed Prussia's power in Central Europe, but keeping the peace meant maintaining a huge standing army.

Besides direct taxation, Frederick raised money by establishing **state monopolies** in the trade of coffee, salt, and tobacco. Citizens were actually required to buy set quantities of these commodities whether they wanted them or not. This was the origin of some of Berlin's most celebrated culinary delicacies: sauerkraut, Kassler Rippchen (salted pork ribs), and pickled gherkins were all invented by people desperate to use up their accumulated salt. Popular discontent was muffled by Frederick's **secret police** and **press censorship**—two innovations which have stuck around in one form or another ever since.

The **Unter den Linden** came into its own during Friedrich's reign as grandiose new edifices like the **Altes Bibliothek** sprang up. Just off the great boulevard the **Französisches Dom** was built to serve the needs of the

Hugenot population, while the construction of Schloss Bellevue in the Tiergarten sparked off a whole new building boom, as the wealthy flocked into the newly-fashionable area.

DECLINE AND OCCUPATION

After Friedrich's death Prussia went into a **decline**, culminating in the defeat of its once-invincible army by French revolutionaries at the Battle of Valmy in 1792. The decline went unchecked under Friedrich Wilhelm II (1744–1797), continuing into the Napoleonic era. As Bonaparte's empire spread across Europe the Prussian court dithered, appeasing the French and trying to delay the inevitable invasion. Life in Berlin continued more or less as normal, but by August 1806 citizens were watching Prussian soldiers set off on the march westwards to engage the Napoleonic forces. On September 19, the king and queen left the city, followed a month later by Count von der Schulenburg, the city governor, who had assured the Berliners that all was going well right up until he learned of Prussia's defeat at Jena and Auerstadt.

Five days later French troops marched through the **Brandenburg Gate** and Berlin was occupied. On October 27, 1806, Napoleon himself arrived to head a parade down the Unter den Linden—greeted as a liberator by the Berliners, according to some accounts. **French occupation** was uneventful, interrupted only by a minor and unsuccessful military rebellion, and ended with the collapse of Napoleon's empire after his defeats in Russia and at the Battle of Leipzig.

THE REBIRTH OF PRUSSIA

With the end of French rule, the Quadriga (the Goddess of Victory in her chariot) was restored to the Brandenburg Gate (see p.39), but the people of Berlin only gained the promise of a constitution for Prussia, which never materialized—a portent of later conflict. The real victor was the **Prussian state**, which acquired tracts of land along the Rhine, including the Ruhr which contained the iron and coal deposits on which its military might was to be rebuilt.

The war was followed by an era of reaction and oppression which did so much to stifle intellectual and cultural life in Berlin that the philosopher Wilhelm von Humboldt resigned from the university in protest at the new authoritarianism. Gradually this mellowed out into the **Biedermeier years**, in which Prussia's industrial fortunes began to rise, laying the foundation of its Great Power status. Berlin continued to grow: factories and railroads and the first of the city's *Mietskaserne* or **tenement buildings** were constructed—foreshadowing what was to come with full industrialization.

REVOLUTION AND REACTION

Berlin enjoyed more than thirty years of peace and stability after 1815, but it shared the revolutionary mood that swept Europe in **1848**. Influenced by events in France and the writings of Karl Marx (who lived here from 1837 to 1841), the Berliners demanded a say in the running of their own affairs. King Friedrich Wilhelm IV (1795–1861) refused to agree. On March 18, citizens gathered outside his palace to present their demands. The soldiers who dispersed them accidentally fired two shots and the demonstration became a **revolution**. Barricades went up and a fourteen-hour battle raged between insurgents and loyalist troops. According to eyewitness accounts, rich and poor alike joined in the rebellion. During the fighting 183 Berliners and 18 soldiers died.

Aghast at his subjects' anger, Friedrich Wilhelm IV ordered his troops to withdraw to Spandau, leaving the city in the hands of the revolutionaries, who failed to grasp the situation. A revolutionary parliament and citizens' militia were established, but rather than assaulting Spandau or taking other measures to consolidate the revolution, the new assembly concerned itself with protecting the royal palace from vandalism. No attempt was made to declare a republic or seize public buildings in what was turning out to be an unusually orderly—and ultimately doomed—revolution.

On March 21, the king appeared in public wearing the black, red, and gold tricolor emblem of the revolution. Having failed to suppress it, he now proposed to join it, along with most of his ministers and princes. The king spoke at the university, promising nothing much but paying lip service to the idea of German unity, which impressed the assembled liberals. Order was fully restored; then in October, a Prussian army under General Wrangel entered Berlin and forced the **dissolution of parliament**. The Berliners either

gave up the fight or followed millions of their fellow Germans into exile.

Suppression followed. Friedrich gave up the tricolor and turned to persecuting liberals, before going insane shortly afterwards. His brother Prince Wilhelm—who had led the troops against the barricades—became regent, and then king himself. **Otto Von Bismarck** was appointed to the chancellorship (1862) despite the almost universal loathing he inspired among Berliners.

Meanwhile Berlin itself continued to grow apace, turning into a cosmopolitan, modern industrial city. Its free press and revolutionary past exerted a liberal influence on Prussia's emasculated parliament, the **Reichstag**, to the irritation of Bismarck and the king (who was soon to proclaim himself emperor, or *Kaiser*). However, Bismarck became a national hero after the Prussian victory at the **Battle of Königgratz** (1866) smashed Austrian military power, clearing the way for Prussia to unite—and dominate—Germany. Although militaristic nationalism caused liberalism to whither elsewhere, Berlin continued to elect liberal deputies to the Reichstag, which became the parliament of the whole nation after **German unification** in 1871.

Yet Berlin remained a maverick city. It was here that three attempts were made to kill Emperor Wilhelm I; the final one on the Unter den Linden (1878) left him with thirty pieces of shrapnel in his body. While the Kaiser recovered, Bismarck used the event to justify a **crackdown on Socialists**, closing newspapers and persecuting trade unionists. The growth of unionism was a direct result of relentless urbanization. Between 1890 and 1900, **Berlin's population doubled** to 2,000,000, and thousands of tenement buildings sprang up in working-class quarters like **Wedding**. These were solidly behind the Social Democratic Party (**SPD**), whose deputies were the chief dissenters within the Reichstag.

By 1890 Wilhelm II had become Kaiser and "dropped the Pilot" (Bismarck), but the country remained predominantly militaristic and authoritarian. Whilst Berlin remained defiantly liberal, it steadily acquired the attributes of a modern capital. Now an established center for commerce and diplomacy, it boasted electric trams, an underground railroad, and all the other technical innovations of the age.

WORLD WAR I AND ITS AFTERMATH

The arms race and dual alliances which gradually polarized Europe during the 1890s and the first decade of the twentieth century led inexorably towards **World War I**. Its outbreak in 1914 was greeted with enthusiasm by civilians everywhere—only confirmed pacifists or Communists resisted the heady intoxication of patriotism. In Berlin, Kaiser Wilhelm II spoke "to all Germans" from the balcony of his palace, and shop windows across the city were festooned with national colors. Military bands played *Heil dir im Siegerkranz* ("Hail to you in the Victor's Laurel") and *Die Wacht am Rhein* ("The Watch on the Rhine") in cafés, while Berliners threw flowers to the Imperial German army or *Reichswehr* as it marched off to war. The political parties agreed to a truce, and even the Social Democrats voted in favor of war credits.

The General Staff's calculation that France could be knocked out before Russia fully mobilized soon proved hopelessly optimistic, and Germany found itself facing a war on two fronts—the very thing Bismarck had dreaded. As casualties mounted on the stalemated Western Front, and rationing and food shortages began to hit poorer civilians, **disillusionment** set in. By the summer of 1915 housewives were demonstrating in front of the Reichstag, a portent of more serious popular unrest to come. Ordinary people were beginning to see the war as an exercise staged for the benefit of the rich, at the expense of the poor who bore the brunt of the suffering. In December 1917, nineteen members of the SPD announced they could no longer support their party's backing of the war and formed an independent socialist party known as the USPD. This party joined the "International Group" of **Karl Liebknecht** and **Rosa Luxemburg**—later known as the Spartacists—which had opposed SPD support for the war since 1915. It was this grouping which was to form the nucleus of the post-war *Kommunistische Partei Deutschlands*, or **KPD**. Meanwhile, fuel, food, and even beer shortages added to growing hardships on the home front.

DEFEAT AND REVOLUTION

With their last great offensive spent, and America joining the Allied war effort, even Germany's supreme warlord, Erich von Ludendorff, recognized that **defeat** was inevitable by the autumn of 1918. Knowing the Allies would refuse to negotiate with the old absolutist system, he declared (on September 9) a democratic, **constitutional monarchy**, whose Chancellor would be responsible to the Reichstag and not the Kaiser. A government was formed under Prince Max von Baden, which agreed to extensive reforms. But it was too little, too late for the bitter sailors and soldiers on the home front, where the contrast between privilege and poverty was most obvious. At the begining of November the Kiel Garrison led a **naval mutiny** and revolutionary **Workers' and Soldiers' Soviets** mushroomed across Germany.

Caught up in this wave of unrest, Berliners took to the streets on November 8–9, where they were joined by soldiers stationed in the capital. Realizing that the game was up, **Kaiser Wilhelm II abdicated**. What Lenin described as a situation of "dual power" now existed. Almost at the same time as Philipp Scheidemann of the SPD declared a "**German Republic**" from the Reichstag's balcony, Karl Liebknecht was proclaiming a "Free Socialist Republic" from a balcony of the royal palace, less than a mile away. In the face of increasing confusion, SPD leader Friedrich Ebert took over as head of the government. A deal was struck with the army, which promised to protect the republic if Ebert would forestall the full-blooded social revolution demanded by the Spartacists. Ebert now became chairman of a Council of People's Delegates that ruled Berlin for nearly three months.

Between December 16 and 21, a **Congress of Workers' and Soldiers' Soviets** was held, and voted to accept a system of parliamentary democracy. However, many of the revolutionary soldiers, sailors, and workers who controlled the streets favored the establishment of Soviet-style goverment, and refused to obey Ebert's orders. They were eventually suppressed by staunchly anti-revolutionary units of the old Imperial army, further indebting Ebert to the Prussian establishment. This itself relied heavily on the **Freikorps**: armed bands of right-wing officers and NCOs, dedicated to protecting Germany from "Bolshevism."

Things came to a head with the **Spartacist uprising** in Berlin during the first half of

January 1919. This inspired lasting dread amongst the bourgeoisie, who applauded when the Spartacists were crushed by the militarily-superior Freikorps. The torture and **murder of Liebknecht and Luxemburg** by Freikorps officers (who threw their bodies in the Landwehr Canal) was never punished once the fighting was over. This hardly augured well for the future of the **new republic**, whose National Assembly elections were held on January 19.

THE WEIMAR REPUBLIC

The elections confirmed the SPD as the new political leaders of the country, with 38 percent of the vote; as a result, Ebert was made President, with Scheidemann as chancellor. **Weimar**, the small country town which had seen the most glorious flowering of the German Enlightenment, was chosen as the seat of government in preference to Berlin, which was tinged by its monarchical and militaristic associations.

A **new constitution** was drawn up, hailed as the most liberal and progressive in the world. It aimed at a comprehensive system of checks and balances to ensure that power could not become too concentrated. Authority was formally vested in the people, and the state was given a quasi-federal structure to limit excessive Prussian domination. Executive authority was shared between the President (who could rule by emergency decree if necessary) and the Reich government in a highly complex arrangement. Reichstag deputies were elected by proportional representation from party lists.

While on the surface an admirable document, this constitution was hopelessly idealistic for a people so unfamiliar with democratic practice and responsibilities. No attempt was made to outlaw parties hostile to the system; this opened the way for savage attacks on the republic by extremists at both ends of the political spectrum. The use of proportional representation, without any qualifying minimum percentage of the total vote, favored a plethora of parties promoting sectional interests. This meant that the Weimar governments were all unwieldy coalitions, whose average life was about eight months, and which often pursued contradictory policies in different ministries.

DADA

World War I smashed prevailing cultural assumptions and disrupted social hierarchies. With politics in ferment, culture became another battleground. The leading exponent of the challenge to bourgeois values was the **Dada movement**, which shifted its headquarters from Zurich to Berlin in 1919. A Dada manifesto was proclaimed, followed by the First International Dada Fair (July & August), whose content aligned the movement with the forces of revolution. The right was particularly enraged by exhibits like a stuffed effigy of an army officer with a pig's head, labeled "Hanged by the Revolution," which dangled from the ceiling. All in all it was an appropriate prelude to the new decade.

BERLIN IN THE TWENTIES: THE WEIMAR YEARS

The history of Berlin in the 1920s is bound up with Germany's—much of which was being dictated by the Allied powers. Resentment at the harsh terms imposed by the **Treaty of Versailles** led to turmoil and a wave of political violence: Matthias Erzberger, leader of the German delegation to Versailles, was amongst those assassinated. On March 13, 1920, Freikorps units loyal to the right-wing politician Wolfgang Kapp marched on Berlin, unopposed by the army. The government left Berlin but returned a week later, when the **Kapp putsch** collapsed. The army had withdrawn its support after protesters called for a general strike.

The early 1920s were a bad time for Berlin. War reparations to the Allies placed a crippling burden on the German economy. As the mark began to plunge in value, the government was shocked by the **assassination of Walter Rathenau**. As Foreign Minister, he had just signed the Treaty of Rapallo, aimed at promoting closer economic ties with the Soviet Union, since the Western powers remained intransigent. Rathenau was killed at his own house in the Grünewald by Freikorps officers. When France and Belgium occupied the Ruhr in response to alleged defaults in the reparations payments, a general strike was called across Germany in January 1923.

The combination of reparations and strikes sent the mark plummetting, causing the worst

inflation ever known. As their savings were wiped out and literally barrowloads of paper money weren't enough to support a family, Berliners experienced the terrors of hyper-inflation. In working-class districts, streetfighting between right and left flared up. Foreigners flocked in to pay bargain prices for carpets and furs that even rich Germans could no longer afford, and fortunes were made and lost by speculators. In the midst of all this, on November 8, Berliners' attention was briefly diverted to Munich when a motley crew of right-wing ex-army officers including General Ludendorff attempted to mount a putsch. It failed, but Berliners were to hear of one of the ringleaders again—**Adolf Hitler**.

Finally the mark was stabilized under a new Chancellor, **Gustav Stresemann**, who proved to be a supremely able politician. Having come to realize that only an economically sound Germany would have any hope of meeting reparations payments, the Allies moderated their stance. Under the Dawes Plan of 1924, loans poured into Germany, particularly from America, leading to an upsurge in the economy.

NIGHTLIFE AND THE ARTS

Economic recovery affected the social life of Berlin. For many people the center of the city had shifted from the old *Regiurungsviertel* (government quarter) around Friedrichstrasse and the Unter den Linden, to the cafés and bars of the Kurfürstendamm. Jazz hit the **nightclubs** in a big way, like drug abuse (mainly cocaine) and all kinds of sex. There were clubs for transvestites, clubs where you could watch nude dancing, or dance naked yourself—and usually the police didn't give a damn. This was the legendary era later to be celebrated by Isherwood and others, when Berlin was briefly the most open, tolerant city in Europe, a mecca for all those who rejected conventions and traditions. The Twenties were also a boom time for the arts, as the Dada shockwave rippled through the decade. **George Grosz** satirized the times in savage caricatures, while **John Heartfield** used photomontage techniques to produce biting political statements. Equally striking, if less didactic, was the work of artists like **Otto Dix** and **Christian Schad**.

Producer **Max Reinhardt** continued to dominate Berlin's theatrical life, as he'd done since taking over at the Deutscher Theater in 1905. **Erwin Piscator** moved from propaganda into mainstream theater at the *Theater am Nollendorf Platz* without losing his innovative edge, and in 1928 **Bertolt Brecht**'s *Dreigroschen Oper* (Threepenny Opera) was staged for the first time. Appropriately, Berlin also became a center for the very newest of the arts. Between the wars the **UFA film studio** at Neubabelsberg was the biggest in Europe, producing legendary films like **Fritz Lang**'s *Metropolis, The Cabinet of Doctor Caligari*, and *The Blue Angel* (starring **Marlene Dietrich**).

Middle- and lowbrow tastes were catered for by endless all-singing, all-dancing **musicals**, featuring platoons of women in various states of undress.

This was also the heyday of the Berlin **cabaret** scene, when some of its most acidic exponents were at work.

THE RISE OF NAZISM

With inflation back under control, Germany experienced a return of relative **political stability**. The 1924 elections demonstrated increased support for center-right and republican parties. When President Ebert died (February 28, 1925) and was succeeded by the former commander of the Imperial army, **General Field Marshal von Hindenburg**, monarchists and conservatives rejoiced. Nevertheless, it was now that the extreme right began gradually gaining ground, starting in Bavaria.

The **National Socialist German Workers' Party** (NSDAP) began as a ragbag group of misfits and fanatics, whose views were an odd mixture of extreme right and left, as the party's name suggests. It was Hitler who synthesized an ideology from existing reactionary theories, modeled the Nazis on Mussolini's *Facisti*, and took a leaf from the Communists when it came to red flags, excessive propaganda, and streetfighting. For this they had the thuggish, brown-shirted **SA** (*Sturmabteilung*) Stormtroopers. As long as "reds" were the victims, the authorities did little or nothing to curb SA violence. The fear of street violence—foreshadowing a return to the anarchy of the post-war years—was calculated to drive the bourgeoisie towards Nazism, which promised drastic "solutions" to Germany's ills.

The Nazis made no headway in staunchly "red" Berlin until the end of 1926, when Hitler appointed **Joseph Göbbels** as *Gauleiter* of the city party organization. Göbbels reorganized the SA with the intention of confronting the Communists and conquering the streets of Berlin. On February 11 the following year, he rented the Pharus hall as a site for a Nazi demonstration in the predominantly Communist suburb of Wedding. A bloody brawl ensued and an **era of violence** began. Marches by the SA and the Communist *Rote Frontekämpfer Bund* (Red Fighters' Front)—often culminating in pitched battles—became a regular feature of street life in Berlin's working-class suburbs. The Nazis were here to stay.

ELECTIONS AND UNREST

In the 1928 elections the NSDAP won 800,000 votes and gained twelve seats in the Reichstag. In May 1929 there was serious unrest in Berlin when Communist workers clashed with armed police in Wedding. Running street battles occurred and thirty-three civilians, many of them innocent bystanders, were killed. Fearful for their lives and property should the Communists gain ascendancy, wealthy bourgeois and the captains of finance and industry donated heavily to the Nazis.

In October 1929 Gustav Stresemann, one of Germany's few capable politicians, died. A few weeks later came the **Wall Street Crash**. All American credit ended, and international recession wiped out what was left of Germany's economic stability. By the year's end **unemployment** had reached 3,000,000, and the poverty of the immediate post-war period had returned with a vengeance. Hindenburg appointed a centrist politician, Heinrich Brüning, as Chancellor, who failed to get any legislation passed in the Reichstag and advised Hindenburg to dissolve it, pending elections. Poverty—worsened by a state-imposed austerity program—polarized society: gangs fought in the streets, while swastika banners and red flags hung from neighboring tenements.

The **1930 elections** resulted in gains for the Communists, and 107 seats for the Nazis. There were anti-semitic attacks throughout Berlin as the newly-elected Nazi deputies took their seats in the Reichstag on October 13. By now the parlia-mentary system had effectively ceased to function and Germany was being ruled by presidential decree. Financial misery and disorder showed no signs of abating, and SA uniforms became a common sight on the streets of central Berlin, where Nazi thugs attacked Jewish shops and businesses, flaunting pornographic hate-sheets like *Der Sturmer*. Their rising influence was confirmed when General Schleicher of the *Reichswehr* General Staff began to court Hitler, envisaging the Nazis as a bulwark against the left. In Berlin—with its predominantly anti-Nazi population—despair began to mount.

At the **presidential elections** of April 10, 1932, Hindenburg gained an absolute majority, but Hitler won 13,500,000 votes. A month later Hindenburg dismissed Brüning for failing to control the economy and disagreeing with his speeches, replacing him with Franz von Papen. Flanked by a Cabinet which the left-wing press pilloried as the "Cabinet of Barons," von Papen announced plans for "reform" which amounted to a thinly disguised attempt to revive the pre-war order. The **parliamentary elections** in July saw street violence on an unprecedented scale, and made the Nazis the largest single party in the Reichstag. Despite a setback at the polls in November 1932, their strength on the streets was increasing—intimidating Berlin's cabarets and left-wing theaters into muted criticism or silence.

Hitler's last steps to power were assisted by conservatives who sought to use the Nazis for their own ends. First, General Schleicher (by now Defense Minister, and less enamored of the Nazis) engineered the removal of von Papen, and personally replaced him as Chancellor. Papen retaliated by instigating a series of **political intrigues**. To Hindenburg he argued that Schleicher was incompetent to govern Germany, whose political mess could best be resolved by making Hitler Chancellor. Von Papen reckoned that the Nazis would crush the left but reveal themselves unequal to the task of government. After a few months Hitler could be nudged aside and power would pass back into the hands of conservatives like himself.

Having come to an agreement with Hitler, he persuaded the virtually senile Hindenberg to appoint Hitler as Chancellor and himself as

Vice Chancellor (January 4, 1933). Knowing nothing of this, people were demanding the departure of Schleicher on the streets of Berlin. Two days after his resignation, they were horrified to see **Hitler sworn in as Chancellor** on January 30. Life in Berlin would never be the same again, despite the fact that three quarters of the city's electors had voted against the Nazis at the last elections.

THE NAZI TAKEOVER

Hitler went immediately to the Reichs' Chancellery to make his first public appearance as Chancellor. Berlin thronged with Nazi supporters bearing torches, and the SA marched in strength through the *Regiurungsviertel* to celebrate their victory. For anti-Nazis in Berlin, it was a nightmare come true.

The Nazi takeover of the state and the suppression of political opposition was spearheaded by **Hermann Göring**. As Prussian Minister of the Interior, he ordered the police "to make free use of their weapons wherever necessary" and built up the secret political department, soon to become notorious as the **Gestapo** (*Geheimestaatspolizei*—"secret state police"). "It's not my business to do justice; it's my business to annihilate and exterminate," boasted Göring. The pretext for an all-out assault on the Nazi's opponents was provided by the **Reichstag fire** (February 28, 1933). Whether this was really caused by the Nazis themselves, or by Marinus van der Lubbe, the simple-minded Dutch Communist whom they accused, is still a subject for debate. But there's no doubt that the Nazis used the Reichstag fire to their advantage.

An **emergency decree** to "protect the people and the state" was signed by Hindenberg the following day. It effectively abolished habeas corpus and provided the legal basis for a permanent state of emergency. The Nazi propaganda machine played up the Red Menace. Communist offices were raided, and the head of the Communist International, Georgi Dimitrov, was accused of instigating the Reichstag fire. In this atmosphere, the **elections of March 5** took place. The Communist vote dropped by 1,000,000, but the Nazis failed to achieve an outright majority, with 43.9 percent of the vote. Nevertheless, Hitler was poised to consolidate his grip on power.

The new Reichstag was opened in the Garrison Church in Potsdam and later transferred to a Berlin opera house. Delegates were asked to approve an **Enabling Act** which would place dictatorial powers in the hands of the predominantly Nazi cabinet. By the arrest of Communist deputies, some of the SPD, and the support of the traditional right, Hitler was only just short of the two-thirds majority he needed to abolish the Weimar Republic quite legally. The SPD salvaged some self-respect by refusing to accede to this, but the Catholic centrists failed to repeat their act of defiance against Bismarck, meekly supporting the Bill in return for minor concessions. It was passed by 441 votes to 84, hammering the final nails into the coffin of German parliamentary democracy.

On May 2, the Nazis clamped down on the unions, arresting leaders and sending them to concentration camps. In a series of subsequent moves opposition parties were effectively banned, and persecution of Nazi opponents was extended to embrace "active church members, freemasons, politically dissatisfied people . . . abortionists and homosexuals." An **exodus from Berlin** of known anti-Nazis and others with reason to fear the Nazis began. Bertolt Brecht, Kurt Weill, Lotte Lenya, and Wassily Kandinsky all left the city, joining the likes of Albert Einstein and George Grosz in exile. The atmosphere of the city was changing irrevocably. Social Democrats, Communists, and trade unionists were being rounded up and sent to **concentration camps**, the first of which was founded in February. The unemployed were drafted in labor battalions, set to work on the land or building *autobahns*.

On April 1, the SA launched an enforced **boycott of Jewish shops**, businesses, and medical and legal practices in Berlin. Meanwhile, the Nazis put their own men into vital posts throughout local governments—in Berlin, and the rest of Germany. This was the first stage of *Gleichschaltung* ("coordination"), whereby the machinery of state, and then society itself, would be nazified. On May 11, they shocked the world by burning thousands of books which conflicted with Nazi ideology on the Opernplatz in central Berlin. After the concentration camps, the **book-burnings** (*Buchverbrennung*) remain one of the most potent symbols of Nazi brutality.

THE NIGHT OF THE LONG KNIVES

In 1934 Nazi savagery was briefly turned inwards. Under **Ernst Röhm**, the SA had grown to 500,000 men, and boasted of swallowing up the smaller *Reichswehr*. The SA felt cheated of the spoils of victory and muttered about a "Second Revolution." "Adolf is rotten. He's betraying all of us. He only goes around with reactionaries . . . Are we revolutionaries or aren't we?," Röhm complained. Big business and the regular army and rival Nazis like Himmler and Göring were united in their hostility towards the SA. Hitler was persuaded that Röhm and his allies were conspiring against him, and ordered a wholesale purge later known as the "**Night of the Long Knives**." On the night of June 30, the SA leaders were dragged from their boyfriends' beds in the resort of Bad Wiessee; taken to Stadelheim Prison and shot in the courtyard by SS troopers; some believed this was an army coup, and died shouting "Heil Hitler!." In Berlin alone, 150 SA leaders were executed. Röhm's final words before being shot in Stadelheim prison were more appropriate: "All revolutions devour their own children."

Other victims included General Schleicher, von Papen's assistants, and the leader of the radical Nazis, Gregor Strasser. Local police and Gestapo chiefs added personal enemies to the death lists. Some of the victims had no connection with politics, like the Bavarian music critic whom the hit-squad mistook for an SA General of the same name. Aside from Hitler, Göring, and the army, the main beneficiaries of the purge were two Nazi organizations under the control of a failed chicken-farmer, **Heinrich Himmler**. His black-uniformed **SS** (*Schutzstaffel*—"Defense Staff"), originally Hitler's personal bodyguard, grew into the nucleus for a Nazi army. Meanwhile, the Party's private intelligence service, the **SD** (*Sicherheitsdeinst* or "Security Service"), established itself as a rival to the Gestapo and the army's *Abwehr*—military intelligence organization.

Following Hindenburg's death later that summer, Hitler merged the offices of President and Chancellor, and declared himself **Führer** of the German Reich. Defense Minister von Blomberg acceded to Hitler's request that all soldiers of the *Reichswehr* swear an oath of allegiance to him personally. Having assured Blomberg that the army would remain the "only bearer of arms in the nation," Hitler took the salute from the *Leibstandarte Adolf Hitler* regiment of the SS, and the Hermann Göring Police Battalion—an indication of how he applied the policy of divide and rule even within the Führer state.

THE NAZI IMPACT ON BERLIN

In Berlin as in the rest of the Reich, **Nazi control** extended to all areas of life—the press and radio were orchestrated by Göbbels; children joined Nazi youth organizations; and every tenement building had Nazi-appointed wardens who doubled as Gestapo spies. It was even decreed that women should eschew make-up as an "un-German" artifice—one of the few edicts that wasn't taken seriously. Anti-Nazi criticism—even of the mildest kind—invited a visit from the Gestapo. Although Germans might avoid joining the NSDAP itself, it was difficult to escape the plethora of related organizations covering every aspect of life—from riding clubs and dog breeders to the "Reich Church" or "German League of Maidens." This was the second stage of *Gleichschaltung* – drawing the entire population into the Nazi net.

As the capital of the Reich, Berlin became a showcase city of banners, uniforms, and parades. An image of order and dynamism, of a "new Germany" on the march, was what the Nazis tried to convey. This reached its apotheosis during the **1936 Olympics**, held at a vast purpose-built stadium in the Pichelsdorf suburb of Berlin. Hitler's expectation that the Games would demonstrate Aryan racial supremacy was humiliatingly dashed when black American athlete Jesse Owen gave the greatest performance of the Olympics. Hitler refused to shake Owen's hand at the grandstand. (It's a less well known, perhaps even sadder fact, that US President Roosevelt also refused to do so back home.)

Like many previous rulers of Germany, Hitler felt uncomfortable in Berlin, probably aware that most Berliners suffered rather than supported him. He also felt the city was insufficiently grandiose for the capital of the "Thousand Year Reich," and from 1936 onwards spent much time with his favorite architect, **Albert Speer**, drawing up extensive plans for a remodeled post-war Berlin, to be called "Germania." Its main purpose would be to serve as a monument to the expected Nazi victory in the forthcoming war, and as the capital of a vast empire thereafter. Hitler's millenial megalomania inspired hours of brooding on how future generations might be awed by Germania's monumental ruins—hence the need to build with the finest materials on a gigantic scale. In the meantime, he preferred to spend his time in the Berghof in Berchtesgaden.

KRISTALLNACHT AND THE ROAD TO WAR

If the Berlin Olympics had partly glossed over the realities of Nazi brutality, "*Kristallnacht*" exposed them to the world. On the night of 9/10 November, 1938, organized **attacks on Jewish shops and institutions** took place across Germany, an escalation in the Nazis' violent anti-semitism. At least 36 Jews were murdered, and thousands injured; in Berlin Jews were beaten on the streets while passers-by looked on, and 23 of the city's 29 synagogues were destroyed. Many of the attacks were carried out by SA men in civilian clothes, to give the impression that these were spontaneous outbursts by German citizens. In the wake of *Kristallnacht* ("Crystal Night"—after the broken glass), new **anti-semitic laws** were brought in, making life difficult and dangerous for German Jews, and paving the way for the greater horrors to come.

Throughout the 1930s the Nazis made **preparations for war**, expanding the army and gearing the economy for war readiness by 1940. Göring bragged of putting "guns before butter," but the real architect of the four-year plan was Hjalmar Schacht, a respected banker. It dovetailed with Hitler's foreign policy of obtaining *Lebensraum* ("living space") from neighboring countries by intimidation. In 1936 the German army occupied the Rhineland (demilitarized under the terms of the Treaty of Versailles) to token protests from the League of Nations. The *Anschluss* (annexation) of Austria in 1938 was likewise carried off with impunity, and a few months later Britain and France agreed to the dismemberment of Czechoslovakia at Munich.

Encouraged by their pusillanimity, Hitler made new demands on Polish territory in 1939. It's probable that he believed there would be a similar collapse of will by the western powers, the more so since he first pulled off the spectacular coup of signing a non-aggression pact with

his ultimate enemy, the Soviet Union, thus ensuring that Germany could avoid a war on two fronts. But two days after the German invasion of Poland began on September 1, Britain and France declared war in defense of their treaty obligations.

WORLD WAR II

The outbreak of **World War II** was greeted without enthusiasm by Berliners, despite German victories in Poland. According to American journalist and eyewitness William Srentr (see "Books"), there were few signs of patriotic fervor as the troops marched off to war through the streets of Berlin, and Hitler cancelled further parades out of pique. On October 11, there was rejoicing of near riot proportions when a radio broadcast on the Berlin radio wavelength stated that the British government had fallen, and an immediate armistice was to be declared. Srentr noted that the Berliners showed more enthusiasm at the military parade to mark the fall of France (July 18, 1940), where German troops marched through the Brandenberg Gate for the first time since 1871. Still, he reckoned that it was the spectacle rather than martial sentiments which attracted crowds of Berliners.

Initially, Berlin suffered little from the war. Although citizens were already complaining of meager rations, delicacies and luxury goods from occupied Europe gravitated towards the Reich's capital. What remained of the diplomatic and foreign press community, and the chic lifestyles of Nazi bigwigs, passed for high life. Open dissent seemed impossible, with Gestapo informers believed to lurk everywhere. The impact of wartime austerity was also softened by Nazi welfare organizations and a blanket of propaganda.

AIR RAIDS

Göring had publicly boasted that Germans could call him "Meyer" (a Jewish surname) if a single bomb fell on Berlin—notwithstanding which, the British RAF dropped some for the first time on August 23, 1940. A further raid on the night of August 28/29 killed ten people— the first German civilian casualties. These raids had a marked demoralizing effect on Berliners who had counted on a swift end to the war, and Hitler had to reassure the populace in a speech at the Sportpalast. Holding up a *Baedeker* guide to Britain, he thundered that the *Luftwaffe* would raze Britain's cities to the ground one by one.

However, these early **bombing raids** caused scant real damage and it wasn't until March 1, 1943, when defeat in the Western Desert and difficulties on the Eastern front had already brought home the fact that Germany was not invincible, that Berlin suffered its first heavy raid. While the RAF bombed by night the Americans bombed by day, establishing a pattern which would reduce Berlin to ruins in relentless stages. "We can wreck Berlin from end to end if the U.S.A.A.F. will come in on it. It will cost us between 400 and 500 aircraft. It will cost Germany the war," the head of Bomber command, Sir Arthur "Bomber" Harris, had written to Churchill in 1943. The first buildings to go were the Staatsoper and Alte Bibliothek on the Unter den Linden. On December 22 the Kaiser-Wilhelm-Gedächtniskirche was reduced to a shell. By the year's end, daily and nightly bombardments were a feature of everyday life.

During the 363 air raids until the end of the war, 75,000 tons of high-explosive or incendiary bombs had killed between 35,000 and 50,000 people, and rendered 1,500,000 Berliners homeless. Yet despite the colossal destruction which filled the streets with 100,000,000 tons of rubble, seventy percent of the city's industrial capacity was still functioning at the war's end.

RESISTANCE AGAINST THE NAZIS

Anti-Nazi resistance within Germany was less overt than in occupied Europe, but existed throughout the war, particularly in Berlin. A group of **Communist cells** run by members of the old KPD operated a clandestine information network and organized isolated acts of resistance and sabotage. But the odds against them were overwhelming, and most groups perished. More successful was the *Rote Kapelle* ("Red Orchestra") headed by Harold Schulze-Boysen, a pre-war Bohemian aristocrat who worked in the Air Ministry on Wilhelmstrasse, with agents in most of the military offices, supplying information to the Soviet Union. Eventually it, too, was identified and broken up by the SD and the Gestapo.

The **Kreisau Circle**, a resistance group led by Count Helmut von Moltke, and the groups around Carl Goerdeler (former Mayor of Leipzig)

and General Beck (ex-Chief of Staff) talked about overthrowing the Nazis and opening negotiations with the western allies, but the most effective resistance came from **within the military**. There had been attempts on Hitler's life since 1942, but it wasn't until late 1943 and early 1944 that enough high-ranking officers were convinced that defeat was inevitable, and a wide network of conspirators was established. The one-armed Colonel von Stauffenberg was responsible for placing the bomb in Hitler's headquarters at Rastenberg in East Prussia, while Bendlerstrasse officers planned to use Fromm's Replacement Army to seize crucial points in Berlin.

On July 20, 1944, six weeks after the Allied invasion of Normandy, the coup was launched. Stauffenberg heard the bomb explode as he was leaving Rastenberg, and signaled for the coup to go ahead. In fact, the **attempt to kill Hitler failed** through bad luck, and the conspirators botched their takeover. First they failed to cut communications between Rastenberg and Berlin, and took their time seizing buildings and arresting Nazis. Göbbels succeeded in telephoning Hitler, who spoke directly to the arrest team, ordering them to obey his Propaganda Minister. Then Göbbels set to work contacting SS and Gestapo units, and reminding army garrisons of their oath of loyalty to the Führer. The final blow came at 9pm, when Hitler broadcast on national radio, threatening to "settle accounts the way we National Socialists are accustomed to settle them."

The ringleaders were either summarily shot, or tortured in the basement of Gestapo headquarters on Prinz-Albrecht-Strasse, implicating others. Several thousand suspects were arrested, and hundreds executed. Fieldmarshal Rommel was allowed to commit suicide and receive an honorable burial, but other high-ranking conspirators went before the so-called People's Court in Berlin for a public show trial (August 7–8). All were sentenced to death by the Nazi judge Ronald Freisler, and hanged on meat-hooks at Plötzensee Prison; their death agonies being filmed for Hitler's private delectation. Almost all of those who would have been best qualified to lead post-war Germany had thus been killed. Freisler himself was killed by an American bomb following a later show trial.

THE FATE OF BERLIN'S JEWS

For Berlin's Jews (and those living elsewhere in Germany) the terror began long before the war, as a noose tightened around their right to exist. Of the 160,564 Jews in Berlin at the beginning of 1933, many left in the first year of Hitler's Chancellorship, when a series of laws banned them from public office, the civil service, journalism, farming, teaching, broadcasting, and acting. Still more left when the so-called **Nürnburg Laws** (September 1936) effectively deprived them of German citizenship, and defined Apartheid-like classifications of "racial purity." Jews who could see the writing on the wall, and had money, escaped while they could (other European countries, the US, and Palestine all restricted Jewish immigration); but the majority stayed put, hoping that things would improve, or simply because they couldn't afford to emigrate. After *Kristallnacht*, their already beleaguered position became intolerable.

Once the war began, the Nazis embarked on outright **genocide**, corraling the Jews of Europe in ghettos, branded by their yellow stars, destined for the concentration camps and eventual extermination. Emigration and murder had reduced the Jewish population of Berlin to about 6,500 by 1945. Roughly 1,400 of the **survivors** were "U-Boats" who lived perpetually in hiding, usually with the help of Gentile friends; the other 5,100 somehow survived in precariously legal conditions, usually by being married to non-Jews, or working as gravediggers in the Weissensee Jewish Cemetery.

THE FALL OF BERLIN

Enjoy the war while you can! The peace is going to be terrible...

Berlin joke shortly before the fall of the city.

By autumn 1944 it was obvious to all but the most fanatical Nazis that the end was approaching fast. Even so, Hitler would brook no talk of surrender or negotiation. Teenage boys and men in their fifties were conscripted to replace the fallen millions, as Hitler placed his faith on "miracle weapons" like the V-1 and V-2, and new offensives. A wintertime counterattack in the Ardennes temporarily checked the Allies to the west, but their advance had resumed by January 1945. Meanwhile, the Red Army had launched the largest offensive ever

seen on the Eastern front, 180 divisions seizing East Prussia within two weeks. The distance between the Allied forces was narrowing inexorably.

On January 27, Soviet forces crossed the Oder a hundred miles from Berlin. Only Hitler now really believed there was any hope for Germany. The Nazis threw all they could at the Eastern front and mobilized the *Volkssturm*, an ill-equipped **home guard** of old men, boys, and cripples. Thirteen- and fourteen-year-old members of the **Hitler Youth** were briefly trained in the art of using the *Panzerfaust* bazooka, then sent to fight against T-34 tanks and battle-hardened infantrymen. As thousands died at the front to buy a little time for the doomed Nazi regime, life in Berlin became a nightmare. The city was choked with refugees and terrified of the approaching Russians; it was bombed day and night; and the flash of Soviet artillery could be seen on the horizon.

Behind the lines, **flying court-martials** picked up soldiers and executed anyone suspected of "desertion" or "cowardice in the face of the enemy." On February 1, 1945, Berlin was declared *Verteidigungsbereich* (a "zone of defense")—to be defended to the last man and the last bullet. The civilian population—women, children, cripples, and forced laborers—was set to work building tank traps and barricades; stretches of the U- and S-Bahn formed part of the fortifications. Göbbels trumpeted a "**fortress Berlin**," while Hitler planned the deployment of **phantom armies** which existed on order-of-battle charts, but hardly at all in reality.

As Berlin frantically prepared to defend itself, the Russians consolidated their strength. On April 16, at 5am Moscow time, the **Soviet offensive** began with a massive bombardment lasting 25 minutes. When the artillery fell silent, 143 searchlights spaced 200m apart along the entire front were switched on to dazzle the enemy as the Russians began their advance. Three army groups totalling over 1,500,000 men moved forwards under Marshals Zhukov, Konev, and Rokossovky—and there was little the vastly outnumbered Germans could do to halt them. By April 20—Hitler's fifty-sixth birthday (celebrated with tea and cakes in the *Führerbunker*—the Red Army was on the edge of Berlin. Next day the city center came within range of their guns, and several people standing in line outside the *Karstadt* department store on Hermannplatz were killed by shells. On April 23, Soviet troops were in the Weissensee district, just a few miles east of the center. The Germans were offered a chance to surrender, but declined.

Hitler's birthday party was the last time the Nazi hierarchy assembled before going—or staying—to meet their respective fates. The dictator and his mistress Eva Braun chose to remain in Berlin, and Göbbels elected to join them **in the Führerbunker** with his family. It was a dank, stuffy complex of reinforced concrete cells beneath the garden of the Reich Chancellery. Here Hitler brooded over Speer's architectural models of unbuilt victory memorials, subsisting on salads, herbal tisanes, and regular injections of dubious substances by one Dr. Morell. To hapless generals and faithful acolytes, he ranted about traitors and the unworthiness of the German *Volk*, declaring that the war was lost and that he would stay in the bunker to the end, after learning that General Steiner's army group had failed to stop Zhukov's advance.

THE FINAL DAYS

By April 25, Berlin was completely **encircled by Soviet troops**, which met up with US forces advancing from the west. Over the next two days, the suburbs of Dahlem, Spandau, Neukölln, and Gatow fell to the Russians, and the city's telephone system failed. On April 27 the Third Panzer Army was completely smashed; survivors fled west, leaving Berlin's northern flank virtually undefended. The obvious hopelessness of the situation didn't sway the top **Nazis' fanatical refusal to surrender**. Never mind that many of Berlin's defenses only existed on paper, or that units were undermanned and poorly armed, with crippling shortages of fuel and ammunition. As the Red Army closed in, Göbbels called hysterically for "*rücksichtsloser Bekämpfung*"—a fight without quarter—and SS execution squads worked around the clock, killing soldiers, *Volkssturm* guards, or Hitler Youth who tried to stop fighting.

In the city the horrors mounted. The **civilian population** lived underground in cellars and air raid shelters, scavenging for food wherever and whenever there was a momentary lull in the fighting. Engineers blasted canal locks, flooding the U-Bahn to prevent the Russians from advancing along it. Hundreds of civilians sheltering in the tunnels were drowned as a result. On April 27, the Ninth Army was destroyed attempting to break out of the Russian encirclement to the south, and unoccupied Berlin had been reduced to a strip nine and a half miles long from east to west, and three miles wide from north to south, constantly under bombardment. Next the Russians captured the Tiergarten, reducing the **last pocket of resistance** to the *Regiurungsviertel*, where fighting focused on the Reichstag and Hitler's Chancellery, and on Potsdamer Platz, only a few hundred meters from the *Führerbunker*, by now under constant shellfire.

Hitler still hoped that one of his phantom armies would relieve Berlin, but on April 28 his optimism evaporated when he heard that Himmler had been suing for unconditional surrender to the western Allies. In the early hours of the following day, he married Eva Braun, held a small champagne wedding reception, and dictated his will. As the day wore on savage fighting continued around the Nazi-held enclave. At a final conference the commandant of Berlin, General Weidling, announced that the Russians were in the nearby Adlon Hotel, and that there was no hope of relief.

A breakout attempt was proposed, but Hitler declared that he was staying put. On the afternoon of April 30, after testing the cyanide on his pet German shepherd dog, **Hitler and Eva Braun committed suicide**; he with a revolver, she by poison. The bodies were taken to the Chancellery courtyard and doused with 200 liters of gas; Hitler's followers gave the Nazi salute as the corpses burned to ashes. Meanwhile, Soviet troops were battling to gain control of the Reichstag, and at 11pm two Russian sergeants raised the red flag from its rooftop.

According to Hitler's will, Admiral Dönitz was appointed Chancellor *in absentia*. In the early hours of May 1, Chief of Staff Krebs was sent out to parley with the Russians. After hasty consultation with Stalin, General Chuikov replied that only unconditional surrender was acceptable. When Krebs returned to the bunker, Göbbels rejected this and ordered the fighting to continue. That night he and his wife killed themselves, having first poisoned their children. The rest of the bunker occupants, with the exception of Krebs and General Burgdorf—Hitler's ADC, who committed suicide—now decided to try and break out. Weidling agreed not to surrender until the following dawn in order to give the fugitives time to **escape from the bunker** and through the railroad tunnels towards northern Berlin. Of the 800 or so who tried, about 100 made it—the rest were either killed or captured. No one is sure about the fate of Hitler's deputy, Martin Bormann.

CAPITULATION AND SURRENDER

At 5am, Weidling offered the **capitulation of Berlin** to General Chuikov, who broadcast his surrender proclamation from loudspeaker vans around the city. At 3pm, firing in the city center stopped, although sporadic, sometimes fierce fighting continued on the outskirts, where German troops tried to break out to the west to surrender to the British or Americans rather than the Russians. Their fears were justified, for the Soviets unleashed an **orgy of rape and looting** on the capital, lasting three days. This was Stalin's reward to his troops for having fought so long and so hard.

The **official surrender of German forces** occurred at a Wehrmacht engineers' school in the Berlin suburb of Karlshorst on May 8, 1945. Wehrmacht forces in the west had already surrendered the day before, and British, French, and American delegates flew in with General Keitel, High Commander of the Armed Forces, to repeat the performance for the benefit of the Russians. Berliners had already emerged from their shelters and started to clear the dead and rubble from the streets. Now the Red Army established field kitchens.

With the final act of surrender complete, it was time to count the cost of the Battle of Berlin. It had taken the lives of 125,000 Berliners (including 6,400 suicides and 22,000 heart attacks), and innumerable German soldiers from the 93 divisions destroyed by Red Army. The Soviets themselves had suffered some 305,000 casualties in the battle, whilst the city itself had been left in ruins, without even basic services.

OCCUPATION

During the immediate post-war months, civilian rations of food, fuel, and medicine were cut to the bone to support the 2,000,000-strong **Soviet occupation forces**. Survival rations were measured in ounces per day, if forthcoming at all, and civilians had to use all their wits to stay alive. The Soviet Union had taken steps towards establishing a civilian, Communist-dominated administration even before the war was over. On April 30, a group of exiled German Communists arrived at Küstrin airfield and were taken to Berlin, where they established a temporary headquarters in Lichtenberg. Directed by **Walter Ulbricht**, the future leader of the GDR's Commmunist Party, they set about tracking down old Berlin party members and setting up a **new municipal administration**. In each city district, they were careful to ensure that control of education and the police went to Communists. This apparatus remained in place even after the arrival of the British and Americans in July.

The **Western occupation sectors** had been demarcated by the Allies as far back as 1943, but the troops didn't move in until July 1–4, when 50,000 British, American, and French soldiers replaced the Red Army in the western part of the city. Here, the food situation improved marginally once American supplies began to find their way through, but public health remained a huge problem. Dysentery and TB were endemic, and there were outbreaks of typhoid and paratyphoid, all exacerbated by an acute shortage of hospital beds. British and American soldiers had endless opportunities to profit on the burgeoning **black market**: trading cigarettes, alcohol, gas, NAAFI and PX supplies for antiques, jewelry, or sexual favors. With less to offer, the Russians simply demanded "*Davai chas*," and took watches at gunpoint. Huge black market centers sprang up around the Brandenburg Gate and Alexanderplatz.

From July 17 to August 3 the **Potsdam Conference** took place at the Cecilienhof Palace. It was to be the last great meeting of the leaders of the Big Three wartime alliance. Churchill took the opportunity to visit the ruins of the Reichs Chancellory, followed by a mob of fascinated Germans and Russians. Mid-conference he returned to Britain to hear the reults of the first post-war election—to be replaced by the newly-elected Labor Prime Minister, Clement Atlee, who could do little but watch as Truman and Stalin settled the fate of post-war Europe and Berlin.

For Germans, the worst was yet to come. Agriculture and industry had virtually collapsed, threatening acute **shortages of food and fuel** just as winter approached. In Berlin they dug mass graves and stockpiled coffins for the expected wave of deaths, and thousands of children were evacuated to the British occupation zone in the west of the country where conditions were less severe. Much to everyone's surprise and relief the winter turned out to be uncommonly mild. Christmas 1945 was celebrated after a fashion, and mothers took their children to the first post-war *Weihnachtsmarkt* (Christmas fair) in the Lustgarten.

STARVATION AND UNREST

Unfortunately the respite was only temporary, for despite the good weather, food supplies remained overstretched. In March rations were reduced drastically, and the weakened civilian population fell prey to typhus, TB, and other **hunger-related diseases**; the lucky ones merely suffered enteric or skin diseases. The Allies did what they could, sending government and private relief, but even by the spring of 1947 rations remained at malnutrition levels. **Crime and prostitution** soared. In Berlin alone, 2000 people were arrested every month, many of them from juvenile gangs which roamed the ruins murdering, robbing, and raping. Trains were attacked at the Berlin stations, and in the countryside bandits ambushed supply convoys heading for the city. The winter of 1946/47 was one of the coldest since records began. Wolves appeared in Berlin and people froze to death aboard trains. There were rumors of cannibalism and Berlin hospitals had to treat 55,000 people for frostbite.

Meanwhile, **political developments** which were to have a lasting impact on Berlin were occurring. In March 1946, the social democratic SPD was forced into a shotgun merger with the KPD, to form the **SED** (*Sozialistische Einheitspartei Deutschlands*— "Socialist Unity Party of Germany"), or future **Communist Party** of East Germany. In the western half of the city, 71 percent of members

voted against union; in East Berlin no voting was permitted, and attempts to hold ballots in Prenzlauer Berg and Friedrichshain party offices were broken up by Russian soldiers. In October 1946, the first city-wide **free elections** since 1933 were held. The SED fared badly and the SPD triumphed, much to the annoyance of the Soviet zone authorities, who abandoned free elections after this setback.

THE BERLIN AIRLIFT

Already the city was becoming **divided along political lines** as the wartime alliance between the Western powers (France had also been allotted an occupation zone) and the Soviet Union fell apart, ushering in a new era of conflict which would all too often focus on Berlin. The Allied Control Council met for the last time on March 20, when Marshal Sokolovsky, the Soviet Military Governor, protested about British and American attempts to introduce economic reform in their occupation zones.

Tension mounted over the next few months as the Allies went ahead with economic reform, while the Russians demanded the right to board Berlin-bound Allied trains, and on June 16 walked out of the four-power Kommandantura which had ultimate control over Berlin. Things finally came to a head with the **introduction of the D-Mark** in the Western zone (June 23, 1948). On that day, the Soviets presented the Mayor of Berlin with an ultimatum, demanding that he accept their own Ostmark as currency for the whole city. The issue was put to the vote in the city's parliament, which voted overwhelmingly against the Soviet-backed currency.

Everyone knew that this was asking for trouble, and trouble wasn't long in coming. On the night of June 23/24, power stations in the Soviet zone cut off electricity supplies to the western half of Berlin, and road and rail links between the western part of Germany and Berlin were severed. This was the beginning of the **Berlin Blockade**, the USSR's first attempt to force the Western allies out of Berlin. SPD politician Ernst Reuter, soon to be Mayor of Berlin, addressed a crowd at the Gesundbrunnen soccer field, promising that Berlin would "fight with everything we have."

There was now only one month's food and ten days' coal supply left in the city. The British and Americans realized that they had to support West Berlin, but were unwilling to use military force to push their way in overland. After some consideration it was decided to try to supply Berlin by air, as it was felt that the Soviets wouldn't dare risk intercepting Allied planes. However, there were serious doubts as to whether it was possible to sustain 2,000,000 people by an airlift. The only previous attempt on a comparable scale—maintaining the German Sixth Army at Stalingrad—had been an utter failure. Berlin's needs were calculated at 4000 tons of supplies per day, yet the available aircraft could carry less than 500 tons.

Nevertheless, the **Berlin Airlift** that began on June 26, 1948, soon gathered momentum. The Soviets maintained their blockade and made it plain that they regarded Germany as divided, and Berlin as the capital of their half. America brought in huge C54 Skymaster transport planes to supplement the smaller C47s and Dakotas that the airlift began with. It soon became an around-the-clock, precision operation. By October, planes were landing every three minutes, bringing in 4760 tons of food and fuel every day. Winter was exceptionally tough. Power cuts and severe food rationing reduced living standards to the level of the immediate post-war period. The Russians made supplies available in the eastern half of the city, but relatively few West Berliners chose to take advantage of them. At municipal elections on December 7, the SPD's **Ernst Reuter** was voted in as Mayor of West Berlin, becoming a kind of human symbol of its resistance.

By the spring of 1949, planes were landing or taking off every thirty seconds, and shifting 8000 tons a day. On Easter, the Allies mounted a special operation to boost morale and thumb their noses at the Soviets. In only twenty-four hours they flew 13,000 tons of supplies into Berlin. Shortly afterwards the Soviets gave up, lifting the blockade on May 12. The first trucks and trains to reach West Berlin received a tumultuous welcome. The airlift was continued for another four months to ensure that Berlin would be supplied should the blockade be resumed at short notice. Though it cost the lives of forty-eight airmen and millions of dollars, the airlift thwarted Stalin's attempt to expel the Allies from West Berlin, and dealt the Soviets a resounding propaganda defeat. It also changed most Berliners' perception of the Western powers, from occupiers to allies.

THE BIRTH OF THE TWO GERMANIES

Within six months, the political division of Germany was formalized by the creation of two rival states. First, the British, French, and American zones of occupation were amalgamated to form the **Federal Republic of Germany** (May 1949); the Soviets followed suit by launching the **German Democratic Republic** on October 5. As Berlin lay deep within GDR territory, its eastern sector naturally became the official GDR capital. However, much to the disappointment of many Berliners, the Federal Republic chose Bonn as their capital. West Berlin remained under the overall control of the Allied military commandants, although it was eventually to assume the status of a *Land* (state) of the Federal Republic.

Although West Berlin's **economic recovery** was by no means as dramatic as that of West Germany, the city did prosper, particularly in comparison to East Berlin. The Soviets had gone in for ruthless **asset-stripping**—removing factories, rolling stock, and generators to replace losses in the war-ravaged USSR—and when they eventually turned to reconstructing the GDR, the emphasis was put on heavy industrial production. West Berlin soon became an attractive destination for East Berliners, who were able to cross the **zonal border** more or less freely at this time. Many came to stay, while others worked in the city benefitting from the purchasing power of the mighty D-Mark. And those who did neither used the city to get the entertainment and culture lacking in the more spartan East.

Political tension remained a fact of life in a city which had become an arena for superpower confrontations. The Soviets and GDR Communists had not abandoned the idea of driving the Allies out of Berlin, and mounted diverse operations against them; just as the Allies ran spying and sabotage operations against East Berlin. In this cradle of **Cold War espionage**, the recruitment of former Gestapo, SD, or *Abwehr* operatives seemed quite justifiable to all the agencies concerned. On one side were Britain's SIS (based at Olympia Stadium) and the American CIA, which fostered the Federal Republic's own intelligence service, the Gehlen Bureau, run by a former *Abwehr* colonel. Opposing them were the Soviet KGB and GRU (based at Karlshorst), and the GDR's own foreign espionage service and internal security police. The public side of this rumbling underground war was a number of **minor incidents** in 1952. An Air France plane approaching West Berlin through the air corridor was fired upon by a Russian MiG; the East German authorities blocked streets leading from West to East Berlin, and expropriated property owned by West Berliners on the outskirts of the eastern sector.

THE WORKERS' UPRISING

The **death of Stalin** (March 5, 1953) raised hopes that the situation in Berlin could be eased, but these were soon dashed. In the eastern sector, the Communists unwittingly fueled smoldering resentment by announcing a 10 percent **rise in work norms** on June 16. For workers already hard-pressed to support their families, this demand to produce more or earn less was intolerable. The first to protest were building workers on block 40 of the prestigious Stalinallee construction project, who downed tools and marched on the city center, being joined by other workers and passers-by. At Strausberger Platz they swept aside *Volkspolizei* units who tried to stop them and headed, via Alexanderplatz, for the Unter den Linden. From here, by now roughly 8000-strong, the **demonstration** marched to the House of Ministeries, occupying Göring's former Air Ministry on Leipzigerstrasse, where they demanded to speak with SED chief Walter Ulbricht and Prime Minister Otto Grotewohl, both of whom declined to appear.

Eventually three lesser ministers were sent out to speak to the demonstrators. Clearly alarmed at the scale of the demonstration, they promised to try and get the work norms lowered. But by now the crowd wanted more, and began calling for political freedom. After declaring a **general strike** for next day, the protestors returned to Stalinallee, tearing down SED placards on the way. Grotewohl's announcement rescinding the new work norms later that day failed to halt the strike, news of which had been broadcast across the GDR by Western radio stations. About 300,000 workers in 250 towns joined in, and by 7am a crowd of 100,000 people was marching through East Berlin towards the House of Ministries.

Ulbricht and Grotewohl feared for their lives and called for Russian help. When **Soviet**

tanks appeared in Leipzigerstrasse before noon, they found their route blocked by a vast crowd which refused to budge. The Soviet commandant, General Pavel Dibrova, warned by loudspeaker that martial law had been declared, and all violators would face summary punishment—but with little effect. Dibrova ordered his troops to move forward with the tanks following in close support, and it was at this point that the shooting started.

The crowd scattered as the first shots rang out, leaving youths to confront the T-34s with bricks and bottles. **Street-fighting** raged throughout East Berlin for the rest of the day, and it wasn't until nightfall that the Soviets re-asserted Communist control. At least 267 demonstrators, 116 policemen, and 18 Soviet troops were killed during the fighting, and it's estimated that 92 civilians (including a West Berliner just passing through) were summarily shot after the **suppression of the uprising**. The Western Allies did nothing to prevent this, nor the subsequent trials of "counter-revolutionaries" at which fourteen death sentences and innumerable prison terms were meted out—final confirmation that Berlin was divided.

Bertolt Brecht, who had returned to Berlin in 1949 and elected to live in the East, wrote an epitaph to this episode in a poem called *The Solution*:

> *After the rising of 17 June*
> *The secretary of the Writers' Union*
> *Had leaflets distributed in Stalinallee*
> *In which you could read that the people*
> *Had lost the government's confidence*
> *Which it could only regain with*
> *Redoubled efforts. Would it in that case*
> *Not be simpler if the Government*
> *Dissolved the people*
> *And elected another?*

Berlin was relatively quiet for the remainder of the Fifties, but important events were taking place **in West Germany** under Chancellor Konrad Adenauer. Foremost amongst these was the so-called "**economic miracle**," which saw West Germany recover from the ravages of war astonishingly quickly, and go on to become the largest economy in Europe, which couldn't help but give a shot in the arm to the fortunes of West Berlin. On the political front the **Hallstein doctrine** of non-recognition for the GDR reigned supreme. This was even stretched to the point of not maintaining diplomatic relations with other countries who chose to recognize the GDR. A pragmatic exception was made of the Soviet Union.

THE BUILDING OF THE WALL

The economic disparity between East and West Germany (and their respective halves of Berlin) worsened throughout the 1950s. **Marshall Aid** and West German capital were transforming West Berlin into a glittering showcase for capitalism, whereas the GDR and East Berlin seemed to languish. Prospects for development in the GDR were undermined by a steady **population drain**, as mostly young and often highly-skilled workers headed west for higher living standards and greater political freedom. Roughly 2,500,000 people quit the GDR during the 1950s, mostly via the open border with West Berlin, where an average of 19,000 East Germans crossed over every month. Both the GDR and Soviet governments saw this as a threat to East Germany's existence.

On November 10, 1958, Soviet leader **Nikita Khrushchev** demanded that the Western allies relinquish their role in the "occupation regime in Berlin, thus facilitating the normalization of the situation in the capital of the GDR." Two weeks later, Khrushchev suggested that the Allies should withdraw, and Berlin become a free city—coupled with a broad hint that if no agreement was reached within six months, a blockade would be re-imposed. The Allies rejected the ultimatum, and the Kremlin allowed the deadline to pass without incident. Tripartite **negotiations** at Geneva (May–September 1959) failed to produce a settlement. Meanwhile, tens of thousands of East Germans continued to cross the border into West Berlin.

By 1961 Ulbricht's regime was getting desperate, and rumors that the border might be sealed began to circulate. In mid-June Ulbricht felt compelled to assure the world that no one had "the intention of building a wall." Simultaneously, however, border controls were tightened. Yet the flood of people voting with their feet continued to rise, in what West Berlin's Springer press dubbed, "mass escapes . . . of avalanche proportions." It was obvious that something was about to happen.

Shortly after midnight on August 13, 1961, East German soldiers, policemen, and Workers'

Militia received orders to close the border with the west. At 2am, 40,000 men went into action, stringing barbed wire across streets leading into West Berlin, and closing U- and S-Bahn lines to create what their commanders called "an anti-fascist protection barrier." Many Berliners were rudely evicted from their homes, while others, marginally less unfortunate, had their doors and windows blocked by bales of barbed wire and armed guards. Although the Allies reinforced patrols, they did nothing to prevent the **sealing of the border**.

Despite earlier rumors, most people in West and East Berlin were taken by surprise. Those who lived far from the border area only learned of its closure when they found all routes to West Berlin blocked. Crowds gathered and the border guards were reinforced to prevent trouble. There was little most people could do other than accept this latest development as a *fait accompli*. Others—including a few border guards—managed to take advantage of loopholes in the new barrier, and flee west. But within a few days, building workers were reinforcing the barbed wire and makeshift barricades with bricks and mortar, creating a **provisional version of the Wall**. As a further measure, West Berliners were no longer allowed to cross the border into East Berlin.

REACTION IN THE WEST

Despite public outrage throughout West Germany and formal **diplomatic protests** from the Allies, everyone knew that to take a firmer line risked starting nuclear war. The West had to fall back on symbolic gestures: the Americans sent over General Lucius Clay, organizer of the Berlin Airlift, and Vice-President Lyndon Johnson, on August 18. The **separation of families** plunged morale in East Berlin to new depths, and caused **economic problems** for West Berlin, which was suddenly deprived of 60,000 skilled workers who formerly commuted in from the GDR. They could only be replaced by creating special tax advantages to attract workers and businesses from the Federal Republic into West Berlin. American support for West Berlin was reaffirmed in August 1963, by President **John F. Kennedy**'s "*Ich bin ein Berliner . . .*" speech, but for all its rhetoric and rapturous reception, the West had essentially come to accept the new status quo.

From 1961 onwards the GDR strengthened its **border fortifications**, completely sealing off West Berlin from East Berlin and the East German hinterland. The Wall became an almost impenetrable barrier—in effect two walls separated by a *Sperrgebiet* (forbidden zone) dotted with watchtowers and patrolled by soldiers and dogs. Border troops had orders to shoot to kill and often did so. Yet despite this, hundreds of successful **escapes** took place before the GDR was able to refine its techniques, and thousands of people passed over, under, or through the Wall by various methods, usually involving extreme danger.

BERLIN IN THE SIXTIES

The **gradual reduction of political tension** that occurred after the Wall had been standing a couple of years was partly due to improved relations between the superpowers, and mostly to local efforts. Under SPD Mayor **Willi Brandt**, talks were opened between the West Berlin Senate and the GDR government, resulting in the **"Pass Agreement"** of December 1963, whereby 730,000 West Berliners were able to pay brief visits to the East at the end of the year. Three more agreements were concluded over the next couple of years until the GDR decided to use border controls as a lever for winning **diplomatic recognition** (which the Federal Republic and its Western allies refused to give under the Hallstein doctrine). Access to West Berlin via routes through GDR territory was subject to official hindrances; on one occasion, deputies were prevented from attending a plenary session of the *Bundestag*, held in West Berlin in April, 1965. New and more stringent **passport and visa controls** were levied on all travelers from June 1968 onwards.

As the direct threat to its existence receded, West Berlin society began to fragment along generational lines. Partly because Berlin residents can legally evade West German conscription, young people formed an unusually high proportion of the population. The immediate catalyst was the wave of **student unrest** in 1967–68, where initial grievances over unreformed, badly-run universities soon spread to embrace wider disaffection with the West Germany's materialistic culture. As in West Germany, the *APO* or **extra-parliamentary**

opposition emerged as a strong and vocal force in West Berlin, criticizing what many people saw as a failed attempt to build a true democracy on the ruins of Nazi Germany. Another powerful strand was anti-Americanism, fueled by US policy in Southeast Asia, Latin America, and the Middle East. Both these viewpoints tended to bewilder and enrage older Germans.

The police reacted to street demonstrations in Berlin with a ferocity which shocked even conservatives. On June 2, 1967, a student was shot by police during a protest against a state visit by the Shah of Iran. The right-wing **Springer press** (deliberately sited just near the Wall) absolved the police and pinned all the blame on "long-haired Communists." When someone tried to kill student leader **Rudi Dutschke** (April 11, 1968), there were huge and violent demonstrations against the Springer press. Although the mass-protest movement fizzled out towards the end of the Sixties, a new and deadlier opposition would emerge in the Seventies—partly born from the West German establishment's violent response to what was initially a peaceful protest movement.

OSTPOLITIK AND DETENTE

The international scene and Berlin's place in it changed considerably around the turn of the decade. Both superpowers now hoped to thaw the Cold War and reach a *modus vivendi*, while elections in the Federal Republic brought to power a Chancellor committed to rapprochement with the GDR. On February 27, 1969, US President Richard Nixon called for an easing of international tension during his visit to Berlin. Soon afterwards, **Four Power Talks** were held in the former Allied Control Council building in the American sector. Against a background of negotiations between West Germany and the Soviet Union, and proposals for a European security conference, the participants decided to set aside broader issues in an effort to fashion a workable agreement about the status of the divided city.

This resulted in the **Quadripartite Agreement** (September 3, 1971), followed in December by inter-German agreements regarding transit routes to West Berlin, and travel and traffic regulations for West Berliners. These were largely due to the efforts of Chancellor

Willi Brandt, whose **Ostpolitik** aimed at normalizing relations between the two Germanies. Treaties were signed with the Soviet Union and Poland in 1970, recognizing the validity of the Oder-Neisse line marking the Polish-German border. Finally, in 1972, the Federal Republic and GDR signed a **Basic Treaty**. Whilst stopping short of full recognition, it bound both states to respect each other's frontiers and *de facto* sovereignty.

In return for abandoning the Hallstein doctrine, West Germans were given access to friends and family across the border, which had been effectively denied to them (barring limited visits in the mid-1960s). However, the freedom to move from East to West was restricted to disabled people and senior citizens. This marked a concession by the new East German leader, **Erich Honecker**, who was regarded as a "liberal" when he succeeded Ulbricht in 1971. Aside from desiring access to West German know-how, markets, and capital, Honecker had a personal reason for wanting closer ties: his own family lived in the Saarland.

THE 1970S

During the Seventies Berlin assumed a new identity, breaking with the images and myths of the past. Thanks to the easing of Cold War tensions West Berlin was no longer a frontline city, and East Berlin lost much of its intimidating atmosphere. Throughout the decade, **West Berlin** had similar problems to West Germany: economic upsets triggered by the quadrupling of oil prices in 1974, and a wave of terrorism directed against the establishment. In addition, West Berlin suffered from a deteriorating stock of housing and rising unemployment—both alleviated to some extent by financial help from West Germany.

East Berlin remained relatively quiet. Under Honecker, living standards improved and there was some relaxation of the tight controls of the Ulbricht days. However, most people regarded the changes as essentially trivial, and escapes continued to be attempted, although by now the Wall was formidably deadly. In 1977 a rock concert in Alexanderplatz turned into a brief explosion of street unrest, which the authorities suppressed with deliberate brutality.

THE 1980S

Throughout the 1970s and early 1980s, the Quadripartite Agreement and the inter-German treaties formed the backdrop to relations between West and East Berlin. The main irritant was the **compulsory exchange** of D-Marks for Ostmarks, which the GDR raised from DM6.50 to DM25 in 1980, deterring significant numbers of vistors. But on the whole, a degree of stability and normality had been achieved, enabling both cities to run smoothly on a day-to-day basis, without being the focus of international tension. Even after the partial resumption of the Cold War, following the Soviet invasion of Afghanistan in 1979, Berlin remained relatively calm. The only notable event was the shooting of an American officer on an alleged spying mission in Potsdam, in the spring of 1985.

As elsewhere in West Germany, Berlin witnessed a crystallization of issues and attitudes, and the flowering of new radical movements. Concern about the arms race and the environment was widespread; feminism and gay rights commanded increasing support. Left-wing and Green groups formed an **Alternative Liste** to fight elections, and a left-liberal newspaper, *Tageszeitung*, was founded. Organized squatting was the radical solution to Berlin's **housing crisis**. In 1981, the newly-elected Christian Democrat administration (elected after a financial scandal forced the SPD to step down) tried to evict the squatters from about 170 apartment buildings, and police violence sparked rioting in Schöneberg. The administration compromised by allowing some of the squatters to become legitimate tenants, which had a big effect on life in West Berlin. For the first time since the late 1960s, the social divisions that had opened up showed signs of narrowing. *Alternative Liste* delegates were elected to the Berlin Senate for the first time in May, 1981, and the same year witnessed a boom in **cultural life**, as the arts exploded into new vitality.

The **early 1980s** saw a resumption of frostiness in US-Soviet relations, and heightened concern about **nuclear weapons**. Anti-nuclear activists protested during the Berlin visit of President **Ronald Reagan** (June 1981). But the tension and saber-rattling that characterized the Cold War of the Fifties and Sixties didn't return to Berlin. In 1985 the USSR broke with its tradition of geriatric rulers when the dynamic and comparatively young **Mikhail Gorbachev** became General Secretary of the Soviet Communist Party. The West was slow to appreciate the full significance of his campaigns for *glasnost* and *perestroika*, and their initial impact on Berlin was slight. The city's status—and the division of Germany into separate states—seemed assured by the Quadripartite Agreement and the Basic Treaty.

Unfortunately, ideological hostility prevented the two halves of the city from jointly celebrating Berlin's 750th anniversary in 1987. Instead, **separate anniversary celebrations** were arranged. In East Berlin, these were preceded by a massive **urban renewal project**, both in the city center and the inner suburbs. The SED boasted that the GDR was a mature socialist state, advancing to the front rank of European nations. It saw no need for *glasnost* or *perestroika*—indeed, it regarded them with deep suspicion.

In West Berlin, the elections of spring 1989 swept the CDU administration from power, and an **SPD/Alternative Liste coalition** took over, with Walter Momper as Mayor. In Kreuzberg, demonstrations against what many regarded as an *Alternative Liste* sell-out were put down with unwarranted force, sparking running street battles. Further violence occurred on May 1, during the now-traditional annual wrecking-spree by anarchists and other far-leftists espousing anti-imperialist, anti-capitalist motives. For once, however, the police refrained from breaking heads, having been told to go easy by their chief.

THE GDR RESISTS PERESTROIKA

In the East there were few visible signs of change as the decade wore on, but things were happening behind the scenes. The **Protestant church** provided a haven for several **environ-mental and peace organizations**, which formed a nascent opposition. But the regime seemed as intractable as ever, dismissing Gorbachev-style reforms as inappropriate to the GDR. The most memorable rebuff was delivered by SED chief ideologist Kurt Hager, who said in April 1987, "You don't need to change the wallpaper in your apartment just because your neighbor is doing his place up." Open dissent was stamped on: in January 1988, a group of protesters who unfurled banners calling for greater freedom at the official demonstration in memory of Karl Liebknecht and Rosa Luxemburg were immediately arrested and imprisoned, later being expelled from the GDR.

Fearful of the changes sweeping the Soviet Union, Hungary, and Poland, the authorities banned the Soviet magazine *Sputnik* and several Russian films from the Sixties, only now released from censorship. As a further insult to their subjects, the GDR's rulers heaped honors on the odious Romanian dictator Nicolae Ceaușescu. Although Poland and Hungary were both embarked on the road to democracy, the GDR was unmoving. SED leader Erich Honecker declared that the Wall would stand for another fifty or one hundred years if necessary, to protect "our republic from robbers." East Germans could only despair.

Few believed any more the endless lies and clichés which spanned the gap between official pronouncements and reality. The SED leadership seemed totally isolated from the mood of the people. There seemed no way out except individual attempts to escape. When Chris Gueffroy was shot dead while trying to cross the border at Neukölln on February 6, 1989, no-one realized that he was to be the last person killed in such an attempt.

Something had to give, and give it did in a manner so dramatic and unpredictable that it surprised the whole world.

1989—DIE WENDE

1989 ranks as the most significant year in German history since 1945. In the space of twelve months a complete and unforeseeable transformation (what Germans call *Die Wende***) occurred. The unification of Germany has suddenly gone from being a remote possibility to an imminent near certainty, forcing everyone to reassess the European order.**

Once again Berlin is at the forefront of historical change, manifested in human terms and emotional scenes which caught the imagination of the world. When the Berlin Wall parted on November 9, 1989, it symbolized the end of an era; the Cold War was finally over, and a lifetime's dream had come true for most Germans— above all, those living in the East.

THE BEGINNING: EXODUS THROUGH HUNGARY

It was reform in another Eastern European country that made the incredible events of 1989 possible. On May 2, the Hungarian authorities began taking down the barbed wire along their border with Austria, creating **a hole in the Iron Curtain**. The event was televised worldwide, and thousands of East Germans saw it as a chance to get out. Aware that new visa laws making travel to Hungary more difficult would come into force in the autumn, they seized their chance during summer, when "holidays" provided a pretext.

It wasn't an easy option. Much of the barbed wire was still intact, and Hungarian troops patrolled the border. The lucky ones made it through the woods and swamps, evading soldiers who sometimes, but by no means always, turned a blind eye. In the early months, those who were caught were deported back to the GDR where jail awaited them. Later the Hungarians merely stamped the passports of those whom they intercepted leaving it to the East German police to deal with them—if they returned home.

Wise to what was going on, the GDR authorities began trying to halt the increasing numbers of would-be escapers. Hungary-bound

travelers were stopped and thoroughly searched. Anyone traveling light was deemed to be making a one-way trip and sent back. The same went for people carrying birth certificates and other important documents. Smart **escapers** began booking round-trip tickets to destinations like Bulgaria, and traveling with baggage as if on a family holiday—only to make an unscheduled stop in Budapest.

The whole process was made slightly easier by the **illness of SED leader Erich Honecker**, which put him out of action from July 8 onwards. No one else seemed able to fill the ensuing power vacuum and enforce measures that would have enabled the state to check the draining away of its population. By August, some 200 East Germans were crossing into Austria every night. Those who were caught could console themselves with the fact that the Hungarians no longer stamped their passports, leaving them free to try again. Many, unable to get through the border and rapidly running out of money, sought **refuge in the West German embassy in Budapest**. The situation was gradually reaching crisis point.

MASS ESCAPE

The first **mass exodus** happened on August 19, when 700 East Germans surged across the border into Austria, unhindered by Hungarian border guards. They got there under the pretext of holding a frontier peace picnic near Sopron; in fact, the whole escape was prearranged by the conservative *Paneuropa-Union*, with the support of the reformist Magyar politician, Imre Pozsgay. On August 24, others were allowed to leave after the Red Cross stamped their documents with a "Permit de Voyage." By now some 6000 people had made it across the border and their success encouraged others to make the journey from the GDR to Hungary. By the beginning of September there were over **20,000 refugees** housed in Hungarian holiday camps and the West German embassy—which was by now overflowing.

Having considered the reactions of East and West Germany, the Hungarian government opted to please the latter, and announced (September 7) that "humanitarian measures" would take place in the next few days. This was diplomatic smooth talk for **opening the border** and allowing all the East Germans to leave. When the instruction was implemented on

September 10, East German refugees heard the news at 7pm. Gyula Horn, Hungarian Foreign Minister announced: "The GDR citizens staying in this country can leave with their own, in other words GDR passports, to a country that is willing to receive them." The border opened at midnight, and 300 cars crossed over within fifteen minutes. A couple of hours later the first East German car crossed the Austro-German border at Passau. For those without transport special buses and trains were laid on. The GDR government could only condemn what it called "an organized trade in human beings," while the West German government—from whom the Magyars hoped for investment—promised it would "not forget this independent decision by Hungary."

Other East Germans had meanwhile made their way to **Prague and Warsaw**, where they took refuge in West German embassy buildings. By the last week of September there were 3500 people in the Prague embassy, while Czechoslovak police and *Stasi* agents tried to hold back the thousands more who hoped to gain admission. Despite strongarm tactics, increasing numbers scaled the fence and swelled the crowd of refugees inside the embassy, where living conditions were daily growing more intolerable. Relief finally came on September 30, when **Hans-Dietrich Genscher**, West Germany's Foreign Minister, who had himself fled East Germany during the 1950s, appeared on the embassy balcony and announced that the refugees were to be allowed to leave. Special trains laid on by the GDR government were to ferry 17,000 refugees to West Germany via East German territory. As the **trains** passed through towns like Dresden, Karl-Marx-Stadt, and Plauen, railroad stations were stormed by people hoping to jump on board, and there were dozens of injuries as the police sealed off the tracks.

THE OCTOBER REVOLUTION

Within the GDR, morale plummeted. While people who had applied to leave and were still waiting for exit permits now despaired, thousands of others who had previously been content to make the best of things suddenly began thinking of emigration. Meanwhile, fledgling **opposition groups** like *Neues Forum* emerged, as East Germans took courage from the regime's evident dissarray.

People risked printing and circulating *samizdat* manifestos calling for reform and dialogue. SED leader Erich Honecker, whom West Germany's *Bild Zeitung* had already assigned to the obituary column, reappeared on the scene in time to join official celebrations marking the GDR's fortieth anniversary. Amongst the honored guests were Mikhail Gorbachev, whom most East Germans eagerly awaited; a delegation from Beijing bearing thanks for the SED's public approval of the massacre in Tianenmin Square; and the Romanian dictator Nicolae Ceauşescu.

There was tension on all sides at the **anniversary celebrations** on October 7. Gorbachev stressed the need for dialogue, receptivity to new ideas, and the West German viewpoint. Honecker took a contrary stance, praising the status quo in stock clichés, seemingly oblivious to growing public discontent. The vainglorious parade of weaponry and floats passed off calmly (only party loyalists were admitted to the televised zone), but side street protests and scuffles took place along the cavalcade route. As the day wore on, these escalated into a huge demonstration, which the police and *Stasi* brutally suppressed. Thousands of arrests were made, and prisoners were subject to degrading treatment and beatings. Simultaneous **demonstrations** in Dresden and Leipzig were dealt with even more harshly. But the people were growing bolder, while the regime's self-confidence diminished.

A week later most of those arrested on October 7 were released, and sections of the press voiced oblique criticism of the party leadership's handling of the crisis. The Politburo offered to talk with the opposition, but refused to legalize it. Monday, October 9 saw **nationwide demonstrations**, which came close to bloodshed in **Leipzig**, where 70,000 people marched through the city. Honecker ordered the local security forces to suppress the protest by any means necessary, including force of arms. City hospitals were alerted, and extra plasma was rushed in to cope with the expected casualties. But the march went ahead and Honecker's orders were never executed. Whether someone in the Politburo countermanded them, or the local party secretary or security boss simply ignored them, remains unclear. The main point was that elements of the regime drew the line at wholesale slaughter.

Indeed, the whole Politburo of the SED had become disenchanted with Honecker's rigidity. He was an obvious target for public hatred, and protests were gathering momentum daily. In Leipzig, now the focal point of opposition, the latest protest brought 150,000 people onto the streets. For the leadership, the strain proved too great: after eighteen years as party secretary, **Erich Honecker was suddenly replaced by Egon Krenz** on October 18. It seems that Honecker threatened to resign unless the Politburo supported his hard line; instead, they accepted his resignation in silence, and he left the room "an old and broken man." Krenz, whom SED-watchers dubbed the "crown prince," was a 52-year-old Politburo member with a hardline reputation of his own; it was he who had congratulated the Beijing government after it crushed the Chinese democracy movement. Confounding expectations, however, Krenz immediately announced that the regime was ready for dialogue, although his reputation was to remain a stumbling block when it came to gaining popular trust.

THE CONTINUING EXODUS

Over the next week, as newspaper reports critical of the government increased in frequency, the opposition gained ground and the exodus of GDR citizens continued. On October 27, the government declared an **amnesty** for those convicted of *Republiksflucht* (fleeing the country) or jailed for demonstrating, but the pressure on the streets kept rising. On November 4, East Berlin witnessed the **largest street protest since the workers' uprising of 1953**, as over 1,000,000 citizens demonstrated. The vast crowd walked from the headquarters of the ADN state news agency to Alexanderplatz, where they were addressed by reformists, writers, and priests. Banners calling for the demolition of the Wall were unfurled. The author Stefan Heym, a long-time critic of the regime, told the crowd: "It's as if someone's thrown open a window after years of dullness and fug, platitudes, bureaucratic arbitrariness, and blindness." Author Heiner Müller added: "If the government should resign during the next week, it will be permitted to dance at demonstrations."

The authorities made hasty **concessions**. The same day, Krenz agreed to allow 5000 East Germans packed into the West German embassy in Prague to leave for the west. It was also announced that GDR citizens no longer required visas to visit Czechoslovakia—in effect, permitting emigration via Czechoslovakia. People swarmed across the border to exploit this loophole, and 15,000 of them had reached Bavaria by November 6. The same day, 500,000 citizens demonstrated in Leipzig, winning fresh concessions—the promise of thirty days' foreign travel a year—which satisfied no one.

Next, the SED tried placating people with **resignations**. The government of Prime Minister Willi Stoph quit on November 7, with the Politburo following suit the next day. On the new executive that replaced it, Krenz and Berlin party boss Günter Schabowski were the only relics from the old order; the new Prime Minister, **Hans Modrow**, had acquired something of a liberal reputation during his previous job as Dresden party chief. Simultaneously, the Ministry of the Interior accepted an application from *Neues Forum* to be considered as a legal group. Across the GDR, hardline officials were resigning in the face of ever-increasing demands from the street, and the exodus of citizens was continuing. By now, 200,000 East Germans had left the country since the beginning of 1989.

THE WALL OPENS . . .

The opening of the Berlin Wall was announced almost casually. On the evening of Thursday, November 9, Schabowski told a press conference that East German citizens were free to leave the GDR with valid exit visas, which were henceforth to be issued without delay. Journalists were puzzled; did this really mean that the Wall was effectively open? As news filtered through to the East German population, they sought confirmation by calling the TV stations, which broadcast Schabowski's announcement several times in the course of the evening. Hardly daring to believe it, citizens started heading for the nearest border crossings, with or without visas. A couple who passed through the Bornholmer Strasse crossing at 9:15pm may well have been the first to leave under the new law.

In both East and West Berlin, people flocked to the Wall. Huge crowds converged on the **Brandenburg Gate**, where an impromptu

street party broke out. As West Berliners popped champagne corks and Germans from both sides of the Wall embraced, the *Volkspolizei* gave up checking documents, and simply let thousands of East Germans walk through into West Berlin, from which they had been barred for 28 years. The scenes of joy and disbelief were flashed around a world taken by surprise. West German Chancellor **Helmut Kohl** had to interrupt a state visit to Warsaw and rush to West Berlin, where the international press were arriving in droves. Inside the GDR, disbelief turned to joy as people realized that the unimaginable had happened.

The opening of the Wall was a hard act to follow, but events acquired even greater momentum. On November 10, the Jannowitz Brücke U-Bahn station re-opened after 28 years, making it possible for East Berliners to go to West Berlin by U-Bahn. On Saturday, November 11, **500,000 East Berliners visited West Berlin**. There were reports of mile-long lines at checkpoints, where 2,700,000 exit visas were issued during the first weekend after the opening of the Wall. West Germans—and TV-viewers around the world—gaped at the streams of Trabant cars pouring into West Berlin, where shops enjoyed a bonanza as East Germans spent their DM100 "welcome money," given to all GDR visitors by the Federal Republic. On November 12, the mayors of the two Berlins, Walter Momper and Erhard Krack, met and shook hands at the newly opened Potsdamer Platz border crossing. Just over two years ago, Krack had spurned an invitation to West Berlin celebrations marking the city's 750th anniversary, saying that West Berlin "does not exist for us."

PROTEST AND FURTHER REFORM

Inside the GDR the pace of protest didn't slacken, although the opposition was as surprised as anyone at the rapid changes. Demonstrations continued across the country; in places like Leipzig (now known as the "hero city of the revolution") they had practically become institutionalized. Feelings were still running high against Krenz and other government figures seen as tainted by their association with old system. Not least of the problems facing Prime Minister Modrow was the **declining value of the Ostmark**. The black market

rate fell from 10=DM1 to 20=DM1, and enforcing the official rate of 1:1 became virtually impossible. A fiscal crisis loomed on the horizon.

On the second weekend after the opening of the Wall, the GDR authorities announced that **10,000,000 visas** had been issued since November 9—an incredible statistic considering the whole population of the GDR was 16,000,000. By now all eyes were on the Brandenburg Gate, where the western media was massing in expectation of a grand re-opening. Their hopes were dashed on November 19, when Krenz announced that the opening of the Gate was a symbolic affair in which he had no interest at the moment. Attention shifted back to events in the GDR, whose parliament, the *Volkskammer*, was asserting itself—particulary the hitherto "tame" parties allied to the SED.

The *Volkskammer* motion **ending the leading role of the SED** was passed (December 1) just as pent-up feeling against the *Stasi* erupted in a series of demos and sporadic attacks on its premises and members. These calmed down with a promise from the government that dismantling of the formidable *Stasi* security service would begin straight away. In the first week of December, **round table talks** between government and opposition began in an attempt to thrash out the future. After some haggling, the government agreed to one of the opposition's prime demands, **pledging free elections on May 6, 1990**—these were later brought forward to March 18.

At a special **SED conference** (December 15–17), the party decided to emulate the Hungarian Communists and repackage itself as the new, supposedly voter-friendly **PDS—** *Partei Democratische Sozialismus* or "Democratic Socialist Party." As one of the last representatives of the old guard, Egon Krenz was consigned to political oblivion. His successor, **Gregor Gysi**, was a previously unknown lawyer who had defended a number of dissidents under the old regime. Almost immediately, Gysi and Modrow had to respond to a new initiative from **Chancellor Kohl**, who visited Dresden on December 19. Addressing a huge, enthusiastic crowd as "dear countrymen," Kohl promised that he wouldn't leave them in the lurch, and declared his **ultimate goal of a united Germany**.

Hans Modrow took Kohl's visit as an opportunity to announce the **re-opening of the Brandenburg Gate**. Initially this was opened to pedestrians only, with one channel in each direction. Almost simultaneously it was announced that the **removal of visa controls and compulsory currency exchange for West German visitors** to the GDR would be implemented ahead of schedule. By the year's end there were further signs of the **two Berlins drawing closer together**. Numerous joint economic, industrial, and cultural projects were under consideration, and East Berlin city maps began to feature S-and U-Bahn stations in West Berlin (which had previously been represented by a blank space).

INTO THE NINETIES

On the face of it Berlin's future has never looked so rosy, and, should the changes sweeping Eastern Europe and the Soviet Union remain (relatively) peaceful, there's probably little to fear in the long term. But the transition stage is fraught with difficulties and uncertainties for Germans on both sides of the fading border, and for those in the East, the new decade began under a palpable shadow of disappointment and fear. Reform seemed too slow in coming, and people suspected that the apparatus of SED control had merely gone underground, biding its time. Hence the outrage in January 1990, when the government proposed establishing a new security service based on the old *Stasi*.

Revelations of **corruption** amongst the former Communist leadership, and the discovery that West Germany's standard of living eclipsed anything offered by the GDR, produced massive disillusionment with the East German state. The notion of **German unification** became increasingly popular, dismaying some of the original opposition activists, who cherished hopes of a maintaining a separate state, pursuing a "third way" between socialism and capitalism. Groups like *Neues Forum* began losing ground to parties modeled on Kohl's CDU, the social democratic SPD, and the far-right Republicans, all of which supported unification in one form or another.

When the GDR's first free elections were finally held on March 18, 1990, the result was a victory for a right wing alliance dominated by the CDU under Lothar de Maiziere. In reality this was a victory for Chancellor Helmut Kohl, the self-proclaimed champion of German unification. It was his promises of financial help and investment that led people back to the CDU in the GDR, and it was to him that people were looking to ease the worsening economic plight.

During the two months following the election it began to seem possible that these hopes would be realized as, after a shaky start, the new government hammered out an agreement with the Federal Republic, leading to the economic and currency union effected on July 2.

East Germans hope that the Deutschmark and West German know-how will substantially improve their standard of living within a few years, and see economic and currency union as the first real step along the road to full recovery. Yet many people are worried that the change from a planned to a market economy will push up rents, close factories, and wipe out the value of pensions and savings. Already, some former owners of apartment buildings in East Berlin are starting to threaten legal claims; and with the Deutschmark so strong, West Germans can buy up anything worth owning.

The likely cost of rebuilding the East's industry and mitigating its appalling environmental blight is already worrying West German taxpayers. Both the SPD and the CDU have to tread a fine line between the voters' patriotism and self-interest. Kohl's fear of losing support to the Republicans caused him to prevaricate about a firm commitment to existing borders—causing alarm in Poland, and testy reactions from the European Community. It was Foreign Minister Genscher who finally impelled Kohl to affirm the inviolability of the Oder-Neisse line and other borders, clearing the way for international negotiations at the highest level.

Diplomatically, much has to be settled. Does Germany remain within NATO (as the CDU pledges) or become neutral (as the SPD advocates)? Will NATO and Soviet forces be withdrawn entirely, or keep a scaled-down presence in their former zones? Everyone favors maintaining and expanding cooperation with other European states, but exactly how, and on what terms, has still to be decided. Yet with all-German elections now timetabled for December 2, 1990 a united Germany within a peaceful Europe seems a realistic prospect. And as and when it happens, Berlin will once again be at the forefront of German—and European—developments.

FROM EAST TO WEST: ONE FAMILY'S STORY

After years of trying to leave his home in Prenzlauer Berg, East Berlin, Victor Schröder, his wife, and young son were allowed to emigrate from the GDR to West Berlin, a few weeks before the East German government relaxed the laws on foreign travel. He is currently living in West Berlin, working in the theater.

THE DECISION TO LEAVE

I started writing this account while sitting in Tegel Airport, West Berlin waiting for a flight to London. For three years we had celebrated the new year in East Berlin with our British friends, hoping that one day we would be able to leave the GDR and celebrate New Year in London.

In 1986, the year in which we made applications to leave the GDR and to be "relieved" of our GDR citizenship, the political and economic situation had reached the point where most intellectual and progressive forces inside the GDR agreed that there was no point in trying to work for a better life there. In purely economic terms things were getting worse all the time. Outside of East Berlin people had problems getting hold of even the most basic necessities. To lay your hands on the simplest things you had to travel to the big towns and stand in line for hours. People were forced to take time off work merely to stand in lines—by late afternoon everything was invariably already sold out. The only things which didn't disappear within hours were the things which went within minutes, if they ever even made it into the shops at all.

And it seemed that as the situation got worse and worse, the hymns of praise to socialism and its economic successes in the newspapers grew more outrageous. Every day you could read about 100 percent fulfillment of production, and goals being exceeded, but all normal people could do was wonder where all these mythical goods were. The figures were completely false.

During this time anger against the regime came to a head. Small scale complaints began to be heard, but usually not for long. The all-powerful and ever-present *Staatssicherheits-dienst*—the *Stasi*—kept people quiet or persuaded them to change their minds. Tentative voices of opposition were usually dealt with by quick arrest and summary trial, at which it was alleged that they were "Rowdies," misled and influenced by the Western propaganda. Little attention was paid to their real political backgrounds.

After sentencing, such people were sent to prison or forced, under threat of receiving an even longer sentence, to make an application for an exit visa. In the latter case they'd spend a few months in jail before being chucked out of the country. Rumors were spread about people dealt with in this way, alleging that their actions had been merely calculated to get them out of the country, and that they had no real interest in changing things in the GDR.

At that time we had a lot of hope in Gorbachev, but, thanks to the domestic and foreign policy of the GDR, this was rapidly shattered as the government told us that the GDR had a totally different economic potential and historical background, and had no need of changes like those taking place in the Soviet Union. The official line was succinctly summed up in a statement from Kurt Hager, the "GDR Göebbels" as he was known, at that time the Minister for Propaganda: "You don't need to change your wallpaper in your apartment just because your neighbor is doing his place up."

Not surprisingly, this all led to uncertainty among the people about what was really going on in the GDR, and increased hatred of the government and the despised *Stasi*. During this time fear mounted, as the *Stasi* was strengthened and anger grew because its operatives and agents earned good money and had access to heavily subsidized western goods in special shops.

Even then we knew about corruption in the GDR and illicit deals with the West. We knew that alcohol was being smuggled into West Berlin, and we suspected that Schönefeld airport was being used as staging post for drug smuggling. We also knew that the GDR government was involved in illegal arms trading, although when this was actually officially proved we were surprised by its extent.

For us, and for many others, the problem was the schizophrenic situation into which we were forced by life in the GDR. School children and students found themselves having to give their teachers and professors a view of their existence which did not correspond to what they actually knew from their own lives, backed up by what they'd heard on Western radio and TV. This in turn led to a build-up of frustration and aggression.

THE FIRST STEPS

We made our application to leave in December 1986. Immediately my wife had to resign from her job as photographic laboratory assistant at the state-run Berlin Water Board, and was made to do a menial job within the same organization—which was so unbearable that she left. The fact that she'd left went on her work record, meaning that there was little likelihood of her being able to find a decent job in the future.

I was saved from this kind of treatment because I was working as a lighting technician in the *Berliner Ensemble* theater, and the government, recognizing the big potential for dissent within the arts, tended to leave people who worked in that area alone. In fact the "culture industry" was generally allowed a limited degree of freedom and given certain financial and material incentives.

That's not to say though that the arm of the *Stasi* didn't also reach us. At one point a lot of their people were placed in the finance department of the theater to keep an eye on things. Paradoxically, these were mainly people who had elsewhere embezzled considerable amounts of money or who had fallen behind on tax payments. Before their official trials they'd been given secret hearings at which they were offered the choice of either going to jail or working for the *Stasi* in an easy job.

Otherwise, people tended to work for the *Stasi* out of conviction—if you could really call it conviction. Mostly it was a case of indoctrination into blind obedience, further encouraged by money and privileges. These were the people who, during the demonstrations of October 7 and 8, reacted most violently, attacking pregnant women and, with total irrationality in this supposedly socialist state, calling people "niggers." It was outbursts like these which showed up more than anything the senselessness of the whole setup.

At the theater we also had *Stasi* people employed in the personnel department, from where they could control who worked in the theater, bringing more of their own people in if necessary. They were also involved in the overall management, from where they had a real say in the running of the theater. I experienced this directly. On several occasions, I was assigned to go to the West on tour. Invariably, just before the journey, I would be turned down with doubtful excuses and consoled with the prospect of being allowed to go—"next time." The first time I was told that I was too young, and the second time that I couldn't go until I'd done my military service—although everyone knew that I was a conscientious objector (to explain how I avoided military service without ending up in jail would be a story in itself, suffice to say that I was very well-organized and I had a very good lawyer who, today, is the Chairman of *Demokratische Aufbruch*, "Democratic awakening," one of the new opposition groups*).

The third refusal was the final straw. Fourteen days before I was due to go to Italy I was summoned to appear before the management, where I was told that the Ministry for State Security had said there was no chance of my being able to go, because there was a "discrepancy between my professional conduct and private conduct." From this point onwards I was convinced of the impossibility of any change in the system in the foreseeable future. We were scared that things would get worse.

The situation had reached the point where no one could see any meaning in socialism. All forms of this "social order" had proved to be totalitarian dictatorship, based on the total physical and psychological exploitation and repression of the working population, and benefitting only a privileged few. We never imagined that the regime could collapse; at best we thought there might be a few cosmetic changes. That was what we thought then. We reckoned it up and it looked like this: we were then both 25 years old with a son of 4. If we decided to stay and devote our lives to trying to achieve change we would have to reckon with 5 to 10 years to reach the point where there would be a chance of the government being overthrown, and during this time we'd possibly have to reckon with jail. After that there'd be a re-building phase as the

---

Editor's note: Wolfgang Schnur, who later resigned after admitting spying for the *Stasi*.

GDR recovered economically. All this would probably have taken another 20 years. According to this calculation we'd be about 50 before we'd be able to start realizing the dreams of 25 years.

Also, there seemed to be no guarantee that you'd actually survive. It seemed quite possible that we'd suffer psychological damage or even death at the hands of the *Stasi*. We wanted to live and give our child a future, in order that he wouldn't have to live in these, or perhaps even worse, conditions. That was why we made an application to leave. Three years of deceit, fear, and trepidation followed. However, in a relatively short time we were able to start realizing what we wanted out of life.

BUREAUCRACY

Once we'd made our application to leave we were summoned time and time again to the Prenzlauer Berg district Department for Internal Affairs where they used all kind of doubtful methods to try to make us change our minds. We were told that that our application hadn't been made in time. When we drew their attention to certain paragraphs in the GDR constitution we were told: "That doesn't apply in your case," and, "Do you really believe everything you read?." Then, when we referred to various UN human rights agreements, we were told that the GDR had indeed signed these international agreements but that rather than being binding they represented an ideal state which it was *hoped* would one day be achieved. On another occasion we were told that our application had been turned down and that we had absolutely no right to bother them any more.

During this time a few things happened which strengthened our resolve to see things through to the end. One example which had a great effect on me personally, although it might not seem so momentous to an outsider, was our effort to throw a New Year's party at the end of 1987, to which we wanted to invite a lot of friends from both home and abroad.

During the course of the year I'd scripted and directed a Super 8 film which I wanted to show at the party. Making a film like this was no easy matter in the GDR, and we'd had to do it more or less secretly. There was no way we'd be allowed to show it publicly without the *Stasi* preventing it, and so a private party like this was the best way to do it. On a previous

occasion I'd been stopped from showing a film I'd made. When I'd asked why I was told not to ask stupid questions, they knew very well what the film was about, which shows the extent to which you were spied on in our society.

In order to throw the party I had to find a room, which was also no easy matter, as in the GDR it was difficult to rent rooms for any private functions other than weddings. Six months in advance we were able to rent a sort of bar with a buffet included. The only condition was that we had to clear everything with the police. I had to take full responsibility for the orderly nature of the party, and provide five people to keep an eye on things. Everything was arranged: I was given the official go-ahead and started sending out invitations.

Then on December 30 I was summoned from work to the local police station where I was told that I'd given false information when applying for permission and that they were going to stop the party. I was now left with seventy guests due the next day and no room. That evening I went to the Interior Ministry, where I was told that nothing could be done. Then I was asked why I couldn't go to one of the many official parties being held in bars and local community/ arts centers, and how come I knew so many people anyway, and whether I knew all their names. Finally, in all seriousness, the official told me that he'd recently celebrated his birthday with some friends, colleagues, and relatives, and that there had been only five people there—and that it had all been very nice.

There was no answer to that. I left because there was really no point in sitting with people like these. In the end we were able to celebrate as a friend made her apartment available, and in the GDR one thing we knew how to do was improvise. It turned out to be one of the best New Year's parties we ever had, in spite of everything. Sadly, the friend who had lent us her apartment for the evening took her own life shortly afterwards, something for which the political situation in the GDR was at least partly to blame.

WAITING

As we waited to hear about our application to leave we kept writing letters to the government and the responsible ministries. All our efforts were completely without success until March 1989. Then, suddenly, we received a summons to the district Department for Internal Affairs, where we were told that we'd have to make a new application. This would then be considered over the course of six months, at the end of which we'd find out whether we had any chance of being allowed to leave the country. After six months had gone by we were summoned once more and told that our application had been accepted—in principle—and that it was now necessary to determine whether our emigration would "damage the economy of the GDR." We were also told that once we reached the West we would almost certainly fall into "the deepest abyss."

After this everything went relatively quickly. We were summoned again and given a so-called *Laufzettel*, a slip which had to be signed at the various banks we used, the housing office, the post office, and so on. We also received notification that we had to give up our apartment. We began to sell off and give away our furniture and possessions, since moving costs from the GDR to the West were extremely high, and had to be paid in hard currency. In a way, I suppose, it was also a psychological move: we wanted to make a completely new start, without dragging all our rubbish from "home."

After we'd handed over our *Laufzettel* we were again told a few times by the authorities that we were taking the wrong path: but, if everything went without problems, then we could reckon on being out within a week. Then the big day arrived when we had to hand over a large wad of cash for the document confirming that we'd given up our citizenship, and sign other bits of paper in which we had to state that we had no interest in visiting the GDR again. Then we handed over our identity cards in return for temporary identity papers which were only valid for the period we were permitted to remain in the GDR—until midnight. On this final day the people at the District Council offices were very polite to us, wishing us good luck. But I had the feeling that they were being very hypocritical, and merely wanted to avoid any complaints against them being registered at Salzgitter*, or that, on the off chance that they might one day be allowed to travel themselves, they wanted to avoid meeting people

who'd spit at them, or (the way I was feeling by then) lynch them in the street.

We left the offices for the last time and went to my wife's sister's house where we drank a lot of champagne and picked up our things to take them to the Friedrichstrasse border crossing. For me the most disappointing experience was that once we'd passed through the frontier onto western territory, everything seemed so normal. I had the feeling that things had never been any different. I think though that this wasn't a general reaction but rather a personal one caused by the hate inside me for the GDR.

We reacted to the opening of the Wall with mixed feelings. At first we thought it couldn't be true. We'd been led around in circles for three years. But we were lucky: others had been hindered for much longer, imprisoned and even murdered, ever since the Wall went up. For others still it went back forty years to the founding of the GDR. Now suddenly everything was normal again. Even now, at the start of 1990, we can't help feeling skeptical about it and worrying that, as long as the high-ranking army officers and *Stasi* people remain unpunished, there will always be the possibility of a *putsch*.

The one thing I know for certain is that, although we've only been in the West for three months, there's no way we'd ever be able to adapt to the new conditions in the GDR, because we didn't see the turnaround ourselves and in our minds the old system is still intact. It's almost impossible to grasp that the changes which we despaired of ever seeing have now become at least a partial reality.

There's no way we would think about going back. The GDR was never our homeland and never will be, unless it becomes economically and politically part of West Germany. Apart from which we don't feel we have time to take part in rebuilding the country which took so many years away from us. And I for one don't think it would be very easy to stomach seeing the spies and scum who made our lives difficult walking the streets freely having managed to escape the punishment due to them. That, however, is a mistake that was made after fascism. But then this kind of communism was nothing but fascism camouflaged with a different ideology—something which recently became all too clear in Romania.

---

*The West German town where a record is kept of crimes committed by the GDR government.

Victor Schröder, January 1990
Translated by John Gawthrop

BOOKS

HISTORY

EARLY AND PRE-WORLD WAR II

Walter Hubatsch *Frederick the Great: Absolutism and Administration* (UK, Thames & Hudson £12:50); **Christopher Duffy** *Frederick the Great: A Military Life* (Routledge, Chapman & Hall, 1988; $16.95). Two contrasting biographies on different aspects of the man who brought Berlin and Prussia to the forefront of German affairs, and to a place among the great powers of Europe.

Alexander Reissner *Berlin 1675–1945* (UK; Oswald Wolff £6.95). Subjective and often highly opinionated history of the city. A stimulating read nevertheless.

Eberhard Kolb *The Weimar Republic* (UK, Unwin & Hyman; available in libraries). The most recent study of the endlessly fascinating but fundamentally flawed state—as yet the only experiment at a united and democratic German nation—which survived for just fourteen years. A bad omen?

John Willett *Weimar Years* (Abbeville Press, $19.95). The man who has brilliantly translated Brecht's works into English here turns his attentions to the wider culture of the Weimar Republic.

Alex de Jonge *The Weimar Chronicle* (New American Library, 1979; $8.95). While not the most comprehensive of accounts of the Weimar Republic, this is far and away the most stimulating. A couple of chapters focus on Berlin, and the book is spiced with eye-witness memoirs and a mass of engaging detail, particularly on the arts in Berlin.

Questions on German History (German Bundestag Press DM6). English translation of the guide to the Reichstag exhibition of the same name. Essential if you're visiting, and, for the price, a good bargain read on Germany and Berlin history from 1800 to the mid-1980s.

RECENT HISTORY AND SOCIAL STUDIES

John Ardagh *Germany and the Germans* (Harper & Row, 1988; $10.95). The most up-to-date (1987) English-language characterization of West Germany and its people, taking into account its history, politics and psyche, and covering almost every aspect of national life. The section on Berlin, while brief, is packed with astute observations and illuminating facts.

Walter Henry Nelson *The Berliners* (McKay o/p). Dated (1969) but all-embracing portrait of the city in the years of psychedelia, student protest, and frequent (and mostly fatal) attempts to cross the Wall.

Werner Hülsberg *The German Greens* (Routledge, Chapman & Hall, 1989; $15.95) An in-depth analysis of Germany's most exciting political phenomenon, this book traces the movement's intellectual and political origins, chronicles the internal disputes, introduces the main characters, and analyses its shortcomings.

Mark Girouard *Cities and People* (Yale University Press, 1987; $24.95). A well-illustrated social and architectural history of urban development that contains knowledgeable entries on Berlin, particularly the eighteenth and nineteenth century periods.

Norman Gelb *The Berlin Wall* (Simon Schuster, 1988; $8.95). The definitive account of the building of the Wall and its social and political aftermath—as far as 1986. Includes a wealth of information and anecdote not to be found elsewhere.

Berliner Illustrierte (Springer Verlag DM7). Glossy account of the 1989 events with historical background and "human interest" material, illustrated by gripping photos. Published by the house responsible for the tabloid *Bild*, it inevitably has a right-wing political bias.

Granta 30 *New Europe!* (Penguin $7.95). Granta's round-up of writing on and from central Europe in spring 1990 contains pieces by Jurek Becker on German unification, and Werner Krätschell on the opening of the Wall.

NAZISM AND THE WAR YEARS

SPECIFIC ACCOUNTS

Martin Middlebrook *The Berlin Raids* (Penguin, 1989; $24.95). Superbly researched account of the RAF's campaign to destroy the capital of the Third Reich by mass bombing. Based on interviews with bomber crews, Luftwaffe fighter pilots and civilians who survived the raids, it's a moving, compassionate and highly exciting read.

Tony Le Tissier *The Battle of Berlin* (St Martin, 1988; $29.95). Soldierly (the author was a lieutenant-colonel in the British army) shot-by-shot account of Berlin's final days. Authoritative, if a little dry.

George Clare *Berlin Days 1946–1947* (UK, Macmillan £12.95). "The most harrowing and yet most fascinating place on earth" Clare begins his account of his time spent as a British army translator. This is Berlin seen at what the Germans called the *Nullpunkt*—the zero point—at which the city, its economy, buildings and society, began to rebuild almost from scratch. Packed with characters and observation, it's a captivating—if at times depressing—read.

Christabel Bielenberg *Christabel* (Penguin, 1989; $6.95). Bielenberg, the niece of Lord Northcliffe, married German lawyer Peter Bielenberg in 1934 and was living with her family in Berlin at the outbreak of the war. Her autobiography details her struggle to survive the Nazi period and Allied raids on the city, and to save her husband, imprisoned in Ravensbrück as a result of his friendship with members of the Kreisau resistance group.

Marie Vassiltchikov *The Berlin Diaries* (Random, 1988; $8.95). Daughter of a Russian emigré family and friend of the Bielenbergs (see above), Vassiltchikov's diaries provide a vivid portrait of wartime Berlin and the July 1944 bomb plot conspirators—whose members also numbered among her friends.

Lali Horstmann *Nothing for Tears* (Houghton Mifflin, o/p). Rather stolidly genteel description of life in a small village on Berlin's outskirts during the war, but successful in capturing some of the fear of those "waiting for the Russians."

GENERAL READING

Alan Bullock *Hitler: A Study in Tyranny* (Harper & Row; $13.95). Ever since it was published, this scholarly yet highly readable tome has ranked as the classic biography of the failed Austrian artist and discharged army corporal whose evil genius fooled a nation and caused the deaths of millions.

William Shirer *The Rise and Fall of the Third Reich* (Simon & Schuster, 1981; $17.95). The perfect complement to Bullock's book: Shirer was an American journalist stationed in Berlin during the Nazi period. Notwithstanding the inordinate length and excessive journalese, this book is full of insights, and is ideal for dipping into, with the help of its exhaustive index.

Hugh Trevor-Roper *The Last Days of Hitler* (Macmillan, 1986; $7.95). A brilliant reconstruction of the closing chapter of the Third Reich, set in the Bunker of the Reichs Chancellery on Potsdamerplatz. Trevor-Roper subsequently marred his reputation as the doyen of British historians by authenticating the forged *Hitler Diaries*, which have themselves been the subject of several books.

Claudia Koonz *Mothers in the Fatherland* (St Martin, 1988; $14.95). Recent and brilliantly perceptive study of the role of women in Nazi German. Includes a rare and revealing interview with the chief of Hitler's Women's Bureau, Gertrud Scholtz-Klink.

James Taylor and Warren Shaw *A Dictionary of the Third Reich* (UK, Grafton £4.99; available in libraries). The handiest reference book of the period, difficult to put down.

Adolf Hitler *Table Talk* (AMS Press, 1979; $49.50). Hitler in his own words: Martin Bormann, one of his inner circle, recorded the dictator's pronouncements at meetings between 1941 and 1944. The early *Mein Kampf* (Noontide, 1986; $6.00), a series of rambling, irrational and hysterical outbursts on every subject under the sun is also of interest, as it constituted Hitler's blueprint for power.

ART AND ARCHITECTURE

Frank Witford *Bauhaus* (Thames & Hudson, 1984; $11.95.) Comprehensive and well-illustrated guide to the architectural movement that flourished in Dessau and included the Berlin architect Walter Gropius.

Wolf-Dieter Dube *The Expressionists* (Thames & Hudson, 1985; $11.95). A good general introduction to Germany's most distinctive contribution to twentieth-century art.

Post-War Berlin (UK, Architecture Design Profile £8). A collection of scholarly essays on how the wartime legacy of destruction has been handled by the architects of East and West Berlin.

Berlin: an Architectural History, Doug Clelland, ed. (St Martin, 1984; $14.95) Excellent—if overly academic—essays on the city's development from the thirteenth century to the present day. Heavy going, but worth the effort.

GUIDES

Karl Baedeker *Berlin and its Environs* (Scribners, o/p, but available in libraries). First published in 1903, the learned old *Baedeker* is an utterly absorbing read to a grand imperial city now long vanished. There's advice on medicinal brine-baths, where to buy "mourning clothes," the location of the Esthonian embassy, and beautiful fold-out maps that enable you to trace the course of streets that survived the war. An armchair treat.

Karin & Arno Reinfrank *Berlin: Two Cities under Seven Flags, A Kaleidoscopic A–Z* (St Martin, 1987; $19.95). Quirky observations on Berlin East and West make this an enjoyable study of the city's background.

Anders Reisen *Planbuch Berlin* (Anders Reizen DM12.80). German-only street-by-street listings of every decent bar, café and restaurant in West Berlin. The entries, however, are scant and rather dated (1987). Anders Reisen's (German only) *Berlin* guide (DM14.80) is a collection of politically clued-up essays on the pre-*Wende* city.

Hans Peter Heinicke *The Secret Sights of Berlin* (Wort & Bild Specials DM19.80). Not quite as intriguing as the title suggests, but has the occasional tidbit of offbeat information.

Outlook Berlin (Informationszentrum Berlin; free). Giveaway official pamplet with a brief illustrated history and dull round up of facts and figures on contemporary West Berlin. Along with other, similar official material, available from the *Informationszentrum*: see "Information and Listings Magazines" in *West Berlin Basics*).

FICTION

Alfred Döblin *Berlin-Alexanderplatz* (Ungar, 1984; $11.95). A prominent socialist intellectual during the Weimar period, Döblin went into exile shortly after the banning (and burning) of his books in 1933. *Berlin-Alexanderplatz* is his weightiest and most durable achievement, an unrelenting epic of the city's proletariat.

Lillian Hellman *Pentimento* (New American Library, $4.95). The first volume of Hellman's memoirs contains *Julia*, supposedly (it was later charged to be heavily fictionalised) the story of one of her friends caught up in the Berlin resistance. This was later made into a finely acted, if thinly emotional, film of the same name.

Ian McEwan *The Innocent* (Doubleday, 1990; $18.95.) McEwan's latest novel brilliantly evokes 1950s Berlin as seen through the eyes of a post office worker caught up in early Cold War espionage—and his first sexual encounters. Flounders in its obligatory McEwan final nasty twist, but laden with a superbly researched atmosphere.

Peter Schneider *The Wall Jumper* (Pantheon, 1985; $6.95). A series of fascinating cameos which describe life under the Wall, and the intrigue, characters and tragedy it caused.

Christopher Isherwood *Goodbye to Berlin* (Random, o/p). Set in the decadent atmosphere of the Weimar Republic as the Nazis steadily gain power, this collection of stories brilliantly evokes the period and brings to life some classic Berlin characters. It subsequently formed the basis of the films *I Am a Camera* and the later remake *Cabaret*. See also Isherwood's *The last of Mr Norris* (Morrow, o/p), the adventures of the overweight eponymous hero in pre-Hitler Berlin and Germany.

Ian Walker *Zoo Station* (Atlantic Monthly, 1988; $7.95). Not really fiction but a personal recollection of time spent in Berlin in the mid 1980s by a British journalist. Perceptive, engaging and well informed, it is the most enjoyable account of pre-*Wende* life in the city available.

Philip Kerr *March Violets* (Penguin, 1989; $17.95). Well-received, detective thriller set in the early years of Nazi Berlin. Though keen on period detail—nightclubs, the Olympic stadium, building sites for the new autobahn—it somehow fails to convince.

Len Deighton *Winter: A Berlin Family 1899–1945* (Ballantine, 1988; $4.95). Fictional saga that traces the fortunes of a Berlin family through World War I, the Rise of Nazism and the Third Reich's collapse: a convincing account of the way in which a typical upper-middle-class family weathered the wars. Better known is Deighton's *Funeral in Berlin* (Berkley, 1984; $3.50), a spy-thriller set in the middle of Cold War Berlin and based around an Eastern chemist's defection, aided by hard-bitten agent Harry Palmer (as the character came to be known in the movie starring Michael Caine). *Berlin Game* (Ballantine, 1984; $5.95) pits British SIS agent Bernard Samson (whose father appears in *Winter*) against an arch manipulator of the East Berlin secret service, and leaves you hanging for the sequels *Mexico Set* and *London Match*.

LANGUAGE

German is a very complex language and you can't hope to master it in a short time. As English is a compulsory subject in West Berlin's school curriculum, most people who have grown up since the war have some familiarity with it, which eases communication a great deal.

Nonetheless, a smattering of German does help. Also, given that the city is occupied by American and British forces who make little effort to integrate into local communities or learn German, people are particularly sensitive to presumptuous English-speakers. On the other hand, most will be delighted to practise their English on you once you've stumbled through your German introduction.

The most useful **dictionary** is the pocket-sized *German-English Dictionary* (Langen-Scheidt, $4.95), while the best **phrase book** for your trip is *Berlitz German For Travelers* (Macmillan, $4.95).

PRONUNCIATION

English-speakers find the complexities of German grammar hard to handle, but pronunciation isn't as daunting as it might first appear. Individual syllables are generally pronounced as they're printed—the trick is learning how to place the stresses in the notoriously lengthy German words.

VOWELS AND UMLAUTS

a as in f**a**ther, but can also be used as in h**u**t

e as in d**ay**

i as in l**ee**k

o as in b**o**ttom

u as in b**oo**t

ä is a combination of a and e, sometimes pronounced like **e** in b**e**t (eg Länder) and sometimes like **ai** in p**ai**d (eg spät).

ö is a combination of o and e, like the French *eu*

ü is a combination of u and e, like tr**ue**

VOWEL COMBINATIONS

ai as in l**ie**

au as in h**ou**se

ie as in fr**ee**

ei as in tr**ia**l

eu as in **oi**l

CONSONANTS

Consonants are pronounced as they are written, with no silent letters. The differences from English are:

r is given a dry throaty sound, similar to French

s pronounced similar to, but slightly softer than an English z

v pronounced somewhere between f and v

w pronounced same way as English v

z pronounced ts

GENDER

German words can be one of three genders: masculine, feminine or neuter. Each has its own ending and corresponding ending for attached adjectives. If you don't know any German grammar, it's safest to use either neuter or male forms.

The German letter ß, the *Scharfes S*, often replaces *ss* in a word: pronunciation is identical.

BASIC WORDS AND PHRASES

Ja, Nein	Yes, No	*Dieses*	This one
Bitte	Please/ You're welcome	*Jenes*	That one
Bitte Schön	A more polite form of *Bitte*	*Gross, Klein*	Large, Small
Danke, Danke Schön	Thank you, Thank you very much	*Mehr, Weniger*	More, Less
Wo, Wann, Warum	Where, When, Why	*Wenig*	A little
		Viel	A lot
Wieviel	How much	*Billig, Teuer*	Cheap, Expensive
Hier, Da	Here, There	*Gut, Schlecht*	Good, Bad
Jetzt, Später	Now, Later	*Heiss, Kalt*	Hot, Cold
Geöffnet, offen, auf	All mean 'open'	*Mit, Ohne*	With, Without
		Wo ist . . . ?	Where is . . . ?
Geschlossen, zu	Both mean 'closed'	*Wie komme ich nach . . . ?*	How do I get to (a town)?
Früher	Earlier	*Wie komme ich zur/ zum . . . ?*	How do I get to (a building, place)?
Da drüben	Over there		

GREETINGS AND TIMES

Auf Wiedersehen/ Auf Wiederhören	Goodbye	*Vorgestern*	The day before yesterday
Guten Morgen	Good morning	*Übermorgen*	The day after tomorrow
Guten Abend	Good evening	*Tag*	Day
Guten Tag	Good day	*Nacht*	Night
Wie geht es Ihnen ?	How are you? (polite)	*Woche*	Week
Wie geht es Dir ?	How are you? (informal)	*Monat*	Month
Lass mich in Ruhe	Leave me alone	*Jahr*	Year
Hau ab	Get lost	*Am Vormittag/ vormittags*	In the morning
Geh weg	Go away		
Heute	Today	*Am Nachmittag/ nachmittags*	In the afternoon
Gestern	Yesterday		
Morgen	Tomorrow	*Am Abend*	In the evening

DAYS, MONTHS, AND DATES

Montag	Monday	*Januar*	January	*Frühling*	Spring
Dienstag	Tuesday	*Februar*	February	*Sommer*	Summer
Mittwoch	Wednesday	*März*	March	*Herbst*	Autumn
Donnerstag	Thursday	*April*	April	*Winter*	Winter
Freitag	Friday	*Mai*	May		
Samstag	Saturday	*Juni*	June	*Ferien*	Holidays
Sonnabend	Saturday	*Juli*	July	*Feiertag*	Bank holiday
Sonntag	Sunday	*August*	August	*Montag, der erste April*	Monday, the first of April
		September	September		
		Oktober	October	*Der zweite April*	the second of April
		November	November		
		Dezember	December	*Der dritte April*	the third of April

QUESTIONS AND REQUESTS

All inquiries should be prefaced with the phrase *Entschuldigen Sie bitte* (excuse me, please). Note that *Sie* is the polite form of address to be used with everyone except close friends, though young people and students often don't bother with it. The older generation will certainly be offended if you address them with the familiar *Du*, as will all officials.

Sprechen Sie Englisch ?	Do you speak English ?	*Die Rechnung bitte*	The bill please
Ich spreche kein Deutsch	I don't speak German	*Die Speisekarte bitte*	The menu please
Sprechen sie bitte langsamer	Please speak more slowly	*Fräulein . . . !*	Waitress . . . ! (for attention)
Ich verstehe nicht	I don't understand	*Herr Ober . . . !*	Waiter . . . ! (for attention)
Ich verstehe	I understand	*Haben Sie etwas billigeres ?*	Have you got something cheaper ?
Wie sagt mann das auf Deutsch ?	How do you say that in German ?	*Haben Sie Zimmer frei ?*	Are there rooms available ?
Können Sie mir sagen wo . . . ist ?	Can you tell me where . . . is ?	*Wo sind die Toiletten bitte ?*	Where are the toilets ?
Wieviel kostet das ?	How much does that cost ?	*Ich hätte gern dieses*	I'd like that one
Wann fährt der nächste Zug ?	When does the next train leave ?	*Ich hätte gern ein Zimmer für zwei*	I'd like a room for two
Um wieviel Uhr ?	At what time ?	*Ich hätte gern ein Einzelzimmer*	I'd like a single room
Wieviel Uhr ist es ?	What time is it ?		
Ist der Tisch frei ?	Is that table free?	*Hat es Dusche, Bad, Toilette . . . ?*	Does it have a shower, bath, toilet . . . ?

NUMBERS

1	*eins*	12	*zwölf*	30	*dreissig*
2	*zwei*	13	*dreizehn*	40	*vierzig*
3	*drei*	14	*vierzehn*	50	*fünfzig*
4	*vier*	15	*fünfzehn*	60	*sechzig*
5	*fünf*	16	*sechszehn*	70	*siebzig*
6	*sechs*	17	*siebzehn*	80	*achtzig*
7	*sieben*	18	*achtzehn*	90	*neunzig*
8	*acht*	19	*neunzehn*	100	*hundert*
9	*neun*	20	*zwanzig*	1989	*neunzehn-hundert-neun-und-achtzig*
10	*zehn*	21	*ein-und-zwanzig*		
11	*elf*	22	*zwei-und-zwanzig*		

SOME SIGNS

Damen/Frauen	Women's toilets	*Vorsicht !*	Attention
Herren/Männer	Men's toilets	*Geschwindigkeitsbegrenzung*	Speed limit
Eingang	Entrance		
Ausgang	Exit	*Baustelle*	Building works
Ankunft	Arrival	*Ampel*	Traffic light
Abfahrt	Departure	*Krankenhaus*	Hospital
Ausstellung	Exhibition	*Polizei*	Police
Auffahrt	Motorway entrance	*Nicht rauchen*	No smoking
Ausfahrt	Motorway exit	*Kein Eingang*	No entrance
Umleitung	Diversion	*Verboten*	Prohibited

GLOSSARIES

ART AND ARCHITECTURE

ART DECO geometrical style of art and architecture prevalent in 1930s.

ART NOUVEAU sinuous, highly stylized form of architecture and interior design; in Germany, mostly dates from period 1900–15, and is known as *Jugendstil.*

BAROQUE expansive, exuberant architectural style of seventeenth and early eighteenth century, characterized by ornate decoration, complex spatial arrangements, and grand vistas. The term is also applied to the sumptuous style of painting of the same period.

BAUHAUS plain, functional style of architecture and design, originating in early twentieth century Germany.

EXPRESSIONISM emotional style of painting, concentrating on line and color, extensively practised in early twentieth century Germany; term is also used for related architecture of the same period.

GOTHIC architectural style with an emphasis on verticality, characterized by pointed arch, ribbed vault, and flying buttress; introduced to Germany around 1235, surviving in an increasingly decorative form until well into the sixteenth century. The term is also used for paintings of this period.

NEOCLASSICAL late eighteenth and early nineteenth century style of art and architecture returning to classical models as a reaction against Baroque and Rococo excesses.

RENAISSANCE Italian-originated movement in art and architecture, inspired by the rediscovery of classical ideals.

ROCOCO highly florid, light and graceful eighteenth century style of architecture, painting and interior design, forming the last phase of Baroque.

ROMANESQUE solid architectural style of late tenth to mid-thirteenth century, characterized by round-headed arches and a penchant for horizontality and geometrical precision. The term is also used for paintings of this period.

ROMANTICISM late eighteenth and nineteenth century movement, particularly strong in Germany, rooted in adulation of the natural world and rediscovery of the achievements of the Middle Ages.

GERMAN TERMS

ALTSTADT old part of a city.

AUSKUNFT information.

AUSSTELLUNG exhibition.

BAHNHOF station.

BAU building.

BERG mountain, hill.

BERLINER SCHNAUZE sharp and coarse Berlin wit.

BRÜCKE bridge.

BURG mountain or hill

DENKMAL memorial.

DOM cathedral.

DORF village.

EINBAHNSTRASSE one-way street.

ELECTOR (*Kurfürst*) sacred or secular prince with a vote in the elections to choose the Holy Roman Emperor. There were seven for most of the medieval period, with three more added later.

FEIERTAG holiday.

FLUGHAFEN airport.

FREMDENZIMMER room for short-term let.

GASSE alley.

GASTARBEITER ("guest worker") anyone who comes to West Germany to do menial work.

GASTHAUS, GASTHOF guest house, inn.

GEMÄLDE painting.

GRÜNEN, DIE ("The Greens") West German party formed from environmental and anti-nuclear groups.

HABSBURG the most powerful family in medieval Germany, operating from a power base in Austria. They held the office of Holy Roman Emperor 1452–1806, and by marriage, war, and diplomacy, acquired territories all over Europe.

HAUPTBAHNHOF main railroad station.

HOF court, courtyard, mansion.

INSEL island.

JAGDSCHLOSS hunting lodge.

JUGENDHERBERGE youth hostel.

JUGENDSTIL German version of art nouveau.

JUNKER Prussian landowning class.

KAISER Emperor.

KAMMER room, chamber.

KAPELLE chapel.

KAUFHAUS department store.

KIRCHE church.

KRANKENHAUS hospital.

KUNST art.

MARKT market, market square.

NATIONALER VOLKSARMEE National Peoples' Army of the GDR

NEUES FORUM Umbrella group for political opposition organizations in the GDR.

OSTPOLITIK West German policy of detente towards the GDR.

PLATZ square.

PRUSSIA originally, an Eastern Baltic territory (now divided between Poland and the Soviet Union). It was acquired in 1525 by the Hohenzollerns who merged it with their own possessions to form Brandenburg-Prussia (later shortened to Prussia); this took the lead in forging the unity of Germany, and was thereafter its overwhelmingly dominant province. The name was abolished after World War II because of its monarchical and militaristic connotations.

RASTPLATZ picnic area.

RATHAUS town hall.

RATSKELLER cellars below the Rathaus, invariably used as a restaurant serving *burgerlich* cuisine.

REICH Empire.

REISEBEÜRO travel agency.

RUNDGANG way around.

SAMMLUNG collection.

S-BAHN commuter railroad network operating in and around conurbations.

SCHICKIE (abbreviation of "Schickie-Mickey") yuppie.

SCHLOSS castle, palace (equivalent of French *château*).

SEE lake.

STAATSSICHERHEITSDIENST the "State Security Service" or secret police of the GDR.

STADT town, city.

STAMMTISCH table in a pub or restaurant reserved for regular customers.

STIFTUNG foundation.

STRAND beach.

STRASSENBAHN tram.

TANKSTELLE gas station.

TOR gate, gateway.

TRABI conversational shorthand for the now famous *Trabant*, East Germany's two-cylinder, two-stroke peoples' car.

TURM tower.

U-BAHN network of underground trains.

VERKEHRSAMT, **VERKEHRSVEREIN** tourist office.

VIERTEL quarter, district.

VOLK people, folk; given mystical associations by Hitler.

VOLKSPOLIZEI the "Peoples' Police," the everyday GDR police force.

WALD forest.

WECHSEL currency exchange office.

WEIMAR REPUBLIC Parliamentary democracy established in 1918 which collapsed with Hitler's assumption of power in 1933.

ZEUGHAUS arsenal.

ZIMMER room.

ACRONYMS

BRD (*Bundesrepublik Deutschlands*) official name of West Germany.

CDU (*Christlich Demokratische Union*) ruling Christian Democratic (Conservative) Party.

DB (*Deutsche Bundesbahn*) national railroad company.

DDR (*Deutsche Demokratische Republik*) official name of East Germany.

FDJ (*Freie Deutsche Jugend*) East German party youth organization.

GDR ("German Democratic Republic") English equivalent of DDR.

NSDAP (*National Sozialistiche Deutsche Abrbeiterparte*), "National Socialist German Workers' Party") official name for the Nazis, totalitarian rulers of Germany in the Third Reich 1933–45.

PDS (*Partei Democratische Sozialismus*) "Democratic Socialist Party." New (post-December 1989) name of the SED.

SED (*Sozialistische Einheitspartei Deutschlands*) "Socialist Unity Party of Germany," the official name of the East German communist party before December 1989.

SPD (*Sozialdemokratische Parteii Deutschlands*) Social Democratic (Labor) Party.

STASI slang term for the *Staatssicherheitsdienst*, the former East German secret police.

VOPO slang for *Volkspolizei* , a member of the East German police force.

INDEX

HELP US UPDATE

With the opening of the Wall and the unification of the two Germanys looming on the horizon, Berlin is bound to undergo a transformation in the near future. Things change almost daily: bars appear and disappear, openings times vary, restaurants close, prices increase – and we'd appreciate any suggestions, recommendations or corrections for future editions of the guide. We'll credit all contributions and send a copy of the new edition (or any other Real Guide, if you prefer) for the best letters.
Send them along to: Jack Holland, The Real Guides, Prentice Hall Trade Division, 15 Columbus Circle, New York, NY10023.